MG,

Thanks so much for your great work on H803 and then H811. It is such a pleasure to plan and execute with you.

Philip

Learning through Language

Learning language and using language to learn are at the core of any educational activity. Bringing together a globally representative team of experts, this volume presents an innovative and empirically robust collection of studies that examine the role of language in education, with a particular emphasis on features of school-relevant language in middle childhood and adolescence and its precursors in early childhood. It addresses issues like how children's linguistic and literacy experiences at home prepare them for school, how the classroom functions as a language-mediated learning environment and how schools can support bilingual students in academic attainment. Each of its three parts – early childhood, middle childhood and adolescence and learning in multilingual contexts – features a discussion from experts in the field to stimulate conversation and further routes for research. Its structure will make it useful for anyone interested in ongoing efforts towards building a pedagogically relevant theory of language learning.

VIBEKE GRØVER is Professor of Education at the University of Oslo, Norway.

PAOLA UCCELLI is Professor of Education at the Harvard Graduate School of Education, USA.

MEREDITH L. ROWE is Professor of Education at the Harvard Graduate School of Education, USA.

ELENA LIEVEN is Professor of Psychology at the University of Manchester, UK.

Learning through Language

Towards an Educationally Informed Theory of Language Learning

Edited by

Vibeke Grøver
University of Oslo

Paola Uccelli
Harvard University

Meredith L. Rowe
Harvard University

Elena Lieven
University of Manchester

CAMBRIDGE
UNIVERSITY PRESS

CAMBRIDGE
UNIVERSITY PRESS

University Printing House, Cambridge CB2 8BS, United Kingdom

One Liberty Plaza, 20th Floor, New York, NY 10006, USA

477 Williamstown Road, Port Melbourne, VIC 3207, Australia

314–321, 3rd Floor, Plot 3, Splendor Forum, Jasola District Centre,
New Delhi – 110025, India

79 Anson Road, #06–04/06, Singapore 079906

Cambridge University Press is part of the University of Cambridge.

It furthers the University's mission by disseminating knowledge in the pursuit of
education, learning, and research at the highest international levels of excellence.

www.cambridge.org
Information on this title: www.cambridge.org/9781107169357
DOI: 10.1017/9781316718537

© Cambridge University Press 2019

First published 2019

Printed and bound in Great Britain by Clays Ltd, Elcograf S.p.A.

A catalogue record for this publication is available from the British Library.

Library of Congress Cataloging-in-Publication Data
Names: Grøver, Vibeke, editor. | Uccelli, Paola, editor. | Rowe, Meredith
L.,editor. | Lieven, Elena V. M., editor.
Title: Learning through language : towards an educationally informed theory of
language learning / edited by Vibeke Grøver, Paola Uccelli, Meredith Rowe,
Elena Lieven.
Description: New York, NY : Cambridge University Press, [2019]
Identifiers: LCCN 2018048869 | ISBN 9781107169357
Subjects: LCSH: Language awareness. | Language and education.
Classification: LCC P120.L34 L435 2019 | DDC 418.0071–dc23
LC record available at https://lccn.loc.gov/2018048869

ISBN 978-1-107-16935-7 Hardback

Contents

Figures

Tables

Contributors

Macarena Alvarado, Servicio Nacional de Capacitación y Empleo (SENCE), Chile

Macarena Alvarado has a master's degree in economics from the University of Chile and a master's degree in public policy and development from the Paris School of Economics, France, and is an external consultant for the Inter-American Development Bank and the Chilean government.

MaryCatherine Arbour, Division of Global Health Equity, Brigham and Women's Hospital, USA

MaryCatherine Arbour, MD MPH, is Associate Professor for Research at Brigham and Women's Hospital and Assistant Professor at Harvard Medical School. She implements and evaluates interventions to promote child development and reduce inequities in the USA and abroad, using a combination of experimental, ethnographic and quality improvement methodologies. She has particular interests in methods for adapting evidence-based practices across diverse contexts and populations, and at scale.

Bernardo Atuesta, Comisión Económica para América Latina y el Caribe (CEPAL), Chile

Bernardo Atuesta is Consultant for CEPAL in Santiago, Chile. He is an economist with a master's degree in economics from Rosario University in Colombia and a master's degree in public policy and development from the Paris School of Economics, France.

Gina Biancarosa, University of Oregon, USA

Gina Biancarosa is Associate Professor and Ann Swindells Chair in Education at the University of Oregon. She earned her EdD in language and literacy from the Harvard Graduate School of Education. Her research interests centre primarily on measuring and tracking growth in reading comprehension and on adolescent literacy, as well as meta-representational skills more broadly.

Elma Blom, Utrecht University, the Netherlands

Elma Blom is Professor in Language Development and Multilingualism in family and educational contexts in the Department of Education and Pedagogy at Utrecht University, the Netherlands. She studies the parallel development of multiple languages in children, linguistic and cognitive effects of bilingualism, predictors of language development and the distinction between language delay and language impairment, and she works on the improvement of diagnostic instruments for multilingual children.

Si Chen, Harvard Graduate School of Education, USA

Si Chen, PhD, is a post-doctoral fellow at the Harvard Graduate School of Education. Her research is primarily concerned with the ways in which language/literacy learning curriculums and environments for young children – in and out of school, monolingual and bilingual – can be designed to support children's development. Much of Chen's research focuses on detecting the effectiveness of randomized literacy interventions in China.

Evelyn Ford-Connors, Boston University, USA

Evelyn Ford-Connors, EdD, is a senior lecturer in the literacy programme at Boston University's Wheelock School of Education and Human Development and the Co-director of the Donald D. Durrell Reading and Writing Clinic. Her dissertation research examined middle school teachers' talk during their classroom-based vocabulary instruction, and she continues to pursue this line of inquiry through research and coaching focused on teachers' talk during literacy instruction.

Vibeke Grøver, University of Oslo, Norway

Vibeke Grøver is Professor of Education at the University of Oslo, Department of Education. She has conducted research on children's peer play, on children's language use in a cross-cultural perspective and on longitudinal relations between language exposure and vocabulary learning in language-minority children. Currently she is undertaking an intervention study of dual language learners and their language learning and text comprehension in urban, multi-ethnic preschools in Norway.

Kenji Hakuta, Stanford University, USA

Kenji Hakuta is the Lee L. Jacks Professor of Education, Emeritus, at Stanford University. His publications are in the areas of theory, policy and practice in the education of English learners.

Paul L. Harris, Harvard Graduate School of Education, USA

Paul L. Harris is the Victor S. Thomas Professor of Education at Harvard University. He obtained a DPhil in experimental psychology from Oxford University. He studies the development of emotion, imagination and cognition in early childhood.

Anna M. Hartranft, University of Maryland, USA

Anna M. Hartranft is a faculty research associate at the University of Maryland, College Park. Her research focuses on reading and writing difficulties for children with or at risk for disabilities. She has conducted research on the development and instruction of comprehension and has recently completed her dissertation, focused on the role of executive functioning in the comprehension of upper elementary students from linguistically diverse backgrounds and/or with disabilities.

Lowry E. Hemphill, Boston University, USA

Lowry E. Hemphill is Clinical Associate Professor at Boston University. She received her doctorate from Harvard Graduate School of Education with a focus on language and literacy learning. Her main research interests are literacy development among low-income children and adolescents and oral language contributions to reading comprehension. She is the main developer of the Strategic Adolescent Reading Intervention (STARI) and helps lead a large-scale clinical trial into its efficacy.

Lotte F. Henrichs, Utrecht University, the Netherlands

Lotte F. Henrichs is a researcher and educational consultant at the Department of Educational Consultancy and Professional Development, Utrecht University. She obtained a PhD in linguistics from the University of Amsterdam, with a focus on academic language development in early childhood. She currently teaches on the topic of teaching diverse classrooms in the Utrecht University Teacher Education Program for primary education. She collaborates with teachers in various practice-oriented research projects.

James Kim, Harvard Graduate School of Education, USA

James Kim is Professor of Education at the Harvard Graduate School of Education. He studies the effectiveness of literacy reforms and interventions in improving student outcomes.

Young-Suk Grace Kim, University of California, Irvine, USA

Young-Suk Grace Kim is Professor at the University of California, Irvine. She received her EdD from Harvard University in human development and psychology with a concentration in language and literacy and a minor concentration in quantitative policy analysis in education. Her primary research areas include development and difficulties in language, cognition and reading and writing skills across languages and writing systems.

Nonie K. Lesaux

Nonie K. Lesaux is Academic Dean and Juliana W. and William Foss Thompson Professor of Education and Society at the Harvard Graduate School of Education. Her research focuses on promoting the language and literacy skills of today's children from diverse linguistic, cultural and economic backgrounds, and is conducted largely in urban and semi-urban cities and school districts.

Paul P. M. Leseman, Utrecht University, the Netherlands

Paul Leseman is Professor of Education in the Department of Education and Pedagogics. He studies language and cognitive development in children with a low socioeconomic status or a migration background. He is involved in intervention programmes to close the early education gap between children from different backgrounds and is currently leading a large cross-national study into the mechanisms of educational inequality and exclusion in Europe.

Robert A. LeVine, Harvard Graduate School of Education, USA

Robert A. LeVine is Roy E. Larsen Professor of Education and Human Development, Emeritus, at the Harvard Graduate School of Education. His research concerns cultural aspects of parenthood and child development in African, Asian, Latin American and other societies. His most recent research finds that across these contexts, much of the effects of maternal schooling on child health and development are due to the language and literacy skills that the mothers learned in school.

Diana Leyva, Davidson College, USA

Diana Leyva is Assistant Professor of Psychology at Davidson College, USA. Her research focuses on how parents support the development of children's school readiness skills in minority communities in the USA and Latin America. She received her PhD from Clark University, was a lecturer in education and a post-doctoral fellow at Harvard University and was project director of *Un Buen Comienzo* (A Good Start), an initiative to improve early childhood education in Chile through a teacher professional development programme.

Elena Lieven, University of Manchester, England

Elena Lieven is Professor of Psychology at the University of Manchester. Her research involves usage-based approaches to language development; the emergence and construction of grammar; the relationship between input characteristics and the process of language development; and variation in children's communicative environments, cross-linguistically and cross-culturally. She is Co-Director of the ESRC International Centre for Language and Communicative Development (LuCiD: www.lucid.ac.uk) at the Universities of Manchester, Liverpool and Lancaster. She is an elected Fellow of the Cognitive Science Society and of the British Academy.

Stefka H. Marinova-Todd, University of British Columbia, Canada

Stefka H. Marinova-Todd is Associate Professor in the School of Audiology and Speech Sciences at the University of British Columbia, Canada. She holds an EdD in human development and psychology from the Harvard Graduate School of Education. Dr Marinova-Todd investigates the language, literacy and cognitive development of bilingual children, both typically developing and with autism.

Marcela Marzolo, Fundación Educacional Oportunidad, Chile

Marcela Marzolo is Executive Director of Fundación Educacional Oportunidad in Chile, which implements *Un Buen Comienzo*, a programme that seeks to improve the quality of early childhood education for at-risk Chilean children. She is an early childhood educator from the Pontificia Universidad Católica de Chile. She is a specialist in learning disabilities from the same university and a specialist in children's attachment and mental health from the Universidad del Desarrollo in Chile.

Ageliki Nicolopoulou, Lehigh University, USA

Ageliki Nicolopoulou is Professor of Psychology at Lehigh University. She is a socio-cultural developmental psychologist whose research interests include the role of narrative in development, socialization and education; the influence of the peer group and peer culture as social contexts for children's cognitive and socio-emotional development; the relationship between play and narrative; the foundations of emergent literacy; and the developmental interplay between the construction of reality and the formation of (gender) identity.

Catherine O'Connor, Boston University, USA

Catherine O'Connor is Professor of Education and Linguistics at Boston University in the Wheelock College of Education and Human Development. She received her PhD in linguistics at the University of California, Berkeley with a focus on language documentation of Northern Pomo, a dormant indigenous language of northern California. Her research in education centres on language use in school settings, including classroom discourse and discussion and its role in literacy development and mathematics learning, and how teachers learn to orchestrate productive classroom discussion.

P. David Pearson, University of California, Berkeley, USA

P. David Pearson is an Emeritus faculty member in the Graduate School of Education at the University of California, Berkeley, where he served as Dean from 2001 to 2010. His current research focuses on literacy history and policy. He also holds an appointment as Professor of the Graduate School and is the Evelyn Lois Corey Emeritus Chair in Instructional Science.

C. Patrick Proctor, Boston College, USA

C. Patrick Proctor is Associate Professor of Literacy and Bilingualism at the Lynch School of Education, Boston College. His research interests include cognitive and sociolinguistic explorations of bilingualism in elementary and middle school–aged children, language and literacy development among linguistically diverse learners, collaborative partnerships with teachers in multilingual classrooms and the intersections between technology and literacy development in urban school settings.

Andrea Rolla, David Rockefeller Center for Latin American Studies, Harvard University, Chile

Andrea Rolla is a post-doctoral researcher at Harvard University and an advisor to the *Un Buen Comienzo* project in Chile, an interdisciplinary partnership with Fundación Educacional Oportunidad. Previously, she worked for four years as Senior Advisor at the Chilean Ministry of Education as well as at the US Department of Education, the UK National Foundation for Education Research and the Pontifical Catholic University of Chile and as a consultant in Costa Rica, Chile, El Salvador, Colombia, Ecuador and the USA. Andrea holds a BA in literature as well as an elementary school teacher certification from Princeton University, a master's degree in educational research from the University of Oxford and a doctorate in education from Harvard University, having specialized in language and literacy development.

Meredith L. Rowe, Harvard Graduate School of Education, USA

Meredith L. Rowe is Professor at the Harvard Graduate School of Education, where she teaches courses on language and literacy development. Her research focuses on uncovering features of parent communication with children that contribute to children's language and cognitive development across early childhood and on translating these findings into intervention programmes for parents.

Sara Rutherford-Quach, Stanford University, USA

Sara Rutherford-Quach is Director of Academic Programs and Research for Understanding Language at the Stanford Graduate School of Education. She received her PhD in linguistic anthropology of education from Stanford University. Her interests include language development, classroom discourse and instructional practice and with respect to bilingual students and their educators.

Robert L. Selman, Harvard Graduate School of Education, USA

Robert L. Selman is the Roy E. Larsen Professor of Human Development and Education and Professor of Psychology in Psychiatry at Harvard University. Currently, he studies the developmental and cultural antecedents of the capacity to form and maintain positive social relationships, as well as ways to prevent negative educational, social, and health outcomes in youth.

Rebecca D. Silverman, Stanford Graduate School of Education, USA

Rebecca D. Silverman is Associate Professor of Early Literacy at the Stanford Graduate School of Education. Her research focuses on language and literacy development and instruction of children in early childhood and elementary school. She has focused especially on vocabulary and comprehension for children from socioeconomically disadvantaged and linguistically diverse backgrounds.

Lauren Skorb, Davidson College, USA

Lauren Skorb graduated from Davidson College, where she worked with Diana Leyva in the Food for Thought programme. After graduating, she worked for two years as a manager of the Language Learning Lab at Boston College, with Joshua Hartshorne. She will start her graduate programme at Georgia Tech University in fall 2018.

Catherine E. Snow, Harvard Graduate School of Education, USA

Catherine E. Snow is the Patricia Albjerg Graham Professor at the Harvard Graduate School of Education. She teaches courses and conducts research on language and literacy development, with learners from preschool through adolescence, and with special attention to learners facing elevated risk of academic failure.

Ernesto Treviño, Facultad de Educación, Pontificia Universidad Católica, Chile

Ernesto Treviño is Professor and a researcher of the Facultad de Educación, Pontificia Universidad Católica de Chile. He was the director of the Centro de Políticas Comparadas, Universidad Diego Portales, in Chile, between 2011 and 2016. He has been Senior Advisor to the Latin American Laboratory of Evaluation of the Quality of Education of UNESCO-OREALC since 2013. He is an economist from the Instituto Tecnólogico y de Estudios Superiores de Monterrey and holds a doctorate in education from the Harvard University Graduate School of Education.

Margaret Troyer, Strategic Education Research Partnership Institute, USA

Margaret Troyer is currently Project Director at the Strategic Adolescent Research Partnership, and she recently earned her EdD from the Harvard Graduate School of Education. Her research interests focus on adolescent struggling readers, reading motivation and teachers' adaptions and implementation of curriculum.

Paola Uccelli, Harvard Graduate School of Education, USA

Paola Uccelli is Professor of Education at the Harvard Graduate School of Education. Her research examines socio-cultural and individual differences in school-relevant language and literacy development in monolingual and bilingual learners. Her projects in the USA and abroad seek to inform research-based pedagogies that empower all learners' voices. Being a native of Peru, she is particularly interested in Latin America, where she collaborates with local schools and organizations to conduct pedagogically relevant research.

Yuuko Uchikoshi, University of California, Davis School of Education, USA

Yuuko Uchikoshi is Associate Professor in the School of Education at the University of California, Davis. She holds an EdD in human development and psychology from the Harvard Graduate School of Education. Dr Uchikoshi's research focuses on the language and literacy development of young children from linguistically, culturally and economically diverse backgrounds.

Josje Verhagen, Utrecht University, the Netherlands

Josje Verhagen is a post-doctoral researcher at Utrecht University and the University of Amsterdam. She studies language development in young children, with a strong focus on bilingual children. In previous studies, she investigated the relationships between phonological memory and language learning in monolingual and bilingual children. More recently, she examined effects of bilingualism on statistical learning and on children's reliance on non-verbal communicative behaviours, such as pointing.

Hirokazu Yoshikawa, New York University, USA

Hirokazu Yoshikawa is the Courtney Sale Ross Professor of Globalization and Education and University Professor in the Department of Applied Psychology, New York University. He co-directs the Global TIES for Children Center at NYU and serves on the advisory boards of the Open Society Foundations Early Childhood Program and the UNESCO Global Education Monitoring Report.

Joonmo Yun, Florida State University, USA

Joonmo Yun received his PhD in education at Florida State University. His research interest is in students who struggle with literacy acquisition.

Qianqian Zhang-Wu, Boston College, USA

Qianqian Zhang-Wu is a PhD candidate in the Department of Curriculum and Instruction at the Lynch School of Education, Boston College. Her major research interests lie in the areas of bilingualism, bilingual education, teacher education and literacy development in K–20 settings. Prior to her doctoral studies, Qianqian received her MSEd in educational linguistics (TESOL) from the Graduate School of Education, University of Pennsylvania.

Foreword

For decades, research on child language acquisition followed a tradition of looking to work conducted in the lab, often with homogeneous samples of children and families, to address questions about typical and atypical patterns and processes of development. Less common was work motivated by questions about the context of language learning – questions about language use and exposure, questions about the influence of specific inputs at home and school on trajectories of learning and questions about the role of second language acquisition. An exception to this trend is the work of Catherine Snow – a scholar who articulated the link between children's early language interactions, whether at the family dinner table or while engaged in joint storybook reading with a parent or caregiver, and their later language and literacy behaviours. Within her expansive and innovative programme of research, Snow has paid special attention to identifying those high-lever interactions – the questions, the types of utterances and the kinds of texts – that are linked with children's vocabulary and language growth.

Tracking with the increasing diversity of the school-age population, including linguistic diversity tied to immigration and globalization, the widening income-achievement gap and a press for policy and practice-based solutions to these challenges for education, Snow's early work, mostly conducted in homes and with young children, was followed by almost two decades of work that has been foundational to a next generation of research focused on examining and describing solutions to the dire need for richer classroom language-learning environments. This body of research ranges from large-scale intervention work in US classrooms serving high numbers of linguistically diverse learners to preschool classrooms in Latin America serving academically vulnerable children.

Fittingly, then, we have before us an unparalleled volume – one that focuses on building a pedagogically relevant theory of language learning. This book is based on the idea that developing an educationally relevant approach to language demands an investigation of language and literacy learning in its diverse cultural contexts, as evidenced by chapters that focus on learning and development in China, Chile, the Netherlands, Norway, Canada and the USA.

Combining methodological rigour and a sophisticated lens on development with both ecological validity and practical relevance, the chapters address how language exposure and language use in early childhood at home and in school are precursors to academic language use and literacy in the school years. The volume goes further to address how academic language and its precursors can be supported through instruction and specific discourse practices at home and in classrooms.

The volume solidifies a new era of research – research that is at once robust methodologically and substantively but equally attentive to issues of context and pressing problems of policy and practice. Today's policy makers and education leaders need guidance on how to improve the forms of language practices to which children and adolescents are exposed at home and in school. And at the same time, much more discussion among researchers is needed about the qualities of language use and competency that prepare all children, recognizing multilingualism as a feature of today's population, to become language and text users in modern societies. The volume, and the trailblazing work on which it is based, is therefore inspirational and much needed; it showcases the fundamental developmental ideas and understandings that have had a profound influence on language and literacy research and practice initiatives taking place in many parts of the world and will serve as a guide for such work in decades to come.

Nonie K. Lesaux

1   Learning through Language

Vibeke Grøver, Paola Uccelli, Meredith L. Rowe, and Elena Lieven

Why This Book?

At knowledge institutions in modern societies, language is an inseparable part of learning. Schools are institutions for building certain types of knowledge, and acquiring this knowledge also involves becoming competent in the language and discourse of schooling. As school content becomes increasingly complex and abstract, novice learners need to continue to expand their vocabulary, their mastery of complex syntax, their knowledge of various discourse structures and their skills in conveying their perspectives and understanding the perspectives of others. Indeed, successful participation in school and academic learning requires not only expanding knowledge but also learning the language to communicate ideas in a precise, concise, logically organized, and reflective manner. Beyond school, being proficient in these ways of using language is important for navigating society as an informed citizen. New information (health, civic or political news) is disseminated publicly via oral or written texts that typically use academic language. Inspired by the advances of recent research that sheds light on the role of language in education, we edited this volume to present a coherent set of empirical approaches that examine language through two lenses: that of *learning language* and that of *learning through language*. Grounded in a social-interactionist, pragmatically oriented, theoretical framework, the chapters in this book span from early childhood to adolescence and address monolingual as well as multilingual development, providing insights of relevance for developmental theory and educational research and practice. Our hope is that the research insights in this collection will be informative for educators, inviting for researchers, and inspiring for practitioner–researcher partnerships that seek to further advance this work.

In this introductory chapter, we first briefly situate the research presented in this book as part of a larger effort towards an educationally informed theory of language learning. Next, as a preview of the insights the reader will find throughout this book, we highlight some of the most salient cross-cutting themes, and we end by posing some new research directions that emerge from this collection.

Towards an Educationally Informed Theory of Language Learning

Though the book has contributors from many universities across several countries, the research agenda that was developed at the Harvard Graduate School of Education under the leadership of Catherine Snow over the past several decades has been particularly influential in shaping the research perspectives adopted in this book. This research agenda involves conducting theoretically and empirically grounded studies geared towards the articulation and refinement of an educationally informed theory of how children and adolescents learn language as well as towards how they use language to acquire knowledge in and out of school. In other words, the research programme seeks to understand language learning with the ultimate goal of informing how to best support learners' knowledge acquisition and socio-cognitive development. Theoretically, the work is anchored in dialogically oriented approaches to language learning and literacy and in the understanding that language develops in the context of achieving pragmatic goals and for the purpose of contact, interaction, understanding and knowledge acquisition (e.g. Ninio & Snow, 1996). Empirically, the work makes use of tools from language and literacy research, merges qualitative and quantitative analytic approaches and seeks to integrate insights from practitioners and researchers to produce practice-based research and to inform evidence-based practices.

Historically, the study of children's language development took an important shift in the 1970s, when researchers started to move beyond the narrow level of the utterance to try to better understand language learning by situating it as part of the larger unit of conversations (Brown, 1973; Halliday, 1975). This turn led to findings that illuminated the different ways in which caregivers' input facilitated children's language development. In studying the speech directed to children, semantic extensions, recasts, and clarification requests, among others, were identified as input features associated with children's language learning outcomes (Newport, Gleitman, & Gleitman, 1977; Snow, 1977a). Beyond conventional measures of vocabulary and grammar, conversational skills, such as regulating turn taking, maintaining a joint topic, and providing sufficient information, became an important object of study (for a discussion, see Pan & Snow, 1999). Gradually, however, cross-cultural and educational researchers called for an expansion of this somewhat constraining conversational lens (Ochs, 1988; Snow, 1991a).

One pedagogically relevant reconceptualization of the study of language learning was advanced by Catherine Snow. She suggested that language learning be studied in relation to 'the tasks that children face when using language, the ways in which performance can vary across tasks, and the manner in which those tasks change as children get older' (Snow, 1991a, p. 67). Moving away from traditional models focused on linguistic levels (phonology, lexicon, morphology, etc.), which served the goals of linguists better than those of developmentalists or educational researchers, Snow (1991a) proposed a 'task-based multidimensional model of language proficiency'. When actual tasks are taken into consideration, language development is studied in relation to the situational demands posed by the increasing variety of contexts that learners navigate throughout life. These demands can be organized along two main dimensions: (1) message and (2) audience (Snow & Uccelli, 2009). First, early in development, young children participate in minimal exchanges (often single utterances) about concrete here-and-now messages (e.g. *I want that!* while pointing to a toy). Gradually throughout development, learners take part in longer language exchanges (with multiple thematically linked utterances) about increasingly abstract and complex there-and-then messages (e.g. a debate about global warming). Second, as children grow older, they also move from interactions with a present, highly supportive, familiar audience with shared knowledge (e.g. a parent) to interactions with distant, unfamiliar and uncooperative audiences with no presumed shared knowledge (e.g. a TED talk). Children's developing socio-cognitive skills, including their growing abilities to consider multiple points of view, serve to strengthen their messages and arguments when they interact with more distant audiences.

In this theoretical framework, language tasks, and thus language learning, are understood as embedded in a particular socio-cultural context and shaped by the cultural norms and expectations of the communities in which children are enculturated. This lens informed studies that shifted the research focus to the speaking child and the complexity of conversations and discussions, typically of multi-party character, at home and in classrooms, across various cultures (e.g. Blum-Kulka & Snow, 2002). School, then, is also seen as a specific cultural context and the language for school learning as the result of the particular cultural and pragmatic expectations of school. The language of school learning also responds to the demands of message and audience, but under particularly challenging conditions. Firstly, messages tend to be abstract or theoretical, typically unfamiliar to students, and in need of extended elaboration. Secondly, the audience or interlocutor is somewhat indeterminate in nature. Learners need to imagine an intangible, non-interactive, academic interlocutor and learn to comprehend and produce language that responds to the cultural expectations of academic communities (Snow & Uccelli, 2009). These demands call for language that is very different from that used in brief exchanges about the here and now (e.g. explaining photosynthesis at school vs. asking for salt at the dinner table).

Within this conceptualization, learning to read and learning to write are understood as extensions of language development (e.g. Hemphill & Snow; 1996; Snow, 1983). The longitudinal Home-School Study of Language and Literacy Development (HSLLD) measured discourse-level skills in children, their teachers, and their parents, highlighting that the oral language–school literacy relations involve more than just vocabulary knowledge. This was visionary, as the HSLLD revealed that, among the many ways of interacting through language, particular interactions, specifically those that involve extended discourse about there-and-then messages (e.g. narratives, explanations), at home and in school contributed to children's later vocabulary knowledge and reading comprehension (Snow, Porche, Harris, & Tabors, 2007; Snow, Tabors, & Dickinson, 2001). While most of the earlier work within this research area was descriptive, recent large-scale experimental studies add evidence supporting these close relations between language and literacy. Today, rigorously tested educational interventions designed through researcher–practitioner partnerships, such as the Word Generation Project (Snow & Lawrence, 2011; see also http://wordgen.serpmedia.org/), provide evidence that students' language proficiencies are malleable throughout adolescence and are influenced by improvable teachers' language practices. This research shows that classroom environments where students are actively engaged with producing extended discourse about complex topics lead to significant gains in students' advanced literacy skills (LaRusso et al., 2016).

Finally, this conceptualization also highlights further opportunities for *learning through language*, or in other words, how engaging orally in academic discussions can help promote literacy skills and knowledge acquisition. As emphasized by Snow, discussion is in itself a key contributor to learning and to reading comprehension. Words and other features of academic language are not easily acquired if not 'embedded in meaningful texts and if opportunities to use them in discussion, debate, and writing are not provided' (Snow, 2010, p. 452). Critical to students' engagement in classroom discussion and debate, in addition to their language skills, are their socio-cognitive skills of considering and evaluating others' perspectives. There is emerging evidence that children and adolescents, through well-designed instructional approaches based on classroom discussion and debate, such as in the Word Generation Project, acquire features of both academic language and perspective taking (Jones et al., in press). Language-minority students have, in particular, proved receptive to instruction that includes diverse perspectives (Hsin & Snow, 2017).

Inspired by this line of research, the present volume illustrates the ongoing efforts towards building an educationally informed theory of language learning by bringing together a body of research that sheds light on the nature of school-relevant language and literacy development and the contextual factors that support learners' academic learning and communication.

School-Relevant Language Development: A Note on Terminology

Researchers who study language learning in relation to school literacy and school achievement use multiple terms, which may require clarification for the reader of this book. Here we provide our definitions of three main overarching concepts. However, it is important to keep in mind that the terms listed below are used somewhat interchangeably in the field and are not the only ones used to refer to these concepts.

Decontextualized discourse/talk/language refers to talk about the there and then (Hemphill & Snow, 1996). As discussed above, learners move gradually from talking about the here and now, i.e. concrete objects, events, or people present in the physical setting of the interaction, to talking about messages that are more remote or abstract (e.g. causal explanations, narratives, pretend play). In discussing non-present messages, language users cannot use non-verbal cues, such as pointing or gestures, to help convey their messages; instead they need to rely more on language itself. It is important to clarify that *decontextualized* refers to the characteristic of messages that are detached from the physical context but does not imply the absence of a larger communicative context. Being able to successfully communicate about the non-present in fact requires attention to the discourse context and involves mastering new language and perspective-taking skills that respond to the complex language and cognitive demands of a non-present message.

Extended discourse refers to 'the use of several [thematically linked] utterances or turns to build a linguistic structure' (Snow, Tabors, & Dickinson, 2001, p. 2). Extended discourse typically entails talk about there-and-then topics (e.g. explanations, narratives, pretend play) and thus is often used to refer to talk that is both decontextualized and extended. However, it is important to clarify that extended discourse could also be about the here and now, e.g. a mother who describes the ingredients and steps for making lemonade, as she and her child prepare it together.

Academic discourse/language, or the language of education, the language of schooling or the language of academic texts, are terms that refer to the language used for learning in schools and universities, in textbooks and scientific communication for argumentation, explanation and information synthesizing and dissemination (Halliday, 2004; Schleppegrell, 2001). Whereas the two terms above are defined as referring to message characteristics (i.e. decontextualized or extended message), academic language is instead typically defined by the context in which this language is found. Discipline-specific, academic language (the language of history, the language of math) refers to the language forms and functions that highlight key concepts and reasoning moves of specific disciplines. Cross-disciplinary, academic language instead refers to the language forms and functions that are used to fulfil goals shared across disciplines, such as precise and concise communication or explicit marking of conceptual relations and of reflective perspectives (Bailey, 2007; Hyland, 2009; Schleppegrell, 2004; Snow, 2010; Snow & Uccelli, 2009). There is, however, no clear-cut way of defining academic language, and the term itself often raises controversy from authors who rightly point to the erroneous and educationally dangerous misconception of academic language as a superior language variety (e.g. Gee, 2014; Valdes, 2004). In response, it is important to emphasize that we view academic discourses as 'cultural manifestations valued by academic institutions embedded in larger socio-political and historical structures' (Uccelli, Phillips Galloway, & Qin, in press). In other words, we view academic language as a pragmatic solution to a particular situational context.

Three important considerations are worth highlighting. Firstly, rather than categorical notions, each of these three concepts falls within a continuum from less to more extended, from contextualized to decontextualized and from more colloquial to more academic discourse (Snow & Uccelli, 2009). The two ends of the continua differ in the demands of the message and audience and, consequently, in the language required to address those demands. At one end, not-extended, contextualized, colloquial language occurs in exchanges with a face-to-face audience about concrete entities or events (e.g. *'Could you pass the salt, please?'* during a dinner table conversation). At the other end, extended, decontextualized, academic language occurs in exchanges with intangible audiences typically about non-present events, entities, or ideas and requires drawing on more advanced lexical, morphosyntactic and discourse resources (Uccelli, Demir, Rowe, Goldin-Meadow, & Levine, 2018).

Secondly, these three concepts offer interrelated but distinct entry points into the study of language learning. To illustrate this, think about a presentation on photosynthesis by a sixth-grade teacher. This presentation is an example of academic language (language for learning at school); it is also decontextualized (photosynthesis represents a non-present abstract message) and requires extended discourse (i.e. multiple thematically linked utterances). Whereas this example illustrates the co-occurrence of these three characteristics, they do not always co-occur: not all decontextualized language is academic (e.g. personal narratives, pretence), and not all academic language is decontextualized (e.g. explaining an experiment while conducting it); whereas decontextualized talk is often extended, it can occur at the level of single utterances; and extended discourse can be highly contextualized and not academic in nature (the lemonade example).

Thirdly, as researchers apply each of these terms to the study of language, they may focus on three different levels of analysis: the level of actual practices, the level of individuals' skills or the level of abstract systems. For instance, academic language can be studied at the level of (1) home and school *practices* in which students participate (then research would focus, for example, on the frequency and quality of student participation in academic practices, e.g. debates, science reports); (2) learners' skills (then research would focus on measuring students' language skills, e.g. knowledge of academic vocabulary or complex syntax); or (3) abstract systems (then research would focus on the characteristic of abstract units of academic language, e.g. the linguistic features characteristic of scientific dissertations). Decontextualized and extended discourse can also be analysed as practices (learners' actual participation in these practices), skills (learners' skills required to successfully participate in these practices) and systems or abstract units (features of decontextualized extended units, such as the linguistic features of narratives). Because researchers are not always explicit in this regard, it is important to keep in mind that studies that use similar terms may be referring to different levels of analysis.

This Volume: Cross-Sectional Themes

This book examines qualities of academic language learning in the school years, as well as its precursors in early childhood, captured through concepts such as decontextualized talk and extended discourse. We asked the contributors to offer a review of the specific field they covered, to present some empirical evidence and to offer suggestions for how this research contributed to an educationally informed theory of language learning. We structured the book into three sections: section I covers precursors of academic language and literacy proficiencies during the preschool and early elementary school years; Section II, academic language and literacy development and instruction during the middle school and early adolescent years; and Section III, multilingual learners' school-relevant languages and literacies during early and later childhood. To encourage discussion, debate, and multiple perspectives, we invited one or two experts in the field to discuss each section's chapters.

In this introduction, instead of referring to each chapter one by one, we articulate some of the core ideas and findings reported throughout the book. These cross-cutting themes are organized below into those related to *language learning across contexts of use, across ages, across skills, across languages, and across instructional settings.*

Across Contexts: The Pragmatics-Based Perspective

This set of findings simultaneously informs and is informed by an understanding of language learning as context dependent and highlights that language learning is influenced by the social interactions and the language environments in which learners participate. Being a skilled language user in one context does not guarantee being skilled in another context. Also, children may be skilled users of different forms of social language (sophisticated personal narratives, complex jokes, rich similes) and yet struggle with the language expected for school literacy and learning. Talk about the non-present and literacy routines takes different forms across cultures.

Language learning relies on intentional communication. On the basis of an extensive review of early language acquisition research and guided by social-interactionist theories, Lieven (Chapter 2) puts forward the argument that children would have a hard time learning language if it were not embedded in communicative contexts. Children's understanding that they can communicate intentionally and that others try to communicate with them offers a foundation for language learning. Consistent evidence from cross-cultural studies documents that children start to communicate intentionally and produce words roughly at the same age across cultures.

Home language environments vary considerably, with some that more closely resemble the language of school. Leseman and colleagues (Chapter 15) report that parents of bilingual children in demographically diverse immigrant groups in the Netherlands (Moroccan Dutch, Turkish Dutch) created linguistic contexts at home that resembled contexts for language learning in preschools: asking questions, expanding on children's utterances, and engaging in extended discourse. However, the variability in the ways and the extent to which children were invited to engage in these practices at home was substantial and reflected parental education, family constellation, and parents' reading skills.

Interactions that support school-relevant language take different forms across cultures. Leyva and Skorb (Chapter 5) show that elaborate discussions that resemble the language of school do not only take place around books; culturally relevant practices, such as narratives around food routines in Latino families, can offer optimal language environments that foster decontextualized skills and prepare children for school literacy. Leyva and Skorb examine how parents incorporate talking, reading, and writing into family routines. These routines have a personal value and are regularly practised. They find that discussion about past events is one of the routines in which Latino parents from low-income communities regularly engage with their children. In doing so, they engage in decontextualized language in a culturally congruent manner.

Societal contexts influence the multilingual practices of educational systems and individuals. Uchikoshi and Marinova-Todd (Chapter 17) high-light the role of the broader societal and educational contexts (United States vs Canada) in the opportunities afforded to bilingual children to use their home languages for school learning, and therefore in the relations that research can detect between oral language and reading in bilingual children. Similarly, Proctor and Zhang-Wu (Chapter 16) suggest that cross-linguistic associations may vary depending on the societal contexts in which bilingual children are raised (such as gender and school type, urban, rural). Moreover, Leseman et al. (Chapter 15) conclude that understanding cross-linguistic relations requires attention to the specific socio-cultural context and power relations within which children live and use their languages.

Across Ages: The Developmental Perspective

Multiple chapters throughout the book examine the contribution of language environments, specific discourse practices, and early language skills to lear-ners' later school-relevant language skills.

Early language skills predict later language and literacy proficiencies. Research has documented not only relations within the early years of language development (Lieven, Chapter 2; Rowe, Chapter 4) but also relations between young children's language skills and practices and adolescent language profi-ciencies (Uccelli, Chapter 8). Rolla et al. (Chapter 7) found that preschool (age four to five years) vocabulary, letter-word identification, and early math skills predicted second-grade academic achievement. Leseman et al. reported that a composite measure of second-language academic language skills at age six was a strong predictor of second-language reading comprehension at age eleven.

Parental input has an impact on child language development. Interestingly, the type of input that is most beneficial varies by age during early language development. As discussed in Rowe's and Lieven's chapters, around eigh-teen months, caregivers tuning in to children's current focus of attention and labelling the objects they attend to supports their expressive vocabu-lary; at age two, caregivers' diverse vocabulary becomes important; and at age three, exposing children to decontextualized talk seems most effective in building their vocabularies. It is not merely the amount of talk but the type of talk that matters. Young children's participation in interactions with their caregivers about the non-present (narratives, pretend play, explana-tions) predict their preschool and kindergarten discourse skills (Rowe, Chapter 4; Leyva and Skorb, Chapter 5) and also their adolescent academic language proficiency (Uccelli, Chapter 8).

Children are co-constructors of their own development. Harris (Chapter 3) argues that infants' pointing is not only a sign of paying attention to something but a request for information which, in turn, elicits lexical input from the caregiver. Uccelli's findings suggest that beyond language input, children's own talk about the non-present is predictive of their adolescent academic language proficiency.

Across Skills: The Language-to-School Learning Continuum

Talk about the non-present requires cognitive, socio-cognitive, and emotional skills in addition to language skills. Participation in talk about the non-present contributes to school-relevant language proficiency.

Perspective taking and other cognitive skills in school-relevant language. Rowe (Chapter 4) highlights that narrative language skills as well as cognitive and socio-cognitive skills such as theory of mind skills, prospection, and information-seeking strategies are essential for school learning. Grøver (Chapter 13) suggests that relations between extended discourse production and perspective taking tap into cognitive developments that prepare children for using language to learn about the world, and that bilingual children in particular may make use of their perspective-taking skills in their second-language narrative production. Kim and Yun (Chapter 6) point in a similar vein to the cognitive underpinning of discourse comprehension and production, such as perspective taking and other higher-order cognitive skills. Biancarosa (Chapter 12), moreover, underlines the importance of inferencing when children make sense of narratives. Hemphill, Kim and Troyer (Chapter 10) selected texts for their STARI project that challenged the middle school reader's skills in resolving diverse perspectives. Thus, it was reading activities that invited the students to respond to contrasting peer perspectives that enriched their reading comprehension.

Language interactions socialize children into ways of talking and ways of thinking. Rowe explains that posing *wh*-questions to two-year-olds elicited a verbal response from the child that fostered reasoning skills. Moreover, between the ages of eighteen and forty-two months, parents use more decontextualized language as children grow older and children were increasingly able to engage in such conversations with their parents. Use of decontextualized language in preschool fosters language and literacy skills but also theory of mind and prospective memory skills. Further, Uccelli (Chapter 8) highlights how the skills in the construct 'core academic language' correspond to expectations of shared scientific reasoning.

Differences in teacher talk afford different learning opportunities. Ford-Connors and O'Connor (Chapter 11) offer a microanalysis of the language input provided by teachers in interaction with their sixth-grade students around new vocabulary relevant for reading. In so doing, these authors reveal the nuanced analyses required to advance the field's understanding of what rich language input entails in the classroom context.

Across Languages: The Search for Cross-Linguistic Relations

In large parts of the world, children grow up multilingually. Several chapters examine under which conditions children may optimally make use of their languages as resources for learning.

Cross-linguistic relations depend on the characteristics of the languages at play. Proctor and Zhang-Wu (Chapter 16) analysed four language pairs (English being present in all four pairs) and found that, across several studies, transfer of code-based skills (phonological, phonemic awareness and word reading) was more likely to occur when languages shared a common writing system. Moreover, they demonstrated that morphological awareness in one language facilitated literacy in the other, pointing to common underlying proficiencies and suggesting that what has been learned in one language does not need to be relearned in a new language.

A certain level of proficiency (in the first and second language) is necessary for positive cross-linguistic relations. Aligned with the threshold hypothesis, originally articulated by Jim Cummins (1979), Proctor and Zhang-Wu find that children need a certain level of proficiency in their second language before the positive impact of their first language vocabulary appears. Similar evidence was offered by Uchikoshi and Marinova-Todd (Chapter 17) in their review of cross-linguistic relations. Relatedly, Leseman and colleagues (Chapter 15) reported that first language skills were positively related to the reading comprehension in the Turkish Dutch group but not related to reading comprehension in the Moroccan Dutch group. These authors suggest, similar to Proctor and Zhang-Wu, that a certain level of first language proficiency is necessary for the first language to facilitate the learning of a second language.

Across Instructional Settings: Emerging Insights for Practice

Multiple chapters examine ways in which multi-dimensional aspects of children's decontextualized/extended/academic talk may be promoted through interaction with parents and teachers at home and in school. Chapters elaborate on how instructional strategies may have differential effects for different learners and how assessments can be designed to inform instructional practice.

At home, narratives, explanations, and pretence support children's school literacy. Rowe's research has informed recent interventions to promote decontextualized extended discourse between children and parents (e.g. narratives, explanations, and pretence) as a mechanism to support longer-term language and literacy outcomes for children. Initial findings are promising.

Home authentic routines and socio-emotional support are key for children's language learning and early literacy. Leyva and Skorb (Chapter 5) demonstrated how everyday routine activities (e.g. grocery shopping, cooking) can provide opportunities for involving children in reading and writing. Their recent intervention research suggested that scaffolding children's writing and reading within culturally relevant activities that have authentic social and communicative functions is both engaging and supportive of children's literacy development. Kim and Yun (Chapter 6) point out the importance of considering socio-emotional support for language learning in instructional practices and shed light on the socio-emotional qualities of adult–child interactions.

Not only language but cognitive skills foundational for language learning are teachable. Kim and Yun report on the effects of teaching higher-order cognitive skills (e.g. comprehension monitoring, perspective taking, and inferencing) through book discussions and argue that teaching of language and cognitive skills can be most effective if it includes exposure, elicitation, extension, and emotional engagement.

Teachers tend to provide a teacher-centred and direct instructional approach. Silverman and Hartranft (Chapter 9), in a follow-up observation study, found that teachers most often used a direct instruction approach; they offered definitions and provided information on relations between words. Less often they encouraged students to make personal connections or invited peer collaboration, and in linguistically diverse classrooms, almost no attention was paid to specific needs of bilingual learners. Silverman and Hartranft's research suggests that gains in reading comprehension are greatest in classrooms in which the type of instruction offered matches student characteristics. They call for more research on differential effects of various instructional strategies for different learners.

Discourse-rich instructional approaches support language development and knowledge building. Ford-Connors and O'Connor (Chapter 11) offer a qualitative analysis of teacher–student interactions to illustrate that vocabulary understanding develops in contextually rich conversations that expand students' knowledge about words and about the world. Teachers in their study took different approaches to vocabulary instruction: a definitional approach (provided word definitions) or a contextual approach (incorporated students' ideas and prior knowledge into a deeper discussion of word meanings). On the basis of their extensive prior research, they advocate for contextual, discourse-rich, instructional approaches which are based on Vygotsky's theory of socialization through language, and they identify language as a tool for sharing knowledge.

Successful instructional approaches for struggling readers advance both basic and higher-order skills via discussion of engaging texts. Hemphill and her colleagues (Chapter 10) present their researcher-designed STARI intervention, a discussion-oriented approach especially designed for struggling adolescent readers in the United States. STARI attends to basic literacy skills (e.g. reading fluency), not as goals in themselves, but as a stepping-stone in support of critical engagement with complex yet accessible texts. This intervention, which promotes a deeper perspective and ownership of texts through discussion with peers, has demonstrated positive impact on adolescents' literacy improvement.

Research-based assessments can be purposefully designed to inform educational practice. Biancarosa (Chapter 12) presents a reading comprehension assessment grounded in theoretical and empirical evidence and designed to be informative for educational practice, in particular to identify readers who struggle.

Text-based discussion and vocabulary instruction that use the first language as a resource support bilingual learners' literacy development. Chen (Chapter 14) reports on a theoretically grounded and carefully implemented book-based language intervention for Uyghur-Chinese bilingual preschoolers in one of the poorest regions in China: Xinjiang. The intervention included three main elements: enriching the classroom literacy environment through carefully selecting and providing bilingual picture books; implementing the curriculum and encouraging shared book reading through small-group discussion, open-ended questions, and vocabulary instruction; and finally, providing professional development to teachers. Chen found a positive impact of teachers' vocabulary instruction on children's first language expressive vocabulary and second language receptive vocabulary.

Future Research

We end this introductory chapter by pointing out some future challenges to research that follow from the social-interactionist, pragmatically oriented theory of language learning and of learning through language that has informed this volume. Many chapters in this volume point out directions for future research that would extend our knowledge of the specific topic the chapter has reviewed. In this final section, we will not echo these reflections but build on them to point out three promising directions for future research.

Examining School-Relevant Language as Contextually Dependent and Multi-dimensional

Future research should seek to further identify the multiple contexts and learning activities in which children encounter and learn language. Learning in and out of school takes place while children use their linguistic resources in one or more languages to communicate and navigate socially. Language is from an early age developed in settings in which the primary focus is not on language learning per se but on communicating, sharing, and expressing intentions. As children grow older, more complex ways of using language to learn appear as they apply their oral and written language skills to discuss, argue, develop a personal stance, and figure out the perspectives of others (for discussion, see Nicolopoulou, Discussion Chapter, Part I). Pearson (Discussion Chapter 1, Part II) extends the contextual perspective on learning through language when he addresses the contextualized versus decontextualized distinction and identifies both terms as complementary and helpful in examining how children encounter words in multiple settings and how such encounters are instrumental to learning word meaning with greater breadth, depth, and precision, pointing out a direction for future research that is anchored conceptually in this distinction. Similarly, Snow in her Afterword suggests that research should seek to further clarify concepts such as decontextualized language, extended discourse, and academic language to help us define quality dimensions in language exposure and how quality of language input matters in children's learning.

Children's language learning experiences are embedded not only in face-to-face social interactional contexts but in macrostructures such as socioeconomic development and power, migration, and multilingualism, structures to which future research on learning through one or more languages should attend more closely (LeVine, Discussion Chapter 2, Part III).

Finally, Selman (Discussion Chapter 2, Part II) helps us identify a future direction for research on school-relevant language as multi-dimensional by emphasizing the significance of the emotions, perspective taking, and social needs, such as affiliation and agency, that children bring along in the interactions within which their language is developed.

*Developing Research Methods and Assessment Instruments Useful for
Studying Language-Mediated Learning*

Several chapters in this volume have presented learning outcome assessments that are closely aligned with the learning-through-language perspective. Extending our understanding of learning through language in diverse sociolinguistic contexts will require further development of research methods that allow multi-level and multivariate analysis (LeVine, Discussion Chapter 2, Part III). It will also require development of assessment instruments that theoretically link ways in which exposure and outcomes are assessed (Rutherford-Quach and Hakuta, Discussion Chapter 1, Part III). For example, if participation in a discussion-based classroom intervention is hypothesized to support learning of content-area knowledge, new ways of participating in discussion and new ways of using content-area relevant vocabulary might represent a more valid outcome than standardized vocabulary measures.

*Instructional Research Focusing on the Content to Be Taught and
Learned*

Finally, and most importantly, we hope this volume will inspire further practice-based research on instruction that supports children's language-mediated learning. Several chapters offer evidence of instructional interventions that have positively affected children and adolescents' learning inside and out of school, such as studies of instruction in multilingual classrooms with young learners in China (Chen, Chapter 14) or in middle school classrooms with struggling and diverse readers in the US (Hemphill et al., Chapter 10). Snow (Afterword) emphasizes the *content of school learning* as the organizational educational principle, with academic language use such as explanatory or argumentative talk being ways in which school content is processed and acquired. We need more research that helps us identify instructional strategies optimizing content learning through language in the diverse linguistic and cultural contexts within which children and young people live – instruction that builds on and further advances their language resources and the perspective-taking and discursive skills that are foundational in participating in and becoming engaged in talk and text at home and in school.

Part I

Learning through Language during the
Preschool and Early Elementary School Years

2   Input, Interaction, and Learning in Early Language Development

Elena Lieven

One thing is certain: if children are not exposed to a language, they will not learn it. On the other hand, while most children learn to talk, they do so in a wide variety of environments, at different rates and to different levels of competence. Although predictive relations are complex, speed and size of early vocabulary as well as the early onset of combinatorial speech have all been implicated in children's abilities with later academic language and literacy. These facts raise a large number of open questions about exactly how early language learning takes place, its consequences for later language development and the influence of the child's environment on this process. In this chapter, I first outline the course of early language development and its impact on later language development before turning to studies of environmental influences on the process of language learning. Throughout this review I will provide evidence both from studies in our LuCiD Centre (www.lucid.ac.uk) and from other research that addresses these issues. The LuCiD Centre is a five-year collaboration between researchers at three Universities in the north-west of the United Kingdom, investigating language and communicative development between six months and six years of age.

The Course of Language Development and Its Relation to Later Outcomes

A lot happens in the first year of life as infants move through a series of stages of developing sensitivity to the language or languages around them. Initially, they can discriminate between different intonation patterns (Nazzi, Bertoncini, & Mehler, 1998) then, at around six months, they start to discriminate the consonants and vowels of the language that they are hearing (Kuhl, 1991). Their babbling also shows a move from sensitivity to more universal, to more language specific, sounds (de Boysson-Bardies & Vihman, 1991). Children who babble early also tend to be children who start to talk early probably because they are practising the sounds of their language as they babble. A longitudinal study of forty-six infants, seen monthly between nine and eighteen months, found that earlier onset of babbling predicted the age at which the children produced their first words (McGillion et al., 2017).

At around six to nine months, infants are able to identify some words in the input (Bergelson & Swingley, 2012) and to start to extract patterns, at least in simple experimental situations (Saffran, 2001). From around eight months, they are beginning to map specific words to concepts. A study by Fernald, Pinto, Swingley, Weinbergy, and McRoberts (1998) showed a major increase between fifteen and twenty-four months in the speed with which infants could match a known name to a known object in a looking task. At fifteen months, infants did not turn to look until after the end of the word; by eighteen months, they could turn at the end of the word; and by twenty-four months, they were turning before the end of the word at the first sound that discriminates the two words (e.g. the 'g sound' in *doggie* from the 'l sound' in *dollie*). If the speed of mapping a word to an object relates more generally to how fast infants can process incoming speech and segment it, then this will affect how fast they are able to learn new words and to map them to concepts (Fernald, Perfors, & Marchman, 2006).

The speed with which words or segments in the input can be identified on the basis of previous experience will also affect infants' ability to abstract the distributional regularities of both structure and meaning that will allow for further learning. Since the input language is heard or seen as a rapidly disappearing series of sounds or gestures, it is going to be far more difficult to divide it into meaningful segments with a low processing speed. And, in turn, 'processing speed' is a proxy for a dynamic system in which how much the infant already knows is going to affect how easily new material can be identified and learned. Thus being able to recognize a word is important in helping to segment the material around it (Frost, Monaghan, & Christiansen, 2016), and detecting patterns is also going to be affected by the speed with which the infant can identify already known material. We know that eight-month-old infants are able to detect patterns in artificial language learning tasks (Saffran, Newport, & Aslin, 1996). In these tasks, infants hear a stream of three-syllable nonsense words (e.g. *babupu, bupada, dutaba, patubi, pidabu, tutibu*) in which the probability between the syllables within the 'words' is higher than the probability of syllable sequences between 'words'. The eight-month-olds in these experiments show that they have detected these probabilities after only two minutes of listening. Although this task is very 'stripped down' compared to what infants have to do to segment incoming natural language, there is also evidence that they are becoming sensitive to regularities in the natural language input that they are exposed to. For instance, a study by Shi, Werker, and Cutler (2006) suggests that at eleven months (but not at eight months), infants could discriminate between real English functors (determiners and possessive pronouns) and minimally different 'nonsense' functors.

To my knowledge, there are no studies that show the relation between these early statistical learning skills and later language development, though Kidd (2012) has shown a relationship between implicit learning skills in four- to six-year-olds and their syntactic proficiency. In an ongoing study, the LuCiD Centre 0–5 project is following eighty children between the ages of six months to four and a half years to investigate the extent to which these early perceptual, processing, and communicative skills are predictive of individual differences in later language development. Measures include visual sequence learning (at twelve months), segmentation and generalization from an artificial speech stream (at sixteen months), speed of linguistic processing (at eighteen months), and word-referent mapping (at eighteen months). The relationship between these measures and language outcomes will be analysed as the children develop.

The Beginnings of Intentional Communication

So far, I have been considering the development of speech and language without worrying about communication. But there is a very strong argument to say that children would have great difficulty learning language unless it was embedded in a communicative context and, equally fundamentally, unless they understand that they can communicate with others and that others are trying to communicate with them. Bruner (1981) was a very strong proponent of this position, and more recently, Tomasello (1999, 2003) has argued that it is the 'nine-month revolution' in children's development of intention reading that is crucial for the breakthrough into language. Intention reading is part of the development whereby infants start to understand both themselves and others as agents with mental goals which are separate from just the instrumental means of obtaining them. It is marked by a move from dyadic interactions (i.e. interactions with *either* people *or* objects) to triadic interactions (in which infants share attention to an object or event with another person and know that they are doing so). Tomasello points out that although children can learn individual words before this, it is only around twelve months, after the development of these intention reading skills, that language learning really takes off.

While turn-taking interactions and various sorts of dyadic exchanges between infants and their caregivers often start from birth, there is a major developmental change around seven to nine months, which sees infants starting to develop a whole range of behaviours which reflect the beginnings of attention sharing and intention reading. These involve not just joint engagement with objects but active sharing of attention with others, often indicated by gaze checking, pointing, showing, and inferences about what the partner knows or does not know (Boundy, Cameron-Faulkner, & Theakston, 2016). For instance, while it might be thought that infants simply point as an expression of their own interest in an object or event, both experiments and naturalistic studies have shown that they also point to share interest with other people as well as to inform them and help them to find things. Infants will persist in pointing or use other methods of drawing the attention of others to events and they will differentiate between situations in which other people have misunderstood their communicative intention, ignored it, or fulfilled it by responding appropriately (Lizskowski, Carpenter, Henning, Striano, & Tomasello, 2004).

Thus infants start to develop the ability to match the forms of language which they have started to extract, to an emergent understanding of the meaning being communicated, and this provides the foundation for the move into developing comprehension and production.

Children seem to be on a developmental trajectory for these early developments in language and communication. Cross-cultural studies suggest that they start producing joint attention behaviours, showing, giving, pointing, imitation, and first word comprehension at roughly the same mean ages across a number of very different cultures. This is true of both naturalistic studies (Lieven & Stoll, 2013; Brown, 2011; Salomo & Liszkowski, 2013) and of semi-experimental studies (Callaghan et al., 2011). Lieven and Stoll (2013) studied the onset of pointing, imitation and giving/showing in a rural Rai culture of East Nepal and a mixed rural/township culture of Germany and found no difference in the mean ages at which these behaviours emerged, with reaching and requesting for children in both cultures noted at eight months and points, imitations, and offering objects at ten months. Brown (2011) compared the rate at which adults and infants initiated interactions in the community of Rossel Island, Papua New Guinea, and a Tzeltal community of the Chiapas in Mexico. These were measured in terms of 'an initiating move, [a] summons to interaction which is not necessarily responded to' (p. 39). Despite very different rates of these initiations with the infants by the adults in the two communities, the rates of initiation by the infants (aged ten to twelve months) were very similar. Finally, Callaghan et al. (2011) conducted a semi-experimental, cross-cultural study in rural communities of Peru and India as well as a town community of Newfoundland in Canada and again found few differences in the mean age at which children manifested these behaviours in the three communities. However, while the mean age of onset of these behaviours shows less variation between cultures, there is considerable evidence, for instance, from the Salomo and Liszkowski (2013) study, that the rate at which children use these behaviours varies both within and across cultures and that this can be affected by caregiver interaction.

It is important not to see these 'intention reading' behaviours as independent from each other but, rather, as reflecting the emergent development of intentional understanding. Thus a study conducted in our Centre showed that infants' showing and giving behaviours with their caretakers, together with the length of the following interaction, predicted the rate at which the infants pointed at twelve months (Cameron-Faulkner, Theakston, Lieven, & Tomasello, 2015). In turn, there is evidence that these communicative gestures, used to share attention, are precursors to language development; early gesture use is a strong predictor of later language ability. For example, babies who start to use communicative pointing early also develop language earlier (Colonnesi, Stams, Koster, & Noom, 2010) and know more words at eighteen months of age (McGillion et al., 2017). I return to the ways in which these developments are influenced by caregiver interaction later in this chapter.

Word Learning

Most children can comprehend more words than they produce. Data from the Stanford Wordbank (http://wordbank.stanford.edu/) show that, by eighteen months, the average American English-learning child understands 262 words, although this varies widely between children (from around 120 to 367 words). First words are produced between nine and fourteen months of age, but there is also great individual variation. At eighteen months, the size of children's productive vocabulary can vary between ten and around two hundred words. American children from lower socio-economic status backgrounds tend to have, on average, smaller expressive vocabularies between sixteen and thirty months than children from higher SES backgrounds, as measured by the Bates-MacArthur CDI – a parent report measure (Arriaga, Fenson, Cronan, & Pethick, 1998).

Relations between early vocabulary measures and later language development are complex. In Rescorla's (2011) study of late talkers, she found that, on the one hand, many late talkers have caught up by school age. In some studies, their performance on language tests can be below a control group of children with no reported early language delay, but these children can perform within the normal range on tests of expressive and receptive language. However, some children who are subsequently diagnosed with language delay do not always show up as late talkers in infancy. Thus evidence from longitudinal studies suggests that the relation between measures of early vocabulary and later language as measured by receptive vocabulary, grammatical scales, and/or narrative ability is not that reliable for individual children (e.g. Henrichs et al., 2011). However, predictive relationships are improved by risk factors such as the presence of both expressive and receptive deficits (e.g. Paul & Roth, 2011) or a family history of language difficulties (e.g. Bishop et al., 2012; Zambrana, Pons, Eadie, & Ystrom, 2014).

Early Combinatorial Speech

Children start to combine words and short phrases when they have learned between fifty and one hundred words. Between the ages of two and three, children learn the basic morphology of their language and increase the length and complexity of their utterances. However, the syntax of what they can say and understand is heavily dependent on the frequency with which these structures appear in the input and on their contexts of use (Ambridge, Kidd, Rowland, & Theakston, 2015). For instance, the verbs that children hear in the input and even the specific form in which they appear are those that children learn first (Naigles & Hoff-Ginsberg, 1998; Theakston, Lieven, Pine, & Rowland, 2004). But frequency is not everything: in a study of specific pronoun–auxiliary combinations (e.g. *I'm, you are, he is*), we showed that while the frequency of third-person combinations in the input predicted the order in which they were recorded in the children's speech, this was not the case for first- and second-person pronouns (Theakston et al., 2005). We argued that this is almost certainly because children want to talk about themselves (*I*) and parents tend to talk about you!

Although structures which are frequent in the input often underpin children's correct use, they can also lead to errors as children start to generalize across the system. In a study of children's errors with first-person pronouns (*me do it, me go there, me sing*), we (Kirjavainen, Theakston, & Lieven, 2009) found that children who heard more complex sentences in the input with *me* placed before the verb (e.g. *Let me help you, Watch me dancing*) were significantly more likely to make these errors. Experimental studies show that when context and frequency are stripped away, even much older children have difficulty understanding more complex syntax, for instance detailed morphology (Dittmar, Abbot-Smith, Lieven, & Tomasello, 2008), complement structures (Brandt, Lieven, & Tomasello, 2010), and relative clauses (Brandt, Kidd, Lieven, & Tomasello, 2009).

We know from the work of Rowe and Goldin-Meadow (2009) that gesture and speech combinations at eighteen months predict sentence complexity at three and a half years. However the precise relations between measures of early vocabulary and of combinatorial speech and later language outcomes are not entirely clear. Interestingly, predictive stability in language measures is more robust between four and fourteen years of age than at the earlier ages from twenty months to four years (Bornstein, Hahn, Putnick, & Suwalsky, 2014). However, a recent study suggests that children who were late in combining words were more likely to have language difficulties later than those who were late to produce their first words (Rudolph & Leonard, 2016), suggesting that measures of combinatorial speech may be more informative than vocabulary measures alone.

Finally, we have to recognize that the balance of importance of the types of language processing skills (e.g. the speed with which children can identify a word in the speech stream) and the intention reading skills (e.g. children's ability to understand the need to share common ground with their interlocutor) outlined in this section may be different for different children. For most typically developing children, language, communication, and interaction almost certainly go hand in hand, each building on the other. However, the existence of children with a clear diagnosis of core autism but good vocabulary and structural language skills suggests that there may be somewhat variable routes into language, though even here strong correlations are reported between children diagnosed with autism but who show relatively good joint attentional skills and language development (Lieven, 2017).

The Influences of Environment and Interaction

Influences of Caregiver Interaction on Precursors to Language Development

Is there evidence for early caregiver effects on the early precursors and predictors of language development outlined above? To say that infants are on a developmental trajectory is, of course, not to say that a child brought up in a world without any interaction would show the same trajectory. On the one hand, children who are not exposed to language do not learn it, but on the other, these children do develop communication skills (Goldin-Meadow, Mylander, de Villiers, Bates, & Volterra, 1984) based partly on their interaction with others but almost certainly also on developments that are initially at least, somewhat independent of language input, for instance knowledge about objects and events and intention reading skills. And neurotypical children who are exposed to very different amounts and styles of language will still learn to use it at least to the levels typical of the community in which they are growing up. But there are widespread individual differences between children growing up in the same culture in the age at which first gestures, words, and multi-word utterances are produced. Since there are a number of studies in which these differences are related to later outcomes in terms of language development, literacy, and school achievement, it is obviously important to know how they are related to children's environments and the kinds of interaction in which they and their caregivers engage. There is a tendency for dichotomized explanations for these differences: they are seen either to result from factors intrinsic to the child (for instance individual differences in pattern recognition, processing speed, memory, executive function) or from aspects of the environment. But it is almost certainly a mistake to make this sharp distinction between intrinsic and external influences on development. Each developmental stage that a child arrives at is the outcome of earlier developmental achievements, and this then affects the child's subsequent interaction with his or her environment.

Thus there is suggestive evidence that children's developmental trajectories for communicative and language skills can be influenced by the nature of their interactions. Hsu and Fogel (2001) found that the thirteen infants in their study, followed from four to twenty-four weeks, vocalized more when caregivers were interacting with them: when mothers were smiling and making eye contact, they produced more syllabic, speech-like vocalizations. This was supported by Bornstein, Putnick, Cote, Haynes, and Suwalsky (2015), who found significantly correlated contingencies between the vocalizations of 684 mothers and their five-month-old infants' vocalizations across communities in eleven countries. Likewise, Goldstein, King, and West (2003) found that mothers who responded to the vocalizations of their eight-month-old infants with interactive behaviours such as smiling and touching had infants who produced more developmentally advanced vocalizations. This suggests that there is a degree of entrainment of infants into interactive communication with their caregivers. Snow's (1977b) paper suggested something similar: she found that mothers responded to their infants' behaviours in turn-taking interactions as if they were communicative but that the behaviours that they responded to changed with the babies' development, with mothers being more likely to respond to more clearly communicative behaviours as the children got older.

There are correlations between caregivers' use of gestures and their children's gesture production in interaction (e.g. Namy, Acredolo, & Goodwyn, 2000), but it is difficult to disentangle cause and effect: children who gesture a lot may attract the attention of their caregivers who then gesture in return. Thus there is obviously the possibility that as the infant develops, this influences caregivers to interact with more focussed communicative interactions and thus the influence is in both directions. However, there is suggestive evidence that the amount of caregiver joint action and gesture use (e.g. Salomo & Liszkowski, 2013) and the length of the caregiver–child interactional sequence following a child's gesture at one developmental time point (e.g. Cameron-Faulkner et al., 2015) predict the onset and/or frequency of children's later gesture use. In a training study, Matthews, Behne, Lieven, and Tomasello (2012) found that, while increasing the amount of maternal pointing had no effect on the rate of pointing in their ten- to twelve-month-old infants, this was predicted by joint attention and the amount of pointing in naturalistic recordings at the beginning of the study. Thus, caregivers who promote shared interaction with their children and who are sensitive to their children's gestures and focus of attention may be more likely to provide the types of contingent interactions that facilitate later gesture use and subsequently language learning. This is supported by Carpenter, Nagell, Tomasello, Butterworth, and Moore's (1998) results, which suggest that the amount of joint engagement between mothers and their infants, as well as the mothers' use of language that followed into the infant's focus of attention, predicted infants' early gestural and language skills.

However, it is not clear whether these findings only apply to certain groups, for instance from cultures with particular ideologies of parenting or for mothers with more school-based education. Richman, Miller, and Levine (1992), in a comparison of mothers' behaviour with infants in Kenyan (Gusii) and Boston communities, showed that mothers responded differently to non-distressed infant vocalizations, the Boston mothers with verbal responses and the Gusii mothers with physical holding and quieting. The Gusii mothers had many fewer years of schooling than the Boston mothers, but there were also major cultural differences in ideologies of parenting between the two groups. Mastin and Vogt (2016) found that the structure of infant attention varied in Mozambican mother–infant interactions as a function of whether they lived in rural or urban settings (see also Rogoff, 2003; Keller, 2013). It may not be sensible to try to disentangle the effects of wider cultural practices from educational level since the two are so closely intertwined.

Influences of Caregiver Language on Children's Language Development

We know that children have to be exposed to language in order to develop it. But this leaves many open questions: how much language, what kind of language, and in what contexts?

Influence of Caregiver Language on Vocabulary Development

There is much research showing correlations between the amount of talk infants hear and their own rate of vocabulary development. So clearly what children hear matters and is related to their language development. On the other hand, most children do develop language appropriate to their social group and often under quite different environmental circumstances. Early studies in non-technological societies reported cultures in which babies were rarely spoken to and others in which there was an emphasis on training them to talk (see Lieven 2013). Although these studies raised extremely interesting questions, it is quite hard to compare them since they did not report quantitative results on the amount of input or on any individual differences in language development that might be correlated with it. In the following, I will therefore confine myself to studies in WEIRD (Western, Educated, Industrialized, Rich, and Democratic) cultures.

There is a wealth of research on the best contexts for word learning. How much language children hear is important: children whose parents talk a lot to them have faster vocabulary development (e.g. Hart & Risley, 1995; Cartmill et al., 2013). A study by Hurtado, Marchman, and Fernald (2008) shows that the amount mothers talk to their eighteen-month-old infants is related to these children's speed of word processing and vocabulary at twenty-four months. This goes beyond showing a correlation over time in the size of children's vocabularies but also suggests a potential mechanism: caregivers who talk a lot to their children promote the speed with which their infants can process what they hear.

However, while amount of talk is important, input quality may be even more important especially beyond the very early stages of word learning. Thus the extent to which caregivers talk about the child's focus of interest (contingency), the variability in the words used to children, and the use of decontextualized talk have all been used as measures of input quality. At the earliest stages of acquisition (e.g. around eighteen months of age), tuning in to the child's current focus of attention and labelling objects of interest is related to children's expressive vocabulary (e.g. Tomasello & Farrar, 1986; Rollins, 2003; McGillion et al., 2017). As children get older (around two years), using a diverse vocabulary including rare or infrequent words becomes more important to enable them to develop a more sophisticated vocabulary (Pan, Rowe, Singer, & Snow 2005). Hoff (2003) shows that SES differences in the language ability of two-year-olds can be explained almost entirely in terms of SES differences in maternal speech and that the crucial difference is in the complexity/lexical diversity of high-SES mothers' speech. At even later ages (from around three years), exposing children to decontextualized talk seems most effective at building their receptive vocabularies (Rowe, 2012).

Influence of Caregiver Language on Syntactic Development

Famously, it has long been a tenet of the Universal Grammar theoretical framework that syntax cannot be learned from the language that children hear. Ultimately, this argument derived from Gold's theorem (reconceived in terms of language acquisition as Baker's paradox; cf. Bowerman, 1988), which states that, without negative evidence – evidence which rules out ungrammatical sentences – overgeneralization cannot be prevented. Since children do not regularly or reliably receive direct correction for ungrammatical sentences, a universal grammar from which they can build their specific language is said to be the answer. The main challenges to this 'no negative evidence' position have centred on two approaches. The first rejects the idea of the child as a hypothesis tester during grammar construction by proposing probabilistic learning in which different strengths of representation compete on the basis of different factors (including frequency, transparency, and communicative relevance; MacWhinney, 2004a; Ambridge, Pine, Rowland, Chang, & Bidgood, 2013).

The second is around the idea of implicit negative evidence. As Sokolov and Snow (1994) argued, children often receive replies to their utterances which are contingent on what they have just said and this could be seen as supplying them with information about the syntax and semantics of their utterances, particularly if, as shown by Chouinard and Clark (2003), caregivers are more likely to provide these implicit corrections when children make errors. This study also shows that children quite frequently take up these recasts and repeat the correct form. However, we know that there is a wide range in the extent to which caregivers provide these kinds of recasts or expansions, and while the extent to which they do this is positively correlated with speed of learning, it is probably better to think of this sort of linguistic information as part of the way that children build up their grammar through developing a network of more or less frequent constructions, which then compete for production and comprehension along a number of different features: pragmatic, semantic etc. To give an example, English-speaking children learn from fairly early on to provide the determiners *a, an*, or *the* before count nouns. At the very early stages, children seem to reflect frequencies in what they hear as to the particular nouns used with either *a* or *the* (Pine, Freudenthal, Krajewski, & Gobet, 2013). They rapidly develop the ability to distinguish between the use of *a* to introduce a noun and *the* to refer to it subsequently in discourse (Hughes & Allen, 2015). However, a full understanding of determiner use takes a considerable time to develop. For instance, we carried out a study in which one of three objects was shared with two- and three-year-olds, who were subsequently asked to '*fetch the X*'. Two-year-olds brought any one of the three objects at chance, while three-year-olds were significantly more likely to bring the object already shared (Schmerse, Lieven, & Tomasello, 2015). And there are many studies showing that children find it difficult in experimental situations to refer in ways that are non-ambiguous (Dickson, 1982; Matthews, Theakston, Lieven, & Tomasello, 2006). However, in a training study, we showed that giving children feedback when they were unclear led to much better performance (Matthews, Butcher, Lieven, & Tomasello, 2012). As well as learning through listening and trying to predict what their interlocutors are referring to, children will be likely to learn through breakdowns in shared reference.

We know from many studies that expanding (or recasting) children's utterances is related to a range of language measures, including question formation (Nelson, 1977), morphology (Farrar, 1990), and vocabulary (Taumoepeau & Ruffman, 2016). The meta-analysis by Cleave, Becker, Curran, Owen Van Horne, and Fey (2015) focuses on the benefits of recasting for children with specific language impairment or who were late talkers. In addition, there is good evidence for the effects of not only lexical diversity but also syntactic complexity in parental speech on language outcomes (Rowe, 2012; Huttenlocher, Waterfall, Vasilyeva, Vevea, & Hedges, 2010). An earlier study by Huttenlocher and colleagues (Huttenlocher, Vasilyeva, Cymerman, & Levine, 2002) found that this also held for teachers: children whose teachers used more complex utterances over a year in the classroom showed greater use of more complex language at the end of the preschool year. In addition to what may be direct effects of the frequency with which constructions are heard, contingent talk, with its possibility of providing a correct grammatical, semantic, or pragmatic model, will affect the child's representations because it changes the relative frequencies of constructions (and therefore contributes to driving out the incorrect forms). But contingent talk will also be highly salient precisely because it is temporally close to the child's own utterance and because it is semantically and pragmatically related to it.

Conclusion

Becoming a fluent speaker, able to express complex thoughts and to achieve pragmatic sophistication, is at the heart of school readiness and later academic achievement. The foundations are laid very early on, as the ability to share common ground in pre-verbal communication, to learn a rich vocabulary, and to be able use syntax to express one's ideas fluently all build on each other at early stages in life. It is clear that the early environment in which children grow up and the ways in which they are spoken to is central to children's language development, though many open questions remain. Most children will learn to talk at least to the level of their surrounding environment under a variety of interactional and communicative situations. But this will not necessarily ensure that they will develop the linguistic and communicative skills required for the literacy and academic attainment that they need. At this stage in our research endeavour, I think the following take-away messages are reasonably secure: contingent communicative interactions involving turn-taking, gesture, and language will enhance a baby's readiness for language learning; following a toddler's focus of attention, talking about what they are interested in and the world around them, will enhance word learning; and using diverse language will help children develop the more complex ways of saying things that will allow them to produce pragmatically nuanced and semantically precise language.

3   Infants Want Input

Paul L. Harris

In her work on language acquisition, Catherine Snow has consistently empha-sized the impact of the type of input that children receive, whether in the form of simplified speech (Snow, 1972), sophisticated vocabulary (Weizman & Snow, 2001), or narratives and explanations (Snow & Beals, 2006). In this chapter, I ask about the early part played by the infant in securing that input. I ask if infants have any impact on the input that they receive, and if so, how? I argue that infants display an interrogative stance – effectively, they 'ask' for information from their caregivers. I first review evidence on the interrogative stance and then discuss individual differences in its emergence.

What Is the Point?

Before they start to talk, infants are able to communicate via non-verbal gestures. Especially in the case of pointing, there is good evidence of a relationship to later language ability (Colonnesi, Stams, Koster, & Noom, 2010). One plausible interpretation of this link is that infant-guided naming episodes reduce the likelihood of mapping errors. On this view, when the infant points, a caregiver's response means that infant and caregiver end up attending to the same object or event. Hence, pointing is likely to ensure that any lexical input from the caregiver that such pointing elicits will be mapped onto a target that is the focus of their joint attention. As such, mapping errors by the infant would likely be reduced. Admittedly, such infant-guided naming episodes might not be essential for language development. When a caregiver names an object, infants can use non-verbal cues – the caregiver's direction of gaze or pointing gesture – to figure out what she is referring to (Baldwin, 1991). Still, any naming that is triggered by infant pointing may be especially helpful in minimizing mapping errors because the focus of the infant's attention is likely to be highly legible for the caregiver whereas infants may be prone to error in determining their interlocutor's focus of attention.

This emphasis on the reduction of mapping errors is plausible, but it may be overlooking another important function of pointing. As several investigators have suggested, pointing can also be embedded in a less symmetrical exchange – one in which the infant points not just in order to invite an interlocutor to jointly look at an interesting object but also in order to elicit information about the object. On this view, the infant is not producing a point simply in order to say something like, 'Wow – look at that!' Rather, the infant is requesting information: 'Wow – what is that?' It is plausible that such epistemic requests have an important linguistic pay off. They are likely to elicit not just caregiver attention but lexical input from the caregiver. And there is ample evidence (reviewed in the chapters by Lieven, Chapter 2 and Rowe, Chapter 4) documenting the plausible notion that input promotes language development.

In the next section, I lay out the case for pointing as an interrogative gesture. I describe five sets of recent studies offering persuasive evidence that infants point in the expectation that they will thereby receive information about the object they have pointed to. I then turn to recent findings that probe individual differences among infants in the manner and frequency of their pointing.

The Interrogative Stance

A growing body of research shows that young children are more likely to seek and endorse information from informants who have proven knowledgeable rather than ignorant or mistaken (Harris, 2012; Harris & Corriveau, 2011; Koenig & Harris, 2005). Begus and Southgate (2012) have demonstrated a similar type of selectivity in sixteen-month-olds. Infants watched as a series of novel objects was presented in full view of the infant but behind a female experimenter seated facing the infant. Infants often pointed the objects out to the experimenter but were less likely to do so if she had proven to be poorly informed. More specifically, they pointed less if she had previously produced the wrong names for familiar objects and appeared unsure of the names of the novel objects. A second study suggested that it was the experimenter's previous errors rather than her current uncertainty that reduced infants' interrogative points. If she had previously offered non-committal (e.g. 'Wow, look at this!') rather than incorrect information, and then appeared unsure how to name the novel objects, infants did point them out to her. In sum, these findings indicate that infants – like preschoolers – rapidly construct an 'epistemic profile' of a potential informant and direct their pointing gestures to someone whom they have found to be knowledgeable rather than the misinformed.

Two studies by Kovács, Tauzin, Téglás, Gergely, and Csibra (2014) show that, even at twelve months old, infants prefer to use pointing to elicit informative rather than uninformative input from an interlocutor. As in the study by Begus and Southgate (2012), infants were presented with a series of attractive puppets likely to elicit pointing. In the sharing condition, the experimenter responded to infant points but without providing any information. She smiled, nodded, said 'Uh huh', and looked back and forth between the child and the puppet. By contrast, in the informing condition, the experimenter offered an evaluation of the object – she expressed a positive or negative emotion via her facial expression and an affective interjection (such as 'Wow' or 'Yuck'). Infants pointed more often in the informing condition, especially on later trials – suggesting that they were gradually constructing a profile of the experimenter as a more or less informative interlocutor. Similar results emerged in a follow-up study in which infants were shown an atypical member of a known category (e.g. a toy racing car rather than a regular toy car) and the experimenter responded to infant pointing with either a predictable and familiar name (e.g. 'car') or with an unpredictable and unfamiliar name (e.g. 'dax'). Infants pointed more in the latter case. Thus, in each study, infants were more likely to point if the experimenter provided new information about the object they had pointed at rather than an uninformative acknowledgement of shared attention.

To the extent that infants appear to monitor interlocutors for their informativeness, we can reasonably expect that information delivered in the wake of a pointing gesture will be more likely to be encoded by infants. To test this possibility, Begus, Gliga, and Southgate (2012) showed sixteen-month-old infants two different objects at once. When infants pointed to one of them, the experimenter demonstrated an action – either with the object that the infant had pointed at or with the other object (i.e. the one not indicated). After a short delay, infants were given the demonstration object and prompted to reproduce the action they had just seen the experimenter perform on it. Infants were better able to reproduce the demonstrated action if the experimenter had performed it on the object that they had pointed at rather than on the alternative object that they had ignored – even though, as further analysis confirmed, they had been equally attentive during the demonstration no matter which object had been used. Thus, consistent with the idea that infants point to elicit information, sought information was better encoded than unsought information.

Is the same encoding effect found when infants are given information about the name of an object rather than shown what to do with an object? Lucca and Wilbourn (2017) presented twelve- and eighteen-month-old infants with two objects on each of three trials. On any given trial, the experimenter waited until the infant expressed some kind of preference for one of the two objects by either pointing, or reaching or looking toward it. The experimenter then brought this target object close to the infant and repeatedly named it (e.g. *This is a Modi! See the Modi! Wow, it's a Modi! Look at the Modi!*). In a test phase, the two objects were placed back on the table and after a brief silent phase, infants were prompted to attend to the target object (e.g. *Where is the Modi? Find the Modi! See the Modi?*). Selective looking during this naming phase was compared to looking during the earlier silent phase, with the expectation that infants would show a stronger bias to look at the named object in the naming phase as compared to the preceding silent phase. The more precise question was whether infants would be especially prone to such a looking bias if they had expressed their initial object preference via pointing rather than via looking or reaching. Indeed, exactly this pattern did emerge, albeit only among the eighteen-month-olds and not among the twelve-month-olds. Thus, eighteen-month-olds were more likely to encode the name of an object if they had been told its name in the wake of a pointing gesture.

Of course, it might be argued that infants who point differ from those who do not – perhaps they are more precocious or have a bigger vocabulary – so that their superior lexical uptake is simply a reflection of such individual differences. But this objection does not apply to the findings of Lucca and Wilbourn (2017) because infants' learning when they had pointed was compared with their learning when they had not. Indeed, further analysis showed that infants who pointed performed no better on the trials when they happened not to point than infants who never pointed. Thus, infants who pointed were not inherently better word learners – their superior learning revealed itself only on trials when they pointed as compared to trials when they did not. Finally, a follow-up study showed that no learning advantage accrued in the wake of infant pointing if the experimenter responded inappropriately – by presenting and naming the object that the infant had *not* pointed at. So, pointing was not associated with a state of generalized readiness to learn. Instead, it was associated with a more targeted disposition to learn, notably to learn about the indicated object. In sum, these findings fit nicely with those obtained by Begus et al. (2012). When infants have pointed toward an object and then learn something from an adult about that object – they are shown its function or told its name – they are more likely to encode that information than if they have not pointed at it.

A plausible interpretation of such superior encoding is that it is a consequence of a state of cognitive receptivity that accompanies pointing. Begus, Gliga, and Southgate (2016) report two studies aimed at identifying the neural signature of such cognitive receptivity. In the first study, eleven-month-olds were familiarized with two adults who differed in the information that they offered about a series of objects. One adult – the so-called Non-Informant – effectively provided no information. She only pointed at the objects or handled them. By contrast, the other adult – the Informant – did provide information. She either named the objects or demonstrated their function. In subsequent test trials, each adult reappeared individually and faced each of a series of novel objects. Theta activity (i.e. EEG oscillatory activity in the theta frequency range), a neural signal associated with cognitive receptivity, was analysed during the initial anticipatory period of each trial when either the Informant or Non-Informant was about to interact with the particular object in front of them but had not yet started to do so. Theta activity proved to be higher when the Informant rather than the Non-Informant reappeared facing a novel object.

In a follow-up study, eleven-month-olds were again introduced to two informants. Both informants supplied the names of several objects, but one informant provided labels in English, whereas the other provided labels in Spanish, a language foreign to all the infants being tested. During the initial anticipatory period of subsequent test trials, theta activity was greater when infants faced the informant they now knew to be a native speaker as compared to the informant who was a foreign speaker. By implication, infants were in a state of greater cognitive receptivity when face-to-face with someone they knew to be a speaker of a language that they understood.

Taken together, these two studies suggest that infants prepare to receive and encode information, especially from those who have reliably supplied it in the immediate past. We do not yet have direct evidence, but it seems plausible that such readiness, as indexed by theta activity, is more likely to be in play when infants point to an object rather than look at it or reach for it. Such findings would consolidate the proposal that when infants engage in pointing, they do so in an interrogative fashion – they want input and are especially receptive to input that they have thereby elicited as compared to input they receive unbidden.

Summarizing, infants prefer knowledgeable rather than inaccurate informants as well as informants who provide unexpected or new information about a novel object as opposed to an uninformative acknowledgement of shared attention. Information about the function or name of an object is better retained if it is provided in the wake of infant pointing. Moreover, faced with a potentially informative interlocutor, infants display a neural signal associated with cognitive receptivity. Taken together, these studies imply that pointing signals an interrogative stance – a request for input from a potentially informative interlocutor and a cognitive receptivity to process and retain that input when it is provided.

Individual Differences in Pointing

As noted in Lieven's chapter (Chapter 2), recent research has identified a relatively stable timetable for the emergence of pointing. Liszkowski, Brown, Callaghan, Takada, and de Vos (2012) studied its emergence in seven different cultures varying in language spoken, average family size, urban versus rural setting, and source of livelihood. The investigators invited caregivers to carry their infants (ranging from seven to seventeen months) on their hips as they walked through an area where there were various potentially interesting items to look at – pictures of animals, a balloon, a blinking light, and so forth. The timetable for the emergence of infant pointing and the morphology of the gesture proved to be similar across the seven cultures. Whole-handed pointing started at around eight months. Index finger pointing, in which the index finger was clearly extended relative to the other fingers, started later – at around eleven months – but eventually became more frequent than whole-handed pointing.

Follow-up studies have added nuance to this apparently stable and universal timetable. Lüke, Grimminger, Rohfling, Liszkowski, and Ritterfeld (2017) observed infants' pointing at twelve months in three different settings: two relatively structured settings and a third, semi-naturalistic setting. One of the two structured settings was designed to elicit declarative pointing – infants were seated in a high chair facing the experimenter and a screen with four windows through which animal puppets could be presented. The other structured setting was designed to elicit imperative pointing – four mechanical or musical toys were presented on a table out of the infants' reach. The third, semi-naturalistic setting was similar to that used by Liszkowski et al. (2012): caregivers were asked to carry their infant through a room containing a variety of interesting objects.

Infants were classified as either index finger pointers or whole-handed pointers. Regression analyses confirmed that the number of points in both the declarative and the imperative setting was a predictor of word production at twenty-four months. However, further analysis showed that this predictive relationship was carried only by index finger points and not by whole-handed pointing. Moreover, when index finger pointers and whole-handed pointers were compared in terms of their language skills at twenty-four months, index finger pointers proved superior in terms of language competence whether assessed via a psychometric test or via parent report. Indeed, when children were classified at twenty-four months in terms of the presence or absence of language delay, the dichotomous classification of their pointing mode at twelve months proved to be a strong predictor. Pointing classification at twelve months led to an accurate prediction of language status (i.e. delayed vs not delayed) at twenty-four months for 85 percent of the sample.

Combining these various findings, a plausible working conclusion is that human infants display a relatively stable transition in which they request, indicate, or ask about objects of interest via whole-handed pointing, and then via an increasing use of index finger pointing as they approach their first birthday. Nevertheless, despite the existence of this transition, the age at which it occurs varies from infant to infant and appears to have down-stream consequences for the child's language status one year later. These findings raise two intriguing questions – what is the nature of the transition from open-handed to index finger pointing, and why might it be consequential for subsequent language development?

One possible answer to the first question is that the shift in gesture morphology is just that – a motoric shift roughly akin to the transition from crawling to walking. However, an alternative possibility is that the shift is part of a more pervasive functional separation between the motor programmes dedicated to practical actions on objects – reaching and grasping – and those dedicated to communication with an interlocutor. On this latter interpretation, index finger pointing is part of a broader realization by infants that an act of communication is *not* a preparation for grasping an object or for being handed an object. Rather, it is directed at an interlocutor who, in principle, will – as argued in the preceding section – communicate about the object indicated. Insofar as such a transition is likely to be consequential for subsequent language development, the second interpretation is more plausible than the first. After all, an infant's shifting conception of gestural communication is likely to have more consequences for subsequent language acquisition than any narrowly motoric adjustment of the fingers.

It is also important to note that – notwithstanding the ubiquity of the shift from whole-handed to index finger pointing – Liszkowski et al. (2012) observed one intriguing type of variation in their cross-cultural study of pointing. Regardless of the age of the infant, there was a two-way reciprocity between caregiver and infant – a point by the caregiver often elicited (within ten seconds) a point by the infant, and vice versa. Indeed, infant and caregiver were equally responsive to one another's points, and this overall pattern or reciprocal responding was evident in each culture. Nevertheless, there was cross-cultural variation in the overall frequency of such reciprocal responding. For example, it was more frequent in Japan, Canada, and Rossel (an island of Papua New Guinea) than in two different Mayan communities of Mexico or in Bali. By implication, even if these early acts of reciprocal communication can be universally observed, they occur at different rates, depending on the culture.

Salomo and Liszkowski (2013) examined this cultural variation more systematically in a follow-up study. They observed infants ranging from eight to fifteen months in three different cultures: Yucatec-Mayan (Mexico), Dutch (Netherlands), and Shanghai-Chinese (China). Infants and their caregivers were observed as they went about their regular activities. This observational strategy meant that, in contrast to the semi-naturalistic setting used in the earlier study (where the presence of a variety of attractive objects deliberately positioned within a relatively small area may have attenuated cultural differences), potential differences in the frequency and reciprocity of infant–caregiver interaction were given more scope to emerge. Indeed, the frequency with which infant and caregiver were engaged with the same object or event (e.g. looking at a book together or playing with toys together) proved greater in China than in Holland and greater in Holland than in Mexico.

A similar pattern of cross-cultural variation emerged for gestures. Hand gestures (including pointing, showing, offering, or placing an object in front of an interlocutor) were more frequent for both caregivers and infants in China as compared to Holland and more frequent in Holland as compared to Mexico. Nevertheless, pointing was the most frequent hand gesture among the infants, especially in China and Holland. Salomo and Liszkowski (2013) plausibly conclude that joint engagement in such object focused-activities serves to promote hand gestures, including pointing. More specifically, infants who have caregivers that respond promptly and reliably to their hand gestures are likely to produce them more often, and this may be especially true of pointing. Still, it is worth specifying in more detail what such responsiveness might involve and how it might reinforce infant pointing.

The previous section suggests a plausible answer. Arguably, caregivers vary in their disposition to view pointing as an interrogative gesture and in how they then respond to their infants' points. Caregivers who view their infants as pointing in an interrogative fashion are more likely to provide information, both evaluative and lexical, about the object indicated and are likely to reinforce the interrogative stance of their infants. By contrast, caregivers who view their infants as pointing in a declarative or imperative fashion may be inclined to offer a simple acknowledgement of the object indicated or to hand the object to the infant. Such reactions may be less effective in nurturing the interrogative stance of their infants. In sum, infants want informative input from their caregivers, and they use pointing to elicit it. It is plausible that they point all the more when they interact with a caregiver who is inclined to attribute an interrogative stance to them.

Conclusions

Infants are not passive recipients of the input that is on offer – they actively signal to a caregiver that input is wanted. The cross-cultural data also indicate that infants vary in their tendency to seek such input, arguably because caregivers do not place a uniform interpretation on those inter-rogative signals. Certainly, in line with a large body of research on pre-schoolers, infants draw up a cognitive profile of the people that they interact with, characterizing some as informative and others as uninforma-tive. They draw up such a profile quickly and efficiently, and they use it to forecast the responsiveness – or more precisely, the informativeness – of a potential interlocutor.

These claims fit into a broader perspective on the nature of early com-munication in infancy. Unlike other non-human primates, human infants are disposed to exchange information with others (Harris, 2017). This disposi-tion is apparent well before children engage in extended conversation. In this chapter, I have focused on the interrogative stance of infants. But alongside this disposition to ask for information, infants also display a willingness to convey information, often via pointing, to those in need of it. Moreover, they take steps to repair communication breakdowns when they occur. Infants want input. More broadly stated, they are motivated to construct a shared reality with their caregivers.

4 Learning More than Language through Language during Early Childhood

Meredith L. Rowe

Research clearly demonstrates that the quantity and quality of communication that caregivers engage in with their children on a daily basis plays an important role in promoting children's vocabulary development during early childhood (e.g., Hart & Risley, 1995; Huttenlocher, Haight, Bryk et al., 1991; Pan, Rowe, Singer, & Snow, 2005). However, less research has focused on what else children are learning from this caregiver input. It is not only vocabulary that children are building through conversations with caregivers but other oral language, cognitive, and social-cognitive skills that are essential for school success. This chapter examines what we know about the role of caregiver input, particularly parent input, in vocabulary development and then extends the review to research on the role of caregiver input on other skills that help children master the academic language challenges of a formal school environment. Empirical evidence is presented from several recent studies as examples of how specific features of caregiver input promote broader learning and school readiness in early childhood. Finally, the relevance of this work for an educationally informed theory of language learning is discussed.

Theoretical Perspective

The argument that caregiver input influences children's language and cognitive development is rooted in sociocultural and social-interactionist theories (Snow, 1972; Bruner, 1990; Vygotsky, 1978) which stress the importance of children's early environments and social interactions in the course of language acquisition and cognitive development. Analyzing caregiver influences on vocabulary in particular is a reasonable place to start investigating these theories, as children need to hear specific words to learn those words, and vocabulary is a measurable skill even early on in development. Yet, Vygotsky's (1978) argument that children's scaffolded interactions with more competent others influence their thinking more broadly sets the stage for investigating what else children learn through their social-communicative interactions with caregivers. Our interest is in the other skills, in addition to vocabulary, that can help children succeed with the academic language challenges of schooling.

Caregiver Input and Child Vocabulary

Since the early 1990s, advances in recording and transcribing capabilities (e.g., the Child Language Data Exchange System, CHILDES; MacWhinney & Snow, 1990), as well as in statistical methods, have led to a growing number of studies providing evidence of relations between caregiver input and child vocabulary, both within and across social-class groups. The work by Hart and Risley (1995) suggested positive relations between socioeconomic status (SES), caregiver input, and child vocabulary development. More specifically, in their study of forty-two families of varying SES, professional parents of higher SES were found to talk more, respond to their child's utterances more, ask more questions, and provide more affirmatives and fewer prohibitives when interacting with their children compared to parents from lower-SES backgrounds. Furthermore, the children of the higher-SES, professional families showed faster vocabulary growth than their peers. At the same time as Hart and Risley were working on their study in Kansas, Janellen Huttenlocher and colleagues were conducting similar work in the Chicago area. They capitalized on state-of-the-art statistical methods to test the significance of the relations between amount of parent input and child vocabulary growth in their entirely middle-class sample of twenty-two families with children between fourteen and twenty-six months of age (Huttenlocher et al., 1991). This was an important study because it not only highlighted the potential uses of individual growth modeling methods but found that even within a relatively homogenous sample, variation in amount of parent input significantly predicted variation in vocabulary growth. In the two decades following these foundational studies, many more studies have replicated and extended these general findings. Hoff (2003) was able to show statistically that the strong relations found in many studies between SES and child vocabulary growth is mediated, or explained, by parent input, particularly the length of parents' utterances. Using similar methods as Huttenlocher and colleagues, we found that even within an entirely low-SES sample of families ($n = 108$), variation in the diversity of vocabulary that parents used with children predicted children's vocabulary growth between fourteen and thirty-six months (Pan et al., 2005). Weizman and Snow (2001), studying a sample of fifty-three low-SES mothers and their five-year-olds, found that mothers who used a larger proportion of rare or sophisticated vocabulary words when talking with their children had children with larger vocabularies in kindergarten and second grade.

The research reviewed here is just a sampling of the studies that show clear links between various features of parent input and child vocabulary development. The studies suggest that within and across SES groups, parents who talk more, use more diverse vocabularies, use more sophisticated vocabulary words, and use longer utterances have children with faster vocabulary growth during early childhood. These findings point to clear implications for interventions aimed at promoting early vocabulary development, especially as vocabulary skill in kindergarten entry in a strong predictor of later reading comprehension skill and school success (Durham, Farkas, Hammer et al., 2007).

Input and Other Developing Skills

While vocabulary is a key ingredient for school success, it is not the only ingredient, and exposure to words embedded in interesting conversations builds other skills as well. Here I review research linking specific aspects of caregiver input to other important school-readiness skills, including narrative skills, theory of mind development, and information-seeking strategies, all skills that should help children handle the challenges of academic language (Snow & Uccelli, 2009), as discussed below.

Decontextualized language, or language that is removed from the here and now (Snow, 1990), is a useful type of parent–child discourse that is found to build vocabulary abilities in children. Common uses of decontextualized language in caregiver input include narrative discussions about the past or future, pretense, and providing explanations about how things work in the world. As discussed in Chapter 1, decontextualized talk differs from extended discourse in that it is not necessarily extended. That is, a single parent utterance about a past event would be considered decontextualized but not extended. Decontextualized talk can be considered challenging for children because discussing abstract topics involves mastering new discourse and perspective-taking skills that respond to the complex language and cognitive demands of a nonpresent message. By exposing children to this type of talk, parents can provide them with practice in the forms of academic language they must come to master in school. Indeed, research has found links between parent uses of decontextualized language and not only children's vocabulary but also their narrative production skills. Much of the work in this area comes from the Home School Study of Language and Literacy Development (e.g., Snow, Dickinson, & Tabors, 2001), which demonstrates relations between the percentage of parent talk that is explanatory or narrative during family mealtimes, with preschoolers and children's narrative and vocabulary skills at age five. These findings suggest that using decontextualized talk with preschoolers engages them in challenging conversations that potentially increase vocabulary knowledge as well as other important extended discourse abilities. Below, I provide a more nuanced review of the literature that suggests that specific types of decontextualized language, when examined extensively and in isolation, can have effects on other important developing skills during early childhood.

A growing body of research has examined one form of decontextualized language, parent–child conversations about the past, in more detail, finding connections between maternal reminiscing with preschool-aged children about shared past experiences and children's cognitive and social-emotional development. More specifically, mothers who are more elaborative in reminiscing with their children, who provide rich information, and who encourage their children's participation in the narrative have children who develop better autobiographical memory skills (e.g., Nelson & Fivush, 2004; Reese & Newcombe, 2007), narrative skills (Peterson, Jesso, & McCabe, 1999), and theory of mind skills (Reese & Cleveland, 2006; Taumoepeau & Reese, 2013; Welch-Ross, 1997). These results are intuitive from a sociocultural or social-interactionist theoretical perspective. For example, if children learn through their communicative interactions with others, and are provided with more opportunities to discuss their previous experiences with an adult who scaffolds them through those discussions, it is not necessarily surprising that those children will gain the skills to provide more detailed and coherent narratives of their own past experiences (e.g., Fivush, Haden, & Reese, 2006). Snow (1983) argued that experience with decontextualized language should theoretically be linked to both children's developing language skills at the time of those conversations as well as children's language and narrative skill in the future. In regard to theory of mind development, or children's developing abilities to represent and distinguish their own and others' mental states, Taumoepeau and Reese (2013) conducted an intervention study to examine whether training parents of toddlers in elaborative reminiscing would influence children's theory of mind development a year later. They found that the training did influence the mothers' use of open-ended elaborative questions and confirmations of children's utterances and that there was an effect of training on children's subsequent theory of mind development for the children in the training group who started with smaller vocabularies. The authors argue that elaborative reminiscing may promote theory of mind because it engages the child in a discussion of perspective sharing and allows the child to reflect on relations between events and mental states.

In sum, engaging young children in elaborative discussions of shared past events can build language skills such as narrative skills, but also other abilities, such as theory of mind. Research uncovering the specific skills necessary to succeed with the challenges of academic language in school highlights the linguistic features of narrative as well as perspective taking as key ingredients for success (Uccelli, Galloway, Barr et al., 2015). Thus, elaborative reminiscing with young children has broad and important effects on children's early development. These findings point to additional directions for research in this area, such as our own ongoing work on future talk described below.

Another form of decontextualized language, specifically the explanations that parents provide to children, has also been examined closely. As noted above, parents' explanatory talk with preschoolers is found to relate to children's subsequent vocabulary abilities (Beals, 2001); however, more recent research extends those findings to important child behaviors such as information-seeking strategies. For example, Frazier, Gelman, and Wellman (2009) found that when toddlers and preschoolers ask *why* and *how* questions of their parents, parents vary in the extent to which they provide explanatory responses. Furthermore, when provided with a causal explanation, children are more likely to ask another question and continue their information seeking than if not provided with an explanation. In a more recent experimental study, the same authors (Frazier, Gelman, & Wellman, 2016) showed that when four- to five-year-olds received causal explanations in response to their explanatory questions, they were better able to recall or learn that information than the information they were provided in nonexplanatory responses. These findings suggest that parents' use of causal explanations with children can help shape children's tenacity in gathering information through questioning, as well as through their learning from those conversations.

The work reviewed above demonstrates that different types of early communicative experiences contribute not only to children's vocabulary development, but also to many other important cognitive, social-cognitive, and oral language abilities. While having a large vocabulary will help children in literacy tasks such as reading comprehension, other more challenging language skills, including perspective taking and understanding of narrative discourse markers such as connectives, predicts reading comprehension over and above vocabulary size (Uccelli et al., 2015). These skills are considered academic language skills yet are also of high utility in many other areas of society. Thus, a greater understanding of how early parent–child interactions can build not only vocabulary but other relevant skills for school success is warranted.

Evidence

To highlight some more specific examples of relations between caregiver input and children's language and cognitive development that build upon this previous body of research, I will summarize the results of some of our recent studies: first, a study that finds relations between low-income fathers' use of questions with their toddlers and the children's vocabulary and subsequent verbal reasoning skills (Rowe, Leech, & Cabrera, 2017); second, a series of studies that show the important role of decontextualized language input with preschoolers for the development of vocabulary, but also narrative, syntax, and later academic language skills (Rowe, 2012; Demir et al., 2015; Uccelli et al., 2018); and finally, a study showing that priming children to talk about their extended selves in the near past or future helps promote their prospection and planning abilities (Chernyk, Leech, & Rowe, 2017).

Example 1: *Wh*-Questions and Toddlers' Vocabulary and Verbal Reasoning

Questions, in particular *wh*-questions, or questions framed with *who, what, where, when, why,* and *how,* are shown to be a beneficial type of input for toddlers' language learning, particularly vocabulary development and children's own use of questions (e.g., Cristofaro & Tamis-LeMonda, 2012; Hoff-Ginsberg, 1985; Rowland, Pine, Lieven, & Theakston, 2003; Ninio, 1980). We explored whether exposure to *wh*-questions may also be useful for fostering children's verbal reasoning skills, as these questions provide children with opportunities to reason and offer verbal explanations.

Our sample consisted of forty-one low-income, African American fathers and their children who had participated in the Father Involvement with Toddlers Substudy (FITS) of the Early Head Start Research and Evaluation Project (EHSRP; Love et al., 2005). Father–child dyads were videotaped in free play sessions at home when children were twenty-four months. The play included a book and age-appropriate toys and lasted for ten minutes. Videotapes were transcribed and reliably coded for sheer quantity of fathers' input (number of utterances) as well as the number of total questions and *wh*-questions fathers produced. Children's productive vocabulary was measured at twenty-four months using the McArthur Bates Communicative Development Inventory MCDI (completed by the mothers), and children's verbal reasoning skills were measured one year later using the Bayley Scales of Infant Development. Thirteen items on the Bayley Scales were combined to form a verbal reasoning factor that reflected children's ability to verbally sequence, compare, and discriminate properties of objects (e.g., color, object location, temporal events).

Results indicated substantial variability in father input within this sample. For example, in the ten-minute free play interaction, fathers averaged 220 utterances, but there was a range from 66 to 378 (SD = 67.8). Fathers asked an average of 17 *wh*-questions per ten minutes, but there was a range from 2 to 38 (SD = 10.5), and fathers asked an average of 32 other questions (mostly yes/no questions) with a range from 3 to 74 (SD = 16.9). The majority of the *wh*-questions were "*what*" questions (69 percent), followed by "*where*" (14 percent) and "*who*" (11 percent) questions. Interestingly, fathers' use of *wh*-questions appeared to elicit more talk from children than their other questions. Specifically, children's responses to *wh*-questions were more frequent than their responses to other questions (49 percent vs. 33 percent), and their

Table 4.1 *Partial Correlations between Father Input and Child Outcome Variables, Controlling for Fathers' Years of Education*

	Child outcomes	
	24-month vocabulary	36-month reasoning
Father total utterances	−.19	−.14
Father number *wh*-questions	.50**	.35*
Father number other questions	.01	.02
Father prop. *wh*-questions	.61***	.44**
Father prop. other questions	.10	.12

Note. From Rowe, Leech, and Cabrera (2017).
   * $p < .05$; ** $p < .01$; *** $p < .001$.

responses to *wh*-questions were more syntactically complex, measured using the Mean Length of Utterance (MLU), than their responses to other questions (MLU = 2.01 vs. 1.62). Finally, as shown in Table 4.1, we found that fathers' use of *wh*-questions (but not overall number of utterances or use of other questions) related to both child vocabulary at that same age as measured by the CDI and reasoning outcomes one year later. Further analyses indicated that the relation between father *wh*-questions and children's verbal reasoning at thirty-six months was partially mediated by children's vocabulary skill at twenty-four months. Taken together, these results suggest that posing *wh*-questions to two-year-olds is a specific type of input that elicits a verbal response from the child, relates to vocabulary ability, and likely fosters verbal reasoning abilities.

Example 2: Decontextualized Language Input and Children's Subsequent Vocabulary, Narrative, Syntax, and Academic Language Skills

As noted earlier, most of the research on parent use of decontextualized language was conducted with parents of preschoolers, yet little work has examined this type of input to younger children. In two studies using the same longitudinal sample (e.g., Rowe, 2012; Demir et al., 2015) we examined the specific role of decontextualized language input to eighteen- to forty-two-month-olds in relation to the children's later abilities at kindergarten entry. We found that in this diverse sample of fifty families from the greater Chicago area, parents increased in their use of decontextualized utterances over the early childhood period. That is, during a ninety-minute interaction in the home at child age eighteen months, only 2.2 percent of parents' utterances were decontextualized (explanations, narrative, or pretend) on average, whereas at thirty months, over 6 percent were decontextualized, and by forty-two months, almost 10 percent of the utterances parents produced were of this challenging nature. Furthermore, parents' use of decontextualized language was associated with children's use of decontextualized language. This result is not surprising but shows that between eighteen and forty-two months, parents use more decontextualized language as children get older and children are increasingly able to engage in decontextualized conversations with caregivers.

We then looked at the relation between variation in parents' use of decontextualized language at child age thirty months and children's subsequent vocabulary, syntax and narrative abilities at age fifty-four months, around the time of kindergarten entry. Kindergarten vocabulary was measured using the Peabody Picture Vocabulary Test (PPVT). Syntax was measured using the Recalling Sentences subtest of the Clinical Evaluation of Language Fundamentals (CELF), and narrative ability was measured by an experimenter-designed task that asked children to watch a short cartoon video and then tell the experimenter the story. The story retellings were coded for narrative structure on a 0–6 scale (see Demir et al., 2015). We found that, controlling for SES, children's vocabulary at thirty months measured as word types produced in the parent–child interaction, and parent contextualized input (all of the utterances parents produced that were not considered decontextualized), parent use of decontextualized language with children at thirty months was a significant positive predictor of children's vocabulary, syntax and narrative skills at fifty-four months. Furthermore, in all of these analyses, it was the decontextualized input only, not the contextualized input, which predicted children's later skills. Thus, these results suggest that engaging children from an early age in conversations about the nonpresent, or providing children with explanations of how the world works, predicts not only their vocabulary skills but their syntactic and narrative skills that we know are also essential for school success. Finally, in a more recent study (Uccelli, Demir, Rowe et al., 2018), we found that variation in these children's early uses of decontextualized language at thirty months was significantly predictive of their academic language knowledge in adolescence, controlling for their early vocabulary, parent decontextualized input, and family factors such as SES. Thus, early experiences around decontextualized language not only play a role in preparing children for school entry, but continue to predict their abilities to handle features of complex academic language in the middle school years.

**Example 3: Talking about the Extended Self and Preschoolers'
Prospection Abilities**

We have recently extended the work on decontextualized input further to
determine whether talking with children about the past or future might also
influence other abilities besides language or theory of mind. In particular, we
were interested in prospection abilities. Prospection, or the ability to act on behalf
of one's future self, is related to uniquely human abilities such as planning, delay
of gratification, and goal attainment (Atance & O'Neill, 2001). While
prospection develops rapidly during early childhood (Atance, 2015) little is
known about the mechanisms that support its development. Thus, we began by
hypothesizing that providing children with experience talking about their futures
might help promote prospective abilities. Because of research showing a link
between cognizing about the past and the future (Schacter, Addis, & Buckner,
2007), we questioned whether not just future talk but also past talk may
potentially relate to prospective abilities as well. Thus, we designed a study to
explore whether encouraging children to talk about their extended selves (self
outside the present context) boosts their prospective abilities (Chernyk, Leech, &
Rowe, 2017). In the study, eighty-one preschoolers participated in a five-minute
interaction with an adult in which they were asked to talk about events in the near
future, distant future, near past, or present. The children were shown a time line
and were shown locations for now, before now, and after now. The experimenter
then told the child they were going to be talking about events that would happen
"after now" (in the near future condition, for example). The experimenter listed
examples of near future events in increasing temporal order ("After now, are
things like right after this game when you will go back to class, later today when
you will go home from school, or even a really long time from now when will you
go to bed tonight"). The experimenter then asked the child to draw a picture of
him/herself in the last exampled future time period: "Can you draw a picture of
yourself going to bed tonight?" After the child completed the drawing, she placed
it on the square labeled "after now" and reaffirmed that it belongs on that square
("We're going to put this right here because this is going to happen after now!").
The experimenter then asked the child to list some events that would happen in
the next twenty-four hours (e.g., "What are some things you'll do right after this
game, like when you back to class?"), posing three cues and stopping when the
child had either stated he or she could not generate further events or generated
five events.

Immediately following this discussion, the children interacted with another
experimenter (blind to condition) who administered several prospection and
planning measures to the children. Tasks were drawn from prior literature and
selected to reflect a broad range of prospective measures appropriate to the

targeted age range. Two measures (prospective memory and mental time travel) had been used extensively in prior work and are known to measure children's planning abilities (e.g., Atance, 2015). The Mental Time Travel Task asked children to reason about a hypothetical planning scenario (e.g., a child pretending to make a plan to walk through a forest); the Prospective Memory Task was an action-based planning measure, in which a child was asked to make a future plan (e.g., remind an experimenter to open a box) and remember to successfully carry out that plan. Our findings indicated that compared with children discussing their present and distant future, children asked to discuss events in their near future or near past were the most effective in eliciting self-projection (use of personal pronouns; Figure 4.1) and displayed better planning and prospective memory skills (see Figure 4.2). Thus, our findings suggest that a short conversation about one's "extended self" in the near past or near future seemed to prime children's prospective memories and planning abilities. This was an experimental design and not based on naturalistic interactions, but the broader implications are that children who have more experience with this type of decontextualized language may have an advantage in developing planning and prospection abilities, as even brief conversations with adults can help scaffold, shape, and activate concepts about one's extended self. Critically, engaging young children in conversations where they are provided with opportunities to cognize, remember, and discuss their extended selves may ultimately help them make future-oriented decisions that benefit those extended selves.

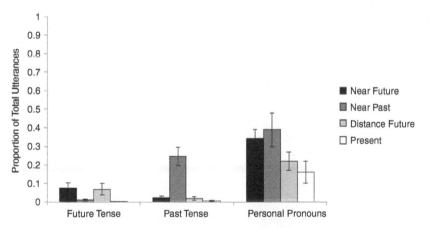

Figure 4.1 Proportion of children's utterances (bars represent standard error) containing future tense, past tense, and personal pronouns across conditions. Reprinted from Chernyk, Leech, and Rowe (2017).

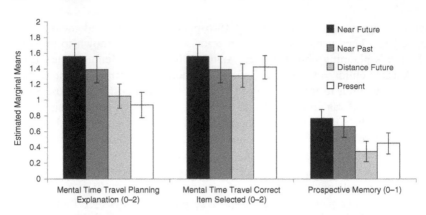

Figure 4.2   Estimated marginal means (bars represent standard errors) of planning explanation and mental time travel correct item selected across conditions. Reprinted from Chemyk, Leech, and Rowe (2017).

These three examples provide additional evidence for how children can learn more than language through language during early childhood. Specific types of parent–child interactions and conversations can foster important skills that will help prepare children for the challenges of school. One implication of these findings is that encouraging parents and early childhood educators to ask children questions, provide causal explanations, and engage children in discussions about past experiences or future plans, should result in positive outcomes for children's early language and cognitive development. While it sounds like a complicated message to send to caregivers, at least more complicated than encouraging "more talk" in general, we have found that it is possible to increase parents' use of decontextualized language through a short training. In a recent study (Leech, Wei, Harring, & Rowe, 2018) we randomly assigned parents of four-year-olds (n = 36) to a decontextualized language training condition or a control condition. The parents in the training condition received a brief intervention introducing them to a term we developed —"READY" talk—which was defined as a broad style of conversation that helps children get ready for kindergarten. We designed READY to be an acronym in order to provide parents with four examples of decontextualized conversation in an easily remembered framework (Recall past events, Explain new words and concepts, Ask lots of questions, Discuss the future), and a message to increase efficacy and motivate parents to incorporate these conversations into their daily interactions with their children (You can make a difference in your child's academic success). We found that compared to the families in the control condition, parents in the training condition significantly increased in their use of decontextualized talk during mealtimes at home and maintained that increase over the month following the intervention. Critically, the children also increased in their use of decontextualized language during the interactions with parents. These are promising results and suggest that caregiver use of decontextualized language is malleable. However, future work should examine whether training caregivers to use more decontextualized talk results in longer-term language and literacy outcomes for children.

Relevance to an Educationally Informed Theory of Language Learning

An educationally informed theory of language learning must encompass an understanding of the early experiences that contribute to skills that are foundational for literacy and school success. We know that vocabulary is one of these foundational skills, but it is not the only one. If we consider reading comprehension the gold standard for attaining success in school, recent work suggests that having a strong vocabulary and strong academic language skills are both essential ingredients (Uccelli et al., 2015). We've shown that certain types of early conversational experiences can help build children's vocabulary as well as academic language skills such as perspective taking and narrative discourse abilities. Furthermore, succeeding in school in general involves a variety of other social-cognitive and motivational abilities (e.g., Snow, Porche, Tabors, & Harris, 2007), including planning skills and the propensity or desire to learn and seek information from others. As we've demonstrated, these skills can also be fostered early on through conversations with caregivers. Thus, an educationally informed theory of language learning should span the entire period from birth throughout schooling – from early language through advanced literacy – and should broaden the definition of "language" early on to encompass other important communication or pragmatic skills, such as, but not limited to, perspective taking, questioning, and discussing the extended self.

5   Food for Thought
Turning Everyday Family Practices into Opportunities to Develop Rich Language and Literacy Abilities in Latino Children

Diana Leyva and Lauren Skorb

Children develop language and literacy abilities through interactions with 'more experienced' members of the community including parents, teachers, and siblings (Vygotsky, 1978). In everyday social interactions, children learn how to master oral and written language, consequently extending their cognitive abilities to become active participants in society (Bruner, 1990). Hence, studying parent–child interactions is central to understanding how children develop language and literacy abilities. Researchers typically assess the quality and quantity of parent–child interactions and examine how these predict and explain variability in child language and literacy abilities. Three main contexts of parent–child interactions have been examined in previous literature: talking, reading, and writing. In this chapter, we review these three contexts, offer evidence on a parent-focused intervention program, and discuss implications for educational settings. We focus on the preschool and kindergarten years, as this is a critical time during which children develop the language and literacy abilities they need to ensure academic success (Duncan et al., 2007).

Talking

The quantity and quality of parent talk is consistently and positively related to children's language and literacy development (Fivush, Haden, & Reese, 2006; Hart & Risley, 1995; Hoff, 2003). The amount of parental talk (i.e., higher quantity) is important for children's language and literacy. Parents who talk with their children more often have children with larger vocabularies than parents who talk with their children less often (Hart & Risley, 1995; Huttenlocher et al., 1991). This association has been observed in parents from different socioeconomic statuses (SES) and ethnic backgrounds. The way that parents talk (i.e., higher quality) is also important for children's language and literacy development. Parents' use of diverse and sophisticated words (i.e., words that children do not commonly hear, such as banquet, voracious or nourish) and *decontextualized language* is related to growth in children's vocabulary (Rowe, 2012; Weizman & Snow, 2001). Decontextualized language is talk that focuses on events, people or objects that are not present (not 'here and now'), elaborates on a single topic, and involves more than a few conversational turns, such as talking about past or future events. Studies specifically examining parent–child talk about past events (reminiscing) have identified *elaboration* as a parent talk style that is related to language and literacy development. Elaborative parents ask many open-ended questions (e.g., what, where, when, and how?) that encourage the child to participate and contribute new pieces of information to the conversation (Fivush et al., 2006). Both correlational and intervention studies have demonstrated that parents who are more elaborative in conversations about past events have preschool children with larger vocabularies (Peterson, Jesso, & McCabe, 1999), narrative skills (Reese, Leyva, Sparks, & Grolnick, 2010), phonological awareness (Leyva, Reese, & Wiser, 2012), print knowledge (Sparks & Reese, 2013; Reese, 1995) and perspective-taking skills (Taumoepeau & Reese, 2013), which are all relevant skills to academic success.

Reading

Both the quantity and quality of shared reading interactions are linked to children's language and literacy development. The frequency with which parents engage children in conversations about books (i.e., higher quantity) matters. Specifically, parents who report engaging in shared book reading more often have children with larger vocabularies than parents who report engaging in shared book reading less frequently (Bus, van Ijzendoorn, & Pellegrini, 1995; Scarborough & Dobrich, 1994). The way that parents engage children in conversations about books (i.e., higher quality) also matters. Although parents may adopt different styles during book reading (Reese & Cox, 1999), one of the most studied styles is *dialogic reading*. The hallmark of dialogic reading is helping children become story narrators through repeated readings of the same book. As children gain familiarity with the book, parents progressively ask more questions that encourage children to predict, explain, infer, and elaborate on the plot of the story (Lonigan & Whitehurst, 1998). Two meta-analyses of intervention studies using dialogic reading indicate that the positive effects of this book-reading style are mainly on children's vocabulary and alphabet knowledge (Mol, Bus, de Jong, & Smeets, 2008, 2009). Importantly, the effects of dialogic reading are smaller for older children (beyond the preschool years) and children from low-income households and ethnically diverse backgrounds. This suggests that other book-reading styles, besides dialogic reading, might be better suited for certain populations. Another highly studied book-sharing style is *print referencing*, that is, asking questions or commenting about print (Justice & Ezell, 2004). Although most parents do not spontaneously engage in print referencing, experimental studies have shown that when parents are explicitly taught to do so, children develop more sophisticated print knowledge (Justice & Ezell, 2004).

Writing

Parents vary in the quantity and quality of their writing support. Parents who report engaging in more explicit teaching of writing at home (i.e., higher quantity) have children with better spelling, decoding, and reading skills in school (Sénéchal & LeFevre, 2003; Sénéchal, LeFevre, Thomas, & Daley, 2011) than parents who report engaging in less explicit teaching of writing. The quality of the parents' writing support depends on the specific strategies they use. One writing-support strategy that has been examined during the preschool and kindergarten years is breaking words into units of sounds. Parents who support their children's writing by breaking words into units of sounds and linking each unit of sound to its corresponding letter have children with more advanced decoding, phonological awareness and reading comprehension skills (Aram & Levin, 2001, 2004; Bindman et al., 2014; Lin et al., 2009; Skibbe et al., 2013).

Taken together, prior research on these three contexts—talking, reading, and writing—indicates that parents vary in whether and how they provide support to their preschool and kindergarten children. Most importantly, all three contexts are central to the development of children's language and literacy abilities.

Talking, Reading, and Writing in Family Food Practices

Some families do have daily routines specifically devoted to conversations, book reading, or writing with their children. However, most families engage in talking, reading, and writing with their children in a more organic and dynamic way, while performing their everyday activities. How do families incorporate these three contexts into their everyday routines? One meaningful set of everyday activities where these three contexts naturally converge is family food practices.

In some communities, food practices are at the heart of what it means to be a family. For example, in ancient Greece, *oikos* (family) meant "those who feed together," indicating the important role that eating together played in defining who was a member of the family (Lacey, 1968, p. 15). Through food routines, families not only nourish but also build relationships, share beliefs and values, and construct their identities. Hence, food selection, preparation, and consumption are important vehicles through which parents may socialize children into becoming competent members of a society (Ochs & Shohet, 2006). Understanding how families incorporate these three contexts (talking, reading, and writing) into everyday routines, such as food practices, is central to designing and evaluating family literacy intervention programs that are culturally sensitive and sustainable in low-income and ethnically diverse communities.

Talking during Food Practices

Observational studies across families from diverse SES and ethnicities show that parents use more diverse and sophisticated words during mealtimes than book sharing (Snow & Beals, 2006). Furthermore, in using diverse and sophisticated words, parents explain these words and tell meaningful stories using this new vocabulary. Both explanatory and narrative talk are foundational to language and literacy development (Beals, 1993; Davidson & Snow, 1995). Explanatory talk involves defining complex words (e.g., "pounds are how much something weighs") but also discussing general knowledge about the world and abstract principles (e.g., talking about why things fall to explain gravity). Narrative talk typically involves telling stories about particular events or personal experiences; some of these stories require using complex words (e.g., talking about the day the child was born can trigger the use of words such as C-section and anesthesia). Both explanatory and narrative talk fall under the category of decontextualized language. Parents who use more complex words as they engage in explanatory and narrative talk during mealtimes with their preschool children have children with larger vocabularies skills six years later (Snow & Beals, 2006). Hence, mealtime conversations provide rich opportunities for parents to foster their children's language abilities.

Reading and Writing during Food Practices

Certain food activities, such as cooking and grocery shopping, are particularly rich settings to foster children's literacy abilities. In these activities, children use reading and writing for authentic (real-life) purposes. For example, one reads a recipe to know what ingredients to add, writes a grocery list to remember what food to buy, and reads food labels and prices to know what food to buy (Purcell-Gates, Duke, & Martineau, 2007). Thus, in food activities, children experience writing and reading as means to serve a social and communicative function.

Reading and writing for the purposes of selecting and preparing food have been pervasive in human history. In fact, a recent study suggests that food practices were closely related to the spread of literacy in the ancient world. In an excavation in Israel, dated about 600 BC, archeologists found notes inscribed in ink on pottery containing ancient shopping lists, indicating that writing and reading, at least for the purpose of requesting food supplies such as oil, wine, and flour, were more prevalent in the ancient world than previously known (Faigenbaum-Golovin et al., 2016).

Studies on parental support during cooking activities have focused on the development of preschoolers' math rather than literacy skills (e.g., Vandermaas-Peeler, Boomgarden, Finn, & Pittard, 2012). These studies suggest that when parents are explicitly asked to discuss sophisticated concepts while cooking (e.g., comparing magnitudes by saying: "Which of these two has more?"), children are more likely to use sophisticated concepts during the cooking activity than when parents are not explicitly asked to discuss them (Vandermaas-Peeler et al., 2012).

Research on parents' reading and writing support in the context of a grocery game (i.e., parent and child make a list together and use it to shop at a pretend store) has identified three strategies central to the development of literacy abilities (Leyva et al., 2012; Leyva et al., 2017). First, parents who dictate and sound out letters for their children while making a grocery list have preschool children with advanced decoding skills (Leyva et al., 2017). Second, parents who encourage children to write and read their list while playing a grocery game (e.g., "we have to get five apples. Do you want to write the word apple?") have preschool children with more advanced emergent writing skills than those children whose parents do not engage in these strategies (Leyva et al., 2012). Encouraging children to write and read their list while playing a grocery game might be similar to print referencing (Justice & Ezell, 2004), a shared book style that has demonstrated positive effects on children's literacy skills. We argue, however, that this strategy goes beyond print referencing, as it helps the child make connections between writing and the social and communicative functions that writing serves. A third parental strategy documented by prior research is engaging in discussions about the purpose of writing with their children while making a grocery list (i.e., "if we don't write, we won't remember what to buy"). Talking about the purpose of writing might be considered a type of decontextualized language, as these conversations involve explanations that go beyond the mechanics of how to write (i.e., beyond the "here and now"). The positive effects of decontextualized language on children's language and literacy skills are well documented (Fivush et al., 2006; Rowe, 2012; Weizman & Snow, 2001).

Taken together, talking, reading, and writing during everyday family food practices are unique opportunities for parents to foster their children's language and literacy development through the use of several strategies including narrative talk (e.g., talking about past events during mealtimes), explanatory talk (talking about the purpose of writing), encouraging the child to read her own writing for authentic purposes (e.g., reading her list to know what to buy), and breaking words into units of sounds or dictating and sounding out letters to support the child's writing.

Evidence from the Food for Thought Program

In this section, we describe the Food for Thought (FFT) program, a family literacy program for low-income Latino parents and their kindergarten children. The data collected in this study provide powerful evidence of how parents who participate in this program foster their children's language and literacy abilities during everyday food practices. The program focuses on family food practices because they are central to family organization and family dynamics in Latino communities (Eisenberg, 2002). Latino families report frequently including children in food preparation activities, such as cooking (Eisenberg, 2002), and consider food preparation to be an everyday family activity (Kermani & Janes, 1999). Furthermore, Latino parents are more likely to provide support for their children and be engaged in the task during food preparation (i.e., baking biscuits) than other activities (i.e., building a block model, playing with a toy track and cars). Specifically, Latino parents discuss more complex concepts promoting cognitive growth (e.g., counting objects, explaining why certain activities are necessary) and are more actively engaged while preparing food with their children than while playing with blocks with their children (Eisenberg, 2002). In addition, Latino parents consistently ask more questions while playing with toy foods with their children than during other forms of play (Tenenbaum & Leaper, 1997). These studies suggest that in more naturalistic, familiar, and meaningful settings, such as food routines, Latino parents are more likely to engage in decontextualized language by asking questions that engage children in the task and encourage children to connect, infer, and explain concepts. Therefore, it makes sense to focus on these everyday activities to promote Latino parents' support of their children's language and literacy during the kindergarten years.

Importantly, family food routines are not the only meaningful and naturalistic context through which decontextualized language can be fostered at home. There are many other routines that families engage in during bedtime, bath time, or other times during the day. As long as the routines have personal value for family members and are regularly practiced (are predictable and part of the family life's organization), they might be good settings to foster children's language and literacy skills.

Program Description

The FFT program consists of four weekly family meetings. Each meeting is ninety minutes and held in a classroom in the child's elementary school during a weekday morning. Each family meeting focuses on a different family food activity: the first meeting is about grocery shopping, the second meeting is about cooking at home, the third meeting is about eating out, and the fourth meeting is about planning a family celebration event.

At the beginning of each family meeting, new strategies fostering language and literacy skills are presented through a PowerPoint presentation and inter-active discussion with the parents. Examples of these strategies include (1) asking open-ended questions to encourage child participation in family con-versations during mealtimes; (2) engaging the child in writing activities at home by asking the child to make a grocery list before going grocery shopping or writing a recipe for the child's favorite dish; and (3) supporting the child's writing skills by breaking words into units of sounds and linking each unit of sound to its corresponding letter or by dictating and sounding out letters.

The parents then proceed to watch a video of other Latino parents imple-menting these same strategies with their children. After the video presentation, the program facilitators encourage parents to consider the strategies they observed and how they could implement them in the interactions they have with their own children. In the last twenty minutes of the meeting, parents practice the new strategies with their children and receive immediate feedback from the program facilitators. At the end of each family meeting, parents receive take-home materials and homework assignments to complete with their children. Throughout the week, the parents receive text messages remind-ing them to practice the new strategies at home (modeled after York & Loeb, 2014).

Program Results

The FFT program was implemented in three public elementary schools (with kindergarten classrooms) serving primarily economically disadvantaged stu-dents located in a southeastern city in the United States. Latino parents of kindergarteners were invited to participate via fliers and schoolwide open houses. Parents received a small incentive at each family meeting and a $50 grocery store gift card at the completion of the FFT program.

Sixty-eight families consented to participate in the program, and thirty-seven parents attended at least one of the four FFT family meeting. Reasons for not attending the family meetings included conflicting work schedules and illness. Demographic information was collected from consenting parents who attended at least one meeting. All participants self-identified as Latino; 50 percent came from Mexico and 50 percent came from a Central American or Caribbean country. In addition, 48.6 percent reported having at least a high school educa-tion. This percentage is slightly below the average reported by others studies; for example, in a study using a nationally representative cohort of children in kindergarten (ECLS-K; NCES, 2001), the percentage of Latino mothers with a high school education or higher was 70 percent (Durand, 2011). The children's ages ranged from sixty-three to ninety-one months at the start of the program ($M = 70.68$ months, $SD = 5.22$).

A subsample of twenty-two parent–child dyads was videotaped while practicing the new strategies learned in the FFT program with their children. The goal of collecting these data was to determine whether it was feasible for low-income Latino parents to use the newly learned FFT strategies with their children. We transcribed these interactions verbatim using CHAT conventions (Child Language Data exchange System, CHILDES; MacWhinney, 2000).

Transcripts of *parent–child conversations about past events* (i.e., talking about something they did the past weekend) were coded at the utterance level using the Fivush et al.'s (2006) elaboration coding scheme. The average inter-rater reliability was 89 percent. First, we examined the extent to which parents and children participated in the conversation (i.e., quantity). On average, out of the total number of utterances produced during parent–child conversations, 40 percent of them belonged to children and 60 percent belonged to the parents. This indicated that parents and children were participating fairly equally in the conversation. Second, we examined how parents and children contributed to the conversation (i.e., quality). We found that 36 percent of children's utterances were unique contributions (i.e., the child provided a new piece of information, typically a response to a parent's question, e.g., the child says: "hotdog" after the parent asks: "What did you eat?"), 29 percent were evaluations (i.e., confirmations of the parent's comments, such as saying "yes" or nodding yes), and 31 percent were place-holders (i.e., saying "uhmm"); the remaining 4 percent were other (e.g., off-task). This means not only that children were participating frequently (i.e., significant quantity) but also that the quality of their participation was substantial as well. We also found that 25 percent of the parents' utterances were open-ended questions regarding new pieces of information (e.g., "What did you do?" "Who did you go with?"), 21 percent were evaluations (e.g., confirmations or negations of the children's utterances), 17 percent were close-ended questions (e.g., "Were you happy?"), and the remaining 37 percent were categorized as "other" (i.e., place-holders and off-task). These data suggest that parents were successfully implementing one of the key strategies taught in the FFT program: asking many open-ended questions to engage their children in the conversation. Our findings are in line with correlational (Leyva, Reese, Grolnick, & Price, 2008) and experimental studies (Reese et al., 2010) showing that low-income Latino parents can talk elaboratively about past events with their children. In doing so, the parents engage in decontextualized language, which is positively associated with language and literacy development.

Below we present an excerpt of a parent–child conversation. The original transcript was in Spanish but was translated to ease readability. This parent implemented one of the strategies learned in the FFT program, and as a result, the child contributes new information to the conversation.

*PARENT:	and what did you like the most about it?
*PARENT:	about those places?
*CHILD:	pizza.
*PARENT:	pizza.
*PARENT:	and what else?
*CHILD:	the games.
*PARENT:	the games.
*PARENT:	what games were they?
*CHILD:	uhm.
*PARENT:	what games are they?
*CHILD:	machines.

Transcripts of *parent–child interactions pertaining to writing* (e.g., making a grocery list, recipe, menu or list of guests for a party) were coded at the utterance level using the following categories: literacy support (e.g., breaking words into units of sounds and linking each unit of sound to its corresponding letter, "tomato, /t/, like the first letter of your name"), math support (e.g., counting and comparing magnitudes such as "one, two and three ... which one is bigger?"), focusing attention (e.g., "Here! look at this"), teaching general knowledge (e.g., "this is the tip, this is the money we leave on the table for the waitress to say thank you"), positive feedback (e.g., "good job"), giving the child choices (e.g., "What should we buy at the store?"), and corrections of the child's writing (e.g., "not like that, the L is like this"). This coding scheme was developed by our lab (see Leyva et al., 2017). The average interrater reliability was 86 percent. First, we examined the extent to which parents used each of the abovementioned categories. Overall, 36 percent of the parents' utterances were literacy support, 17 percent were math support, 19 percent were focusing attention, 19 percent were general knowledge, 4 percent were giving the child choices, 4 percent were correcting the child's writing, and 1 percent was positive feedback. Second, we explored associations among the different categories (e.g., literacy support, math support, focusing attention). Parents who provided more literacy support were not necessarily providing more math support ($r = .22, p > .10$). Parents who used more literacy support were more likely to teach general knowledge ($r = .64, p < .001$) and provide positive feedback ($r = .48, p < .01$). However, parents who provided more literacy support were also more likely to correct their children's writing ($r = .65, p < .001$). These data suggest that parents were successfully implementing the specific literacy strategies taught by the FFT program. It is noteworthy that almost 20 percent of parents' utterances focused on spontaneous teaching of general knowledge (e.g., "we have to bake it at 400 degrees, this means that the oven must be that hot"), which is a type of decontextualized language known as explanatory talk (Beals, 1993). It is also remarkable that parents provided literacy support in conjunction with other strategies that support children's cognitive and socioemotional skills (e.g., general knowledge and positive feedback). Similarly to prior research conducted with low-income families (Aram & Levin, 2001; but see Bindman et al., 2014), parents who provided more literacy support also engaged in "correction." This makes sense given that with increased support of the child's independent writing, the child is provided with more opportunities to make mistakes; consequently, the parent is more likely to correct the child's writing.

Below is an excerpt of an interaction illustrating a parent providing significant literacy support while the child writes a recipe that includes the word "margarine," a word fairly hard to spell for kindergarten children.

*PARENT: mar ... ga [parent breaks word into units of sounds].
*PARENT: /a/ [parent sounds out the letter A].
*CHILD: O?
*PARENT: no, otherwise it'd be "margo."
*PARENT: but we're saying "marga."
*PARENT: ga ... ga [parent breaks word into units of sounds].
*PARENT: think.
*CHILD: A.
*PARENT: aha!
*CHILD: it's A?
*PARENT: it's A!
*PARENT: yes.
*CHILD: [child writes the letter A].
*PARENT: would you like me to help you in English?
*CHILD: no.
*CHILD: in Spanish.
*PARENT: alright.
*PARENT: so ...
*PARENT: mar ... ga ... ri [parent breaks word into units of sounds].
*PARENT: ri ... ri [parent breaks word into units of sounds].
*CHILD: R!
*PARENT: aha!
*PARENT: that one.
*PARENT: this word has a lot of letters!

Taken together, data collected by the FFT program suggest that it is feasible for low-income Latino parents to implement the strategies learned in the FFT program with their children. Using the strategies seems fairly viable regardless of variability in the children's skill levels and the parents' educational levels. An important caveat to our findings is that these videos were collected during the FFT family meetings; we did not collect pretest data on quantity and quality of parent–child interactions. It would be useful to collect not only evidence on whether and how parents implement these strategies during FFT meetings but also at home, as well as collect baseline data on how parents interact with children around writing and in conversations about past events before the start of the FFT program.

Implications for Education and Literacy Programs

Educators have long advocated for the incorporation of environmental print and meaningful activities involving reading and writing into daily preschool and kindergarten classrooms, as demonstrated by the use of activity centers such as the post office or the grocery store (Lonigan, Schatschneider, & Westberg, 2008). The evidence discussed in this chapter indicates that food practices provide unique opportunities for adults to develop children's language and literacy abilities during the preschool and kindergarten years. Although the current data involve a fairly small sample size and do not lend themselves to causal conclusions, they suggest that it is feasible for parents to use certain kind of behaviors or strategies that support language and literacy skills during everyday food practices. Hence, teachers might consider including some of the same writing and reading activities (e.g., writing a grocery list and writing the recipe of a favorite dish) in preschool and kindergarten classrooms and using similar strategies to those taught to parents in the FFT program to foster children's language and literacy skills (e.g., breaking the word into sounds and linking sound units to letters or dictating and sounding out letters). Some of the strategies teachers might use are (1) implement reading and writing activities in the classroom that have clear social and communicative functions (e.g., we need to buy some food at the store); (2) talk about the purpose of writing while children engage in writing (e.g., if we don't put it on paper how many apples we need, we'll forget); (3) encourage children to use their own writing to guide their actions (e.g., your list tells you what to buy at the store; let's read it!); and (4) break words into units of sounds and link letters with their corresponding sounds as children write.

Most of the parent-focused literacy interventions involve techniques for parents to read books or talk with their children at home. Very few interventions focus on joint writing at home (but see Aram & Levin, 2004). The evidence provided here suggests that parents might also benefit from learning strategies on how to support children's writing during the preschool and kindergarten years, particularly when these strategies are used in everyday family routines such as cooking, eating, and grocery shopping. Therefore, researchers and practitioners working in literacy intervention programs might encourage parents and children to use writing in the context of food practices at home. Future research should examine whether these kinds of programs focused on supporting language and literacy through family food practices are generalizable to other populations beyond low-income Latino families living in the United States. It is possible that in other communities where families are less likely to cook or eat at home, this type of program might have different effects.

We are currently conducting an experimental evaluation of the FFT program. We have randomly assigned participants to intervention or control groups to determine whether the FFT program has significant effects on children's language and literacy skills and whether these causal associations remain after controlling for other potential factors that can account for growth in these skills, such as home literacy practices and parental education. Once the experimental evaluation is concluded and causal associations are identified, the next step is to disseminate these results and help inform policies in the United States aiming at improving education for Latino students. Language and literacy are areas where Latino students have traditionally fallen behind when no early intervention is provided. Hence, one way to meet the needs of Latino students in schools is to incentivize federally funded early intervention programs to capitalize on cultural practices such as food routines in order to give Latino children a chance to develop the skills they need to succeed in school on par with their non-Latino peers.

Acknowledgments

This study was funded by the Brady Education Foundation and Davidson College (Abernethy grant). We would like to thank the families, teachers, and school administrators (for participating in the study); Varenya Hariharan, Rhea Costantino, and Allyson Arocha (for transcribing, coding, and analyzing the parent–child data); and Anna Davis, Allie Lowe, Clarise Ballesteros, Marlene Arellano, and Mary Frith (for recruitment, data collection, and data entry).

6 Theory- and Evidence-Based Language Learning and Teaching for Young Children
Promoting Interactive Talk in the Classroom

Young-Suk Grace Kim and Joonmo Yun

An essential part of knowledge acquisition is the meaning-making process. Oral language skills play a critical role in this meaning-making process, interacting with cognitive and social skills (Dickinson, Golinkoff, & Hirsh-Pasek, 2010). Much of learning is mediated by oral language such that accessing complex thoughts and ideas requires command of oral language. Even when learning is primarily mediated by print or written texts (i.e., reading or writing), one's oral language skills underpin this learning process (Berninger & Abbott, 2010; Catts, Adlof, & Ellis Weismer, 2006; Hoover & Gough, 1990; Kim, 2015, 2017; Kim et al., 2014; Kim & Schatschneider, 2017). With this in mind, the primary goals of the present chapter are to examine (1) theoretical and empirical accounts of factors influencing children's oral language development during preschool and early elementary years, (2) their implications and evidence-based instructional strategies in preschool classrooms, and (3) future directions in research.

The preschool years are a crucial period when children rapidly develop many important language (e.g., foundational vocabulary and syntactic abilities) and cognitive skills (e.g., perspective taking), both of which are foundational for later literacy and academic achievements. In fact, the period from ages three to five is the period during which children develop an organized language system (Tomasello & Brooks, 1999). Large individual differences have been reported in oral language skills at this age, and these individual differences are fairly stable such that children's oral language abilities in the early years are strongly related to their later oral language skills (Cain & Catts, 2016; Hart & Risley, 1995; Snow, Porche, Tabors, & Harris, 2007) and to later literacy acquisition (Cain & Catts, 2016; Hart & Risley, 1995; Snow et al., 2007). This high stability and fairly strong predictive power of later literacy acquisition have critical implications – attention to oral language development during the early years is crucial for ensuring successful oral language and literacy acquisition. This implication has significance especially for children who are at risk of weak oral language skills, which, in turn, put them at a greater risk for difficulties with literacy and academic achievement.

Factors Influencing Language Acquisition: Theory and Empirical Evidence

Cognitive Underpinnings

Oral language is a broad construct, consisting of lexical, sentence-level, and discourse-level skills. Discourse-level oral language (i.e., discourse comprehension or production) is the highest level in the hierarchy of oral language and draws on a complex set of cognitive skills and lower-level oral language skills. Successful discourse comprehension or production (also widely referred to as text comprehension or production[1]) requires construction of a precise situation model – a mental representation as described by the text (Graesser, Singer, & Trabasso, 1994; Kintsch, 1988; van den Broek, Rapp, & Kendeou, 2005). The situation model is established through construction and integration processes (e.g., Graesser et al., 1994; Kintsch, 1988; van den Broek et al., 2005), which involve representing words and phrases in memory (called surface code representation); constructing initial, local propositions called textbase representation; and integrating propositions across the text and with one's background knowledge to establish a coherent situation model. In these processes, multiple language and cognitive skills are involved: foundational cognitive skills such as working memory, inhibitory control, and attentional control; foundational oral language skills such as vocabulary and grammatical knowledge; and higher-order cognitive skills such as inference, perspective taking (theory of mind), and comprehension monitoring (Florit, Roch, & Levorato, 2014; Kendeou, Bohn-Gettler, White, & van den Broek, 2008; Kim, 2015, 2016, 2017; Kim & Phillips, 2014; Kim & Schatschneider, 2017; Lepola, Lynch, Laakkonen, Silvén, & Niemi, 2012; Strasser & del Rio, 2014; Tompkins, Guo, & Justice, 2013). Notably, recent evidence using structural equation modeling indicates that these multiple language and cognitive skills can be mapped onto the three levels of mental representations (surface code, textbase, and situational model) and have direct and indirect relations among each other and with discourse-level oral language (see Figure 6.1) (Kim, 2015, 2016, 2017; Kim & Schatschnedier, 2017). That is, foundational or domain-general cognitive skills are necessary for foundational oral language skills, which, in turn, are necessary for higher-order cognitive skills – and all these language and cognitive skills are necessary for discourse-level oral language skills.

---

[1] Theoretical models of discourse comprehension do not differentiate oral texts from written texts in terms of processes. However, discourse comprehension has primarily been studied in written texts (i.e., reading) until recently. Recent studies suggest that highly similar set of skills are involved in discourse comprehension of oral texts and written texts (see Kim, 2015, 2016; Kim & Pilcher, 2016).

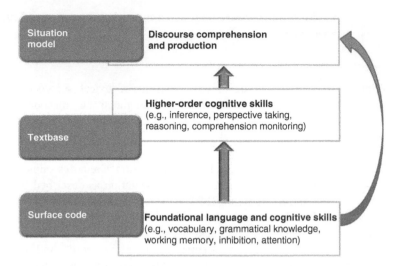

Figure 6.1   Direct and indirect effect model of text comprehension (DIET), illustrating the mappings between mental representations (situation model, text base, and surface code) and language and cognitive skills. From Kim (2016). Reprinted with permission.

Environmental Factors

Input frequency. While cognitive processing or internal mechanism is necessary to extract and abstract linguistic structures, categories, and relations from language input, cognitive processing is useful only to the extent of available external input of linguistic stimuli – the opportunity to hear and use oral language (Hart & Risley, 1995; Hoff, 2006; McMurray, Horst, & Samuelson, 2012). While many studies focused on home environment for the role of external input (see other chapters), environment is not limited to homes but includes any entities that provide systematic and contingent input and exposure, including schools, community, and even culture (e.g., parent–child linguistic interactional norms vary across cultures; see Hoff, 2006). Therefore, differences in teacher's language input frequency in the school settings would explain individual differences in language ability. Evidence indeed supports the hypothesis. Preschool teachers' use of varied vocabulary (Bowers & Vasilyeva, 2011; Dickinson & Porche, 2011), meaning-focused activities such as book reading (Connor, Morrison, & Slominski, 2006), and teachers' use of decontextualized talk during book reading (Hindman, Wasik, & Erhart, 2012) were positively related to children's vocabulary. Variation in syntactic complexity of teacher's language was also related to preschool children's syntactic skills (Huttenlocher, Vasilverva, Cymerman, & Levine, 2002).

Input styles (quality). Language acquisition, of course, is not simply an input frequency = output process. It occurs in the context of achieving communication goals and in the context of social interactions (Snow, 1983; Vygotsky, 1978), and thus, quality of oral language input would be important for language acquisition. Research suggests that children's language acquisition is enhanced when their immediate interests are recognized and extended (Burchinal et al., 2008; Landry, Anthony, Swank, & Monseque-Bailey, 2009; Landry, Smith, Miller-Loncar, & Swank, 1997; Wasik & Hindman, 2011). Directly relevant is the caregiver's responsiveness, such as semantic contingency and scaffolding (Snow, 1983). Semantic contingency refers to "an immediate matching of the adult utterance to the topic or content of the child's utterances" (Rice, 1989, p. 153), and is achieved via various means such as expansions, extensions, clarification questions, and answers to questions. Evidence supports teachers' employment of semantic contingency principles for children's oral language development. Teachers' child-oriented strategies (wait and listen and follow child's lead), interaction-promoting strategies (e.g., asking a variety of questions, encouraging turn taking), and language modeling strategies (expand and extend) were positively related to children's number of utterances and multiword utterances (Girolametto & Weitzman, 2002). In Head Start classrooms, children whose teachers discussed new words, asked questions, and expanded beyond text during book reading had greater vocabulary, particularly for children who started the year with low vocabulary (Gerde & Powell, 2009). Similarly, teachers' quality feedback and language modeling were positively related to children's vocabulary after controlling for overall instructional quality and many demographic factors (Hamre, Hatfield, Pianta, & Jamil, 2014; Mashburn, 2008).

Socioemotional support. The social interactional aspect of language learning points to the importance of child's relations with the caregiver (including teachers) to promote engagement in language-learning opportunities and activities. Quality of teacher–child interactions was positively related to children's oral language skills (Burchinal, Vandergrift, Pianta, & Mashburn, 2010; Cabell et al., 2011; Curby et al., 2013; Guo, Piasta, Justice, & Kaderavek, 2010; Jones, Bub, & Raver, 2013; Schmitt, Pentimonti, & Justice, 2012). Emotional support appears to be especially facilitative for children from at-risk backgrounds (i.e., lower parental education; Peisner-Feinberg et al., 2001), African American children (Burchinal, Peisner-Feinberg, Pianta, & Howes, 2002), or children with low initial oral language skills (Gosse et al., 2014). Furthermore, teacher–child relationships and oral language development have a reciprocal relation such that teacher–child relationships and teachers' responsiveness predicted children's oral language development, and children's oral language predicted the quality of teacher–child interactions (Split et al., 2015).

Implications and Evidence-Based Instructional Strategies

The theoretical and empirical evidence reviewed above suggests that instruction to promote oral language development should explicitly target both cognitive skills and environmental factors. Below is a summary of instructional implications and associated evidence.

Directly and Indirectly Teach Oral Language

One important mechanism of children's oral language acquisition is interactions with caregivers (i.e., parents and teachers). Moreover, certain interactional features promote oral language development. Despite robust evidence, however, oral language interactions such as quality conversations and book readings are less than ideal in many early childhood classrooms (Burchinal et al., 2008; Dickinson, 2001; Gest, Holland-Coviello, Welsh, Eicher-Catt, & Gill, 2006), particularly for children who are considered at risk for later academic difficulties (LoCasale-Crouch et al., 2007).

To ameliorate this, oral language should be intentionally and explicitly taught (Collins, 2012; Wasik & Bond, 2001). Several approaches, such as the Language-Focused Curriculum (Bunce, 1995) and the Learning Language and Loving It approach (Weitzman & Greenberg, 2002), have been developed, implemented, and found to be effective in changing teachers' language behaviors and improving children's oral language skills, at least for subgroups of students (those who had higher attendance and were in the intervention condition [Justice et al., 2008]; those with higher initial expressive vocabulary [Cabell et al., 2011, 2015]). Teachers who received training on quality conversational strategies produced a greater number of utterances and turn-taking behaviors (Girolametto, Weitzman, & Greenberg, 2003), open-ended questions, and responsive statements (Milburn, Girolametto, Weitzman, & Greenberg, 2014), and their children generated a greater number of utterances, multiword combinations, and peer-directed utterances (Girolametto et al., 2003).

Furthermore, a large-scale teacher training has produced positive outcomes on children's achievement including oral language. Landry, Swank, Smith, and Assel (2006) conducted a quasi-experimental, statewide study in which Head Start preschool teachers (500 in treatment and 250 in control) were trained on rich oral language instruction, interactive book reading, emergent literacy skills (phonological awareness and alphabet knowledge), and classroom management. The teacher training had a positive effect on children's oral language, but

the effect varied – larger effects were observed for teachers with more education, for teachers who participated for two years, and in sites where language/
literacy-focused curriculum was used. The effects of teacher training also
varied as a function of child characteristics such that cumulative effects of
teacher training (i.e., two years of training vs. one year of training) had a higher
effect, particularly for children tested in Spanish (Landry, Swank, Anthony, &
Assel, 2011).

Shared or interactive book reading is a useful medium to provide rich and
interactive extended discourse opportunities, and to expose children to informative topics, content, and advanced language forms (e.g., Hayes & Ahrens,
1988). Interactive storybook reading has been found to be particularly beneficial for vocabulary enhancement in preschoolers (Girolametto, Weitzman,
Lefebvre, & Greenberg, 2007; Hindman, Erhart, & Wasik, 2012;
Schwanenflugel et al., 2010; Sénéchal, Cornell, & Broda, 1995; Whitehurst
et al., 1994). For example, preschool teachers in Head Start programs received
training on how to ask open-ended questions, how to explicitly teach vocabulary, and how to connect events and actions during interactive book reading.
Teachers who received the training talked more and asked more open-ended
questions during book reading, and their children had higher receptive and
expressive oral language skills with moderate to fairly large effect sizes (Wasik,
Bon, & Hindman, 2006).

Explicitly Teach Cognitive Skills

As shown in Figure 6.1, foundational cognitive skills such as working memory,
inhibitory control, attentional control, and higher-order cognitive skills such as
inference, perspective taking (e.g., theory of mind), and comprehension monitoring are critical to discourse-level oral language skills. Albeit limited,
evidence does indicate that cognitive abilities such as working memory are
malleable for school-aged children (Karbach, Strobach, & Schubert, 2015;
Loosli, Buschkuehl, Perrig, & Jaeggi, 2012). Evidence is also emerging
about how to improve higher-order cognitive skills for young children in oral
language contexts. Collins (in press) focused on inferential thinking using book
reading with seventy Portuguese and English dual-language learners. For
children in the treatment condition, book reading was followed by either
discussion on literal comprehension questions or discussion on inferential
comprehension questions, depending on the books. Children in the control
group were read to without discussion. After a third reading of each book,
children were assessed on their comprehension. Results revealed that discussion on inferential comprehension questions yielded higher performance on
both literal and inferential questions, with a greater effect on inferential
questions.

Furthermore, we found that comprehension monitoring can be taught to preschool-aged children. We provided brief daily explicit instruction on comprehension monitoring to prekindergartners from low socioeconomic backgrounds. After ten weeks of five-minute instruction four days a week, children in the treatment condition were superior in comprehension monitoring in oral language contexts (Kim & Phillips, 2016). Bianco and her colleagues (2010) focused on both inference making and comprehension monitoring to improve oral language comprehension for preschool children. Children received instruction in a thirty-minute session per week for fourteen to sixteen weeks per year; children who received oral language training for two years in prekindergarten and kindergarten had significant, positive oral language outcomes, and this effect remained nine months after the training was completed (see Bianco et al., 2010, for further details). Studies also found that perspective taking, as operationalized as the theory of mind, can be taught and improved. Guajardo and Watson (2002) provided a training to preschool-aged children on the theory of mind in a book reading context, highlighting and discussing characters' thoughts in a story. After a five-week (twelve to fifteen sessions) training period, children in the treatment condition had superior performance on theory of mind than those in the control condition.

Other studies encouraged teachers to ask cognitively demanding questions to children (e.g., Gerde & Powell, 2009; Hamre et al., 2014). For example, Girolametto and her colleagues (2012) focused on increasing teachers' use of decontextualized talk in a preschool environment. Decontextualized talk involves talking about "the remote and the abstract" beyond the concrete here and now (Snow, 1983, p. 175), and many aspects of oral language development and literacy are characterized as decontextualized. In Girolametto et al.'s study, decontextualized talk was operationalized as comments or questions that relate the story events or actions to children's own experiences (e.g., Have you ever been scared before?) and those that promote analysis and evaluation of story events ("Do you think that the rabbit is bad?" "What is going to happen next?" "What would happen if the moose got into the house?"). The number of decontextualized utterances significantly increased for teachers and children in the treatment condition.

Create a Positive and Nurturing Environment

Given the socioemotional nature of language acquisition, positive and close teacher–child relations and a positive, nurturing environment are enabling conditions for acquisition of cognitive and language skills. Emotional engagement enables cognitive processes to be employed aptly for language acquisition. Therefore, creating open and warm environments conducive to learning is part and parcel of promoting successful oral language acquisition. While this is

Table 6.1 *Definition and Application of E^5 Principle Components*

E^5 principle	Definition	Application
Exposure	Increasing exposure to varied and advanced oral language	Directly teach and provide language models, employing lexically rich and cognitively demanding language and decontextualized talk at the discourse level
Elicitation	Eliciting children's responses and talk beyond a single utterance; level of abstraction of teachers' questions is related to the level of abstraction of children's responses (Tompkins et al., 2013)	Ask literal questions, inferential questions, abstract questions (prediction, problem solving), relational questions (relation to personal lives) (e.g., Schawanenflugel et al., 2010)
Extension	Building on a child's utterances and topic and provide more information or explanation (Justice et al., 2008)	Engage children in extended discourse by adding further information on the given topic and using varied language forms
Emotional engagement	Building a positive relation with children to engage children in language-learning opportunities	Employ warm and responsive interactions

important for all learners, this appears to be particularly important for children from low socioeconomic backgrounds (Peisner-Feinberg et al., 2001) with low initial oral language skills (Gosse et al., 2014).

Summary and Future Directions

E^5 (Expose, Elicit, Extend, and Emotionally Engage) Principle for Language Teaching

While reviewing theory and evidence, we found common threads in instructional practices among various approaches. We will refer these as the E^5 principles for language teaching, which include *Exposure, Elicitation, Extension*, and *Emotional Engagement*. These are aligned with the importance of semantic contingency and scaffolding principles for supporting children's language development (Hirsh-Pasek et al., 2015; Snow, 1983). Of course, this is far from the comprehensive approaches detailed in several studies reviewed above. However, we believe that E^5 provides relatively simple but essential and powerful guidelines for teachers to act as expert language users, modeling, encouraging, and engaging children in rich oral language exchanges. See Table 6.1.

Remaining Research Questions

Much research has contributed to our understanding about factors, processes, and mechanisms involved in language acquisition. Studies also have revealed that many cognitive and environmental factors are malleable and, consequently, can be directly and indirectly taught to young children. Despite this advancement in our understanding, however, several important questions remain. First, many studies have shown that intervention effects vary as a function of factors. For instance, the effect of teachers' use of varied vocabulary and increased amount of talk on children's language outcomes varied as a function of the child's language learner status (Bowers & Vasilyeva, 2011). Intervention was effective for children with low initial oral language skills (e.g., Gerde & Powell, 2009) or high initial oral language skills (e.g., Cabell et al., 2011). In other studies, the effect of teacher training varied as a function of teacher characteristics (e.g., education level) and curriculum used in the school (Landry et al., 2006). Therefore, a clearer, nuanced understanding is necessary about what instructional approaches are beneficial for which children under what conditions.

A related, second question relates to closing the gap between children weak in oral language skills (either due to environmental factors or neurological factors) and those with typically developing oral language skills. Although previous studies have shown that teacher training makes a positive impact on teacher's instructional practices and children's oral language outcomes (e.g., Cabell et al., 2015; Landry et al., 2006), the level of intensity or dosage necessary to close the gap and to ensure successful subsequent development in oral language and literacy acquisition remains unclear. This information would be particularly lacking for discourse-level oral language outcomes despite its importance in language and literacy acquisition (e.g., Berninger & Abbott, 2010; Catts et al., 2006; Kim, 2016, 2017; Kim & Schatschneider, 2017).

Other important considerations that merit attention in research, although not reviewed in this chapter, include scaling up, sustainability, and teacher training. A few large-scale studies have shown that in-service teacher training can have positive effects on children's oral language outcomes (see Landry's work; but see Yoshikawa et al., 2015). However, these large-scale studies are limited, and efforts are needed to inform what it takes to scale up evidence-based best practices and to promote sustaining effects on teachers' instructional practices (e.g., cumulative effect of training) and children's language skills. Finally, evidence is sparse about how to get the information about effective oral language instruction to classrooms. Prior research on in-service training does provide a model for in-service teaching, but further understanding is needed about cost-effective in-service training and effective and systematic preservice training programs.

Closing

Early childhood, including preschool, is an important time to develop and help develop children's oral language abilities. Large gaps have been observed in the oral language skills and academic achievement of children from various backgrounds. Oral language is a complex system (Snow, 1983), and as such, learning takes a prolonged time to develop and requires sustained attention and efforts by multiple stakeholders (e.g., caregivers at home, school, community). Research reviewed here indicates that preschool teachers play a critical role in promoting oral language and cognitive development for children and that efforts should include direct teaching of oral language and cognitive skills and indirect teaching via intentional language modeling to promote linguistically rich, cognitively demanding, and emotionally supportive learning environments.

7   The Relationship between Early Childhood Development and Later Elementary School Performance in Chile

Andrea Rolla, Macarena Alvarado, Bernardo Atuesta,
Marcela Marzolo, Ernesto Treviño, Hirokazu Yoshikawa,
and MaryCatherine Arbour

The relationship between early childhood skills and second-grade reading ability is of substantial developmental and policy import. This chapter explores the nature of that presumably cumulative relationship, in that stronger skills in preschool beget stronger skills in elementary school; the chapter goes on to describe the association between four- and five-year-old children from the *Un Buen Comienzo (UBC)* study in Chile and their second-grade standardized reading test scores (SIMCE), controlling for family background characteristics. We found that children's preschool-age vocabulary, early reading, and early math skills positively predicted second-grade reading scores. Self-regulation and low problem behavior as well as inhibitory control positively predicted later reading test scores. Other socioemotional and executive function variables, such as attention, pro-social behavior, and positive behavior did not predict reading scores in these analyses, similar to the results from the United States, Canada, and the United Kingdom in the Duncan et al. (2007) study. The influence of other developmental domains such as socioemotional development, early mathematics, and self-regulation skills on later literacy development is important to study, and the originality of this research in Spanish monolinguals is important to highlight as a contribution to the field. This chapter ends with a discussion of the implications of this work for practice, contributing to an "educationally informed theory of language learning".

Early childhood development across a range of domains, in particular language and literacy development, form a basis for further development in elementary school and beyond (Snow, Burns, & Griffin, 1998; Duncan et al., 2007). It is important to understand, in particular in at-risk children, what early childhood skill levels are important to ensure future academic achievement, across such domains as cognitive, language, emergent literacy and numeracy, executive function, and socioemotional skills. In addition, it is important to understand how these trajectories develop over time, for example, beginning with preschool skills and then early elementary reading, a fundamental skill that will provide the basis for academic language and reading comprehension for children as they continue to grow and develop over the years (Uccelli et al., 2015). Research has examined the relationship between young children's initial skill levels and their second-grade skills in the United States (e.g., Duncan et al., 2007), but these relationships have not been examined in the context of monolingual Spanish speakers in a Latin American context, to our knowledge. The study discussed here, using *Un Buen Comienzo* and national Chilean test data, was designed in part to fill this gap.

Using six longitudinal data sets from Canada, Great Britain, and the United States, Duncan and colleagues (2007) estimated links among three fundamental elements of school readiness – school-entry cognitive, attention, and socio-emotional skills – and later school reading and math achievement. In an attempt to isolate the effects of these school-entry skills, the authors controlled skills measured prior to school entry, as well as a host of family background measures. Across all six studies, the strongest predictors of later achievement were school-entry math, reading, and attention skills. A meta-analysis of the results showed that early math skills had the greatest predictive power, followed by reading and then attention skills. By contrast, measures of socioemotional behaviors, including internalizing and externalizing problems and social skills, were generally insignificant predictors of later academic performance, even among children with relatively high levels of problem behavior (Duncan et al., 2007). Interestingly, Grimm et al. (2010) reanalyzed three of the data sets and argued that, in fact, attention measures were more predictive than behavioral measures of elementary achievement, but that behavioral measures still exhibited small to moderate associations with academic achievement. Two studies we found replicated the Duncan analyses with a different population, French speakers from Quebec, Canada. The first examined similar constructs such as cognition, attention and socioemotional development for kindergarten school readiness (Pagani et al., 2010). Most of the coefficients were similar to the original study, with math skills predicting strongly consistently, followed by attention, receptive language, attention problems, and behavior.

The second study also chose to replicate and extend findings from the original Duncan et al. (2007) study with Canadian data in two sets of analyses (Romano et al., 2010). The first set examined the influence of kindergarten literacy and math skills, mother-reported attention, and socioemotional behaviors on third-grade math and reading outcomes. Similar to Duncan et al., math skills were the strongest predictor of later achievement, and literacy and attention skills predicted later achievement. However, some kindergarten socioemotional behaviors, specifically hyperactivity/impulsivity, prosocial behavior, and anxiety/depression, were significant predictors of third-grade math and reading.

A study conducted in the United States examined younger children and the link between one- to three-year-old-children's behavior problems and poor levels of second-grade reading (Gray et al., 2014). Reports of inattentive and overactive behaviors at ages one to three years and changes in inattention through toddlerhood predicted reading achievement in second grade. The effects of early inattention on reading appear to be most robust. Findings underscore the contribution of social–emotional development to school readiness and the importance of early identification of children with externalizing problems, as early interventions designed to reduce externalizing problems may improve later reading skills, an interesting contradiction to the Duncan and other studies with older preschool children. It is interesting that with younger children, socioemotional behavior was found to be an important predictor of second-grade reading.

In addition to looking at younger children, authors have looked at kindergarteners and the relationship between their school readiness skills and such important outcomes at the other other end of the educational spectrum as high school completion (Hickman et al., 2008). The authors of this study found that students in northeaster Arizona who had dropped out of high school had lower achievement skills and worse behavior problems as early as kindergarten (and possibly sooner, but they didn't have the data); the authors postulated that in part this could be due to their greater absenteeism, a topic which will be discussed in the discussion of the *Un Buen Comienzo* intervention, which evolved to intervene in absenteeism, which our own work had indicated was affecting Chilean students' outcomes.

We will also conclude with a brief summary of other studies that have conducted similar analyses but with different age ranges than the ones examined in this chapter and/or not usually assessing with as comprehensive a battery of preschool skills and also predominantly with children from the United States, not allowing for a great deal of linguistic and/or sociocultural diversity. For example, Claessens, Duncan, and Engel (2009) examined the relationship between kindergarten skills and fifth-grade outcomes, finding that mathematics, language and literacy skills, and attention were the best predictors of fifth-grade outcomes, while socioemotional skills were not as strong predictors. Hair et al. (2006) did find that low socioemotional skills in kindergarten were predictive of lower reading skills in first grade, unlike other studies already cited. In New Zealand, researchers found that four-year-olds' executive function skills predicted their mathematics achievement at age six (Clark, Pritchard, & Woodward, 2010).

Given the predictive power of specific kinds of preschool skills, such as mathematics, early reading, attention, and potentially behavior, socioemotional skills, and executive function, it is important to examine which skills are the best predictors of later achievement in order to guide future interventions that can prevent later academic difficulties. It appears that age of study may be important – in this case, children, were examined at the beginning of prekindergarten, four to five years of age, and in second grade, seven to nine years of age. At the same time, however, replicating these kinds of studies in other populations is fundamental, as the sociocultural and linguistic context may be important.

Chilean Context

Preschool education in Chile is mandatory beginning in prekindergarten (four years of age) and seeks to promote integral development and relevant learning in young children. In terms of access, Chile has lower rates than the OECD average but higher than the average of Latin American countries. Spending on preschool education in Chile represents a percentage of the GDP equal to the OECD, average increasing considerably from 0.4 percent of the GDP in 2004 to almost double or 0.75 percent in 2013. The only nationally representative measurement of young children in Chile under the age of six is the Encuesta Longitudinal de Primera Infancia (ELPI), which was first applied in 2010 and then again in 2012. Results indicated the existence of favorable psychomotor development of children relative to other Latin American results but in general low levels of cognitive and language skills; in general, children from wealthier backgrounds outperform their at-risk counterparts (Centro de Estudios, Ministerio de Educación, 2013; Berlinski & Schady, 2015). Given the weak preschool skills described and the lack of competitive academic skills Chile shows in comparison to other OECD countries, it is important to examine more specifically what preschool skills are associated with better academic outcomes in the elementary years in this population.

After this review of the research on preschool skills predicting early elementary reading and some contextual information on Chile and a rationale for doing this work in Chile, we will now describe the research interest that guides this chapter, namely, to what degree stronger skills in certain domains in preschool beget stronger skills in elementary school reading.

Evidence

Our goals for working with the *Un Buen Comienzo* longitudinal data were to explore the relationship between incoming prekindergarten skill levels with a rich data set and national elementary school outcomes in the Chilean population.[1] Our first question was in regard to children's incoming skills. We asked, what is the association of prekindergarten levels of language, mathematics, socioemotional development, and executive function on elementary school reading outcomes in low-income children living in Santiago, Chile?

---

[1] The intervention variable was used as a control in all of the analyses described.

This question aimed to answer how much of children's elementary school performance is predicted by what children bring to the public prekindergarten classroom, essentially their skills, controlling for family background characteristics.

Our hypotheses were that prekindergarten emergent language and literacy skills would predict elementary school reading (Claessens, Duncan, & Engel, 2009); the relationship between preschool socioemotional development and second-grade reading would be weaker or nonexistent (Hair et al., 2006); and prekindergarten mathematics skills and executive function would predict second-grade reading (Clark, Pritchard, & Woodward, 2010; Claessens, Duncan, & Engel, 2009).

To reach the objectives explained above, we used SIMCE databases, which provide national test results in reading for all Chilean children in second grade. We analyzed individual and family initial characteristics at the preschool level. We then analyzed the relationship between the characteristics mentioned above and SIMCE reading performance in second grade, controlling for cohort, treatment status (UBC or control), gender, and family background characteristics.

Intervention and Measures

Un Buen Comienzo (A Good Start; UBC) is a two-year professional development intervention for early childhood educators in Chile, with the objective of enhancing children's language, literacy, health, and socioemotional outcomes. A cluster-randomized trial was implemented to determine the impact of the program on classroom quality and on multiple domains of child development. The study of sixty-four municipal schools in Chile followed three cohorts of prekindergarteners in the following years: 2008–2009, 2009–2010, and 2010–2011 (Leyva et al., 2015; Yoshikawa et al., 2015). We did not include the first cohort in this study because it was a much smaller sample.

The Chilean children who participated in this study attended public prekindergarten and kindergarten and then continued on to elementary school. We used the preschool-age data of the 2009–2010 and 2010–2011 cohorts to analyze the relationship between initial characteristics at the preschool level – namely, children's language, literacy, math, socioemotional development, and executive function – and student performance in second grade in reading. More details about the original sample and the context can be found in Yoshikawa et al. (2015). By merging the two UBC cohorts, before merging with the second-grade SIMCE data, we obtained a sample of 5 municipalities (two in the 2009 cohort), 58 schools (29 in each cohort), 79 classrooms (41 in the first cohort), and 1,583 students.

Preschool-age or initial characteristics are those that were measured at the beginning of the intervention (2009 or 2010 in each case). The UBC databases contain information about the initial characteristics of the sample in preschool and the SIMCE database provides information about elementary school characteristics.

The preschool-age variables we considered are (and detailed in Yoshikawa et al., 2015) child performance in language and math, as measured by the Woodcock–Muñoz (WM) in Spanish (Vocabulary, Letter-Word Identification, Dictation, Passage Comprehension, and Applied Problems); child socioemotional development and executive function, as measured by the battery administered in the study (as detailed in Yoshikawa et el., 2015); and family characteristics such as maternal and paternal educational, socioeconomic status, educational expectations, number of children and adults at home, and presence of father/mother at home.

Posttest or final characteristics are those that were measured the year in which the SIMCE was administered to the children in the sample in 2012 and 2013, when the children were in second grade of primary school, respectively, depending on their cohort. The Measurement System of Educational Quality (SIMCE)[2] is a national assessment system of the Chilean Ministry of Education, and its objective is to provide information on achievement levels. SIMCE is a standardized test in which second-grade reading comprehension is assessed. The SIMCE database contains school-level and student-level information (test scores and socioeconomic status).[3]

To understand the generalizability of our sample to other low-income municipalities in Santiago, Chile, Yoshikawa et al. (2015) conducted analyses comparing elementary school students in the five selected municipalities to those in municipalities that were eligible but not selected. These analyses showed that there were no significant differences in the national academic test scores (SIMCE scores measuring fourth-grade reading and math skills) between elementary school students living in municipalities that participated in the study and children from other candidate low-income municipalities. Similarly, no significant differences were found in students' household socioeconomic status. Hence, the sample of municipalities is considered representative of other municipalities in Santiago with similar characteristics.[4]

---

[2] More information can be found at www.simce.cl.

[3] The database includes information about the students, their parents and families, and their schools: (1) student information such as gender, age, and test scores; (2) family information such as parental education levels, income per capita, and knowledge about school; and (3) school information such as administration, socioeconomic composition, number of students, and area of localization.

[4] Characteristics required to participate in this study were (1) a minimum of 20 percent of children at risk in the primary grades (see Yoshikawa et al., for details), (2) a minimum of eight municipal schools with prekindergarten and kindergarten classrooms, and (3) location in the Metropolitan

By merging the aforementioned UBC and SIMCE databases, we found that 77.7 percent[5] of children from the original UBC study had a second-grade SIMCE reading score resulting in a sample size of 1,230. All the children's initial schools were municipal/public. The socioeconomic level was measured with a scale from 1 to 5, in which 1 is a low socioeconomic level and five is a high socioeconomic level. The average level, 2, shows that the schools were mostly of a medium to low socioeconomic level.

Results

We analyzed the relationship or correlations between the initial child variables and SIMCE results. The relationship between SIMCE reading scores and (1) the language, literacy, and mathematics subtests; (2) socioemotional development results such as pro-social and positive behavior, self-regulation, and low problem behavior; (3) variables related to parental stimulation at home; (4) variables of executive function; and (5) the treatment variable (a control variable)[6] are positive and significant. Overall, around 32.6 percent of the variance in second-grade reading variance is accounted for by prekindergarten-entry child skills, controlling for family and child characteristics.

To better estimate the correlation of initial characteristics on child development, we used Hierarchical Linear Modeling (HLM), which accounted for the nesting of students within classrooms, classrooms within schools, and schools within municipalities (Bloom et al., 2008; Hedges & Hedberg, 2007; Raudenbush & Bryk, 2002).

Summarizing the variables that were predictive of later reading, we found that with the Woodcock–Muñoz (WM) subtests Vocabulary, Letter-Word Identification, and Applied Problems are all positively predictive of SIMCE reading scores. In particular, an increase of one point in the WM Vocabulary subtest and in the WM subtest of Letter-Word Identification[7] is associated with a respective increase of 0.043 and 0.056 standard deviations in SIMCE reading scores, while an increase of one point in the WM Applied Problems[8] is

---

Region of Santiago. Fourteen municipalities met these selection criteria and were invited to apply to participate in the UBC program and its evaluation. Then, interviews with municipal representatives from mayors' offices and departments of education and health were conducted to make sure the goals of the program were clear, to explain the evaluation design, and to answer any questions. In this stage, six municipalities were ultimately selected.

[5] This could be because schools select/exclude some children from taking the SIMCE exam or children had been retained a year in school or the child was absent the day of testing due to illness or other reasons.

[6] Once background variables were controlled for, this variable was no longer significant.

[7] Which represent about 5 percent and 19 percent of the overall mean, respectively.

[8] Which represent about 14 percent of the overall mean.

correlated with an increase of 0.02 standard deviations in SIMCE reading scores.

Among the socioemotional and executive function variables, self-regulation and low problem behavior and inhibitory control are significantly correlated with reading test scores. In particular, an increase of 1 point in the self-regulation and low problem behavior variable predicts an increase of 0.31 standard deviations in reading, and an increase of 1 point in the Walk-a-Line task is associated with an increase of 0.26 standard deviations in reading.[9]

Conclusions and Implications

This kind of study, which examines preschool mathematical skills and socio-emotional development in addition to early language and literacy skills to test what skills predict second-grade reading scores in Chile in a large sample of low-income Spanish monolinguals, makes a unique contribution to the field because it helps to determine precursors to later reading comprehension in a language other than English and in a middle-income country. In this chapter we described an analysis of the 2009–2010 and 2010–2011 cohorts of the UBC intervention for early childhood educators in Chile and their corresponding reading test results (SIMCE) in order to analyze the relationship between initial characteristics at preschool level, namely, children's language, literacy, math, socioemotional development, and executive function and students' perfor-mance in reading in the second grade, controlling for other background characteristics.

We found that the Woodcock–Muñoz (WM) subtests of Vocabulary, Letter-Word Identification, and Applied Problems all positively predict SIMCE read-ing scores. As for the other socioemotional and executive function variables, self-regulation and low problem behavior as well as inhibitory control posi-tively predict reading test scores. Other socioemotional and executive function variables, such as attention, pro-social behavior, and positive behavior, are not significantly associated with SIMCE reading scores in these analyses. Again, overall, around 32.6 percent of the variance in second-grade reading variance is accounted for by prekindergarten-entry child skills, controlling for family and child characteristics. These findings suggest that working on these skills in an integrated fashion at the preschool level should lead to promising results at the elementary level.

Similar to Duncan et al. (2007), we found that preschool math, language, and literacy predicted later reading. On the other hand, attention was not predictive

---

[9] This does not necessarily mean that the self-regulation and low problem behavior variable is more "important" than the Walk-a-Line task because their measurement scales are not the same. In this case, the main message is that both variables predict reading scores controlling for other background characteristics.

in our study, while some socioemotional and executive function variables did positively predict reading scores. The first obvious conclusion, our initial hypothesis, is that incoming skills beget later skills; therefore, the focus many times needs to be on at-risk children who enter preschool without the foundational skills that will lead to later academic success. The other potential but much more tentative conclusion is that different executive function and socioemotional skills may be necessary precursors in different sociocultural contexts; in the Chilean context, where class sizes are larger, socioemotional and executive function skills may be more important for later academic achievement.

It seems evident that emergent language and literacy skills will predict later reading – that almost goes without saying. What is interesting is that in Chile, as in other countries, the finding is also replicated that strong math skills predict reading in early elementary. This may have to do with the fact that at this young age, some math skills simply require reading-like abilities – the ability to recognize numbers as opposed to letters, for example – or it may have to do with the fact that throughout the academic careers of students, there is often an important correlation between language and mathematics achievement.

That the importance of socioemotional skills as well as executive function is similar in terms of executive function has not been replicated as frequently with socioemotional skills. It would appear that in the Chilean context, these skills are indeed important, indicating that not only is there an executive function component which may be universal but there may also be a social component which is important culturally.

As professionals who have worked in professional development and classrooms in Chile for many years, it is our impression that there are a great deal more whole-group activities and a teacher-centered pedagogy in Chile, which would suggest that children's learning in the classroom would require more socioemotional and executive function skills than American preschool and early elementary classrooms, which have smaller class sizes and would seem to promote greater autonomy through center work, for example. One potential implication from this study in Chile is that an "educationally informed theory of language learning" needs to understand the educational practices in diverse contexts and how those practices may draw more or less upon specific skills, thus diminishing or increasing the importance and role of those skills in later academic success.

An issue of concern from this study is that our intervention, *Un Buen Comienzo*, begins in prekindergarten, while these results indicate that our students already exhibit important differences among themselves – and these are students who are relatively similar in terms of socioeconomic status. If we were to obtain a nationally representative sample, we would probably find greater achievement gaps between the advantaged and those at risk.

The project over the years has taken steps to provide professional development to give students more access to the learning experiences they need by providing teachers with structured lesson plans that incorporate specific elements of language and literacy instruction and effective interactions based on the CLASS observation instrument (Pianta, LaParo, & Hamre, 2012), and strategies for increasing instructional time and improving school attendance. The CLASS observation instrument can be used as an instrument for professional development, helping classroom teams focus on improving the emotional support, classroom organization, and instructional support they provide through their interactions with children in the classroom (Early et al., 2017). We have also introduced Continuous Quality Improvement (CQI) (Arbour et al., 2015), a methodology to involve stakeholders; help them take ownership of their change at the classroom, school, and district level; and use data to monitor their improvement over time based on clearly defined goals. Attendance is one of the clear inputs that have been shown to have a positive impact on our students' outcomes (Arbour et al., 2015). We have shown impact on improving quality classroom interactions and on student outcomes in kindergarten, but we are waiting to see if these results continue in elementary school with our more recent cohorts (Universidad Diego Portales, 2016). Ultimately, we hope the research presented here, coupled with our professional development and collaboration with public schools in Chile, will help foster the necessary early skills that preschool children will need to succeed in school and will contribute to an "educationally informed theory of language learning."

Discussion

Reflections on Learning through Language from Infancy to Preschool and Early Elementary School Years

Ageliki Nicolopoulou

The six chapters in Part I provide comprehensive and up-to-date overviews of the key factors that are significant in promoting young children's oral language skills starting from infancy and extending to later preschool and elementary school years. The chapters fit together well and build on each other, since all the authors espouse some version of a social-interactional and sociocultural theory of language acquisition. Such theories view the role of verbal (and nonverbal) input in the context of socially communicative interactions between caregiver and child as critical for the child's successful acquisition of language competence. Thus, these chapters illustrate well the current state of child language research, which Catherine Snow (2014) – a major proponent of the social interaction position – has described as showing that "the basic environmentalist/social-interactional position on language acquisition has achieved respectability if not dominance" (p. 119).

In addition, all the chapters are nicely targeted to educators and other professionals whose understanding of the key factors in promoting language in a social context can have important implications for children's lives, since such knowledge can help them to select and adopt, and perhaps to create, appropriate interventions for either home or school settings. Key topics addressed by the six chapters in Part I include the following: (1) how early processes of nonverbal communicative interaction during infancy serve as precursors and foundations for the acquisition of language; (2) the role and significance of caregiver input, including the use of decontextualized language, for the development of strong oral language skills during the early preschool years, and the implications for successful early interventions; and (3) how a complex set of oral language skills combined with cognitive skills and other environmental factors affect the acquisition of early literacy during the preschool and early elementary years, and the implications for teacher interventions in school settings.

Communicative Interactions and Early Language Development

The chapters by Elena Lieven and Paul Harris address the complex interplay between individual development, adult–child interaction, and sociocultural context in language acquisition by infants and toddlers. There is evidence that these processes in early childhood serve as important precursors and foundations for later language development. One theme emphasized by Lieven and Harris is that, while the quantity and quality of input from adult caregivers play a crucial role in promoting the acquisition and mastery of language, even very young children are not simply passive recipients of adult input. They participate from the start in reciprocal processes of communicative interaction, including communication by preverbal gestures, that are essential for early language development. In this respect, the analyses in these chapters accord with the social-interactional approach advocated consistently by Catherine Snow, illustrated by Snow's (1977) insistence that "language acquisition is the result of the process of interaction between mother and child which begins early in infancy, to which child makes as important a contribution as the mother" (p. 31).

Elena Lieven's chapter offers a comprehensive overview of what current research suggests about the dynamics of language acquisition during the early years. Human babies come equipped with universal sensitivities to process any language, but during the first year of life, they become attuned to the specific kinds of linguistic input to which they are exposed, and they develop increasing capacities for processing it. But that is only part of the story. It is now widely accepted that in order for infants to develop language comprehension and eventually speech effectively, their linguistic input needs to be embedded in communicative interactions with significant others with whom they can establish "shared intentionality" (Tomasello, 2008). As Lieven has explained elsewhere (Lieven, 2013), shared intentionality requires not only understanding that others have intentions and goals but also the ability to focus attention and pursue intentions jointly with others. For this purpose, infants must develop not only specifically linguistic and cognitive skills but also social-interactional abilities for attention sharing and intention reading. The hallmark of shared intentionality is that infants can participate in "triadic interactions" in which they share attention to objects or events with other persons and are aware of doing so. Increasingly, they can also draw adults' attention to objects by nonverbal gestures such as pointing while drawing inferences about the adults' attention and knowledge. In other words, children increasingly act as if they are expecting the adult to be a communicative partner. In this respect, a major developmental breakthrough typically occurs around seven to nine months, which in turn helps set the stage for accelerated language acquisition.

At every stage, children's developing mastery of language comprehension and speech, including richness of vocabulary and syntactical competence, is influenced by the amount and quality of linguistic input they receive as well as the communicative and interactional contexts of language use. Lieven's discussion goes on to outline what we know about the typical developmental trajectories of early language acquisition, the complexities of individual variations and of "variable routes into language," and the factors that affect them. The quantity and quality of linguistic input, as well as children's abilities to process this input, are influenced by children's interactions with caregivers, and these are shaped in turn by larger sociocultural contexts, including cultural differences in ideologies of parenting as well as other relevant factors. Lieven argues that although both the quantity and the quality of input are important for promoting children's language learning, input quality is probably more important, especially in the earliest stages. And on the basis of existing research (in relatively affluent, educated, industrialized societies), the most valuable characteristics of adults' linguistic input appear to be the degree of contingent talk, addressing the child's focus of interest and attention; the variability and complexity of vocabulary in adult language; and the use of decontextualized language.

Paul Harris zeroes in on one of the topics highlighted in Lieven's overview, the developmental importance of reciprocal communicative interaction between preverbal infants and adult caregivers, and explores it in greater depth and detail. In particular, Harris analyzes the significance and implications of infants' pointing as a preverbal communicative gesture. He reviews current research which provides evidence that infants point not only to establish joint attention with the adult, implying "Wow—look at that!" but also to request information about the object: "Wow—what's that?" In other words, pointing does not simply signal children's desire to establish joint attention with their caregiver, but also attests to the infants' *interest* in a specific object and their request for *information* about that object. This interpretation is supported by the fact that when adults name or demonstrate the function of an object that infants have pointed to, infants retain this information better than other information communicated by adults. As Harris puts it, baby's pointing may be seen as signaling "an interrogative stance," "a request for new information and a readiness to process it when provided." Furthermore, children's retention of information is influenced by the *type* of pointing they use to request it: index-finger pointing develops later than whole-hand pointing and is associated with greater retention of requested information. There is also evidence that infants can distinguish between adults who provide requested information reliably and those who prove less likely to do so. Again, this analysis identifies even very young children as active participants in a reciprocal process of communicative interaction that helps promote their own language acquisition, and it indicates that children begin to contribute to this process using preverbal communicative gestures even before they can talk themselves.

Next Harris, like Lieven, considers whether and how the frequency and consequences of infant pointing are influenced by individual and cultural differences. The larger question is whether the prelinguistic communicative sociocognitive abilities that form the stepping-stones for language development are universal and appear in roughly the same timetable all around the world, or are influenced by differences in sociocultural contexts from the beginning. While carefully controlled studies with substantial cross-cultural samples are still rare, a handful of studies conducted during the last decade point to some intriguing tendencies. The timetables for the emergence of infant pointing and for the shift from whole-hand to index-finger pointing appear to be roughly similar across cultures. But the frequency of children's deictic gestures (including pointing) varies considerably, in ways that are influenced by patterns of adult–child interaction that, in turn, are influenced by differences in cultural context. For example, those are some implications that can be drawn from a study conducted by Salomo and Liszkowski (2013), who carefully selected three cultures that differed systematically in the typical amounts of joint adult–child attention and in the frequency of deictic gestures (including pointing) by adults to which infants were exposed. They found that infants began to engage in these types of pointing at about the same ages, and in all three cultures, these gestures were part of reciprocal interactions between caregivers and infants, in which pointing by one generated a response from the other. But the frequency of infant pointing varied considerably between cultures. It appears that when caregivers initiate joint attention more frequently, and when they respond more quickly and reliably to infants' hand gestures, the infants generate such gestures more frequently. And these patterns vary between cultures.

In short, research suggests that there may be certain universal patterns in the trajectories of young children's language development from preverbal to verbal stages, but differences also emerge based on patterns of adult–child interaction – especially communicative interaction—which in turn are influenced by cross-cultural variations. Further cross-cultural studies of the earliest phases of language acquisition, including preverbal communicative interactions, can help us to examine the complex interplay between species-wide and sociocultural factors and at the same time to clarify more precisely the processes and mechanisms by which young children begin to acquire language. The chapters by Lieven and Harris provide a usefully informative, stimulating, and thought-provoking picture of current research and debates in this area.

The Role and Significance of Decontextualized Language Input during the Preschool Years

The chapters by Meredith Rowe and Diana Leyva extend this picture of early language development in social context portrayed by Lieven and Harris, focusing on the quality (not just quantity) of caregiver input with a specific emphasis on the role of decontextualized language in promoting vocabulary and other literacy-related skills. The role of caregiver input in language and literacy development has been an important research topic for several decades now, with Catherine Snow being one of its main proponents (cf. Snow, 1977a, 1983, 1993). A distinctive aspect of Snow's line of research in this context is that the acquisition of early oral language is seen as a foundation for early literacy – an emphasis echoed in these two chapters as well.

Rowe provides a useful overview of an accumulating line of research that focuses on the types of parent input that promote vocabulary development. She also extends this overview to other aspects of oral language, including narrative, as well as some cognitive and social-cognitive skills that are significant for school success. The aspect of parental input on which she particularly focuses is "decontextualized language," a concept introduced by Catherine Snow several decades ago (Snow, 1983; Snow et al., 1989) and researched extensively by Snow and her colleagues (Snow, Tabors, & Dickinson, 2001). Following up this research tradition, Rowe defines decontextualized language as language "removed from the here and now" that is commonly encountered in parents' narrative conversations about the past or future, in providing explanations about how things work in the world, and in pretend play. A powerful illustration of this line of research is provided by Rowe (2012), which focuses on the quantity and quality of caregiver input in promoting vocabulary growth for a diverse sample of fifty parent–child dyads from eighteen to fifty-four months. The results indicate that, while diverse and sophisticated vocabulary by the caregivers was a good predictor of children's vocabulary growth, decontextualized talk also contributed to growing vocabulary abilities. Furthermore, the results supported a nuanced developmental picture showing that quantity of input is most important during the second year, the diversity and sophistication of the vocabulary during the third year, and decontextualized talk such as narrative and explanations during the fourth year of life. Rowe provides several other examples from her own research in this chapter.

In addition, Rowe expands the review of decontextualized language in the context of caregiver–child input by recasting previous research as also, in effect, tapping this type of language use. For example, she argues that elaborative reminiscing parent–child talk about the past, book-reading elaborative talk, and explanations that parents provide to children's information-seeking questions are special forms of decontextualized language, which in turn promote autobiographical memory and other sociocognitive skills. This is an interesting application of the study of decontextualized language use that has the potential to open promising new lines of research.

It may be worth noting that the concept of "decontextualized language" used by Rowe differs somewhat from the original formulation of this concept by Snow and her collaborators (e.g., Snow, 1983; Snow et al., 1989; Snow & Dickinson, 1991). Language use is "decontextualized," in the technical sense of Snow's original concept, to the extent that it involves explicitly constructing, conveying, and comprehending information in ways that are not embedded in the supportive framework of conversational interaction and do not rely on implicit shared background knowledge and nonverbal cues. Information is conveyed in ways that can, in principle, allow it to be understood "across a wider variety of contexts" by more unfamiliar, impersonal, or generalized audiences (Snow & Dickinson, 1991, pp. 185–186). Decontextualized discourse in this sense thus raises greater demands than "contextualized" discourse for semantic clarity, planning, and linguistic self-monitoring. Examples of decontextualized language use include various forms of coherent extended discourse such as narratives, explanations, and other monologues, as well as metalinguistic operations such as giving formal definitions and monitoring the grammatical correctness of speech (Snow, 1983). Although this range of examples may seem rather heterogeneous, there is evidence to support the claim that the cognitive and linguistic skills underlying these activities are, in fact, highly interrelated and form a mutually supportive cluster. There is also evidence supporting claims that "skill at the decontextualized uses of language predict[s] literacy and school achievement better than skill at other challenging tasks that are not specifically decontextualized" (Snow & Dickinson, 1991, p. 185).

By contrast, Rowe's criterion for characterizing language use as "decontextualized" refers to an aspect of the content of the discourse – i.e., that it deals with subjects removed from the immediate setting of the communication, the not here and now. It seems to me, therefore, that Rowe's conceptual formulation and operational application of decontextualized language accentuates one element of Snow's earlier distinction between contextualized and decontextualized language while attenuating others. This is also true of the ways that Rowe is extending her concept of decontextualized language to reinterpret other research (e.g., on elaborative talk). My point is not to suggest that the original definition is the right one and that modifications or adaptations of this sort should necessarily be rejected. On the contrary, Rowe's research findings and the interventions she describes in this chapter indicate that these newer formulations of the concept of decontextualized language capture important aspects of the quality of caregivers' language use and the ways they can promote children's development. However, it is also useful to acknowledge explicitly the differences between Snow's original formulation of this concept and the modified version used by Rowe – both because grasping these distinctions can give us a more precise understanding of the research and the issues it addresses and because the original concept also remains a useful, illuminating, and fruitful basis for research.

The issue I have raised about the shifting meaning associated with the term "decontextualized" language applies equally to the chapter by Leyva, who uses a definition similar to the one used by Rowe and also attempts to extend it in a similar way to elaborative talk. In this chapter, she discusses the significance of three family-related language and literacy activities that are critical in promoting language and literacy during the preschool years: talking, reading, and writing. Taking its inspiration from the research by Snow and Beals (2006) that describes the significance of family mealtime conversations, Leyva introduces a family literacy program for low-income Latino parents and their kindergarten teachers called the Food for Thought program. She also describes a preliminary intervention study she conducted that incorporated this family program into a preschool setting and tested the feasibility of this program with sixty-eight parent–child dyads, twenty-two of which were videotaped while participating in the program. The results were encouraging in that the Latino parents used the language- and literacy-based strategies taught in the program. As pointed out by Leyva, the next step will be to systematically test whether the families indeed learned these strategies during the intervention program, whether they could use them effectively beyond the duration of the short program, and whether these had some lasting effects in promoting strong oral language and literacy skills in the children.

Fostering Preschoolers' Oral Language Skills and Their Relationship to Early School Success

The next two chapters, by Kim and Yun and by Rolla and colleagues, build on the picture of children's basic oral language skills provided so far by the previous chapters and further enrich it. The authors take a broader view by examining the various language and cognitive factors that contribute to building strong oral language skills (extended discourse) during preschool and early elementary years (Kim and Yun) and by examining whether preschool oral language (and other) skills can predict reading comprehension during the early elementary years (Rolla et al.).

Kim and Yun start by presenting a model of various language and cognitive factors that have been shown to affect oral discourse comprehension and production during the preschool years, which in turn affect later oral language skills that underpin children's abilities for text comprehension (a similar type of argument can be seen in Snow, Griffin, & Burns, 1998).

The authors enrich this model by differentiating between foundational cognitive skills (working memory, inhibitory control, and attentional control), foundational oral language (vocabulary and grammatical knowledge), and higher-order cognitive skills (inference, perspective taking, and comprehension monitoring), all of which contribute to promoting complex oral discourse and oral listening comprehension. They argue, though, based on empirical evidence presented elsewhere (Kim, 2015, 2016), that these different levels interact with one another such that foundational cognitive skills are necessary for foundational oral language skills, which in turn are necessary for higher-order cognitive skills.

After introducing this model, Kim and Yun go on to discuss the environmental factors that can affect children's performance in building strong oral language abilities during the preschool and early elementary years. While they examine interactional factors such as frequency and quality of input in general, they pay particular attention to the impact that teachers' frequency and quality of input as well as socioemotional support can have in promoting children's complex oral language skills. They also review many interventions that have been shown to be successful in promoting various aspects of oral discourse production and comprehension. And they finish by providing a useful set of principles to teachers in helping them to promote language learning, which they call E^5 principles (explore, elicitation, extension, and emotional engagement). This chapter provides an excellent example of what an educationally informed theory of language learning should look like. While based on a solid review of psychological and educational research, it is directed to educators and other professionals, and I believe it has the potential to be a very useful guide for them.

The study by Rolla and colleagues also casts a wide net by testing not only whether preschool language and literacy skills can predict second-grade reading scores but also whether these reading scores can be predicted by preschool mathematics and socioemotional development, including executive function. These authors used a large sample of more than a thousand Spanish monolinguals in a Latin American context (Chile) with children coming from diverse family backgrounds. They found that preschool language, literacy, and mathematics scores predicted second-grade reading scores, replicating findings from previous research conducted in different countries (Canada, Great Britain, and the United States). They also found that socioemotional variables, such as low problem scores and high self-regulation, predicted higher reading scores at second grade, but these results were different from the socioemotional variables found in previous studies. The significance of this study is that Spanish monolingual children were tested replicating the significance of language, literacy, and mathematics in predicting reading achievement during early elementary school using non-English-speaking students in a Latin

American context. These results are intriguing, and it will be important to further theorize and test the influence of the domains that go beyond language and literacy, as the authors suggest.

In closing, the six chapters in Part I offer comprehensive overviews of the various factors in caregiver–child interaction that contribute to strong early language competence from infancy to later preschool and elementary years. The chapters build well on each other in providing a comprehensive review of the major phases during this period and offer up-to-date information regarding conceptual and practical issues that can be useful to educators and policy makers. They also justly celebrate the work of Catherine Snow, who, as I have tried to indicate throughout my commentary, is often the key inspiration for a great deal of the research discussed in these chapters.

Part II

Learning through Language during the Middle School and Early Adolescent Years

8 Learning the Language for School Literacy

Research Insights and a Vision for a Cross-Linguistic Research Program

Paola Uccelli

As the result of globalization, immigration, and worldwide increases in student enrollment, educational systems are charged to educate ever more linguistically and socioeconomically diverse populations (Varghese, 2014). At the same time, schools are pressed to equip students with advanced literacy skills to navigate an information-based society, where access to educational and professional opportunities, as well as to health, politics, civic, and even social news, relies more than ever before on individuals' literacy skills (Wagner, 2015). Yet, today many schools around the world struggle to adequately support their adolescent students' literacy achievement. In the United States, by the end of middle school, a disquieting majority of students perform below expected proficiency levels in reading and writing (National Center for Education Statistics, 2015b). Adolescents' reading levels are of major concern also in many other countries, where, as in the United States, reading performances display marked socioeconomic discrepancies. Indeed, these unsatisfactory and inequitable educational results call for research-based solutions to address adolescents' literacy.

Motivated by this reality, this chapter discusses academic language as a promising research area to better understand why so many adolescents struggle with reading comprehension. The term *academic language* is widely used to refer broadly to the language of science, the language of schooling or the language of school literacy and learning. The language used in these contexts is characterized by prevalent functional resources (e.g., connectives, such as *consequently;* stance markers, such as *it is uncertain if . . .*) deployed to support precise, concise, and reflective communication of complex abstract ideas (Halliday, 2004; Schleppegrell, 2001). Paradoxically, these language features meant to support precise communication may constitute major roadblocks for text comprehension if readers are unfamiliar with them. The potential contribution of academic language proficiency to reading comprehension has been theorized in educational research focused on bilingual learners for several decades (Cummins, 2000). However, this hypothesis remained untested for too long, and the construct of academic language proficiency, too underspecified to inform instruction. Recently, a newly proposed operational construct, Core Academic Language Skills (CALS), has guided a program of research that empirically assesses an array of cross-disciplinary language skills and their contribution to adolescents' reading comprehension (Uccelli et al., 2015).

This chapter focuses on adolescents' CALS and is organized in four sections. In the first section, I situate the study of language and literacy within a sociocultural pragmatics-based theoretical framework, defining academic language proficiency as a component of a larger construct, the language for school literacy. In the second section, I briefly review research on adolescents' language and literacy relations. The third section presents selected findings from two studies: one focused on CALS as predictor of adolescents' reading comprehension and a second focused on young children's decontextualized language as predictor of adolescents' CALS. Finally, this chapter calls for a cross-linguistic research enterprise to investigate language and literacy relations. A CALS-based vision is presented just as an entry point into a vaster area in need of creative research with potentially profound implications for literacy assessment and instruction.

A Sociocultural Pragmatics-Based Theoretical Framework

A sociocultural pragmatics-based theory of language learning integrates insights from ethnographic research on language and literacy (Heath, 1983; Levine et al., 1996; Ochs, 1988), pragmatic development studies (Blum-Kulka, 2008; Ninio & Snow, 1996), and functional linguistics research (Berman & Ravid, 2009; Schleppegrell, 2004) to conceptualize language learning as inseparable from context. Through a cross-cultural lens, ethnographies document practices across cultures and contexts, shedding light on congruencies and incongruencies between home – or out-of-school – language and literacy practices and those valued at school (Cazden, 2002; Heath, 1983, 2012). Through a pragmatics-based interactional lens, specific language interactions have been shown to support literacy development, e.g., toddlers' participation in co-constructed, decontextualized language (e.g., narratives, explanations) with supporting caregivers (Hemphill & Snow, 1996). Through functional analyses, text and developmental linguists have identified linguistic features distinctive of academic texts (Berman & Ravid, 2009; Schleppegrell, 2001).

Three key developmental implications emerge from these combined insights. First, language development continues throughout adolescence, and under normal circumstances, language learning continues for as long as learners expand the language-mediated social contexts that they navigate. Second, being a skilled language user in one social context does not guarantee linguistic dexterity in a different social context. Speakers are enculturated at home into the language of face-to-face interaction, which typically prepares them well for colloquial conversations in their respective communities. Despite their fluency in informal communication, many adolescents encounter limited opportunities to learn school-relevant language practices, and consequently, academic language poses higher challenges for them (Cazden, 2002; Cummins, 2000; Heath, 2012). Third, language is a powerful socializer: by learning language, children also learn how to interact with others, how to comprehend, and how to learn in ways that are culturally shaped (Heath, 1983; Ochs, 1988).

In a sociocultural pragmatics-based framework, language and literacy proficiencies are conceptualized as the result, to a large extent, of an individual's history of participation in specific contexts and sociocultural discourses (Bruner, 1983; Ochs, 1988). Language development is understood as the expansion of "rhetorical flexibility," i.e., the ability to flexibly use an increasing repertoire of language forms and functions in an ever-expanding set of social contexts, orally and in writing (Ravid & Tolchinsky, 2002). Consequently, learning the language of school entails not only acquiring discrete language skills (e.g., lexical, morphological) but also being able to participate in authentic discourse practices (e.g., debates, persuasive essays). For instance, beyond understanding the connective *however,* students need to learn how to use it to link ideas between sentences and in argumentative texts. They also need to understand –implicitly or explicitly – that school discourse is driven by particular situational expectations shaped by the Western scientific tradition (e.g., marking logical connections explicitly). Overall, adolescents need to understand that, in contrast to the communicative expectations of many of their out-of-school practices, school discourse is expected to be lexically precise, grammatically concise, and explicitly logically connected (among other expectations) (Schleppegrell, 2001). Understanding these typically hidden expectations supports the learning of academic language, not as formulaic, but as a means toward effective communication.

Academic language skills thus constitute only one component of the much larger process of developing proficiency in the Language for School Literacy, defined as "the academic language skills and sociocultural academic discourse practices that learners internalize gradually as they flexibly enact the situational expectations of school reading, writing, and learning in interactions with texts or with other language users" (Uccelli, Phillips Galloway, & Qin, in press). This chapter calls for more research on school-relevant language skills as intimately related to discourse practices. Whereas academic language skills and decontextualized language practices, for instance, have been studied mostly independently from one another – the former in adolescents, the latter in young children – their joint investigation promises to contribute to a pedagogically relevant theory of language learning.

- Academic language refers to the language used for reading and writing academic texts, language-mediated school learning, and scientific communication (Halliday, 2004; Schleppegrell, 2004). Academic language is further divided into discipline specific (i.e., the language features distinctive of particular disciplines) and cross-disciplinary (i.e., the language features of high utility across disciplines). Cross-disciplinary academic language is also relevant beyond school to access scientific knowledge, health information, and civic opportunities communicated orally or in writing. Similar to school texts, these messages are crafted for wide dissemination and are therefore populated with many of the same academic language features that support precise and concise distant communication.
- Decontextualized language is defined as extended discourse about the there and then, in other words, talk that refers to content removed from the surrounding physical context of the interaction, or the here and now (Snow, 1991a). During the first years of a child's life, decontextualized talk is typically found in the form of narratives, comments about future actions, pretend play, or explanations in the context of highly scaffolded interactions with caregivers (Rowe, 2013).

The overlap across both constructs justifies the investigation of a developmental continuity hypothesis, in which early participation in decontextualized talk would lead to early learning of decontextualized language skills, which, in turn, would serve as precursors of later academic language skills. Certainly not all decontextualized language is academic (e.g., personal anecdotes, pretend play), and not all academic language is decontextualized (e.g., explaining an experiment while conducting it). Yet, both have been described as more lexically diverse and morphosyntactically complex than their counterparts, contextualized talk (Demir, Rowe, Heller, Goldin-Meadow, & Levine, 2015; Rowe, 2012) or colloquial language (Halliday, 2004; Schleppegrell, 2001). Both are understood as part of a continuum, with the two ends of both continua differing in purpose and structural complexity (Snow, 1991a; Snow & Uccelli, 2009). Whereas at one extreme, contextualized and colloquial language entails talk about concrete entities or actions, with communication supported by the surrounding physical environment through pointing, gestures, and other nonverbal cues, at the other extreme, decontextualized and academic language entails discussing invisible entities, nonpresent events, or abstract ideas, with language functioning as its own context and, consequently, requiring more autonomous resources.

In the next sections, after a brief synthesis on adolescents' language and reading relations, I share selected findings from two CALS-based studies: one on adolescents' academic language skills as predictors of reading comprehension, the second on young children's participation in decontextualized language practices as predictor of adolescents' academic language skills.

Language and Reading Relations

In the last decades, considerable research has shown that after the early years, once basic, code-focused skills (e.g., identifying letters) no longer pose a major challenge for most readers, language proficiency becomes a primary contributor to text comprehension. Overall, studies reveal that vocabulary is one of the strongest predictors of reading comprehension, such that readers with larger and deeper vocabulary repertoires tend to be more skilled text comprehenders (Stahl & Nagy, 2006). Furthermore, adolescents' morphological skills and syntactic skills (e.g., morphological decomposition/derivation; understanding complex sentences) contribute significantly to reading comprehension, even after controlling for vocabulary knowledge and reading fluency (Kieffer, 2014; Kieffer & Lesaux, 2012; Kieffer, Petscher, Proctor, & Silverman, 2016; Nagy, Berninger, & Abbott, 2006). Nevertheless, these relations are not always found to be significant across grades or groups of English-proficient and emergent bilinguals (Foorman, Koon, Petscher, Mitchell, & Truckenmiller, 2015; Geva & Farnia, 2012; Nagy, Berninger, Abbot, Vaughan, & Vermeulen, 2003). Most studies, however, measure global language skills classified by only formal linguistic levels (i.e., lexicon, morphology, syntax) without attending to which language skills are specifically called upon for school literacy (for a detailed review, see Uccelli et al., in press).

Moving beyond acontextual skills, recent intervention studies have targeted a specific subset of school-relevant or academic vocabulary as a mechanism to improve adolescents' reading comprehension. Insightful findings reveal that beyond discipline-specific academic vocabulary, i.e., words with specialized technical meanings (e.g., *antioxidant, rhombus*), large proportions of students struggle with cross-discipline academic vocabulary, i.e., high-utility words prevalent in texts across content areas (e.g., *process, structural*) (Hiebert & Kamil, 2005; Nagy & Townsend, 2012; Snow, Lawrence, & White, 2009). Disappointingly, though, save only a few exceptions, the majority of vocabulary-focused interventions have resulted in gains in taught words, but only in modest – if any – gains in reading comprehension (Elleman, Lindo, Morphy, & Compton, 2009). These results, which are consistent with those of morphology-focused interventions (Goodwin, 2016), suggest that beyond isolated skills, targeting constellations of language skills used together to create the fabric of authentic academic discourse might be more promising.

The realization that improving vocabulary or morphological skills may be insufficient to facilitate access to texts heavily populated by a wider range of potentially challenging grammatical and discourse features has motivated newer initiatives. One innovative approach grows out of the long history of US English proficiency assessments designed to identify emergent bilinguals, i.e., those learning English as an additional language who have not yet achieved grade-appropriate proficiency (also called "English learners" in the United States, where federally mandated English learning services are provided to these students) (García, 2009). The latest generation of US English proficiency assessments has moved from testing general language skills to measuring instead discipline-specific academic language skill sets relevant for literacy and learning in specific content areas. Assessments, such as the Academic English Language Proficiency instrument (Bailey et al., 2007) or the WIDA-ACCESS (Boals et al., 2015) or ELPA21, now measure vocabulary, morphosyntactic, and discourse skills characteristic of grade-specific and content-area-specific texts and tasks. These assessments have proven informative to design targeted pedagogical practices that prepare students for content-area-specific speaking, listening, reading, and writing demands.

The CALS research program, to which I turn in the next section, is a recent and complementary initiative that seeks to understand cross-disciplinary academic language skill sets in relation to school literacy.

Core Academic Language Skills

The CALS research was motivated by the long-standing, yet untested, hypothesis that adolescents' variability in academic language skills would predict reading comprehension. Given the lack of an inclusive definition, we had to start by proposing an operational definition of academic language skills. Two strategic decisions were made in delimiting this construct. First, instead of focusing on discipline-specific skills, we sought to delineate a cross-disciplinary skill set, which, if identified, would be particularly salient for the period of early adolescence (grades 4–8) and, if proven to be associated with literacy, would have pedagogical implications that transcended a single content area. Second, instead of exclusively investigating bilingual students, we hypothesized that differences in CALS would be relevant across bilingual and monolingual populations.

We define CALS as follows:

> **Core Academic Language Skills (CALS)**
> a constellation of the high-utility language skills that correspond to linguistic features prevalent in oral and written academic discourse across school content areas and infrequent in colloquial conversations

The CALS construct comprises seven theoretically and empirically grounded skill sets, understood as crucial, but not exhaustive (see Figure 8.1). Far from referring to what some call academic gibberish or unnecessarily intricate structures that obscure communication, CALS capture proficiency in the high-utility academic language resources that

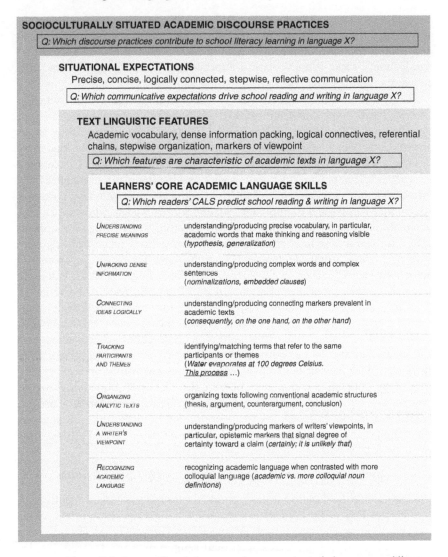

Figure 8.1 A cross-linguistic research program to study language and literacy relations. Adapted from Uccelli, Phillips Galloway, and Qin (in press).

support precise communication and learning. Informed by anthropological and interactional linguistics studies which reveal that children not only learn language but learn how to learn through language, CALS represents proficiency in an array of linguistic markers that correspond to core expectations of scientific discourse and shared scientific thinking. If, arguably, a major goal of schools is to socialize students into ways of individual and shared thinking in scientific communities, then the CALS construct would likely make these scientific expectations more visible for students, educators, and researchers.

The CALS Instrument (CALS-I). The development of the theoretically grounded and psychometrically robust CALS-I was the result of a six-year investigation of the Academic Language Project, which was part of the larger project Catalyzing Comprehension through Discussion and Debate funded by the Institute of Education Sciences and awarded to the Strategic Educational Research Partnership. In collaboration with psychometrician Christopher Barr, former doctoral advisee Emily Phillips Galloway, international colleagues Alejandra Meneses and Emilio Sánchez, and former student Christina Dobbs, our multidisciplinary team implemented a rigorous assessment development plan informed by the most recent theories from various functional linguistic traditions, developmental empirical findings, and the latest psychometric guidelines (Uccelli, Barr et al., 2015). This work began with an extensive research synthesis that identified an array of linguistic features prevalent in texts across disciplines, followed by a research-driven hypothetical developmental map of evolving language skills to guide the design of tasks and items. This work was conducted in partnership with urban public schools across two US states. During the design phase, we gathered extensive feedback from students and teachers in an iterative process of design, testing, and refinement. Guided by qualitative and quantitative studies, the final group-administered paper-and-pencil CALS-I includes two vertically equated forms (Form 1: grades 4–6; Form 2: grades 7–8) and norms for English-proficient students attending urban public schools in grades 4–8.

Study 1: Adolescents' CALS Predict Reading Comprehension

Our quantitative studies reveal that individual variability in CALS significantly predicts reading comprehension in grades 4–8 (Uccelli, Barr et al., 2015; Uccelli, Phillips Galloway, Barr, Meneses, & Dobbs, 2015). To illustrate these findings, data from a cross-sectional sample of 3,563 students (grades 4–8) are displayed in Figure 8.2. This sample was representative of US urban public school populations, where data were collected: approximately balanced by gender (48 percent female), with a majority of students (82 percent) from low socioeconomic backgrounds (as indexed by eligibility for free/reduced-price lunch at school); most students were English proficient (only 10 percent were designated as English learners) and represented a variety of ethnicities (mostly African American, White, and Latino, with only 4 percent Asian students and 2 percent belonging to other ethnic or mixed groups).

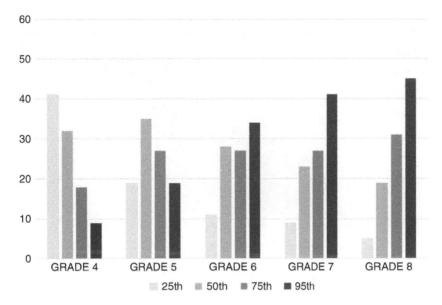

Figure 8.2 Proportion of students by CALS percentile levels and grade (*n* = 3,563).

Participants were administered the following measures:

- CALS-I: fifty-minute, paper-and-pencil, group-administered Form 1 (grades 4–6; α = .90) and Form 2 (grades 7–8; α = .86). Factor scores – on a vertically equated metric – were generated.
- Global Integrated Scenario-Based Assessment (GISA) (α = .89): computer-based reading comprehension assessment that provides students with a reading purpose (e.g., is a wind farm a good idea for a community?) and a set of texts with literal, inferential, and multiple-text integration questions (Sabatini, O'Reilly, Halderman, & Bruce, 2014). Factors scores, reported on a common, cross-form scale, were used.

We found an upward trend in CALS-I scores across higher grades, yet also enormous within-grade variability (see Figure 8.2). As observed in Figure 8.3, a strong relation between CALS and GISA revealed that students with higher academic language skills displayed higher levels of reading comprehension. This is consistent with prior studies that reveal that the contribution of CALS remains significant even after controlling for word recognition skills, vocabulary knowledge, and students' sociodemographic characteristics (Uccelli, Barr et al., 2015; Uccelli, Phillips Galloway et al., 2015; Uccelli & Phillips Galloway, 2016).

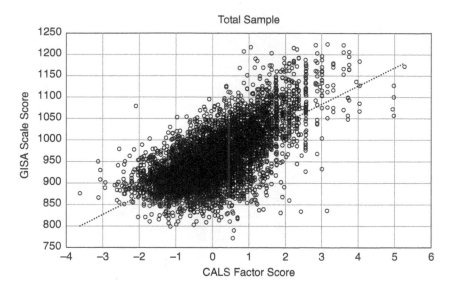

Figure 8.3   Scatterplot of academic language proficiency (CALS) and reading comprehension (GISA) (*n* = 3,563). From Barr and Uccelli (2016).

Also consistent with prior findings, CALS were positively associated with students' socioeconomic status (SES), with considerable variability across and within SES groups (see Figure 8.4). Prior analyses with samples that were administered additional measures have shown that controlling for word recognition skills, when CALS and academic vocabulary are added to the regression model, the contribution of students' SES to reading comprehension is no longer significant (Uccelli, Phillips Galloway, Kim, & Barr, 2015). These results are promising as they suggest that the CALS-I is capturing language skills that tend to be unequally distributed across socioeconomic lines and, consequently, may be relevant to inform literacy interventions that seek to achieve excellence and equity. Among many questions raised by these findings, an important developmental one is which early language experiences might function as precursors or predictors of adolescents' CALS.

Study 2: Young Children's Decontextualized Language Practices Predict Adolescents' CALS

One hypothesis worth exploring is if young children's opportunities to participate in decontextualized language (i.e., narratives, pretend play, explanations) constitute a developmental precursor of later adolescents' CALS. In Uccelli, Demir-Lira, Rowe, Levine, and Goldin-Meadow (2018), taking advantage of

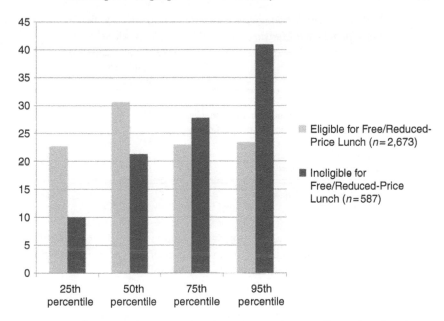

Figure 8.4 Distribution of students by CALS percentile levels and SES (eligibility for free/reduced-price lunch).

Goldin-Meadow and Levine's longitudinal Chicago project (Goldin-Meadow et al., 2014), we examined if young children's (age thirty months) production of decontextualized language in highly scaffolded interactions with their care-givers would predict seventh-grade academic language proficiency (age twelve).

A total of forty-two typically developing monolingual English-speaking children and their main caregivers participated in this study. Participants were selected from the larger sample if data from the home visit at child age thirty months and the child's seventh-grade CALS-I scores were available. Families' SES, indexed by a composite of family income level and primary caregiver's educational attainment, was representative of the socioeconomic diversity of the Chicago area. According to parental reports, twenty-four children were Caucasian, eight were African American, six were Latino, and four were of mixed race/ethnicity. During the home visit, the child and primary caregiver were videotaped for ninety minutes engaging in ordinary daily activities (e.g., toy play, book reading, mealtimes). The unit of transcription for videotaped interactions was the utterance, i.e., a sequence of words pre-ceded and followed by a pause, a change in conversational turn, or in intona-tional contour. Dictionary words, evaluative sounds (e.g., *uh-oh*), and

Table 8.1 *Correlations between Child Seventh-Grade CALS and Video-Based Measures at Child Age Thirty Months*

	Child academic language
Parent SES	.56***
Parent proportion of decontextualized utterances	.42**
Child proportion of decontextualized utterances	.56***
Child word tokens	.32*
Child receptive vocabulary	.48**
Child syntax comprehension	.19

***$p < .001$. **$p < .01$. *$p < .05$.

onomatopoeic sounds (e.g., *woof-woof*) were counted as words. Reliability was calculated on 20 percent of the data, with two transcribers agreeing on 95 percent of the utterances. The measures included the following:

Child age thirty months

- Child and parent proportion of decontextualized utterances: videos were coded for decontextualized utterances (i.e., narrative, pretend, explanation utterances) as described in Rowe (2012). Interrater reliability yielded a Cohen's kappa of 0.73. Given the variability in quantity of talk, proportions of decontextualized utterances (out of the total utterances produced by each interlocutor) were generated.
- Child word tokens: number of words.
- Child receptive vocabulary: Peabody Picture Vocabulary Test-PPVT-III (Dunn & Dunn, 1997).
- Child syntax comprehension: Huttenlocher's and Levine's adaptation of Huttenlocher, Vasilyeva, Cymerman, and Levine's (2002) task; children had to select – out of three or four options – a picture that corresponded to sentences read aloud by the experimenter.

Child in seventh grade:

- CALS Instrument, Form 2 ($\alpha = .86$).

Table 8.1 displays associations between measures at child age thirty months and children's seventh-grade CALS-I scores. Child syntax comprehension was the only measure found to be nonsignificant. Parents' SES and parents' decontextualized utterances were significantly associated with CALS-I scores. Interestingly, regression analyses revealed that children who produced a larger proportion of decontextualized utterances at thirty months displayed, on average, significantly higher levels of CALS in seventh grade, even accounting for the contribution of socioeconomic status, parent decontextualized utterances, child amount of talk, vocabulary, and syntactic comprehension. Moreover, child proportion of decontextualized talk made a relatively greater contribution to CALS scores than any of the other language skills (Uccelli et al., 2018). We interpret these findings as the result of the variability in language environments across children and the relatively high stability of language environments throughout development within child. Indeed, parent and child decontextualized talk were highly correlated ($r = .81$; $p < .001$), indicating their co-occurrence and highlighting the need of interpreting both as dimensions of a single interactional space.

Far from offering definitive answers, these results illustrate a promising line of research into developmental continuities in learning the language for school literacy. Interestingly, pragmatic research on early language focuses mostly on discourse practices (e.g., decontextualized talk) that predict literacy, whereas research in the later years mostly measures language skills (e.g., academic language skills) to predict literacy. It seems timely to integrate not only the two developmental phases but also the investigation of interactional discourse practices and learners' language skills to study them from the early years to adolescence. We stand to gain a deeper understanding of how to scaffold proficiency in the language for school literacy by focusing on the discourse practices that lead to gains in academic language skills. Although text-based discussions are emerging as a promising mechanism to improve reading comprehension, more research needs to investigate which classroom discourse practices are likely to promote meaningful growth in academic language and literacy and why. Microanalysis of interactions could illuminate which characteristics of text-based discussions are particularly effective (e.g., teacher moves, students' participation levels) (O'Connor & Michaels, 2015).

A Cross-Linguistic Research Program

I close this chapter with a vision for a cross-linguistic and pedagogically relevant research program on language and literacy relations. In contrast to the extensive investigation of code-based skills across languages and orthographies (Verhoeven & Perfetti, 2017), cross-linguistic research on the contributions of language proficiency to reading comprehension is still minimal. Psychological research reveals that reading comprehension is a multicomponent process (including decoding, fluency, vocabulary, etc.) dynamically influenced by the characteristics of a specific text, reader, and activity (Snow, 2002; Kintsch, 2004; Perfetti & Stafura, 2014). Yet, neither the role of languages as distinct systems (e.g., Spanish, Mandarin) nor the role of academic language within and across language systems has been theorized in detail.

A CALS-based cross-linguistic research program seems promising in light of findings from Spanish-speaking adolescents' CALS and their contribution to reading comprehension. Aligned with findings in English, Spanish CALS have been shown to predict early adolescents' reading comprehension even after controlling for school effects, students' vocabulary knowledge, and decoding skills (Meneses et al., 2018). In Spanish, given its many structural similarities with English, all original CALS-I skill sets were hypothesized as relevant and indeed found to be predictive of Spanish reading comprehension. Alternatively, in languages that are structurally more distant from English, the skills required to process language-specific text features might differ more saliently. Based on linguistic descriptive data, for instance, knowledge of connectives may be less relevant for reading Mandarin Chinese given the strict syntactic order and reduced frequency of connectives documented for written Mandarin. Rather than taking the CALS construct at face value, this enterprise entails investigating to what extent CALS would need to be adjusted as language-specific or may be generalizable across some languages.

A first consideration would be to understand (through textual linguistics research) which – if any – language features distinguish colloquial and academic discourse in a target language. If the CALS construct is indeed deemed potentially relevant, then, as displayed in Figure 8.1, this research would entail questions at each of the four levels of analysis of the language for school literacy. In this so far minimally elaborated outline for this vision, it would be critical to consider that (1) socioculturally situated academic discourse practices are manifestations of (2) particular situational expectations or communicative norms that, in turn, influence which (3) functional text linguistic features are prevalent in academic texts, which, consequently, delineate the (4) academic language skills that readers need to learn in order to comprehend those potentially challenging linguistic features of academic texts. Languages and the specific contexts in which they are used might vary at any of these four levels. Change might also occur within a language over time due to evolving scientific paradigms or new technology that alter prevalent text features (e.g., digital texts with embedded internet links). Additional, more ambitious questions would address the relative contribution of CALS to reading comprehension across languages and their respective orthographies, and the relevance of a cross-linguistic CALS construct for biliteracy development and instruction.

In sum, the research reviewed in this chapter reveals that reading to learn at school entails the continuous expansion of discipline-specific and cross-disciplinary language skills in both bilingual and monolingual students. Whereas it is perhaps not surprising that language skills would be predictive of adolescents' reading comprehension, the innovation of the CALS work resides in having identified and shown the predictive value of a theoretically and empirically tested set of high-utility, cross-disciplinary language skills associated with text comprehension. Instead of aiming at the discipline-specific language of a single content area, the CALS construct captures an array of skills relevant for reading texts across disciplines and also likely to be of high utility to access informational texts in the larger society. CALS emerge as a componential skillset of reading comprehension that is especially relevant to theory and practice due to its associations with both literacy and students' SES. From a theory-building perspective, this work further specifies the role of language in psychological models of reading comprehension and offers an entry point to further explore language and literacy relations across languages. From a pedagogical perspective, this research has the potential to inform the design of literacy interventions and instruments that help promote not only excellence but also educational equity by illuminating which rich opportunities to learn lead to proficiency in the language for school literacy for all learners. Many questions remain to be answered.

Acknowledgments

I thank all the participants and colleagues who contributed to the projects presented in this chapter. The English CALS-I was developed by Paola Uccelli, Christopher D. Barr, and Emily Phillips Galloway, with support from the Institute of Education Sciences of the US Department of Education through grant R305F100026 awarded to the Strategic Education Research Partnership as part of the Reading for Understanding Initiative. The Spanish CALS-I was developed by Paola Uccelli and Alejandra Meneses, with support from the David Rockefeller Center for Latin American Studies at Harvard University. The longitudinal study presented was possible thanks to the Eunice Kennedy Shriver National Institute of Child Health and Human Development of the National Institutes of Health grant P01HD040605 awarded to Susan Goldin-Meadow and Susan C. Levine and to the collaboration of their team, including Meredith L. Rowe and Özlem Ece Demir-Lira.

9 Observational Research on Vocabulary and Comprehension in Upper Elementary School Classrooms

Rebecca D. Silverman and Anna M. Hartranft

At least since the publication of the Report of the National Reading Panel (NRP; NICHD, 2000), which was commissioned by the US Congress to identify evidence-based practices of reading instruction, there has been a strong focus on experimental reading research. This focus has led to numerous studies showing the effects of reading programs and interventions in tightly controlled trials, but it ignores reading instruction in millions of everyday classrooms where teachers are using the curricula and materials they have on hand or can find on the internet, often with little guidance and support. While observation research is messier than experimental research, it provides insight into what works in typical classroom circumstances.

Despite major educational reforms since the publication of the NRP report, only 36 percent of US fourth graders scored at or above the proficient level in reading on the 2017 US National Assessment of Educational Progress (NAEP; NCES, 2017). How could this be? It could be that reform efforts, which focused mainly on early elementary school, have not adequately prepared students for reading in upper elementary school. It also could be that more attention is needed on instruction in the upper elementary grades. As students in these grade levels become more independent readers, with the expectation that they have mastered basic decoding skills, they are faced with increasingly complex texts and ever more advanced academic content. Many students who had not exhibited early reading difficulties present for the first time in upper elementary school with late emerging reading difficulties (e.g., Catts, Compton, Tromblin, & Bridges, 2012; Snow, 2002). Understanding the relationship between instruction and reading outcomes for students in these grade levels is, therefore, particularly important.

Many of the children who experience late emerging reading difficulties in U.S. schools are children whose home language is other than English and who are learning English, particularly academic English, in school. Though a variety of terms have been used to describe this population (i.e., English Language Learner and Language Minority Learner), we use the term emerging bilingual (EB) in the remainder of this chapter. Often EBs, particularly EBs who speak a home language that is phonologically or orthographically similar to English, have little difficulty learning to decode but have substantial difficulty learning vocabulary and comprehension skills to acquire content area knowledge in school (August & Shanahan, 2006). Observation research aimed at understanding the relationship between teachers' instruction and students' outcomes for EBs can contribute to future reform efforts aimed at improving EB students' reading achievement.

Observation research in upper elementary schools has accumulated since at least the 1970s when Durkin (1978/1979) published a groundbreaking study of reading instruction in grades 3–6. Subsequent research (e.g., Connor, Morrison, & Petrella, 2004; Pressley, Wharton-McDonald, Hampson, & Echeverria, 1998) added to the collective understanding of reading instruction over the years. Given that standards, curriculum, and instruction in the United States have changed in the past few decades in response to the NRP report and the release of the Common Core State Standards (CCSS; National Governor's Association Center for Best Practices & Council of Chief State School Officers [NGACBP & CCSSO], 2010), there is a need for ongoing observational research to investigate instruction in the US context. Furthermore, with the continuously expanding EB population in US schools, there is a need to focus on the relationship between instruction and outcomes for EBs in particular.

In the present chapter, we provide a review of key upper elementary observational studies (i.e., grades 3–6). Then, we describe a recent observational study (Silverman et al., 2013) conducted in linguistically diverse US classrooms and discuss findings and implications of this study. Finally, we discuss theoretical and practical implications as well as directions for future research focused on understanding the relationship between teacher instruction and student outcomes in upper elementary school.

The Theoretical Relationship between Teachers' Instruction and Students' Learning

The importance of investigating the relationship between teachers' instruction and students' outcomes is grounded in Vygotskian theory, which suggests that more knowledgeable others mediate learning through linguistic and instructional support (Vygotsky, 1978). In classrooms, by providing specific direction or modeling for students, teachers can guide students to learn words they have never heard before or understand texts that are more challenging than those which can be understood without support (Duke & Pearson, 2002). Over time, the goal is for students to internalize this direction and modeling such that they are able to integrate knowledge of new words or tackle complex texts more successfully on their own. Thus, theoretically, teachers' instruction should be related to students' vocabulary and comprehension development over time. In fact, empirical evidence supports this theory (Murphy, Wilkinson, Soter, Hennessy, & Alexander, 2009).

Following ecological theories of development such as those proposed by Bronfenbrenner (e.g., Bronfenbrenner & Morris, 2007), the relationship between teachers' instruction and students' learning may be complex. The relationship may depend on the amount and type of instruction as well as the background and abilities of the students. Given that instruction takes place in a particular context and is often responsive to changes in policy, standards, and curriculum, teachers' instruction and the relationships between instruction and student outcomes may change over time. Understanding the interplay of teachers' instruction and students' characteristics within a given educational context is essential for informing future teacher training and professional development as well as curriculum and intervention design (Shavelson & Towne, 2002).

Observational Research

Durkin's (1978/1979) study was one of the first studies to emerge from the US National Institute of Education's newly funded Center for the Study of Reading at the University of Illinois, which was charged with focusing on issues related to improving reading comprehension. Durkin determined that "finding, describing, and timing comprehension instruction" was "central to the mission of the Center, since it is impossible to improve instruction until what goes on now, and with what frequency, is known" (p. 484). Prior to observing, Durkin developed a definition of comprehension instruction to guide her observations. The definition she settled on defined comprehension instruction as what teachers do "to help children understand or work out the meaning of more than a single, isolated word." Teacher questioning related to helping children understand text was included as a form of comprehension instruction. Durkin's study included observations during reading and social studies periods in thirty-six classrooms across several schools throughout an academic year. The unit of analysis was the percentage of minutes observed devoted to particular activities. The major finding from Durkin's study was that "practically no comprehension instruction was seen" (p. 520). Durkin also noted that there was limited attention to other comprehension-related skills such as decoding, vocabulary, and structural analysis. Teachers were primarily "interrogators" (p. 520), asking students questions and evaluating their answers as right or wrong. Cazden (2002) would later describe this kind of instruction as the Initiate, Respond, Evaluate (IRE) model of instruction in which teachers initiate questions, students respond to those questions, and teachers evaluate students' responses.

Durkin's observations were a "wake-up call, motivating research on how instruction might increase students' reading comprehension" (Pressley, Brown, El-Dinary, & Afflerbach, 1995, p. 215). Over the next couple of decades, a flurry of experiments aimed at improving reading comprehension were conducted, and by the 1990s there was a substantial body of research on instructional practices to support comprehension. Specifically, research had accumulated to the point that there was considerable agreement in the field that instruction on comprehension strategies and explicit vocabulary instruction were important to support reading comprehension for all students and particularly for struggling learners. In 1998, Pressley et al. published a study investigating the literacy practices of ten fourth- and fifth-grade teachers considered to be effective by their district level administrators. Observations took place during language arts twice a month across the school year. The researchers took field notes to capture in detail classroom literacy practices. Using qualitative methods to identify common instructional practices, the researchers found that there was little instruction on how to use comprehension strategies to understand text. Pressley et al. (1998) declared,

Comprehension-strategies instruction appears to have made little progress since Durkin (1978–1979) described it 20 years ago. Researchers and teacher educators need to help teachers bridge the gap between knowing that comprehension is important and knowing how to teach strategies to accomplish it. (p. 186)

An observational study of vocabulary instruction conducted by Watts (1995) in six fifth- and sixth-grade classrooms published around the same time as the Pressley et al. (1998) study also showed little progress in instruction to support word knowledge. Watts conducted roughly two observations per month for four months of the school year to determine how teachers taught vocabulary during the reading period in upper elementary schools. Field notes and transcripts from audiotapes capturing instructional dialogue during the observations were coded for patterns and emergent themes. Findings suggested that teachers provided students with definitions of words and presented students with examples of words in context. However, findings revealed that other researcher-based instructional practices such as activating prior knowledge about words, providing multiple exposures to words, guiding semantic and structural analysis of words, and teaching strategies to figure out words in context were largely absent from instruction. Watts concluded that "characteristics associated with effective instruction in the research literature ... were not prevalent" (p. 422). Pressley et al. (1998) noted that the evident gap between research and practice in the area of comprehension found in their study highlighted "the failure of the research community to communicate with the teaching community" and called for "more effective ways of disseminating research and developing ways to apply it in the classroom, where it counts" (p. 189). The study by Watts (1995) showed that the research to practice gap was present in the area of vocabulary as well.

In the decade that followed the Pressley et al. (1998) and Watts (1995) studies, there was a concerted effort by researchers to bridge the divide between research and practice. For example, a practice guide for US teachers entitled *Put Reading First* (Armbruster, Lehr, & Osborn, 2001) was developed to communicate findings from the NRP report. Subsequently, the US Institute of Education Sciences initiated regional technical assistance centers and practice guides for teachers to help translate research into practice. Around the same time, and possibly in response to the increased focus on student assessment following the US federal legislation known as No Child Left Behind, observational work began to emerge that not only described the extent to which instruction in everyday classrooms aligned with research-based practice but also investigated the relationship between classroom instruction and students' outcomes.

In 2004, Connor et al. published a study investigating teachers' instruction and students' reading comprehension in third grade classrooms. Connor et al. conducted observations in forty-three classrooms and assessed a small number of children (i.e., one to five) in each classroom. Observations were conducted three times across the school year. Observers recorded timed written narratives of instructional activities lasting at least one minute in duration, and these timed written narratives were coded for type of instructional activity using a system similar to the one used by Durkin (1978/1979). Types of instructional activities were grouped according to dimensions of instruction: explicit versus implicit, teacher managed versus child managed, and word level versus higher order. Connor et al. found relatively little teacher-managed explicit higher order instruction, which included discussion of text, strategy instruction, and vocabulary instruction, in the observed classrooms. Interestingly, though, relatively small differences in the amount of this kind of instruction predicted substantial differences in students' reading comprehension. Specifically, teacher-managed explicit higher order instruction was associated with positive differences in reading comprehension, particularly for students with average or below-average reading comprehension at the beginning of the study. The Connor et al. (2004) study underscored the fact that what teachers do in everyday classrooms makes a difference in how students' progress in reading in school. Echoing these findings in similar observational research with third graders, Carlisle and colleagues note that the cumulative impact of differences in teacher instruction can have a significant impact on student outcomes (e.g., Carlisle, Kelcey, Berebitsky, & Phelps, 2011).

A decade later, Connor and her colleagues (2014) published another observational study set in third grade classrooms. This study used both a global measure of the quality of the classroom learning environment (CLE) and a specific measure of the types of instructional activities teachers implemented in their classrooms. Similar to the previous work by Connor and her colleagues (2004), instructional activities were characterized as teacher or child managed and meaning focused or code focused. Findings showed that "students showed the greatest gains in vocabulary and comprehension when their teachers provided a high-quality CLE and they spent greater amounts of time . . . in teacher/child-managed meaning-focused instruction" (p. 770). Looking more closely at the data on comprehension instruction, Connor et al. (2014) note that teachers used more than twenty different types of comprehension instructional activities, and in general, the instruction observed was aligned with NRP recommendations. Despite wide variability across classrooms, it seemed teachers were spending more time on research-based practices to support comprehension and vocabulary. Ness (2011), in her descriptive study of reading comprehension instruction in grade 1–5 classrooms, came to a similar conclusion that the amount of comprehension and vocabulary instruction in classrooms has risen dramatically since Durkin's original research. However, Connor et al. and Ness both cautioned that the strategies that received more attention (e.g., comparing and contrasting, highlighting, and using graphic organizers) focus on surface-level understanding of text and the strategies that received less attention, such as inferencing, are needed for understanding texts at a deeper level.

The work by Connor and colleagues (2004, 2014) focused not only on how different dimensions of instruction are related to student outcomes but also on how these relationships depend on student characteristics. As noted, in the Connor et al. (2004) study, the authors found that children with average or below-average reading comprehension skills grew more in comprehension in classrooms in which there was more time spent on teacher-managed explicit instruction (e.g., teacher-led discussions about text). Conversely, children with above-average reading comprehension skills grew more in comprehension in classrooms in which there was more time spent on child-managed explicit instruction (e.g., writing a response to reading individually or in pairs). The Connor et al. (2014) study was implemented within the context of a larger study of an intervention system that focused on matching instruction to student characteristics.

Mostly absent from the body of observational work that has been conducted in upper elementary schools to date is a focus on teachers' comprehension and vocabulary instruction in linguistically diverse populations. Some studies actively excluded EBs (Connor et al., 2004), while other studies simply did not detail whether or how many EBs were included in the samples (e.g., Connor et al., 2014; Pressley et al., 1998; Watts, 1995). Though Carlisle and colleagues and Ness indicated the number of EBs in their samples, they did not investigate the quality or quantity of instruction in consideration of EB students. Some intervention research suggests that instructional approaches have similar effects for EBs and non-EBs (Carlo et al., 2004; Proctor et al., 2011); however, other intervention research suggests that EBs and non-EBs may respond differently to instruction (Silverman & Hines, 2009). Thus, observation research must include and compare findings for EBs and non-EBs.

A Study of Teachers' Instruction and Students' Vocabulary and Comprehension

To address the gaps in the literature, our research team conducted an observation study in thirty-three grade 3–5 classrooms from two US public school districts (Silverman et al., 2013). The study focused on teachers' instruction and students' growth in vocabulary and comprehension across an academic year. Most teachers were female and Caucasian. Teachers had an average of eight and a half years of teaching experience, and two-thirds of the teachers held master's degrees. The study also included 274 students: 52 percent male, 44 percent EB, 74 percent receiving free or reduced-price meals (i.e., an indicator of low income status). In this study we defined EBs as students who spoke a language other than English in addition to or instead of English in the home.

Teachers were observed during their language arts instruction on three occasions across the school year. Observations included audiotapes capturing student dialogue and field notes describing classroom activities. Transcribed audiotapes and field notes were coded using an iterative content analysis approach (Neuendorf, 2002). We started with a list of codes derived from syntheses of best practice (e.g., Shanahan et al., 2010), then we added codes as they emerged from the data. We developed definitions of codes and chose illustrative examples of codes before conducting a final round of coding. See Tables 9.1 and 9.2 for the final list of codes used in analyses as well as descriptions and examples of the codes. The unit of analysis for coding was the utterance. Crookes (1990) defined the utterance as a unit of speech under a single "breath group" or intonation contour that is bounded by pauses on either side (p. 194). Using this unit of analysis, we found that 75 percent of all utterances were teacher utterances, and teacher utterances were, on average, more than 4 times as long as student utterances.

Two research assistants (RAs) were trained on the coding scheme. Interrater reliability was established (Cohen's *kappa* above .80), and the RAs coded the data. Once coding was complete, we calculated the frequency for each code in each lesson and prorated codes to their relative frequency within a standard sixty-minute lesson. Then, we calculated the average frequency for each code across observations by classroom.

Table 9.1 *Vocabulary Codes*

Code	Description	Examples
Definition	Teacher provides a brief definition or asks students what a word means. Teacher asks students to use the dictionary, glossary, in-text definition to look up a word. Teacher labels a picture, an object, or a concept.	T: A *union* is a group that is formed to protect workers in certain fields.
Application across contexts	Teacher guides or shows students how to apply word meaning by providing an example of the word, using the word in a sentence, illustrating the word (drawing or acting it out), or making a connection to the word by using other text, personal experiences, or previous lessons.	T: (in discussing the word *exhausted*) OK, so maybe like after you've just worked out really hard, and then you're just like, oh, so tired, and you're at the gym, and you spread out.
Word relations	Teacher calls attention to the relations among words by discussing synonyms, antonyms, related words, multiple meanings of a word, native language translations, or cognates of a word.	T: *Confused* is a synonym for *bewildered*.
Morphosyntax	Teacher calls attention to morphological or syntactical facets of a word. May include attending to inflectional endings of words, breaking apart or putting together compound words, attending to prefixes, suffixes, and word derivations, discussing how a word fits syntactically in a sentence, or explaining how to using a word in a grammatically correct way.	T: What does that prefix *sub* mean? T: What's the subject of the sentence?
Context clues	Teacher teaches or asks students to use an explicit strategy to determine word meaning from clues in the text.	T: There's a context clue right in the text that tells us what a *trial* is.

Note. From Silverman et al. (2013, p. 57). Copyright 2013 by the International Literacy Association. Reprinted with permission.

Table 9.2 *Comprehension Codes*

Code	Description	Examples
Literal comprehension	Teacher guides or asks students to ask or answer questions about literal details in the text.	T: Then what was the last thing that she did after she removed the rocks out from in front of the canoe?
Inferential comprehension	Teacher guides or asks students to use context clues to figure out the meaning of a sentence or event in the text. Teacher provides an inference or has students provide an inference about the text.	T: We don't really know why she is we can just make an inference why maybe based off of your experiences.
Comprehension strategies	Teacher models or has students use one of the following comprehension strategies: • previewing • activating background knowledge/making connections • monitoring • visualizing • summarizing	T: So we need to stop and tell me what you've read up until that point.
Text elements	Teacher guides students to discuss features of text, including story elements (setting, mood, conflict, etc.), genre, organization of text, and text structures (bold font, captions, titles, headings, etc.).	T: The main event is what I really want you to be writing about, some things that happened, like, the climax that involves all the characters, involves a problem, a solution, right?
Decoding/fluency	Teacher calls students' attention to letter–sound correspondence/ phonics skills to read a word, or teacher directs attention to reading with fluency or asks students to read with fluency.	T: Remember, stop at a period, you take a short breath and you keep reading so I know each sentence is a complete thought, alright?

Note. From Silverman et al. (2013, pp. 57–58). Copyright 2013 by the International Literacy Association. Reprinted with permission.

Results showed that teachers' vocabulary instruction consisted of providing explicit definitions (30 percent), directing students to apply word knowledge across contexts (46 percent), highlighting relations among words (15 percent), focusing student attention on the morphological and syntactical properties of words (8 percent), and guiding students to use context clues to figure out unknown words (1 percent). Teachers' comprehension instruction consisted of scaffolding students' literal comprehension (30 percent) and inferential comprehension (23 percent), guiding students to use comprehension strategies

Table 9.3 *Summary of Findings*

Relationships	Vocabulary	Comprehension
Positive relationships	Definitions Word relations Morphosyntax	Attention to inferential comprehension
Negative relationships	Application across contexts Attention to literal comprehension	
Interactions with language status		Attention to comprehension strategies

(23 percent), focusing students' attention on text elements (19 percent), and supporting students' decoding or fluency (5 percent). Surprisingly, there was negligible attention paid to EB supports such as using translation, cognates, and nonverbal aids. In addition to observations, we administered student assessments in the fall and the spring of the academic year. All assessments were published, standardized measures. Four measures were related to vocabulary, and three measures were related to comprehension. These observed variables were used to create latent variables. Analyses were conducted to explore relationships between instructional variables and fall to spring change in latent vocabulary and reading comprehension.

Table 9.3 provides a brief summary of findings from the study. Findings revealed that instruction devoted to providing explicit definitions of words, highlighting relations among words, and focusing student attention on the morphological and syntactic properties of words had positive effects on change in vocabulary. However, instruction that included directing students to apply word knowledge across contexts and supporting students' literal comprehension had negative effects on change in vocabulary. The findings also showed that scaffolding students' inferential comprehension was related to positive change in comprehension and that guiding students to use comprehension strategies to understand texts was related to positive change in comprehension for EBs but not non-EBs. The results showed no effects of instruction that targeted using context clues to figure out words, focusing student attention on text elements, or supporting decoding and fluency on vocabulary or comprehension.

Given the substantial body of research supporting explicit vocabulary instruction (NICHD, 2000), we were not surprised to find that providing students with definitions had a positive effect on vocabulary. However, we were surprised that guiding students to apply words across contexts had a negative relationship with vocabulary. We hypothesized that this kind of instruction may have led students off track and distracted them from learning the words teachers were targeting. We surmised that, beyond providing students with definitions, guiding students to understand relations among words and focusing students' attention on the morphology and syntactical properties of words provide students with leverage to learn more words that they encounter in school, leading to the positive effects associated with these instructional practices. Given that there was relatively less instruction focusing on word relations and morphology and syntax, these may be areas to target in future intervention research. Finally, we theorized that the negative relationship between literal comprehension instruction and vocabulary may be due to the fact that too much focus on literal information in texts may take away from time that could be spent on discussing words in text.

We were delighted to see that scaffolding inferential comprehension was prevalent in teachers' instruction and that this instruction was related to positive growth in comprehension. In light of the attention to interpreting text and providing evidence to support interpretations in the CCSS, instructional attention to inferential comprehension will be more critical than ever before. We were intrigued by the finding that comprehension strategies instruction had a positive effect on comprehension for EBs but not for non-EBs. We posited that EBs may need more teacher explanation on how to implement comprehension strategies than their non-EB peers due to their limited proficiency in English. More research exploring differential effects of various areas of instructional focus are needed to appropriately differentiate instruction for specific groups of students. Indeed, differentiated instruction was largely absent in our study. The null findings for the relationship between instruction focused on decoding or fluency and comprehension may also have been a result of the lack of differentiation. Likely some students need this kind of instruction and others don't (Kieffer & Vukovic, 2013), but teachers did not often vary instruction depending on students' needs. Instruction focused on literal comprehension and features of text may not have had an influence on comprehension because teachers may not have provided students with an understanding of how to use information readily available in the text and text features to further their general comprehension of the texts at hand.

As a follow-up to our published observation study, we conducted additional qualitative analyses of the data on teacher instruction to better understand what characterized specific types of instruction found to be positively and significantly related to change in vocabulary and comprehension (Silverman, Proctor, Harring, Hartranft, & Guthrie, 2014). First, we identified teachers ($n = 8$) with frequent use of types of instruction found to be positively related to vocabulary or comprehension. Then, we conducted within- and cross-case analysis using a constant comparative method (Stake, 2006; Yin, 2009) to explore specific incidents in the data that helped us refine our understanding of the instructional practices and their relationships to student outcomes.

Teachers varied in how they implemented the instructional practices found to be related to positive vocabulary and comprehension outcomes for students. We noticed that in providing students with explicit definitions of words, determining the relations among words, and attending to the morphological and syntactic properties of words, teachers most often took a direct instruction approach. They told students definitions; they provided students with information about relations among words; and they instructed students on how word parts changed the meaning of words. Less often, teachers encouraged students to make personal connections to words they were learning, asked students to collaborate to come up with definitions and determine relations among words, and engaged students in playing games to figure out words or reinforce word knowledge. In the area of comprehension, teachers commonly asked students to make inferences or use comprehension strategies. Less often, teachers used think-alouds to show students how to make inferences or use comprehension strategies or scaffolded students' attempts at making inferences or using strategies through purposeful questioning. Rarely did teachers engage students in in-depth discussion about inferences or the meaning of text. These additional observations about vocabulary and comprehension instruction revealed that even within the instructional practices shown to be effective with students, more research is needed to understand how to best implement those practices and how students respond to various ways of implementing research-based instruction.

Together, the quantitative and qualitative analyses we conducted offer a glimpse into typical third- to fifth-grade classroom instruction offered to linguistically diverse students in US schools. Much more research is needed to provide a comprehensive picture of the current instructional landscape and the effects of instruction as implemented in everyday classrooms. However, studies such as the one we conducted can serve to inform theoretical and practical implications and directions for future research.

Theoretical Implications, Practical Implications, and Future Directions

The extant observational research described earlier in this chapter, as well as the empirical study we conducted support the theoretical notion that what teachers do and say in everyday classrooms makes a difference in how students develop in language and literacy. It also reinforces the theory that relationships between teachers' instruction and students' learning may be complex, depending on the amount and type of instruction as well as the background and abilities of the students.

Practically, the research presented in this chapter suggests that teacher practice is becoming ever more aligned with research, resulting in a narrowing of the research to practice divide. However, as observational research becomes increasingly advanced, continued research is needed to monitor the alignment of research and practice and to inform the extent to which findings from experimental research hold in everyday classroom settings. According to research described in this chapter, to support vocabulary and comprehension in everyday upper elementary classrooms, teachers can and should provide ample research-based meaning-focused instruction that includes attention on word meanings, word relations, morphological and syntactical properties of words, inference-making, and comprehension strategies. Additionally, more focus on differentiation in upper elementary school may be needed. Future intervention research can take these findings into account. In fact, Connor and colleagues (2014) have used their observational research to guide an intervention in which, based on student profiles, teachers receive specific guidance on the amount and type of instruction to provide to individual students. Furthermore, based on our previous observational research, our team (Proctor, Silverman, Harring, Jones, & Hartranft, 2018) has developed and found positive effects of intervention targeting vocabulary and comprehension for EBs in particular.

If the past few decades are any indication, the context of language and literacy instruction will continue to change. As these changes take place, it is important to capture snapshots of instruction to determine what works for whom and under what conditions. Continually updating what we know about the classroom is imperative to ensure that teacher training, professional development, and curriculum and intervention design are responsive to the needs of teachers and students over time.

10 Improving Struggling Readers' Literacy Skills through Talk about Text

Lowry E. Hemphill, James Kim, and Margaret Troyer

While earlier acquired skills are critical in the transition to later reading, the complex texts and more sophisticated reading tasks of secondary school require new kinds of reading and language competencies (Fang, 2012; Goldman & Snow, 2015). By early adolescence, readers are expected to decode morphologically complex words, apply specialized background knowledge, integrate information across texts, and critique and evaluate, not simply summarize and recall what has been read, expectations instantiated in recent national standards (e.g., Council of Chief School Officers, 2010). In a humanities curriculum widely implemented in the United States, for example, twelve-year-olds are asked to read and evaluate highly varied print and digital texts about global water policy. Students encounter words like *aqueous, primordial*, and *impersonate* and cultural references to Dickens, Aristotle, and the Holocene epoch. Students are expected to record critical notes on each text and integrate these into individual positions on water management policy (New York State Education Department, 2014).

Struggling Readers, Higher Expectations

Against this background of higher expectations for engagement with text, many older readers are left behind, struggling to read multisyllable words, parse complex sentence structures, construct inferences, and formulate critical responses (Barth et al., 2015; Scott & Balthazar, 2010). In the most recent national assessments of reading in the United States (NAEP; National Center for Educational Statistics, 2015a), two-thirds of thirteen-year-olds performed below proficient, the level at which young adolescents can infer the purpose of an argumentative text, for example. More alarming is the substantial percentage of adolescents who score *below* basic, the level at which readers can extract literal information from moderately complex texts. Close to a quarter of US thirteen-year-olds could not reach this expectation for reading performance, with much higher proportions of adolescents from low-income families scoring below basic. In similar findings from international assessments, more than 30 percent of fifteen-year-olds could not integrate several pieces of textual information in generating an overall understanding (PISA; OECD, 2014). In the sections that follow, we explore the nature of reading difficulties among adolescent readers and describe an innovative program for improving struggling readers' competency across a range of literacy domains.

What kinds of language and literacy gaps are characteristic of adolescents who struggle to meet basic reading expectations? Decoding difficulties limit access to text for at least a third of struggling adolescent readers (Brasseur-Hock et al., 2011; Catts, Hogan, & Adlof, 2005). Inaccurate or inefficient decoding can affect adolescents' ability to extract literal propositions as they read, the first step in building up the literal textbase, a prerequisite for deeper comprehension (Kintsch, 1998; van Dijk & Kintsch, 1983).

Within the array of challenging words that adolescents encounter in text, morphologically complex words are especially important because they often convey thematically central content. As adolescents encounter words like *interstellar* and *disenchantment*, they need to be able to both pronounce and access the meaning of roots and prefixes (Goodwin, Gilbert, & Cho, 2013), integrating these into an overall understanding. Skilled readers are also able to assign syntactic roles to complex words through recognizing derivational suffixes, for example, the adjectival suffix (*-ar*) and nominalizing suffix (*-ment*), a process that contributes to sentence comprehension (Tyler & Nagy, 1990) and to overall passage comprehension (Foorman, Petscher, & Bishop, 2012; Kieffer & Box, 2013). Struggling readers show particular vulnerabilities in morphological awareness, however (Nagy, Carlisle, & Goodwin, 2014), vulnerabilities that can affect both decoding accuracy and meaning construction with complex text (Gilbert et al., 2014).

Inefficient and effortful decoding and weak morphological awareness have consequences for reading fluency, the ability to read smoothly, at an adequate rate, and with expression (Barth, Catts, & Anthony, 2008). Fluent reading draws upon effective word recognition but requires that students also interpret sentence structure as they read (Poulsen & Gravgaard, 2016) and use prosody to signal meaning (Veenendaal, Groen, & Verhoeven, 2016). Recent empirical studies identify an important role for reading fluency in supporting older students' ability to read with understanding (Geva & Farnia, 2012; Trapman et al., 2014) and underscore the significance of fluency-related vulnerabilities for less skilled readers.

Beyond text reading ability, to successfully comprehend the less considerate texts that typify adolescent reading (Armbruster & Anderson, 1988), linguistic and cognitive resources become critical (Foorman et al., 2015; Oakhill & Cain, 2012). Students who developed reading confidence in the early years are advantaged in the meaning construction tasks set in secondary school. They have acquired a sizable stock of academic vocabulary as well as efficient vocabulary-learning strategies that make them better able to acquire and retain new words (Cain & Oakhill, 2011). Because they read more both in and out of school, confident readers' receptive vocabularies are enriched by steady exposure to novel words in more challenging texts (Cain & Oakhill, 2011; Mol & Bus, 2011). Wide reading has also contributed to stronger readers' development of school-relevant background knowledge, a critical resource in interpreting and evaluating academic texts.

Struggling readers, in contrast, bring more limited academic vocabulary and background knowledge to their encounters with complex text. Although they use reading strategies that help in repairing comprehension breakdowns (e.g., rereading, adjusting reading rate), they are less able to integrate information within and across texts and infrequently evaluate texts as they read (Barth et al., 2015; Denton et al., 2015b). Confronted with texts above their current reading levels, often the context in secondary school content lessons, struggling readers further reduce their use of integrative and inferential strategies (Denton et al., 2015a), resulting in understandings that are often fragmentary or superficial.

Supports for Reaching Higher Expectations

What supports are available for struggling readers to advance their literacy competence? Typical instruction in secondary schools provides only limited opportunities for sustained engagement with text. In content area classrooms, even in the comparatively text-rich disciplines of social studies and English, students have been observed actually reading text for just 10 percent to 15 percent of total lesson time (Swanson et al., 2016). Secondary teachers infrequently engage in practices that support students' access to complex text: previewing, building background knowledge, monitoring understanding, and promoting text-based discussion (Swanson et al., 2016). Particularly in schools where large numbers of students struggle, teachers respond to literacy limitations by reducing the reading demands of content lessons, for example reading text aloud to students, or substituting worksheets for more complex texts (Greenleaf & Valencia, 2016).

When curriculum reforms are implemented that raise the bar for adolescent literacy (e.g., the Common Core Standards in the United States), foundational reading skills, particularly in decoding and fluency, are rarely addressed, even though gaps in these skills will prevent many students from reaching higher standards (Faggella-Luby et al., 2012). Given the interdependence of lower- and higher-level processes in effective reading (Perfetti & Stafura, 2014; Verhoeven & van Leeuwe, 2008), sizable groups of adolescents will need to improve their word and sentence level skills in order to understand and respond critically to challenging texts.

Impacts of Adolescent Reading Interventions

Because secondary school content lessons provide insufficient support for struggling readers, schools have increasingly implemented specialized reading interventions for students reading below grade level (Biancarosa & Snow, 2003; Kamil et al., 2008). The impacts of existing adolescent reading interventions have often been modest, however, especially for students who are more than two years behind their peers (Edmonds et al., 2009; Scammacca, Roberts, Vaughn, & Stuebing, 2015; Solis, Miciak, Vaughn, & Fletcher, 2014). Some well-designed adolescent reading interventions demonstrate no or virtually no impact on key components of skilled reading (Somers et al., 2010). Impacts appear least promising for reading comprehension, the key focus for efforts to raise skills for struggling readers. In a recent meta-analysis of reading interventions for older readers, for example, effect sizes for comprehension outcomes averaged only .10 (Wanzek et al., 2013).

While targeted interventions often demonstrate only limited impacts, all adolescents bring broad strengths to the enterprise of reading for understanding. Across all levels of reading skill, adolescents are capable of sustaining attention on engaging and complex topics (Ivey & Broaddus, 2001). By the start of secondary school, students have acquired the social cognitive skills needed to consider multiple perspectives (Diazgranados & Selman, 2016; Martin, Sokol, & Elfers, 2008), both within a text (e.g., contrasting diverse character stances in fiction) and about a text (e.g., noting one's own and classmates' differing evaluations of a text-based claim). In addition, adolescents are developing the discourse skills for participation in more sophisticated talk about text, for example, the ability to present textual evidence in support of a claim or to rebut another speaker's claim. These developmental accomplishments provide adolescents, including struggling readers, with resources that can be tapped in moving beyond surface and fragmentary responses to a text.

Discussion-oriented approaches to literacy take advantage of adolescents' growing capacity for sophisticated talk about text. Research on the impact of classroom talk about text on reading competencies points to particular benefits for students with initially weaker comprehension skills (e.g., Murphy et al., 2009). However, discussion-oriented approaches are rarely combined with literacy supports that also address gaps for many adolescents in foundational reading skills.

STARI: A New Approach to Reading Intervention

STARI, the Strategic Adolescent Reading Intervention, is a supplemental reading program for eleven- to fifteen-year-olds whose literacy skills place them at least two years behind their peers. Designed to also address vulnerabilities in decoding, morphological awareness, and fluency, STARI focuses on critical engagement with complex but accessible texts. Core texts are selected for characteristics of cognitive challenge, the degree to which readers must work through ambiguities, resolve diverse perspectives, and use specific background knowledge to bridge gaps in the text. Peer talk about text is used as both a social motivation for reading engagement and as a resource for moving beyond limited and literal interpretations of what is read. STARI classroom activities reflect "dialogically oriented" approaches to meaning construction (Nystrand, 1997; Reznitskaya & Gregory, 2013) in which students construct and deepen personal stances on a text through dialogue with peers. Teachers participate in a summer institute to learn these classroom practices and then deepen their understanding in regular meetings with other STARI teachers and coaches. Coaches visit classrooms regularly to support teachers.

STARI units are organized around an essential question, such as "how can we find a place where we really belong?" Essential questions link highly varied fiction and nonfiction texts, promoting readers' ability to integrate information across a diverse set of readings. Each STARI unit includes a central novel and one or more full-length works of nonfiction. Unit topics, such as sports in society, the war in Iraq, and the immigration debate, are designed to be of high interest, personally relevant to adolescents, and complex enough to support varied personal stances, discussion, and debate. Because complex texts make substantial demands on readers' background knowledge, STARI's design builds topic-specific vocabulary and schemata through linked text sets. For example, before reading the novel *Ask Me No Questions,* in which a Bengali immigrant family faces deportation in the aftermath of the September 11 tragedy, students read shorter nonfiction about the worldwide refugee crisis, US immigration policies, and the political and social climate in New York following the September 11 attacks.

To build reading stamina and fluency, important prerequisites for engagement with longer text, partners engage in timed, repeated reading of short topical passages linked to unit themes (Rasinski, Homan, & Biggs, 2009). Morphological and spelling patterns characteristic of academic language (e.g., nominalizing suffixes) are taught using vocabulary linked to unit topics (e.g., *deportation, detention*).

Unit debates are organized around questions on which students might legitimately disagree, e.g., should nations limit immigration? In debate teams, students reread unit texts, collecting evidence to support their position, and prepare and present debate speeches. Responding to contrasting peer perspectives, a practice supported in varied reading activities in STARI, has been demonstrated to enrich readers' understanding of what they have read (Newell, Beach, Smith, & VanDerHeide, 2011).

Distinctive features of the STARI intervention include integration of basic skills instruction into thematic units; engaging and cognitively challenging texts; use of short texts to build background knowledge, fluency, and confidence for longer texts; multiple opportunities for students to talk about text meaning; and a focus on developing and contrasting personal stances on text content.

Method

Our analysis of STARI's impacts was guided by the following questions:
- Can regular classroom teachers implement a novel literacy program with fidelity?
- Does an intervention design focused on talk about text produce gains in components of skilled reading?
- Can struggling readers engage in more complex talk and reasoning about text?

STARI was implemented through a clinical trial in two large US urban districts and two US rural/suburban districts, all with moderate to high levels of family poverty. In each of the eight participating schools, students scoring below proficient on the state English assessment were eligible for the study. Eligible students scored at or below the 30th percentile for all test takers in the state.

We assigned students to STARI classrooms using random numbers. Students with lower random numbers, the comparison group, were assigned to "business as usual" instruction, which varied across sites. Most comparison group students received an alternative literacy course, such as Wilson Just Words (a structured intervention focused on word recognition) or a teacher-developed comprehension program. Other comparison students received some form of general academic support (e.g., state test preparation, or study skills training).

The twelve teachers who implemented STARI were teachers of middle school English, reading, and special education. Teachers were introduced to the program through a summer institute on traits of struggling adolescent readers and STARI strategies for teaching decoding, morphological analysis, fluency, and comprehension. Teachers received in-school support from program literacy coaches and participated in monthly discussions of practice with other STARI teachers in their district. Regular network meetings brought together teachers across districts to focus on key practices within STARI, including specific strategies for promoting peer talk about text.

Teacher Practices and Student Participation in Text-Based Talk

Research assistants observed each STARI classroom at least twice to assess whether teachers were incorporating core STARI lesson components,

Table 10.1 *STARI Core Instructional Practices*

Fluency

1 Fluency work happened/Did not happen
2 The teacher circulates during fluency work and offers support with the process
3 Students are grouped into partners for fluency work
4 Both partners have a chance to read a passage aloud during fluency work
5 Students record elapsed time and WPM during fluency work
6 Students in the class work in more than one fluency level, A–D
7 Students read phrase-cued passage or challenging phrases and words out loud
8 Students record answers to comprehension questions about fluency passage

Guided reading

9   Students sit in a group with the teacher with copies of the guided reading book
10 Teacher talks about the new words in a meaningful context
11 Students read silently as directed
12 Students participate in discussion of guided reading novel
13 Teacher directs students to silently read particular text chunks and then stop for discussion
14 Teacher poses literal ("right there") questions
15 Teacher poses "search and think" questions

Partner work with novel

16 Students work in partners with the novel and workbook pages
17 Students read the novel and/or record responses in the workbook
18 Students discuss the passage or comprehension questions for the novel with their partner

promoting student talk about text, and successfully engaging students in text-based talk. Analysis of the observations showed that teachers implemented all or nearly all of eighteen core STARI lesson elements, with a range of sixteen to eighteen core practices observed across each study classroom. Table 10.1 lists the core lesson elements for STARI.

Observers also assessed whether teachers promoted student talk about text, for example through circulating among reading partners during fluency work to promote partner conversation about the texts read, or through explicitly connecting different students' discussion contributions in guided reading. Table 10.2 lists nine teacher practices that were theorized to support student talk about text. Across STARI study classrooms, teachers were observed engaged in an average of 8.58 of these 9 talk-promoting practices.

Observers noted whether students were engaging in partner and group talk about text or in activities that supported the ability to talk about text (e.g., tagging and annotating text in preparation for discussion). Table 10.3 lists six types of text talk behavior that were assessed. Across study classrooms and observation time points, an average of 5.83 of these 6 student text talk behaviors were observed.

Table 10.2 *Teacher Practices That Promote Talk about Text*

Fluency
1　Teacher circulates during fluency work and offers support with the process

Guided reading
2　Students are seated so that they face each other and the teacher
3　Teacher leads a summary discussion of the preceding day's guided reading passage
4　Teacher uses a whiteboard or projector to introduce new words before reading
5　Teacher sets a purpose for reading the next section of the novel
6　When directing students to silently read a chunk of the novel, teacher provides a context or a purpose for reading that chunk of text
7　Teacher asks students to reread or refer back to text
8　Teacher asks follow-up questions to elicit fuller or clearer student responses
9　Teacher explicitly connects speakers' contributions to each other

Table 10.3 *Student Text Talk Behavior*

Fluency
1　Students ask each other and answer follow-up questions or comment to partner after reading fluency passages

Guided reading
2　Students use materials to record new words/mark quotes
3　Students participate in summarizing the previous day's guided reading passage
4　Students participate in discussing the new words for the guided reading passage
5　Students provide extended responses during discussion of the novel
6　In discussion of passage meaning, students reference text explicitly

In sum, observations indicated that STARI teachers implemented core lesson elements supporting word reading, fluency, and comprehension; engaged in a range of practices designed to promote student talk about text; and fostered students' text talk during lessons.

The Reading Inventory and Scholastic Evaluation (RISE)

Using an assessment developed by Educational Testing Service (O'Reilly, Sabatini, Bruce, Pillarisetti, & McCormick, 2012; Sabatini, Bruce, Steinberg, & Weeks, 2015), we examined students' growth in key domains of skilled reading: (1) word recognition/decoding: identifying a stimulus as a word, a decodable nonword, or a pseudohomophone; (2) vocabulary: selecting a synonym or word that is topically associated with the target word; (3) morphological awareness: choosing which of three morphologically related words fits the syntax and meaning of a given sentence; (4) sentence processing: selecting the most appropriate word to complete sentences of increasing length and complexity; (5) efficiency of reading for basic comprehension: selecting appropriate words to fit sentence and passage context in three nonfiction passages; and (6) reading comprehension: answering multiple-choice questions about the same nonfiction passages.

Results

RISE performance. To examine whether STARI contributed to growth in reading skills, we compared the beginning and end of the year RISE subtest performance for STARI and comparison students. At the beginning of the school year, before students participated in STARI or a business as usual intervention, there were no significant differences between the two groups in any of the RISE subtests (all p values less than 0.05). Across the school year, comparison students, those receiving a business as usual intervention, made very small gains in reading comprehension, morphology, and sentence processing. Comparison students also made only modest gains in efficiency of basic reading comprehension, word recognition, and vocabulary.

Students randomly assigned to STARI outperformed comparison students on end of the year measures of word recognition (Cohen's $d = 0.20$), morphological awareness (Cohen's $d = 0.18$), and efficiency of basic reading comprehension (Cohen's $d = 0.21$). STARI students also showed greater gains in sentence processing (Cohen's $d = 0.15$), vocabulary (Cohen's $d = 0.16$), and reading comprehension (Cohen's $d = 0.08$), although these differences did not reach statistical significance. STARI students showed the most progress relative to comparison students on aspects of reading that received the most emphasis and practice within the curriculum: recognizing words, analyzing word structure in complex words, reading fluently, and reaching a basic understanding of what was read. Contrasts were less marked for areas that received less emphasis in the STARI curriculum: analyzing sentence structure, giving synonyms for words, and answering multiple-choice questions about a text. Results suggest, however, that STARI participants developed competencies that are critical for reading with understanding.

Reasoning and talk about text. Key components of STARI's design, open-ended and accessible texts, integration of higher- and lower-level skills, and peer collaboration and voice are reflected in STARI participants' talk about text. In partner work in an eighth-grade classroom for example, two students – Rakim, an African American boy, and Jenny, a Latina girl – discuss the novel *Game* by Walter Dean Myers. The main character, Drew, has been assessing his team's chances of making the city basketball tournament:

> RAKIM: [reading aloud the question from the unit workbook] What does he think the Roosevelt team are doing? Drew thinks –
>
> JENNY: Drew thinks that the Roosevelt team are playing around, like they're playing around and not taking the game serious.
>
> RAKIM: Yeah, I think they're taking it like a joke. But then again I think they still might play them in the state finals, so they're taking this game as a joke, so I think Baldwin could win a game so then when they really face them, the other team –
>
> JENNY: They could win?
>
> RAKIM: Yeah, they could win and show them that they was just like joking with them.
>
> JENNY: So which one do you want to write, mine or yours? How about you write yours and I write mine?

This brief excerpt illustrates students' ability to consider multiple perspectives, in this case, the perspective of the text's main character, Drew, and that of Drew's opponents on the Roosevelt High team. Together, the students speculate about stances within the text, and talk through similarities and differences in each other's interpretations. Their discussion demonstrates the ways in which STARI texts and literacy tasks push students beyond very limited understandings, for example, the literal conclusion that one team simply played poorly and lost the game.

Students' written work also demonstrates some of these core features of STARI. In a unit focused on memoir and biography, STARI students are asked whether Muhammad Ali was right to refuse to serve in the Vietnam War, a prompt which required them to integrate, critique, and evaluate content across unit texts.

Several unit components prepared students to respond to this question. First, students built background knowledge on the Vietnam War and the draft through reading short nonfiction passages. They practiced morphological analysis rules for understanding words important to the unit like *deferment* and *resistance*. As students engaged in guided reading of an Ali biography, teachers posed the questions, "When Ali stood up to the government, how did people react? What do you think? Was Ali being courageous or cowardly?" and encouraged contributions with text-based reasoning.

Students' written responses reveal their successful engagement with this sophisticated literacy task. For example, Joseph, a white boy from a low-income family who received special education services, responded,

In my opinion, Muhammad Ali did the right thing he was following his beliefs he knew that he might need to go to jail and lose his title but that was not stopping him. Everyone knew he loved to fight.

Casey, a white girl from a low-income family, responded,

In my opinion, Muhammad Ali was wrong because if he wanted people to like him better and appreciate him for the way he is, then he should have served in the army. Then people might like him for the way he is. But if he didn't go, like in real life, then people wouldn't like him, like real life.

Finally, Ariane, a girl from a multiracial background, responded,

In my opinion, Muhammad Ali you should have gone into the war because you knew you were going to lose your title and you could have gone to jail but you still stood for what you thought was right because you believed war was bad and not a good idea and the man was calling you Cassius Clay.

These student responses illustrate key features of the STARI curriculum. Students grappled with complex and conflicting ideas, integrating information across multiple sources, and offering inferential interpretations of text. For example, Joseph argued that Ali cannot be viewed as cowardly, since due to his achievements as a boxer, "everyone knew he loved to fight." Instead, Joseph posited, Ali's actions are courageous since he was "following his beliefs," despite full awareness of the consequences. Casey drew on different evidence to argue the opposite point of view: since Ali's boxing career depended on his popularity, he should not have risked that popularity by taking an unpopular stand. Ariane expressed a more balanced perspective, beginning by stating a belief that Ali should have served in Vietnam because the consequences of refusing to serve were too great, but concluding with an acknowledgment that despite these risks, Ali "still stood for what he thought was right."

These responses provide evidence of students' developing abilities to take a personal stance toward text, a key goal of STARI, rather than viewing the purpose of reading as finding correct answers to questions set by teachers, a more typical literacy practice in schools (O'Brien, Stewart, & Beach, 2009). Students' differing views demonstrate that diverse stances were welcomed. Furthermore, these responses document students' engagement with the kinds of texts and questions that STARI offered. Their language reflects passion about the topic ("but that was not stopping him," "you still stood for what you thought was right," "the man was calling you Cassius Clay") and personal engagement with written text. Finally, while these students' writing was underdeveloped, their complex thinking about text is apparent.

Discussion

Although traditional remedial curricula rarely target students' ability to develop and advance personal stances on a text, excerpts from student talk and writing in STARI point to emerging skills for responding to sophisticated text-based questions when presented with engaging texts and collaborative tasks. Alongside the shifts in reading engagement that STARI promoted, students also began to improve more basic competencies. Decoding, morphological awareness, and efficient reading for comprehension, the areas in which STARI students significantly outperformed comparison students, are critical foundations for deep comprehension. STARI's meaning-focused approach appeared to be more effective in promoting components of skilled reading than the narrowly focused curricula that were implemented in "business as usual" classrooms in the study.

STARI exposed students to the kinds of tasks that reflect contemporary expectations for literacy – integrating information across texts, marshaling textual evidence for a debate, and critiquing, rather than simply summarizing a text. Among the varied approaches to adolescent reading intervention, STARI is unusual in its emphasis on developing more sophisticated literacy competencies in addition to foundational skills. Assessments, however, document that STARI students and indeed most adolescents, still have considerable progress to make in fulfilling policy makers' expectations for fully proficient reading, writing, and argumentation.

11 Classroom Conversations as Support for Vocabulary Learning

Examining Teacher Talk as Input for Student Learning

Evelyn Ford-Connors and Catherine O'Connor

As the connection of vocabulary to students' reading comprehension and long-term academic achievement has become increasingly apparent, vocabulary knowledge has become an area of growing interest among researchers and educators (Cunningham & Stanovich, 1997; National Reading Panel, 2000; Stahl & Fairbanks, 1986). Moreover, the 'opportunity gap' (Milner, 2012) for students from marginalized groups, those with learning disabilities, and English language learners has been linked, in part, to differences in the vocabulary knowledge that children bring to school (Biemiller & Slonim, 2001; Proctor, Carlo, August, & Snow, 2005).

Relationships among vocabulary knowledge, reading proficiency, and academic success are easier to understand when one considers what it means to know a word. Dale's (1965) influential framing of the problem described vocabulary knowledge as successive stages, from the learner never having heard the word, to having heard it but not knowing what it means, to recognizing its relationship to a category or idea, to finally understanding its meaning. To this, Paribakht and Wesche (1996) added a fifth level of mastery or 'ownership', signifying the ability to readily use the word when speaking and writing.

Representations of vocabulary development as 'stages' or 'levels' provide a useful framework for understanding how knowledge of words grows and highlight the gradual way in which learners acquire not only knowledge of a word's meaning but also knowledge *about* the word, e.g. appropriate contexts for its use, level of formality, relationships to other words and categories, function or role in a sentence, and derivatives (Nagy & Scott, 2000; Nation, 1990).

Word knowledge extends far beyond simple definitions (as 'vocabulary' is frequently conceptualized in classroom instruction) to a deep network of information about the world, with connections to language development and growth in general knowledge. This complex vision of word knowledge illuminates the reasons for the impact of vocabulary on students' reading comprehension, or ability to make meaning and monitor their understanding as they actively engage with text during the reading process (e.g. Snow, 2002). These understandings further highlight the fundamental role of vocabulary in general knowledge acquisition and reveal the complexity of what it means to know a word.

Against this backdrop, it's clear that classroom instruction should include contexts and interactions that will support this complex learning. And not surprisingly, numerous researchers and educators have sought to identify instructional approaches of greatest benefit to students' vocabulary learning. Beginning in the 1980s, a series of studies with fourth-grade students conducted by Beck, McKeown, and their colleagues (McKeown, Beck, Omanson, & Perfetti, 1983; McKeown, Beck, Omanson, & Pople, 1985) revealed the importance of 'rich instruction' that incorporated *both* definitional information *and* contextual information about words, provided multiple exposures to focal words in varied contexts, and encouraged students to make associations among related words.

Over time, these instructional ideas have been distilled into general principles that include (1) engaging students in wide reading; (2) fostering students' *word consciousness*, i.e. their awareness of and interest in the words around them and how they are used to communicate ideas; (3) providing in-depth instruction in a few high-utility or conceptually rich words; (4) developing students' strategic knowledge about word parts (e.g. roots and affixes) and approaches for determining the meanings of unfamiliar words encountered in text; and (5) creating rich and varied language experiences through discussion, reading, and writing (e.g. Blachowicz, Ogle, Fisher, & Watts-Taffe, 2013; Stahl & Nagy, 2006). Taken together, these principles form the framework of 'rich instruction' in vocabulary learning.

Yet, despite these insights about the kinds of instruction that facilitate learning, little has changed in recent decades in actual practice. Instruction generally consists of teachers mentioning words, providing synonyms, assigning words to look up in the dictionary, and asking students to write sentences based on those definitions (e.g. Hedrick, Harmon, & Linerode, 2004; Scott, Jamieson-Noel, & Asselin, 2003). Wright (2012) observed vocabulary instruction in fifty-five kindergarten classrooms, both urban and suburban, and found that teachers' instruction consisted primarily of brief explanations of words. Another observational study of vocabulary instruction in forty-four economically disadvantaged third-grade classrooms (Carlisle, Kelsey, & Berebitsky, 2013) noted that teachers' predominant instructional method was to ask students to use focal vocabulary words in a sentence. These studies suggest that little has changed in teachers' approaches to classroom vocabulary instruction. Given what we understand about vocabulary development and the multi-dimensional character of vocabulary knowledge, it's not surprising that these approaches, focused primarily on *definitional* information about words, have proven largely ineffective (Nagy & Scott, 2000).

Given that knowledge about words emerges incrementally through productive interactions with authentic texts, tasks, and talk (e.g. Beck, McKeown, & Kucan, 2008, 2013; Blachowicz, Fisher, Ogle, & Watts-Taffe, 2006), one line of research gaining traction has focused on the role of *classroom discussions* in supporting vocabulary learning and language development (Ford-Connors & Paratore, 2015). Discussion (sometimes called classroom conversations, dialogic discourse, or academically productive talk) can be seen as an ideal setting for instruction focused on word exploration. It creates contexts of rich oral language known to strengthen vocabulary development and promote students' word consciousness, or interest in and awareness of words and their meanings (Stahl & Vancil, 1986; Beck et al., 2013). In these settings, students hear words put to use in authentic ways and explore words' meanings linked to relevant concepts and ideas. Such approaches are *contextually focused* and incorporate situational and communicative contexts in which words can be used and understood (Graves, 2016; Nagy & Townsend, 2012; Stahl & Nagy, 2006). Moreover, through these contextually rich conversations, students gather knowledge *about how words work* across contexts. Knowledge of a word includes not just the ability to recognize it but also *how to do things with it*.

There are parallels here with lexical learning before school. While some concrete and highly imageable words (e.g. *dog, jump*) are learned first, more abstract, less imageable words (e.g. *yesterday*) are acquired largely through conversation about experiences – experiences with objects, people, and events encountered in family life (Nelson, 1998; Maguire, Hirsh-Pasek, & Golinkoff, 2006). Through these constant interactions, children move up the word learning ladder from level 1 or 2 (non-recognition) to level 3 or 4 (recognizing that the word is connected with a category or idea, or understanding its meaning) and eventually 5 (mastery). So what are possible analogues in classroom discourse? There, the teacher is aiming to quickly familiarize students with academic words – and even more so than ordinary nouns and verbs, these words correspond to complex concepts that cannot simply be pointed to but must be learned within complex contextual scenarios.

Teachers can catalyse this process by setting up and managing students' interactions with words through intentional facilitation and strategic use of talk (e.g. Boyd, 2012). Such a discourse-rich approach to instruction is rooted in the work of Vygotsky (1978), who held that language serves as the principal tool for sharing knowledge and creating common understandings. That is, students develop the 'inner language' that enables thought through interactions with 'knowledgeable others' within a social community (Resnick, Levine, & Teasley, 1991). With this theoretical orientation as a backdrop, classroom discussion can offer a language-rich community in which to engage with others to explore words' meanings and uses and to tie important vocabulary to texts and content. In this way, discussion serves as a setting for the 'rich instruction' known to support students' word learning.

Such productive interactions are facilitated by a knowledgeable teacher who helps students connect new words to networks of related semantic and associative knowledge (Applebee, 1996; Blachowicz et al., 2006; Wolf, Crosson, & Resnick, 2005). Furthermore, such discussion-based explorations of words and related ideas extend beyond word knowledge to advance students' *academic language*, or the knowledge and skills related to school-based language and its appropriate use (Uccelli, Phillips Galloway, Barr, Meneses, & Dobbs, 2016). So as teachers engage students in these classroom conversations, they promote the discursive interactions that provide a platform for a *contextual* focus in vocabulary learning and promote students' acquisition of the academic register.

Word Generation: A Contextual Focus on Academic Words

A variety of instructional approaches now exist to help teachers harness the powerful engine of classroom discourse in order to give students greater access to the many dimensions of word meaning (e.g. Beck et al., 2013; Carlo et al., 2004; Graves et al., 2014; Lesaux, Kieffer, Faller, & Kelly, 2010). One such approach, Word Generation (WG), was developed by Snow, White, Donovan, and colleagues, in collaboration with the Strategic Education Research Partnership (2009). The WG curriculum (http://wordgen.serpmedia.org/) is designed to develop middle school students' academic language and knowledge of high-utility vocabulary items through a combination of direct instruction about those vocabulary items and engagement in discussion and writing that give students opportunities to deploy those words. General purpose academic words (e.g. *prime, compile, eligible*) are drawn from the Academic Word List (Coxhead, 2000) and support students' ability to engage productively with academic tasks and texts across content areas. Each WG unit is built around a current and controversial issue, with a discussion or debate question at the centre. Target words appear in brief reading passages and are included in a variety of content-specific lessons through which students have the opportunity to hear and use target vocabulary in meaningful ways.

Other chapters in this volume focus on adult language input to children's language acquisition at various stages in life. In our view, teacher talk in classroom conversations may also function in this way. The WG curriculum provides an ideal site for an examination of *teacher language viewed as input to student learning of school-relevant language, particularly academic vocabulary*. Drawing from a larger study (Ford-Connors, 2011), we present analyses of transcript data featuring teachers' implementation of the Word Generation curriculum. The two teachers whose classroom interactions we cite and analyse had participated in professional development to support their implementation of the curriculum, to engage students in discussions about the passages, and to encourage students to use target words during the lessons. Yet, as their lessons unfolded, we saw that these teachers' practices in implementing the curriculum varied greatly from one another. In the next section, we examine the kinds of input and interactions students experience in these episodes. Finally, we suggest implications for an educationally informed theory of vocabulary learning.

Structuring Students' Interactions with Words: A Definitional versus a Contextual Approach

In this section we share excerpts from two sixth-grade classrooms and consider the approaches that teachers took to structure students' interactions with words. These classrooms reside in different schools located in the same school district, within the same large city in the north-eastern United States. Students in these classrooms were also similar in terms of their socio-economic backgrounds and high percentages of non-native English speakers (ranging between 50 percent and 65 percent). Teachers in both classrooms teach math and were observed as they implemented the Word Generation curriculum. Both teachers taught their lessons by following a similar pattern: they first introduced the target vocabulary words for the week; then asked students to solve word problems from the curriculum that contained the target words; and, finally, led whole-class discussions of a related, 'high-interest' topic included in the lesson. Despite these similarities, the teachers took very different approaches in the ways they structured students' interactions with target words. They illustrate two different approaches to exploring word meaning that we characterize as *definitional* and *contextual*.

We begin with Ms. Parker. In her class, students typically read aloud the definitions contained in the WG materials, put these definitions into their own words, and called upon their understanding of each word's meaning to create an original sentence that they shared with the class, as in the following example with the target word **compile**:

Ms. Parker's Definitional Approach: Example 1
T: *Another word? The words we have on the board for today? [Does] someone want to give me the definition? And a sentence? Magdalena?*
S1: Compile?
T: *Compile.*
S1: It means [reads WG definition:] to put together or to collect.
T: *to put together or collect.*
S1: I have two sentences.
T: *Okay.*
S1: One is about math and one is not.

T: *Okay.*

S1: I compiled all the parts from the junkyard to make my bike. And I compiled data to find the class's favorite color.

T: *The class's favorite color. Good . . . and my example would be, Miss Farrell asked the students to choose five of their favorite books on Tuesday. And on Wednesday, she compiled the data to find out what the favorite books were. Okay? Anybody else have a good sentence for <u>compile</u>? Justin?*

S2: My sentence was: 'We compiled our brainstorm to get one great idea.'

T: *We compiled . . . ?*

S2: our brainstorm to get one great idea.

T: *Compiled our brainstorm . . .*

S2: Maybe our brainstorming ideas, compiled our brainstorming ideas?

T: *Right. Yeah, that sounds better. Can you say that again?*

S2: We compiled our brainstorming ideas to get one good idea?

T: *Good. Do you have a sentence?*

S3: Yup. According to the regulations, I have to compile a campsite in a minimal amount of time.

T: *Compile the campsite? Do you mean like put it together? Okay. . . .*

The primary focus of Ms. Parker's instruction was to maintain students' attention on the word's meaning as depicted through both the simplified definitions from the WG materials and through students' examples of word use in sentences. For the most part, Ms. Parker responded to students' contributions by acknowledging and affirming their participation with a simple '*okay*' or '*good*'. By structuring her students' interactions with this 'definitional' focus in mind, Ms. Parker consistently directed students' attention toward information that is commonly associated with dictionary definitions, including brief statements of meaning, synonyms, and examples of usage. In turn, students, by and large, focused on definitional information in their responses, as they read definitions from the materials, sometimes restated them in their own words, and then created sentences to illustrate each word's use, as in the following example:

Ms. Parker's Definitional Approach: Example 2

T: *So does somebody want to tell me what the first word is and give me a definition. Michaela?*

S1: *(reads WG definition from her WG activity book)* Interfere: to get in the way.

T: *Okay good. What did you use as an example? Can you put it in a sentence?*

S1: Parentheses interferes with the answer to the number sequence.

T: *Okay. Someone else have a sentence? Go ahead. Justin?*

S2: I interfered with the conversation.

T: *Good. Grace?*

S3: There was an interference in the game, so the point didn't count.

T: *Very nice. Let's go on to the next word.*

These interactions in Ms. Parker's class are easily recognizable as embodying the 'definitional' approaches to vocabulary instruction that are common in many classrooms: students are provided with what are sometimes referred to as 'student-friendly definitions' that explain words' meanings and roles using everyday language that is accessible to students (e.g. Beck, McKeown, & Kucan, 2013) and are given the opportunity to try words out by generating a sentence or two (either orally or in writing) containing the word. This approach offers a starting point, yet it lacks the input needed to support students' knowledge *about* the words. Nor does it help them to connect words to either the larger world or to specific academic content. As a result, these common activities limit the kinds of interactions that may situate the words, for students, within networks of relevant knowledge.

While not denying the importance of definitional information about words, we argue that this approach, alone, is inadequate (e.g. Blachowicz et al., 2006; Graves, 2016). An alternative can be seen in the next example, from Ms. Jenson's classroom. We present two excerpts that illustrate her contextual approach in action. In the first lesson, one of the week's target words was **ratings**, which related to both the general topic (whether movie ratings were helpful sources of information) and to the math word problem that asked students to determine connections between movies with top ratings and gross box office sales. Ms. Jenson initiated the conversation about the week's focal topic in preparation for understanding the word problems that the class would be asked to solve:

Ms. Jenson's Contextual Approach: Example 3

T: *Alright, so what was the topic this week? What are we talking about? Xavier.*

X: We're talking about if ... why ... if they should ... whatchamacallit ... **ratings** ... we're talking about 'Do **ratings** matter?'

T: *Alright. Should ratings on movies matter? And what are they **rating** ... what does it mean to **rate** something? Joel.*

J: *Like R **rated** movies for only adults or PG-13 for kids*

T: *And what else do we **rate**? Do we **rate** just movies? What else do they have **rating** systems for these days?*

S1: TV shows.

T: *Yeah, TV shows, and what else do they **rate**? Aaron?*

A: Video games.

T: *Video games and what else?*

S2: Music.

T: *Music. So they have all kinds of **rating** systems for*

S3: *(overlapping)* Websites too.

T: *For what?*

S3: Websites.

T: *Websites. Wow, websites have **rating** systems?*

S3: Yeah.

T: *Huh, I didn't know about that one yet, that's new to me. So we were talking about this yesterday, what did they say, why do they **rate** movies? Why do they **rate** movies? Johnson, why do you think they give movies **ratings**?*

J: For little kids not to watch.

T: *For little kids not to watch it, but they have kind of another reason, too. So like you said, it's to keep kids from watching wrong stuff, bad stuff, right? But what was the other reason they were talking about? That maybe it's a more complex or difficult issue that's not appropriate for young children, right? So rating systems give a heads-up or warning about the content. So people know whether something in the movie or on the website might be a problem or might be about something that little kids shouldn't be exposed to. Or maybe with music, it's the words, the lyrics, that have swear words or bad ideas. So ratings are intended to protect us or at least to inform us. So now let's look at the math problem.*

J: *[reads problem]* Jeffrey and Gabriella are studying how the movie ratings might be related to how much money the movies make at the box office. Jeffrey says that a G rating tells people that nothing often occurs in the movie.

T: *Hold on one second. Can you read that sentence one more time: 'Jeffrey says?'*

J: Jeffrey says a G rating tells people that nothing, wait, offensive occurs.

T: *There ya go, offensive occurs in the movie – what does offensive mean?*
[Students raise hands.]

T: *What does offensive mean, Amber?*

A: It's something like say you say something to someone, it'd be like offensive.

T: *Okay, so it's offensive to say something rude or something awful or upsetting to someone. So you could offend someone. So in the movies, an offensive event might be profanity. It might be violence, or it might be mature content. In real life, you could offend someone by saying something nasty to them, being impolite, or spreading rumors. So that is offending or talking about their skin color, their sex, their gender, any of that stuff. So G ratings, there's nothing offensive that happens, right? We're talking about Thomas the Tank Train Engine, we're talking about Barney the Purple Dinosaur – nothing offensive about Barney. So ratings let us know if there's something that might be offensive.*

Here we can see that Ms. Jenson's interactions do not involve long turns on the part of students, nor do they involve sustained interactions with one student. They consist of brief, back-and-forth exchanges in which she is clearly determining the path. In some ways, Ms. Parker's class might be argued to give more room for independent student thinking than Ms. Jenson's – each student must provide his or her own example. But we would suggest that Ms. Jenson is doing something else which is perhaps more important. She is creating an extended *scenario* within which the target word, 'ratings', could be used. In doing so, she attempts to provide students with a deeper experience with one word, rather than eliciting multiple one-sentence exemplars of where the word might be used. And although the students do not use the word much, she uses it again and again.

This may be indirectly analogous to early word learning within a family. Words are learned in an experiential context that is rich and multi-faceted. Here Ms. Jenson appears to be attempting to build a rich experiential context through her words – a context that students can relate to, that reflects their own experiences. And she builds it with some input from them, asking for examples similar to movies, where ratings are used. In the final few turns, we observe her bringing in another word, 'offensive', to enrich the experiential context, the 'ratings' scenario.

A second example from another week in Ms. Jenson's classroom shows this contextual emphasis in action again with the target word **eligible,** which students would encounter later as part of a word problem about minimum GPAs as determiners of student eligibility to participate in middle school sports. Here, for the first thirty turns, she builds the 'eligible' scenario around a student contribution:

Ms. Jenson's Contextual Approach: Example 4

1. T: *What were some of your vocabulary words that were new this week? Vidraia?*
2. V: **Eligible.**
3. T: What is it? *Eligible. What does eligible mean, Vidraia?*
4. V: Like to be able to do it?
5. T: *To be able to do it. So, I can tie my shoes. Am I **eligible** to tie my shoes?*
6. SS: Yes.
7. T: *Really? Do I say, 'I am **eligible** to tie my shoes!'*
8. SS: No, that would not make sense.
9. T: *Who can use **eligible** in a different way? Because **eligible** does mean 'to be able', but it's got a little bit of a twist in its meaning. (Hands go up) Ohh I see lots of people excited. Maikeesha?*
10. M: I am **eligible** to pass the 6th grade.
11. T: *How do you become **eligible** to pass the 6th grade? That's a very good use ...*
12. M: By paying attention.
13. T: *By paying attention? What kinds of things do you have to do to be **eligible**? (Other students raise hands). Do you want to call on somebody to help you out?*
14. s6: Homework and class work.
15. T: *And what does your homework and class work help with? Amada?*
16. A: Um, to be **eligible** also has something to do with, um, requirements.
17. T: *Okay, so requirements. So what are the requirements for passing 6th grade? (hands go up). Isaiah?*
18. J: To do your homework everyday.
19. T: *To do your homework everyday? And what does doing your homework everyday allow you to do? What do you get 4 times a year? Regina?*
20. R: Good grades?

21. T: *Good grades. So if I gave homework every single day, and somebody did it everyday, then they would get what?*
22. SS: Good grades. A's. Passing.
23. T: *They'd be passing, they'd get good grades, they'd get A's and B's, they'd do all their class work, they'd pass all their tests ...*
24. S: Make Honor roll ...
25. T: *... they'd make honor roll. They would definitely be **eligible** to pass 6th grade. If they didn't do their homework, that would mean they didn't understand the work, which means they didn't understand the tests, which means they didn't do well ... what kind of grades would that person get?*
26. SS: F's.
27. T: *If you get F's, you wouldn't be **eligible** ...*
28. S: *... for sports ...*
29. T: *... not only for sports, but ...*
30. SS: to pass ...
31. T: *for me to put my stamp of approval on you, and to say this child is **eligible** to enter the 7th grade, they know, they have met the requirements to get into 7th grade?*

By eliciting and incorporating students' ideas into the discussion of words, Ms. Jenson situated new words within 'the known' – linking words and their meanings to students' prior knowledge and experience. But instead of limiting their contributions to a single turn, one scenario per student, minimally described, she drew them out, eliciting student contributions to elaborate the whole class's central scenario. She did this again at turn 32 (not shown), when another student suggests a scenario about eligibility for skiing; she builds and elaborates that scenario in a similar way.

Taken as a whole, Ms. Jenson's contextual approach created more opportunities for input by emphasizing relationship building: between new words and students' experiences, between new words and students' existing knowledge, and between the words and the content. Ms. Jenson's contextual approach also led to lengthier conversations about words and greater numbers of student contributions than in Ms. Parker's classroom. By creating 'space' in the discussion to accommodate a variety of student voices and experiences, Ms. Jenson gathered a range of student contributions. Her expectations and encouragement of widespread participation were likely consequential for student learning, since participation is considered a marker of students' cognitive engagement and active processing of content (Blachowicz & Fisher, 2011; Wolf et al., 2005). Moreover, even *anticipating* participation has been identified as a contributor to learning, even when students are not actually called on by the teacher (Stahl & Clark, 1987). Finally, widespread student participation and elicitation of student ideas positioned students both as academic contributors and as sources of valuable information for their peers.

Reflection: Constraints on Language Input (and Output) in the Classroom

In examining Ms. Parker's and Ms. Jenson's teaching, some might object that neither one looks much like an actual context of word learning. In Ms. Jenson's class, the students don't use the words much, if at all. We acknowledge the gold standard of vocabulary instruction to be students' ability to correctly use newly taught words. However, if we return to the stages of vocabulary development proposed by Dale (1965) and Paribakht and Wesche (1996), we note that several stages lie along the continuum from 'never having seen a word' to the final level of 'full ownership'. Students who recognize a word's relationships to a general category with a sense about its position within their larger 'knowledge network', or who understand its meaning but don't yet hold the word firmly in working vocabulary, will still be equipped to develop the gist of a passage or of a classroom conversation, using the print-based or oral input that the context provides.

Although close analysis of the discourse in Ms. Jenson's classroom shows only occasional use of target words by students, there was routine evidence of students' 'online' processing of concepts and ideas that enabled their participation with relevant contributions and topically appropriate remarks. Participation also signalled students' growing conceptual understanding and knowledge *about* focal words. Absent frequent use of target words as markers of learning, students' increasing familiarity with word meanings may be surmised, in part, through their active participation and the *relevance* of their utterances during discussions of words and concepts. The relevance of students' examples and comments thus constitutes a valuable form of *output* (Anthony, 2008; Swain, 2005) that suggests a developing knowledge about target words, even in the absence of consistent production. Other studies have illustrated the benefits of the Word Generation curriculum and its instructional emphases, which have led to measurable gains in students' word learning (e.g. Hwang, Lawrence, Mo, & Snow, 2014; Snow, Lawrence, & White, 2009).

When looking at any teacher's practice in terms of his or her capacity to orchestrate and sustain discussion, it's important to bear in mind the many constraints that all teachers face, in all grades. As described at more length in O'Connor and Snow (2017), any episode of instruction features at least five 'constant concerns' that the teacher must keep in mind, and these contribute to the delicate balancing act that is teaching. These include (1) clarity and intelligibility, (2) coherence and correctness, (3) engagement, (4) equity, and (5) time. Together, these goals or constant concerns can conspire to make certain forms of discourse productive – or unmanageable. In academic vocabulary instruction, as in many other content areas, the need for time, clarity, and coherence/correctness can work in opposition to the goals of engagement and equity. We would suggest that for many teachers, a solution to these 'simultaneous equations' of instruction looks like the traditional forms displayed in Ms. Parker's class. In contrast, in Ms. Jenson's class, her building of a central vocabulary scenario with tightly managed student contributions is one skilful solution that solves for time, clarity, coherence, engagement, and equity. We suggest that future research on vocabulary instruction using discussion should open up examination of these dimensions in the context of research into student outcomes, in order to bring the field closer to finding optimal solutions to this important challenge of practice.

12   Measurement of Reading Comprehension, Processing, and Growth

Gina Biancarosa

What is reading comprehension? How can we measure it? How can we tell when it improves? This chapter defines reading comprehension (RC), reviews a variety of historical approaches to measuring RC, and delves into two current frontiers in measuring RC: the measurement of oral reading fluency as a proxy for RC and the development of an innovative measure of RC. The chapter concludes with implications for future RC measurement practice and research.

What Is Reading Comprehension?

The RAND Reading Study Group (Snow, 2002) defined RC as "the process of simultaneously extracting and constructing meaning through interaction and involvement with written language" (p. 11). The implications of this definition for measurement are profound.

First, RC is a *process*, not a stable product or phenomenon. Prior to the turn of the twentieth century, RC was not considered an active undertaking by the reader, but as the natural or inevitable product of other processes specific to reading (e.g., vision, word recognition; Venezky, 1984). Thorndike (1917) was the first to investigate RC as an active process. Though he described reading as "reasoning" and the process of reading with comprehension as "elaborate" (p. 323), his definition and interpretation of his findings relied on a notion of "correct reading" wherein comprehension had one correct pathway and outcome (p. 326). Even so his work began a long line of inquiry acknowledging RC as a process in which reader interactions with the text are central.

The active role of the reader is expanded in the RAND definition. Meaning resides not in the text alone, but rather the reader, who actively *extracts* meaning from the text and *constructs* meaning by drawing from her store of knowledge. Readers build mental models as they read a text (e.g., Wilson & Anderson, 1986). These models, often called situation models (Kintsch, 1998), represent a text's meaning based on the reader's interpretation of it. In building a situation model, the reader relies on two types of processes:

memory-based processes and strategic processes (e.g., Cook & Guéraud, 2005). Readers rely not only on their knowledge of the world generally and substantive topic knowledge specifically, but also on their knowledge of language and written conventions, including understanding of vocabulary, syntax, grammar, writing conventions, genre structures, stylistic and rhetorical devices, and many other text-based types of knowledge (e.g., Cook & Guéraud, 2005). Readers also almost involuntarily utilize their background knowledge to fill in gaps in a text's message and to elaborate on that message (e.g., Wilson & Anderson, 1986). Thus, differences in stores of knowledge, as well as in the efficiency and effectiveness of the memory-based and strategic processes that utilize them, can hinder comprehension.

These factors come into play whether listening or reading, leading many to speculate that RC is just listening comprehension plus the ability to read words on a page. Indeed, the final element of the RAND definition for measurement is that RC involves written language. Strong listening comprehension is no guarantee of strong RC (e.g., Hoover & Gough, 1990). However, the difference between them is more than merely decoding. Written language has both hindrances and affordances not shared by spoken language (Snow, 1983). For example, written texts lack pragmatic signals and accommodations such as tone of voice, body language, and in-the-moment adjustments to the listener's exhibited comprehension (Snow, 1983). Conversely, texts offer a permanent record of the communicated message, allow readers to control the pace and flow of incoming information, and enable readers to use visualizations of ideas (e.g., illustrations, tables, figures) and textual cues (e.g., italics, headers) that oral messages do not include (Duke & Carlisle, 2011).

The amount of experience readers have with any of these aspects of written language influences their ability to cope with a particular text. As a result, although correlations between listening comprehension and RC increase across the elementary years (e.g., Tilstra, McMaster, van den Broek, Kendeou, & Rapp, 2009), studies of normative development demonstrate that RC begins lower than and is poorly predicted by listening comprehension (i.e., before decoding is mastered; e.g., Diakidoy, Stylianou, Karefillidoe, & Papageourgiou, 2005). Over time, it becomes more equivalent to listening comprehension (e.g., Diakidoy et al., 2005) and eventually exceeds listening comprehension by the end of middle school (i.e., grade 8 in the United States; e.g., Diakidoy et al., 2005).

Depictions of the RC process in graphical form rely on many arrows flowing in many directions between distinct components of RC (e.g., Perfetti & Stafura, 2014) or abandon all attempt at conveying directionality and depict processes and bodies of knowledge as interweaving strands in a rope (Scarborough, 2009). Visual models help illustrate that RC is a complex process. A reader must recognize orthographic units (i.e., letters) and associate the appropriate phonological units (i.e., sounds), thereby decoding the represented words. This process stimulates and is aided by accessing lexical meanings (i.e., vocabulary) given each word's context within a sentence (i.e., syntax). The process also draws on and contributes to the reader's evolving mental model of the text and ability to make inferences. It further draws on and builds the reader's knowledge of the world (i.e., general background knowledge) and specific knowledge of the linguistic and writing systems used. A breakdown in any of these processes or stores of knowledge can result in poor comprehension and therefore each must be taken into account in some manner when assessing RC.

Measuring Reading Comprehension

Recent calls for improvement in RC measurement highlight the necessity of developing measures that take the myriad features of RC into account (e.g., Cain & Oakhill, 2006; Pearson & Hamm, 2005; Snow, 2002; Sweet, 2005). Improved RC measures will reflect the process, not just the end state of understanding after reading. They will also capture individual differences in the processes and knowledge stores underlying RC and share the affordances and hindrances of authentic texts.

Currently, the field continues to use measures that fall short in numerous ways. Most standardized RC assessments like the Gates-MacGinitie or Neale Analysis of Reading Ability report a single score conveying whether a reader is better or poorer at RC. Most current assessments treat RC as a product rather than a process, conflate RC with its requisite components (e.g., vocabulary knowledge, background knowledge, decoding), and provide little to no information about how RC develops over time (Sweet, 2005). Instead, assessments used in schools today tend to measure memory for text, ability to make inferences about word and text meanings, and ability to summarize or derive the gist of texts (e.g., Pearson & Hamm, 2005). Additionally, results to a multitude of research questions differ depending on the measures used, suggesting that no one measure alone will ever do (e.g., Keenan & Meenan, 2014). While some measures relate more strongly to word-level components of RC (i.e., decoding) versus semantic components of RC (i.e., language comprehension), the opposite is true for other measures (e.g., Keenan & Meenan, 2014). These shortcomings in currently available RC assessments hinder both teachers' and researchers' ability to understand what students understand from what they read and how students' RC evolves over time.

RC's interactive and complex nature makes assessment extraordinarily challenging. The biggest challenge is the translation of the mental processes involved in RC into some more observable form (Pearson & Hamm, 2003). Whether selecting answers to multiple-choice questions, retelling or summarizing what one has read, or writing an evaluative essay, other cognitive and linguistic skills must be employed by the reader to convey comprehension. The translation to another form can obscure comprehension that actually occurred or scaffold comprehension after reading is complete (e.g., García, 1991). For example, a reader may comprehend well but cannot communicate that comprehension in writing. Alternatively, a reader may not comprehend well, but a multiple-choice question enables the reader to arrive at the right answer. These and similar assessment scenarios do not represent the RC process.

Efforts to develop RC process measures are not lacking. The most popular measures of comprehension processing rely on self-report of comprehension processes. Retrospective interviews ask readers about what they thought while reading (e.g., Jiménez, Garcia, & Pearson, 1995), but represent a modest improvement over more typical measures because RC processes are still assessed after reading. Alternatively, the think-aloud procedure (e.g., Crain-Thorenson, Lippman, & McClendon-Magnuson, 1997) requires training readers to state aloud what they are thinking *during* reading. Although think-alouds improve upon retrospective interviews by tapping RC as it occurs, both measures share the shortcoming that a reader must not only execute RC processes, but also monitor and explain their RC processes orally (Nisbett & Wilson, 1977). Moreover, simply receiving training in think-alouds can improve readers' monitoring and thereby improve RC (e.g., Laing & Kamhi, 2002) leading to the instructional use of think-alouds for modeling and practicing RC processes (e.g., Block & Johnson, 2002). From a measurement perspective the influence think-alouds have on the RC process reduces their assessment value for RC.

Other RC process measures circumvent the problem of verbalization by having readers perform tasks while reading. Most commonly in educational practice, readers fill in missing words on maze measures – when candidate words are provided – or cloze measures – when they are not (Pearson & Hamm, 2003; Shin, Deno, & Espin, 2000). Although obviating the need for verbalization, readers must still perform an additional task beyond RC itself, thereby again altering the RC process. Moreover, research suggests that these measures assess lower word-level and sentence-level comprehension better than higher text-level comprehension processes (e.g., January & Ardoin, 2012). Thus, they may only represent part of the RC process.

In addition, all the approaches thus far share a limited ability to measure RC growth (e.g., Snow, 2002; van den Broek & Espin, 2012). Previously noted shortcomings are only compounded when repeated measures are involved. Hence, while options for measuring RC as a process are limited, the options for measuring growth are even more so.

Frontiers in Reading Comprehension Assessment

The failure of current measures to address the complexity of the RC construct have led some to stop trying to assess RC directly at all. In US schools, a frequent substitute for directly measuring RC is oral reading fluency (ORF), which is the number of words read aloud correctly per minute (i.e., correct-words-per-minute) from a standardized grade-level passage (e.g., Shin et al., 2000). Alternatively, many researchers have turned toward capturing RC component processes.

Oral Reading Fluency as Reading Comprehension (Growth) Proxy

Curriculum-based measures (CBMs), which are brief assessments designed specifically to track student progress over time, are one of the most popular measures of RC growth (van den Broek & Espin, 2012). RC CBMs are typically either multiple-choice or maze measures. However, many now use ORF CBMs as a proxy for RC (Fuchs, Fuchs, Hosp, & Jenkins, 2001). ORF works as a proxy because of automaticity's role in reading. LaBerge and Samuels (1974) theorized that automaticity in lower-level reading processes signaled that conscious attention was no longer necessary to their successful execution, allowing readers to focus on deriving and retaining meaning. ORF captures automaticity.

In contrast to direct measures of RC, ORF CBMs are comparatively unobtrusive. A passage is read aloud and the number of words read correctly within a minute is tracked. Within each grade, passages are of average grade-level readability. Readers do not have to verbalize their comprehension or complete other tasks. Critical to their practical utility, ORF CBMs are inexpensive and quick, usually taking three minutes or less to administer. Moreover, ORF is correlated moderately to strongly with comprehension, though some research suggests the relationship weakens slightly in the middle grades (e.g., Fuchs et al., 2001). In practice, ORF CBMs also predict performance on later measures of RC and English language arts better than CBMs intended as direct measures of RC (e.g., Reschly, Busch, Betts, Deno, & Long, 2009). Additionally, the measurement qualities of ORF are remarkably consistent across studies and measures (e.g., Kilgus, Methe, Maggin, & Tomasula, 2014). Most importantly, ORF is sensitive to growth in reading, although more so for longer-term than for shorter-term measurement purposes (i.e., a minimum of five or six weeks or as many as twelve weeks depending on the stakes associated with decision made based on the data; Ardoin, Christ, Morena, Cormier, & Klingbeil, 2013). However, studies of ORF as a measure of reading growth have rarely gone beyond grade 6 in the United States. Thus, while ORF presents a window on RC growth, its adequacy beyond the middle grades is less certain.

ORF within-year trends, or the nonlinearity of growth. Nese, Biancarosa, and colleagues (Nese et al., 2013) have found that within-year ORF growth in a cross-sectional sample of grade 1–8 students followed for one academic year proceeds in a quadratic pattern from grade 1 to grade 7 with a leveling off occurring in grade 8. Grade 2–8 students were administered ORF passages approximately monthly throughout the school year, while grade 1 students took ORF assessments once at the beginning of the school year and five more times during the second half of the year. Passages were at students' grade level.

Results reveal periodicity to ORF growth. In most grades, growth is steeper initially than later in the year (see Figure 12.1). However, this pattern is less apparent in grades 1, 5, 6, and 8. These findings may be an artifact of unmeasured differences between the grade-level cohorts, the result of summer setback, or a curriculum issue, among many other possibilities. They may also derive from intrinsic properties of the ORF measures used (e.g., ORF probes increase in readability and difficulty with each subsequent grade). Another explanation, which finds resonance in research more

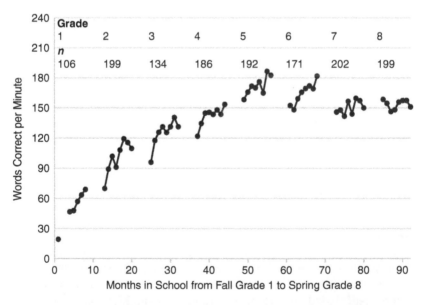

Figure 12.1 Within- and across-year growth in oral reading fluency by assessment occasion from grades 1 to 8. Adapted from Nese et al. (2013).

broadly, is that development typically follows a decelerating learning curve over long developmental periods (i.e., quadratic growth with a negative quadratic effect when speed rather than time is the scale; e.g., Logan, 1992). The general quadratic trend in average growth both within and across grades suggests the latter may be the case. Note in Figure 12.1 how growth in ORF was generally steeper in earlier grades than in later grades. This decelerating growth pattern is also consistent with between-year growth observed across several, direct, standardized RC measures (Bloom, Hill, Black, & Lipsey, 2008). Despite the appeal of the developmental explanation, a multiyear longitudinal study longer than one academic year is required to determine the best explanation for these findings.

ORF and direct CBM measures and growth in reading comprehension.
Another study examining the predictive validity of CBMs in a cross-sectional sample of more than twenty-eight hundred seventh and eighth grade students provides some support for the developmental account (Baker et al., 2015). Baker, Biancarosa, and colleagues' (2015) findings suggest that both ORF and RC CBMs predict performance on a state test of RC well ($r = .6-.7$), confirming the utility of ORF as an index of RC broadly speaking. However, the CBMs also show different patterns in terms of how scores varied across the year. A distinctive feature of this study was that although ORF growth models included only benchmark assessment periods (i.e., fall, winter, and spring), multiple passages were administered at each time point and incorporated into the growth models. Therefore, variance can be separated into three sources: student, period and passage.

Results demonstrate that between 84 percent and 90 percent of variance in ORF scores is between students, suggesting ORF's utility for capturing inter-individual differences in grades 7 and 8. Findings also reveal that only 6 percent and 2 percent of variance in scores was due to change over time in grade 7 and 8, respectively, whereas 10 percent and 8 percent of variance, respectively, is due to passage effects, or the within-period differences in ORF between passages – something that could not be accounted for in the Nese et al. (2013) study. In addition, ORF scores predicted 49 to 53 percent of the variance in a criterion measure of RC (i.e., the state test; $r = .67-.69$ depending on period and passage).

In contrast, about half the variance in RC scores was due to period. However, because RC was assessed using a different, single assessment form at each period, passage and growth effects are confounded for this measure. Figure 12.2 presents the average ORF scores by passage and period and RC scores by period and suggests some consistency with Nese et al. in that growth is apparent in grade 7 but not grade 8, even when passage effects are modeled. Nevertheless, the overall pattern for the RC CBM in these grades is one of

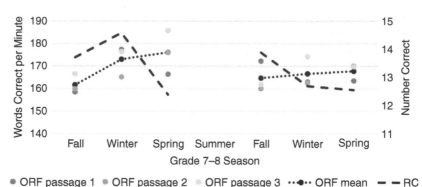

Figure 12.2 Oral reading fluency (ORF) by passage within-period and reading comprehension (RC) scores by time period across grades 7 and 8.

questionable within-year growth (i.e., note the erratic patterns of the dashed RC CBM line in Figure 12.2). Similar to ORF, RC scores predicted the criterion measure of RC well, but with slightly less magnitude ($R^2 = .42–.51$).

Subsequent multiple regression analyses utilizing both CBMs to predict performance on the state RC test indicated that both add significantly to the prediction of state test scores. Moreover, semipartial correlations from these models indicate that the variance explained by either CBM is relatively similar when the contributions of the other CBM are controlled. However, depending on the period in which a CBM was given, the ORF correlation is generally the slightly stronger unique predictor.

The conflicting proportion of within-year growth for ORF and RC CBMs and the similar but unique contributions each makes to prediction of a state RC test suggest several possibilities. First, ORF and RC CBMs do not capture entirely the same information about middle grade reading. Second, because CBMs are time-efficient to administer and score relative to the types of tests they are used to predict (i.e., state and other, longer, standardized reading tests), predictive power may be better served by using both RC and ORF measures rather than one alone. Importantly, despite declining developmental trends in ORF growth over the middle grades, ORF scores appear to be at least as predictive as RC scores. Ultimately the cross-sectional nature of this study and the lack of multiple RC CBM forms administered in each period obscures which measure better captures RC and its growth.

Nonetheless, a recent dissertation study (Park, 2015) investigating similar questions with a single cohort of students followed longitudinally from grades 3 to 4 suggests the latter explanation may be more reasonable. Using the same CBM measurement system, students were assessed on ORF and RC in fall, winter, and spring of their third- and fourth-grade years. Results again demonstrate curvilinear growth in ORF within and across years, and more importantly, ORF growth parallels RC growth (see Figure 12.3). Although correlations between the two measures were strong ($r = .56–.64$), they were by no means perfect, and, perhaps more critically, they were somewhat weaker than the first-order correlations observed in Baker et al. between ORF and the state criterion RC measure (2015; $r = .67–.69$).

Taken together, these results suggest that while ORF does not perfectly represent RC or its growth, it is a solid proxy for use in the elementary, intermediate, and middle grades. While ORF's predictive relationship to RC is strong across these grades, its equivocal relationship to RC depending on the RC measure used in grades 7–8 suggests its ability to capture growth in RC requires ongoing research, particularly in middle school. Related to the mixed grade 7–8 findings, a major impediment to this line of research is the continued inadequacy of existing criterion RC measures. Researchers must assume that criterion RC measures, whether state tests or CBMs, adequately represent RC.

Innovative Approaches to Measuring Reading Comprehension

Rather than relying on CBMs, many researchers have turned to developing diagnostic measures of component RC processes. For example, Snow and colleagues (e.g., Francis et al., 2006) have developed the Diagnostic Assessment of RC (DARC) for grade 2–6 students. The texts employed are a series of logical, relational statements rather than more common narrative and expository forms. Designed to minimize the influence of decoding skills and

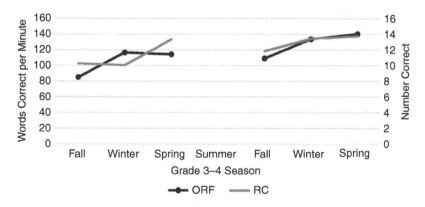

Figure 12.3 Oral reading fluency (ORF) and reading comprehension (RC) scores by time period across grades 3 and 4. Adapted from Park (2015).

vocabulary on scores by using simple concepts and common vocabulary words, DARC attempts to isolate cognitive processes and stores of knowledge in RC.

Similarly, Biancarosa and colleagues (Biancarosa, Davison, Carlson, & Seipel, 2016; Carlson, Seipel, & McMaster, 2014) have attempted to develop a diagnostic RC measure that isolates inference making related to causal coherence. The Multiple-choice Online Causal Comprehension Assessment (MOCCA) builds on theory suggesting that *necessary* inferences in narratives are those that establish and maintain causal coherence (e.g., Trabasso & van den Broek, 1985). Without these inferences a narrative does not entirely make sense. MOCCA uses a maze approach where the penultimate sentence from a short story is deleted, and readers must choose among three sentences that which best completes the story (see Figure 12.4 for a sample item). All MOCCA answer choices (i.e., the candidate sentences) are consistent with the story and make a certain amount of sense, but only the correct answer fills the causal gap in the story due to the missing penultimate sentence thereby establishing a coherent story. The background knowledge and logical relations needed to recognize the causally coherent inference are tightly constrained.

MOCCA distractors are unique because they fail to establish a fully coherent narrative *and* represent comprehension processes on which poor comprehenders are known to rely when reading: either paraphrasing or making lateral

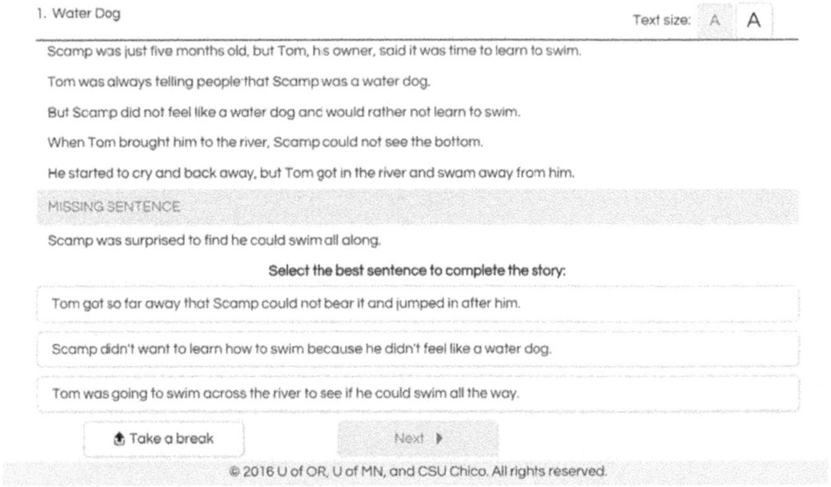

Figure 12.4 A sample MOCCA item with answer choice types labeled in italics. When a candidate sentence is clicked, it appears where the words "missing sentence" now appear. The test does not move on until the student clicks "next." Reprinted by permission of the University of Oregon.

connections (e.g., elaborations, associations, explanations; Carlson et al., 2014). When readers pick a wrong answer, their choice between the paraphrase and lateral connection is informative. Thus, MOCCA yields three scores: number of correct responses, number of paraphrases, and number of lateral connections. MOCCA utilizes these scores in two item response theory models that estimate RC ability (i.e., the main measurement dimension) and comprehension process preference (i.e., a second measurement dimension). Reliability for these two dimensions is at .9 or above for the main measurement dimension and .77 or above for the second dimension. When students fall below a threshold on the first dimension, teachers receive diagnostic categorization of their comprehension process preference. When finalized, MOCCA will enable teachers to determine not only a student's ability to maintain causal coherence, but also what a student tends to do when failing to maintain causal coherence.

Research by McMaster et al. (2012) suggests that knowing what readers do in place of making causally coherent inferences offers leverage for intervention. Their findings demonstrate that students who rely on paraphrases respond differentially to intervention than those who rely on lateral connections. Paraphrasers benefit more than the lateral connectors from a general questioning intervention designed to encourage them to make general connections during reading. In contrast, lateral connectors benefit more than paraphrasers from a causal questioning intervention designed to encourage them to make causally coherent inferences during reading. Although these findings require replication and expansion, they suggest that MOCCA can be instructionally relevant by identifying readers who struggle with RC in different ways. These students are otherwise not easily identified because existing RC assessments do not offer this kind of detail on RC processes.

Implications for Education

Much of the knowledge around the relations between listening and reading comprehension relies heavily on single measures of each. These measures almost always suffer from a bias toward measuring the products rather than the processes of comprehension. Development of process measures for listening comprehension, as well as RC, remains an important goal in future research. Measures are needed that enable us to understand not just *what* children comprehend, but *how* they come to comprehend it and how the capacity to comprehend develops over time. Future studies investigating the nature and dimensionality of RC can be improved by including diagnostic measures of RC, such as MOCCA or DARC (Francis et al., 2006) in addition to more traditional measures of component decoding and language skills. Future research should also prioritize longitudinal rather than cross-sectional designs.

More practically, the results shared here reinforce the idea that CBMs, which are used broadly in the United States and other contexts, do not offer a complete picture of RC development. Though both direct and indirect measures can predict performance on criterion RC measures, neither alone nor together do they completely explain individual RC differences. Both researchers and educators seek to understand individual differences, and innovative measures like MOCCA and DARC hold the potential to provide more complete information about students' linguistic comprehension and its development, as well as helping to expose the roots of poor comprehension.

Beck and McKeown (1999) call RC the sine qua non of reading. Reading without comprehension is not reading in any widely accepted sense. Despite comprehension being the essence of reading, RC measurement has made few advances in the last century. Since 2005, a resurgence in RC measurement research has occurred. While validity evidence continues to accrue for easy-to-administer RC proxies like ORF, innovation in how RC is measured has also progressed. ORF has obvious advantages, which accounts for its popularity in practice, but new measures like MOCCA offer easy-to-administer alternatives that tap directly into the RC process.

Still, no one measure will ever adequately cover the complex multidimensional construct that is RC. As a result, teachers should insist on using multiple measures to assess their students' status and growth in RC. Robust as ORF is as a predictor, it is by no means perfect. Exciting as MOCCA's premise is, it focuses on one important process within the RC process. Just as ocean or space navigators must triangulate data points, teachers and researchers must triangulate data from multiple measures to ascertain their students' progress in RC. Reliance on any one measure is the equivalent to sailing or flying blind.

Discussion 1
Time, Complexity, and the Enduring Importance of Words
Key Themes in Language Learning in the Middle Years

P. David Pearson

When I was a graduate student at the University of Minnesota in the late 1960s, the cognitive revolution in our understanding of language and comprehension, which was less than a decade old, was still finding its sea legs. Chomsky (1957, 1959, 1965) had published three milestone pieces that had shaken the roots of our behaviorist explanations of language acquisition and performance, and many of us in language research had substituted a nativist notion of a hard-wired language acquisition device (LAD) to replace behaviorism's byzantine "learning-by-gradual-accretion" approach as our best explanation of how children acquire and use their native oral (and for some of us, written) language.

Armed with this innate LAD, all children needed to acquire the language of the culture in which they were reared was "data" – a corpus of language to listen to, use, receive feedback about, and, eventually, master. There was also a widespread (almost nativist-like) belief that by roughly the time students started formal schooling, they had pretty much acquired the bulk the syntax they would need to listen and speak effectively and, more importantly, learn about the world in which they lived. Granted, there would be a few arcane, and even a few not so arcane, structures, such as adversatives (Although I tried hard, I lost the game), negative conditionals (Unless you [or If you don't] try hard, you won't win the game), and nominalizations (And all of these links in the chain play a key role in the theory of *transubstantiation* as we know it today). But hanging about in schools with knowledgeable teachers and peers pouring over content – both written and oral – would provide the "data" students would need to acquire mastery of these syntactic tools so that they would be there for learning the stuff (both the content and the vocabulary to talk about it) of the disciplines of the humanities and the sciences that they would face in secondary and tertiary education.

It is also worth noting that some (certainly not all!) of us believed that the acquisition of written language could be accomplished in a comparably effort-less way if adults could just structure the tasks of learning to read and write as naturally as they (albeit unintentionally) structured the task of learning to speak. Many embraced the idea that reading and writing were little more than natural extensions of learning to talk. Certainly this was the cause célèbre of psycholinguistically oriented scholars such as Ken Goodman (1965) and Frank Smith (1971). The parallelism with oral language development was based on some key principles:

1 Learning to read, like learning to speak is more of a language than it is a perceptual process.

2 Students need strong motives for learning to read. One is surely access to the world of information and insight available through books. A second is "cryptoanalytic intent" (Gough & Hillinger, 1980), an almost irrepressible desire to decode the cipher that maps print onto speech.

3 Students need "data" (i.e., a wide world of print) in order to infer that very print to speech cipher.

Even I, in 1973, stuck my oar in the water when I gave an invited address at UC Berkeley entitled, "Learning to Read, Learning to Speak: Are the Processes Parallel?" Those who have rightly pigeon-holed me as a member of the radical middle of reading instruction can rightly infer that I took a balanced position, pointing to many continuities and a handful of pretty major discontinuities.

But the very existence of such a perspective demonstrated the powerful influence of the nativist stance toward *all* forms of language acquisition, oral and written. It was all quite natural – in the nature of things, if you will. Historically, it should be noted that there were recurring counters to this very naturalist perspective. Even as Chomsky's position gathered momentum within linguistic and psycholinguistic circles, there were voices that suggested that a more contextualized perspective in which the forms of early language were framed and shaped by the functions they served in live discourse. Scholars like Snow (Snow 1972, 1977b; Snow & Ferguson, 1977), for example, presented compelling data showing that children's language acquisition at both the very earliest stages (between six and twenty-four months of age) and later (e.g., ages six and ten) – as well as the language use of their mothers – were shaped by highly contextualized attributions of intentions to both real and imagined responses, suggesting that language in use mattered more than language in the abstract. Snow concluded that the changes in linguistic input of mothers during interactions with their children were driven by their perceptions of children's readiness to engage in new and more sophisticated forms of conversational partnership. This more pragmatic view of language acquisition provided a contextualized critique of the more automatic, "natural" view presented by Chomsky. So too were there challenges to the "natural" view of reading and writing acquisition: first in the 1960s (see Chall, 1967), just as it was being put forward; again in the 1980s, as scholars like Phil Gough (Gough & Hillinger, 1980) were working out the theoretical details of what became known as the simple view of reading (reading comprehension is the product of decoding ability times oral language comprehension – $RC = D \times LC$); and again in the mid-

1990s through the late 2000s (see Adams & Bruck, 1995; Lyon, 1995) in the heyday of Scientifically Based Reading Research (No Child Left Behind [NCLB], 2002), the National Reading Panel (NICHD, 2000), and No Child Left Behind (NCLB, 2002).

This historical excursion into LAD and allegedly "natural" approaches to language learning provides a useful backdrop to assess the contributions of the insightful chapters on language growth covered in what I have come to call the "later learners" section (to distinguish it from the section on early learners) of the volume that I have been asked to review – namely, the section on "Learning through Language during the Middle Childhood and Adolescent Years." In light of the prevailing views of language learning (really *acquisition* because intentional learning or teaching seemed to have little to do with it) at the dawn of the cognitive revolution, there are several remarkable features – mainly contrasts – in the underlying view of language learning guiding this volume (or at least the section I was reviewing).

First, it is clear that the views of language learning or acquisition in the current volume assume, in fact often explicitly state, that once children enter school, they have many major language learning tasks ahead of them. The learning task confronting them in schooling, especially as discipline-based curriculum becomes more dominant in their school lives, is more than learning the technical vocabulary used to "name the knowledge base" of each discipline. More sophisticated, as well as discipline-specific, syntactic structures and the discourse features that define the "culture" of each discipline (those unique ways of talking, arguing, observing, and thinking) await them on the pathway to independent learning in science, history, and literature.

Second, it is likely that what students still need to learn after age six may be easily acquired by *some* learners, specifically those who grow up in homes and communities where they learn to *talk* like a book and how to *do* school. By contrast, many if not most learners will require carefully guided and often relentlessly consistent instructional intervention on the part of teachers. It is true that the data for acquiring these discourses of schooling, what we have come to call academic language (to capture their essential school-based and, to a great degree, print-based roots), are certainly out there "for the taking" in the world of school and books. Even so, their successful acquisition will require both *attention* and *intention* on the part of students and their teachers. That is the challenge that this book, especially this section, addresses: learning *through* language in a phase of schooling in which the disciplinary challenges increase in both conceptual and linguistic complexity.

There is good news in this book! The authors in our section offer us particular ways of conceptualizing how to think about learning through language, and more importantly, how to create, select, and/or adapt pedagogical approaches to promote such learning. My job as a reviewer – indeed the role the editors asked us commentators to assume – is to "offer some thoughts about how the chapters may contribute to a theory of language learning and to offer suggestions and future directions for research and practice aimed at better preparing children to succeed in school."

My goal is to offer my reading of the *data* that are offered in this collection of chapters – what they say to me when I read across chapters looking for common threads and insights. But I need to begin working toward that goal by sharing with you the *data* that I harvested from each of these chapters by sharing the briefest of summaries of nuggets of wisdom from each chapter; these are summarized, all too briefly, in Table DC.II.1.1. Then the synthesis of insights across the chapters.

Looking across the entire set of five chapters in the "Later Learner" section, three themes emerge for me – *time, complexity*, and *words*. Most of my analysis will focus on the time question, but I will at least point to the need for teachers to embrace the complexities of language learning and teaching and to the absolutely central role that words play in the language learning process.

Time

The most obvious – but no less important – insight, is that students have much language learning to accomplish between the day they enter kindergarten and the day they leave middle school. This is a major theme in four of the chapters (those authored by Uccelli, Silverman & Hartranft, Ford-Connors & O'Connor, and Hemphill, Kim, & Troyer), and somewhat more implicit in the Biancarosa chapter. This emphasis should not surprise us in a book with the phrase *learning though language* in the title. But it is more than learning *through* language in this book. Hearkening back to Halliday's (1993) language learning triad specifying that we *learn language*, we *learn through* language, and we *learn about* language, there are elements of all three of these faces of language learning in these chapters.

In the Uccelli chapter, the summaries of the validation of the CALS prominently feature both learning *language* (CALS assesses a lot of words and structures that must be learned!) and learning *about* language (CALS assesses the functions that words and structures play in both receptive and productive communication). Interestingly, there is little if any assessment of learning *through* language, which is understandable given CALS' focus on decontextualized language features that operate across disciplines, e.g., *evidence* or *counterclaim* is more likely to show up than *transpiration* or *gerrymander*. By contrast, learning *through* language is inherently contextualized; it's the content and the knowledge that counts. CALS intentionally focuses on those generic facets of language that travel across contexts. Given the elaborate construct validation that CALS has undergone, along with its strong

Table DC.II.1.1 *Summary of Key Findings from the Later Learner Chapters*

Author(s)	Topic	Nuggets
Uccelli	Core academic language skills (CALS)	• In addition to discipline-specific academic language, there is a useful set of CALS that operate across disciplines to explain variance in literacy, especially reading comprehension. • Assessments of CALS predict complex measures of RC, such as scenario-based assessment.
Silverman and Hartranft	Observational research for vocabulary and comprehension	• Compared to twenty plus years ago, today's teachers employ a higher percentage of research-based instructional practices for both L1 and L2 learners. • Both teacher-managed (more explicit instruction and modeling) and student-managed (student monitoring) have a role to play in diverse classrooms.
Hemphill, Kim, and Troyer	Improving literacy through talk about text: STARI	• A comprehensive curriculum that emphasizes decoding, vocabulary, morphology, syntax, comprehension, and multiple perspective building may be just what low-achieving readers need. • Regular ELA teachers can handle the curriculum. • Growth in outcomes varies according to curricular emphasis; we tend to get what we pay for.
Ford-Connors and O'Connor	Conversation in support of vocabulary learning	• Teachers vary in terms of the style of vocabulary talk they promote, with definitional focus (the most common approach) and contextual (somewhat less common) eliciting different participation rates and structures. • Contextually driven conversations bear a strong discursive similarity to early language interactions between mothers and toddlers on the brink of language use. • Ironically, definitional approaches may elicit more learner turns in the flow of conversation, but contextual approaches, characterized by more teacher talk, may provide learners with better models and feedback for enhancing breadth and depth of word learning.

Table DC.II.1.1 *(cont.)*

Author(s)	Topic	Nuggets
Biancarosa	Measuring reading comprehension	• Advances in comprehension theory and pedagogy notwithstanding, we still struggle to create measures of RC that are both valid and useful. • Over the past twenty years, we have witnessed progress in developing and evaluating the construct validity of both direct measures (looking at key infrastructural processes) and proxies (e.g., oral reading fluency) of RC. • For the foreseeable future, multiple measures are our safest pathway toward trustworthy measurement of RC.

relationships with other language, especially reading, variables, it has great potential as a diagnostic tool and appears to be a plausible guide for designing language interventions in school settings.

One of the most provocative aspects of the work of Uccelli's chapter involves a small scale *postdictive* (not predictive) validity study of CALS, taking advantage of sample of forty-two seventh graders who had, when they were thirty months of age, participated in Goldin-Meadow and Levine's longitudinal Chicago project, yielding data on a range of measures of language competence and participation. Summing over many complexities, the astounding finding is that the proportion of decontextualized "school-like" talk that both students and parents engaged in at two and a half years of age actually predicted their scores on the CALS test in seventh grade – even when other factors, including socio-economic status, were controlled. The encouraging news in all of these correlational relationships is that several of these key indicators of early academic language prowess are amenable to both development and pedagogical intervention.

In Biancarosa's account of new developments in reading comprehension assessment, there is little in the way of a prima facie presence for language in her review of the uses to which oral reading fluency (ORF) has been put in providing a working proxy for RC. That said, it lurks just beneath the surface because we know that text complexity, which is largely indexed by linguistic complexity, shapes our judgments about fluency, even when texts are judged to be equivalent in grade-level designation (Toyama, Hiebert, & Pearson, 2017). And in her analysis of newer RC developments, namely, the Diagnostic

Assessment of Reading Comprehension-DARC (Francis et al., 2006) and the Multiple-Choice Online Causal Comprehension Assessment – MOCCA (Biancarosa, Davison, Carlson, & Seipel, 2016; Carlson, Seipel, & McMaster, 2014), language is prominently featured because the key variables that distinguish among items in the assessments are really language features masquerading as conceptual/logical relations among key ideas in the texts. In terms of the Hallidayan triad of language learning, the perspectives within Biancarosa's analytic framework present us assessments of learning *through* and *about* language.

Ford-Connors and O'Connor's work on discussion surrounding the Word Generation vocabulary intervention presents us with one of the most transparent analyses of the role of language. They begin by pointing out that despite mounting evidence on the efficacy of talk about words, we still find precious little of it in classrooms, save for providing or eliciting definitions. Their close discourse analysis of two teachers, one emphasizing definitional (providing or eliciting definitions) approaches to discussion and the other more contextual approaches (examining the use of words in different verbal settings), offers a fascinating if ironic contrast. Contrary to (at least my) default expectations, the definitional teacher actually promoted a much higher proportion of student talk than the contextual teacher, often asking students to produce and refine their own definitions. By contrast, the contextual teacher was a more dominant presence in the classroom conversations, providing a lot of modeling of how to use context and questions that challenged students' conceptions (and misconceptions) of word meanings. While the contextual teacher did some of the talking for the students (in a way that is analogous to the expansion parents do with toddlers), the talk was instructive in the sense that it promoted greater depth of word meaning than, for example, privileging vague or possibly inaccurate definitions. Their account has elements of all three facets of the language learning triad – learning *language* (new words and meanings), *through* language (the talk was the vehicle for vocabulary growth), and *about* language (meta-knowledge about the role of language as a vehicle for learning more language).

Silverman and Hartranft provide us with a solid review of what we have learned from observational studies of teachers' instructional moves (e.g., Connor, 2004; Durkin, 1978/1979; Watts, 1995), focusing on how teachers interact about comprehension and vocabulary. Echoing a point made by Ford-Connors and O'Connor, they point out that when it comes to providing instructional guidance, our knowledge base documenting effective pedagogical practices far outstrips our capacity to help teachers adopt, adapt, and enact these practices. Against this backdrop of studies, they focus on a recent study of their research team that emphasized vocabulary and comprehension practices in classrooms with a relatively high incidence of emergent bilingual learners

(EBs). The results in and of themselves are interesting because they document a consistent set of practices associated with increases in achievement for EB and Non-EB learners in grades 3–5. Most notably, several practices predicted vocabulary growth (explicit definitions, relations among words, and morphological elements), but the most obvious one (applying word knowledge across contexts) did not. Nor, by the way, did decoding or fluency instruction affect growth in vocabulary or comprehension. Focusing on inferential comprehension helped all students, but strategy instruction was helpful only for EBs. In terms of our language learning triad, the focus of the Silverman and Hartranft work stretches across all three facets. Students learn *language* (words) as a consequence of talk, both theirs and their teachers. Students learn *about* language when they acquire strategies for manipulating language on the way to comprehension. And they learn *through* language in response to the talk about text that they engage in during comprehension interactions.

The last of these five chapters, Hemphill, Kim, and Troyer's analysis of the STARI intervention, balances a clear focus on language (conversations that promote the acquisition of word meaning, comprehension, and multiple perspectives on key social and cultural issues) with attention to more foundational decoding and fluency skills. In the conversations about words and texts, there is clear attention to learning *language* and learning *about* language. What is most distinctive about this chapter on STARI, perhaps more so than any other chapter, is the focus on learning *through* language – as students encounter multiple perspectives on controversial social issues in the various novels and informational texts that are at the core of the intervention.

Complexity

It is a truism to say that learning of any sort is complex. Because language is so much more complex than other phenomena, the complexity label truly fits. It is complex for a range of reasons. First, it is a growth phenomenon, not a mastery phenomenon. No matter how good you get at using language, you could always get better. No matter how many words you know, you could always learn more. No matter how much syntactic complexity you can handle in comprehending or producing language, you could always handle more. In fact, this volume portrays this facet of language learning complexity in a remarkably vivid way, with its account of just how much students need to learn once they get to school. Second, language is more of a *tool* than an *entity* in and of itself. Its value lies in its capacity to represent human experience – to "put a name to things" in the world, to convey feelings and ideas, to explain how things work in the world, or to communicate, even argue, with one another. Third, we can and do invent language to talk and write about language – meta-language if you will – that permits us to talk about talk. This sort of language is likely to be doubly complex in that it represents representations. Fourth, the entities that language represents can range from simple to complex; as sense makers, we need to use complex representations to represent complex phenomena. Fifth, humans exhibit a range of individual, social, and cultural differences in their capacity to learn language, even if we regard language as a universal human capacity. Thus what works for one individual, group, or community won't necessarily work for others. Almost inevitably, we will experience individual differences in our learning trajectories.

However, we cannot, as language scholars and teachers, let the complexity paralyze us. Instead, we must not only deal with these complexities, we should actually embrace them (Duffy, 1993) and make a virtue out of the challenge, both for ourselves and our students.

Words

There was a time in the late 1970s and early 1980s when an intentional emphasis on words was viewed as a misguided curricular practice stemming from a fundamental misconception about language learning. In the heyday of the Whole Language movement, emphasizing words in any decontextualized manner or setting – lists, discussions of word meanings, dictionaries, workbook pages – was viewed as theoretically bereft. Word learning, both pronunciation and meaning, would occur quite naturally in the process of reading texts that provided rich contexts for inferring their sounds and meanings.

In fact (true story!), two of my whole language colleagues accosted me at a professional meeting in 1978 (I had just published a book entitled *Teaching Reading Vocabulary* with Dale Johnson), asking how could I possibly be co-author a book about words – "words don't really exist," they said! And there was a palpable impact, a real de-emphasis on vocabulary, in the late 1980s and 1990s. The literature-based basals of that era downplayed systematic, explicit vocabulary instruction (Hoffman early 1990s). But clearly words have made a comeback in every way, shape, and form; we talk about everyday words, academic words, technical words, shades of word meaning, and tiers of vocabulary. These five chapters attest to this renaissance in an emphasis on words, and I am pleased to see their return to a central curricular and assessment role. But it is also clear that the authors of these chapters possess an inherently *contextualized* view of vocabulary *as it is used* to render language meaningful. Words are not the point of words – meaning and, ultimately, knowledge are.

In my view, it is not contextualized versus decontextualized that matters but multiple encounters in multiple settings. I prefer to regard each and every setting in which we encounter words, even those that are allegedly decontextualized, as simply *additional* contexts in which to bump up against a word's meaning. The more different contexts, the better, because each type of context –

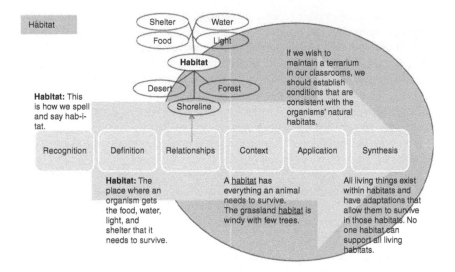

Figure DC.II.1.1 Visual depiction of the various contexts in which a student should meet a word in order to gain control of its meaning. As a student moves from left to right, she moves from decidedly passive to increasingly active control of the concept underlying the word. From Cervetti et al. (2008). Reprinted with permission.

and each encounter in a given type of context – has the potential to reveal another facet of a word's meaning, leading to greater depth, breadth, and precision of knowledge about individual words – and, most important, the ideas for which those words serve as markers. My colleagues at Berkeley's Lawrence Hall of Science captured these contexts in what I regard as a useful visual representation (see Figure DC.II.1.1). So thanks to the authors of the later learning section for finding a key role for word learning in their work.

Coda

I want to end this essay where I began, by reflecting on the foundations of the language work portrayed in this volume. I began by contrasting the 1960s psycholinguistically based notions of early and relatively effortless acquisition of basic oral language capacity with what I took to be the underlying view in this volume, namely, that the acquisition of at least some discourses, such as the generic and discipline-specific discourses of schooling as we know it, require more time (well into the adolescent years) and more effort (intentionally crafted curriculum, pedagogy, and assessment) on the part of learners and teachers.

I hope my account of the research summarized and analyzed by the authors of the later learner section of this volume provides ample evidence for this claim about another model of language learning.

Looking back across the chapters, another consistent theme is that the authors share what is best described as a pragmatically driven view of language – that whatever else (phonetics, semantics, morphology, or syntax) counts, what counts most is our examination of language in use. This common grounding accounts for all of the emphasis on the role of talk – because talk is action that has consequences (Searle, 1969), the emphasis on words as representations of our knowledge, the intimate linking of form to function, and, of course, the underlying commitment to the language learning triad – learning *language*, learning *through* language, and learning *about* language (Halliday, 1993).

Discussion 2
The Road – via Education – to Humane Social Relationships Is Driven by Language (and Literacy)

Robert L. Selman

No one would deny, academically speaking, that one learns quite a lot through language – at any age. But, I wish to specifically address the question, how can the work on language and literacy being done in each of the research labs directed by the authors in section II be understood to contribute in new, and perhaps even unintended ways, to better understand how youth, through the medium of language learning in schools, can establish stronger social relationships. How do early adolescents in particular, as Uccelli in her chapter puts it, "learn how to interact with others . . . in ways that are culturally shaped." This interest of mine is built on a well-respected conceptual framework, one that has existed for over fifty years across many disciplines within the broader social sciences, especially in fields with a strong commitment to understanding the nature (and nurture) of human development, e.g., sociocultural models of literacy (Lewis, Enciso, & Moje, 2007); social cognitive models of human agency (Bandura, 2008); personological models of psychology (McAdams, 1988); sociological models in philosophy (Allen, 2002); evolutionary models of human nature (Bowlby, 1969); and cultural/developmental models of social communication and interaction (Selman, 2007).

This conceptual framework points to three fundamental human needs constantly requiring fulfillment: a need for affiliation (e.g., a sense of cultural identity and moral empathy), a need for safety (or, if you will, to have the power to protect), and a need for agency (to be effective in meeting one's goals, be they individual or social). In this context, from a coevolutionary perspective, one reason language development matters so much is that, it probably developed in prominence out of its contribution to homo sapient efforts toward the "continual attainment" of the three aforementioned needs. Perhaps it is a big leap, but for education today to really matter, educators must address how what they teach – and how they teach it – will help their students better understand how to attain some degree the *satisfaction* of each of these needs. As with the development of any form of comprehension, for reading comprehension skills to be important to students, it must hold personal and shared meaning for them.

In my comments, I attempt to demonstrate how we can draw, from each chapter, evidence that students need to understand how literacy, e.g., reading, writing, clear communicating, will help them in their own striving toward safety, affiliation and agency. I will use the concept *need-based social satisfaction* as a proxy for these universals. In the next paragraphs, I will offer my perspective on each of the chapters in this section.

The Chapters

I was surprised, and, as an outsider, even a bit shocked, to hear from Silverman and Hartranft that until recently observational studies of reading instruction in classrooms were few and far between. Like these authors, I can understand why, in the historical context of the field, educational researchers in the last three decades have wanted to import without any delay the rigorous program evaluation models and designs developed in fields of medicine and public health. However, like these authors, I would have thought descriptive observations in classrooms to be the primary kind of research on the role of language in the context of literacy, not an empirical afterthought. What really caught my attention was their observation that today, in the United States, in actual practice, as distinct from work in the educational research community, reading instruction is still limited, in their words, to "surface level comprehension of text, e.g., compare and contrast, highlight and graph." They conclude that "(middle elementary grade) teachers should have two aims. First, to provide (more) *meaning focused instruction* (my emphasis), i.e., ways to help students understand the deeper and more essential meaning words have in the print context. Second, to figure out the best ways students can express what, as students, they mean when they use their newly learned words to communicate with others."

My perspective. Silverman and Hartranft exhort that teachers need to pay more attention, both in the lessons they take from research, and in their own practice, to strategies that promote their students' deeper level comprehension gained through three I's: identification, inference making, and interpretation. These are, especially in early adolescence, the contributions language makes to *need-based social satisfaction*. If these skills do not develop in an individual by early adolescence, it will be very hard for a young person to develop a stable yet flexible identity, a sense of how to achieve agency, and how to maintain their own safety in the context of their social relationships.

Gina Biancarosa's chapter "Measurement of Reading Comprehension, Processing, and Growth" reminded me that over fifty years ago, in his 1964 book *Understanding Media*, Marshall McLuhan found lasting fame by boldly proclaiming for all to hear, but for few to comprehend, that beyond its role as the messenger, media had in effect become the message. Today, this meme is not hard to understand. One might ask, in a somewhat analogous way, will Biancarosa's claim that in the field of reading comprehension evaluations, process needs to become a product? I take Biancarosa to mean that it is important to have measures to assess ways that a piece of comprehension emerges as a skill in the moment (i.e., as an assessment of performance), and it is also important to study how comprehension processes themselves develop across a range of units of time, from those occurring in the reading moment, to those that occur across the many moments of processing text over months and the years. Designed in the Biancarosa lab, the MOCCA uses a "maze" approach to assess comprehension processes; students read the first five of seven sentences that tell a short story. But when they arrive at the sixth of the seventh sentences, they must decide which way to go in the maze. That is, they find three alternative sentences from which to choose. Each might bridge to the final sentence in the plot, but from the perspective of the story's fullest comprehension, one of the three is a better bridge. They can see sentence seven in the distance (across the metaphorical three bridged river). One sentence 6 simply paraphrases earlier information but does not bring the story narrative forward, a second sentence 6 provides lateral information, but does not really move the plot along to a causally logical conclusion. Biancarosa says we need ways to assess the developmental process students travel from their choice of these two sentences that represent a less developed levels of comprehension to the understanding of sentence that provides a causally clear process to push the story along to its completion, its full meaning.

My perspective. But what are the sentences in the story about? A girl who tends her mother's grape vines (1), is crying because the crows are eating the grapes (2), worries that if the grapes are all eaten, there won't be any to sell (3), meaning hard times for the family, so, in sentence four (4) she decides to build a scarecrow. In sentence five (5) she shares with the reader how she built it, in sentence (7) seven, her mom is happy there are grapes to sell. So, what happened in sentence (6) six? No matter here, you can go back to the essay to check. To me, the measure is primarily interesting because the story is fundamentally social. It assumes the reader's interest in a story about a deep social state of being, where the girl cares about her mother (wants to belong), tries to please her, strives to be responsible, realizes the dire straits the family will be in if no solution is found (she/they needs to feel safe). And she engages her own sense of agency and power to successfully perform her task, which allows the hidden author to satisfactorily complete her story. Social relationships and the human striving for *need-based social satisfaction* drives this story, and make the measure engaging.

The work Lowry Hemphill and her colleagues have undertaken approaches the alchemist's ambition: how to turn poor readers into good ones. The Strategic Adolescent Reading Intervention, aka the STARI project, is a story of five years of programmatic work that involves the following pieces: (1) a (basic) developmental theory: that academic language, complex reasoning, and social perspective taking skills are the basic, but malleable, developmental processes needed so that students can improve upon their academic discussions and their deep (reading) comprehension capacities; (2) the transmutation of this conceptual theory into a theory of educational change: that engaging stories and their discussion by peers, under teachers' guidance, have the power to promote the development of these malleable skills, and as such; (3) the implementation of an evidence based curriculum and instructional approach designed specifically for adolescents with reading challenges to demonstrate the change is not fool's gold: in this case, adolescents eleven to fifteen whose literacy skills lag at least two years behind "grade level" are, on average, better readers of material that requires deep comprehension.

My perspective. The STARI lab claims that regular classroom teachers, given adequate preparation and support, can implement novel literacy practices that improve the reading comprehension of students who struggle in this enterprise. But what are these key additional preparations and supports? Hemphill et al. note. "Although traditional remedial curricula rarely target students' ability to develop and advance *personal stances* on a text, excerpts from student talk and writing point to emerging skills for responding to sophisticated text-based questions, when presented with engaging texts and collaborative tasks." I cannot emphasize strongly enough the importance that "personal stances" play in making a connection for students to their own need for safety, power, and affiliation. The alchemist's magic can be found in each of the steps of/that? the project STARI lays out, but one essential ingredient is in the ways in which teachers use the *need-based social satisfaction* stories that engage students to strive to improve their comprehension of text and their communication with others.

Evelyn Ford-Connors and Catherine O'Connor provide an important coda for the STARI symphony, modest in scope from a practice perspective, but major in significance from a conceptual argument. Their topic, vocabulary acquisition, is major (in the language and literacy field) but perhaps (mistakenly) minor in the fields that take on *need-based social satisfactions*. They claim that the acquisition of vocabulary words can be taught through what they distinguish as "definitional" versus "contextual" approaches. In their comparative case study, Teacher A, the "describer," works with her class on two vocabulary words, *compile* and *interfere*. Teacher B, the "contextualizer," takes on in her class the introduction of the word *rating*. Like the words, *compile* and *interfere*, the word "*rating*" has a wide range of meanings, some deeply social, some not so deeply social, some hardly social at all. The authors advocate for the methods used by Teacher B who consistently asks her students to contextualize the word in vivo.

My perspective. For Ford-Connors and O'Connor, one might say, all word definitions and usages need to be meaningfully taught, but some methods allow words to be learned in a more meaningful way than do some others. When Teacher B's class discusses the meaning of the word, *ratings*, it is in the context of the students' own *need-based social satisfaction*. To describe the meaning of the word "Rating," as in "the quality of razor blades," is weak for students who don't shave or care about shaving. "Ratings, as in the appropriateness of whether a movie is rated PG, R, or X," is very meaningful for adolescents who want access to power, individual choice, a sense of what is appropriate for adolescents as a group, and what is or is not a safe movie for them to see. I suspect, more than the abstraction "context" alone, student engagement in the activities to which the word refers is the strong wind that carries the conversation forward. All words, to be powerful, must have at least some basis in terms that relate to how the learner sees these words being able to help them with their need for safety, power, or belonging. Of course, even a word like "amoeba" can fulfill this requirement for a student bound for a scientific career. However, vocabulary words, like "ratings" or "interfere," become most engaging, and hence better understood, by adolescents when they are used in ways that directly focus on the personal or shared meanings they signify or symbolize for in their social lives. Shades of Paulo Freire.

Paola Uccelli's chapter on the conceptualization – and operationalization – of a set of cross disciplinary academic language skills provides a look into a program of research designed to study the role these skills might play as contributors to the improvement of early adolescent reading comprehension. Yet Uccelli goes further to identify three implications that I find essential to the theme of my discussion:

1 "Language development continues throughout adolescence and ... continues for as long as learners expand the language-mediated social contexts that they navigate."

Across disciplines in the field of prevention science there is a strong line of evidence that supports the claim that early adolescence is a critical period for social and academic health and wellness. Research indicates that if negative health and educational risks such as violent behavior, drug experimentation, and academic disengagement and disappointment are not checked during this phase of life, either individually or within the peer culture, these disruptive and negative forces will much more likely solidify into anger and despair, at either the psychological or sociological level. Developmental malleability begins to decline if not kept supple. Language development is crucial to maintaining the challenges of early adolescence.

2 "A skilled language user in one social context does not guarantee linguistic dexterity in a different social context."

One way to insure suppleness is through engagement with others through moderated discussions. Youth are more likely to be successful in securing their own safety, maintaining and developing their own healthy social relationships, and achieving their own varied goals in life, if they can talk with one another with agency and empathy. But it is often the case that the skills that promote these proficiencies are not practiced sufficiently in those academic disciplines where they can directly and meaningfully inform early adolescent youth in ways they can develop ethically and emotionally. Take the case of middle grades and history courses. These are places of great opportunity. We must realize, in Uccelli's terms, that a history course is a prime "language-mediated social contexts" where students can learn to navigate their own autobiographies. This means, if youth are to be expected to connect the lessons of history to their own current and future actions they will need linguistic dexterity. This will be difficult for them to achieve on their own.

3 "By learning language, children also learn how to interact with others, how to comprehend, and how to learn in ways that are culturally shaped."

This last comment provides me with the opportunity to make a final comment. For over sixty years, researchers in the fields such as moral development and education have understood the importance of discursive interactions among peers in classrooms and schools as a major mechanism for well-informed social engagement. But few educators or policy makers listened to their pleas for even a modest pedagogical revolution that would increase the opportunity for youth to practice these skills. Moral education has never been a priority of educational policy makers, at least not in the past 125 years. But now, with the emergent work of this group of researchers, new evidence begins to build, new measures begin to be validated, and new, and innovative, theories begin to garner attention. We are more secure in our claims that: interpretive skills need attention; discussion skills are essential; awareness of context helps to build vocabulary; comprehension, be it through text or via other media, is a process with very strong developmental features. Yes, these are new directions, but one thing they all have in common is that they follow a line of theorizing and empirical research that can be traced to the antecedent and concurrent work researched, practiced, and advocated for many years by Snow (O'Connor & Snow, 2017; Snow, 1991b, 2002). Without this strong advocacy for the importance of language in literacies of all kinds, without this strong empirical evidence for the importance of disciplinary based discussions that build academic language, without a clear pragmatic analysis of social communication, the field of educational research in language and literacy might have turned in this direction eventually, but the turn would have been much slower and the movement would have been much less vibrant than we can see in the works of this section's scholars.

Part III

Learning through More than One Language

13 Young Bilinguals' Extended Discourse Skills
The Role of Perspective Taking

Vibeke Grøver

Extended discourse skills develop rapidly during the preschool years. Children's early extended discourse skills are demonstrated when they talk about topics beyond the here and now in talk segments that extend single utterances and accommodate to recognizable discourse structures, such as when they offer explanations, present definitions, make arguments, or – as is the focus of this chapter – tell a narrative to a listener based on a wordless picture book. The early extended discourse that young children participate in is likely to be conversational (Grøver Aukrust & Snow, 1998; Snow, 1991b; Snow, Tabors, & Dickinson, 2001), but children soon start demonstrating skills in producing extended discourse with less conversational support, such as when they on their own use a picture book to tell a narrative. While previous research has documented concurrent and predictive relations between preschool children's extended discourse participation with parents and teachers and their vocabulary learning, later literacy skills, and school achievement (see e.g. Rydland, Grøver, & Lawrence, 2014; Snow, Porche, Tabors, & Harris, 2007), recent research has addressed relations between children's extended discourse participation and their perspective-taking skills, that is, their skill in comprehending and providing a perspective or stance on what is talked about. Research on relations between extended discourse participation and perspective taking thus taps into linguistic and cognitive developments that may prepare children for using language to learn about the world. Studies to be reviewed below have suggested that skills in perspective taking may be of particular significance when it comes to understanding bilingual children's extended discourse participation and production. While these studies typically have compared bilingual and monolingual learners and demonstrated more developed perspective taking skills in bilinguals, the second part of this chapter will add to the existing body of research by examining relationships between perspective-taking skills and experienced variability in bilingual language use in a sample of young bilingual children. The chapter will explore whether the form of bilingual language use they experience may impact the perspective-taking skills they demonstrate in extended discourse production.

More specifically, the first part of the chapter will review research on young children's perspective taking, its development in multilingual settings, and its relation to other competencies. The second part will present a study examining bilingual children's perspective taking in relation to vocabulary, narrative skills, internal state explanations, and bilingual language use when children individually tell and retell a narrative based on a wordless picture book. Finally, the chapter's concluding section will discuss perspective taking from an instructional perspective.

Perspective Taking in Early Childhood

Children participate from early on in interactions that may support their development of perspective taking, such as when they respond to others' conversational initiations and repair conversational breakdowns (Pan & Snow, 1999). At a young age, children demonstrate non-verbal perspective taking when they follow others' attention and establish rudimentary forms of intersubjectivity (Bråten, 1998). Two-year-old children understand that what they see may sometimes differ from what another person observes (Moll & Tomasello, 2006). Children's engagement in pretend play is another example of developing skills in taking the perspective of others. By the late preschool years, children use a variety of linguistic and non-linguistic means to signal a shift from the real world to a pretend world (Pan & Snow, 1999).

Research on children's developing theory of mind is another source of information about children's development of perspective-taking skills. Studies have documented a social cognitive skill that, assessed using a false-belief test, develops around the age of four (e.g. Goetz, 2003; Wimmer & Perner, 1983). Recently, children around the age of two (Southgate, Senju, & Csibra, 2007) and even younger (Buttelmann, Carpenter, & Tomasello, 2009) have been found to demonstrate false-belief understanding when they were assessed in a situation that invited a behavioral rather than a verbal response. Thus, the verbal competencies that assessments of children's perspective-taking skills commonly require may have impacted our understanding regarding children's sensitivity to the perspectives of others. More important, these studies extend our knowledge of children's developing perspective taking beyond what is assessed using traditional false-belief tests.

In a study of four- and five-year-olds, Pelletier and Astington (2004) revealed relations between the children's age, language ability, theory-of-mind development, and ability to coordinate story characters' internal states and actions, using wordless picture books. In this chapter, children's perspective-taking skills are examined in terms of their developing capacity to switch narrative perspectives when they individually produce narratives based on a wordless picture book. Children demonstrate a capacity to step outside their own perspective and adopt the perspective of a principal protagonist when they recall a story, even when they are as young as three or four years old. Rall and Harris (2000) found that children accurately recalled verbs of motion (come/ go, bring/take) that were consistent with the protagonist's perspective. Conversely, they made errors in deictic verbs that were inconsistent with the protagonist's perspective. The study offered evidence that children are sensitive to and able to adopt a narrative perspective. Moreover, a possible interpretation of the study is that the presence of a protagonist is critical to perspective taking – supported by empathic identification – in young children. Rall and Harris concluded that when children start producing narratives about what is not here and now, the task of maintaining a consistent point of view becomes more complex. In a similar study that examined somewhat older children, Ziegler, Mitchell, and Currie (2005) found systematic errors in the recall of deictic terms from a narrative. The pattern of mistakes suggested that the children tended to adopt a perspective within the narrative that supported their recall. Children in the experimental narrative condition that included a principal protagonist were cued and supported in adopting a perspective compared to children in the condition in which there was no principal protagonist.

Rall and Harris (2000) as well as Ziegler et al. (2005) concluded that the young children they studied adopted the principal protagonist's perspective. Aldrich, Tenenbaum, Brooks, Harrison, and Sines (2011) demonstrated that children's ability to shift narrative perspective from the main protagonist to a rival within a story about jealousy was more developed in older (seven- to eight-year-olds) as compared to younger children (five- to six-year-olds). The older children more often relayed story information by simultaneously taking into account the perspectives of the different story characters (both the protagonist and the rival), using emotion explanations to organize their narratives in a coherent way related to the theme of the story.

Another expression of perspective taking in preschool children is their judgment about the listener's need for background information when they tell a story, make an explanation, or produce an argument. Even three- and four-year-olds can make adjustments to the amount of information they provide for listeners who have some background knowledge versus those who do not (Pan & Snow, 1999). Moreover, the choice of language code in multilingual environments indicates the child's awareness of the interlocutor. Recent research, which will be reviewed next, has suggested that bilingual children may have more developed perspective-taking skills than their monolingual counterparts because they regularly have to attend to their interlocutors' language skills and understanding. Bilingual children are thus a particularly interesting group to study when examining perspective-taking skills in relation to other competencies that young children use when they produce narratives.

Is There a Bilingual Advantage in Perspective Taking?

Although several explanations for a potential bilingual advantage in perspective taking have been proposed, such as greater inhibitory control and cognitive flexibility in bilinguals (for a discussion, see Akhtar & Menjivar, 2012; Goetz, 2003), the potential advantage has also been explained by greater social sensitivity in bilinguals resulting from communication with interlocutors who do not speak one of their languages. Genesee, Tucker, and Lambert (1975) found that compared with monolingual learners, bilingual children (from kindergarten to second grade) educated in a non-native language were more sensitive to the communication needs of their listeners and seemed more able to take the role of others when experiencing communication difficulties. From very early on, bilingual children can use their languages differentially depending on whom they talk with (Nicoladis & Genesee, 1996), and they can repair breakdowns in communication due to language choice (Comeau, Genesee, & Mendelson, 2007). Studying older preschool children, Siegal, Iozzi, and Surian (2009) documented a bilingual advantage in three- to six-year-old children's pragmatic skills and attributed this advantage to their daily experiences with interpreting the intentions of others. In a similar vein, Yow and Markman (2011) reported that bilingual preschool children, compared with monolinguals, were more skilled at taking the perspective of the listener. Likewise, Goetz (2003) demonstrated a bilingual advantage when monolingual and bilingual three- and four-year-olds were compared on perspective-taking and false-belief tasks. Studying older children attending middle school Hsin and Snow (2017), found that students with a language-minority background more often applied social perspective taking in their academic work, compared with monolingual students. The language-minority students used more explicit language when they related claims to arguments and the authors asked if the students did so because their bilingual upbringing had supported their understanding that others might not immediately make the connections that they did themselves.

Some recent studies have suggested that it is not being bilingual per se but rather growing up in a bilingual or multilingual environment that affects perspective taking. Liberman, Woodward, Keysar, and Kinzler (2016) found that early exposure to multiple languages enhanced sixteen-month-olds' communication skills and that this advantage was also observed in children who were monolingual but learned in a multilingual context. They found that even minimal multilingual exposure enhanced these skills. They suggested that the social experience of being raised in a multilingual environment might provide children with practice in taking other people's perspectives. Similarly, Fan, Liberman, Keysar, and Kinzler (2015) found that multilingual exposure promoted effective communication by enhancing perspective taking. Four- to six-year-old bilingual children and children who were monolingual but exposed to a multilingual environment did significantly better on a perspective-taking task than monolingual children who were not exposed to multiple languages. Fan et al. argued that exposure to diverse sociolinguistic environments provided children with unique experiences that enhanced their communicative skills. To conclude, while several studies point to a bilingual advantage in perspective taking, we do not know the nature of relations between exposure to two or more languages and perspective-taking skills. The study presented in the second part of this chapter extends the body of research on bilingualism and perspective taking by exploring whether variability in the bilingual language use experienced by young immigrant children identified as bilingual by their parents and growing up in highly multilingual communities was related to their perspective-taking skills.

Perspective Taking and Word Learning Embedded in Extended Discourse

Previous research has documented correlations between vocabulary and narrative skills in monolingual preschoolers (Tabors, Roach, & Snow, 2001) as well as in bilingual kindergartners (Uchikoshi, 2005). Snow et al. (2007) found that kindergarten narrative production predicted receptive vocabulary longitudinally in the fourth and seventh grade. Conversely, children depend on their vocabulary when they produce a narrative from a picture book. A rich mental state vocabulary has for example been reported to support storytelling (Pelletier, 2006). Support for relations among vocabulary, narrative, and perspective taking was found by Lohmann and Tomasello (2003), who related young children's vocabulary development to their understanding of others' minds, and by Donahue (2014), who found relations between children's social perspective taking and narrative comprehension.

Comprehending and using words in sophisticated ways presupposes a capacity to take into account the listener's perspective of the message and consider how the message will be understood. Many words that young children learn, even some of their first words, are not learned in an ostensive way such that the word's reference in the world can be pointed out. To comprehend the meaning of the word, the child has to take the speaker's perspective and identify what the speaker has paid attention to. Children's word learning can thus be compared to a social puzzle in which they look for interpretation support in the social and linguistic context, applying early perspective-taking skills (Akhtar & Tomasello, 2000). Although word learning and perspective taking are deeply interrelated theoretically, their relationship has not been entirely explored. A purpose of this chapter is to further examine relations between vocabulary and perspective-taking skills in young bilinguals.

Some studies have suggested that bilingual children rely more on their perspective-taking skills than monolingual learners when they participate in extended discourse. Pelletier and Beatty (2015) concluded that theory-of-mind skills contributed to narrative understanding beyond the contribution of general vocabulary in a sample of kindergartners who were mostly second-language learners. Pelletier (2006), who studied monolingual and bilingual learners in two age groups (from kindergarten to second grade and fourth grade), found that theory-of-mind skills accounted for unique variance in reading comprehension in bilingual learners, particularly those with low reading skills, but not in monolingual learners.

The linguistic features that children adopt when they tell a story, such as the use and recall of perspectival words (e.g. 'this' versus 'that' and 'come' versus 'go'), reflect the identification of a principal narrative protagonist (Rall & Harris, 2000; Ziegler et al., 2005). Rather than examining how word choice may reflect children's growing awareness of perspectives, the study presented in the second part of this chapter examined bilingual children's perspective taking as demonstrated by their response to an invitation to change narrative perspective when they retold a story based on a wordless picture book. In particular, they were asked to change perspective from that of the principal protagonist in the first telling to that of a more distant character. Relations between bilingual children's narrative perspective taking on the one hand and their vocabulary and narrative skills on the other were examined as they told and retold the story. Children with more advanced narrative skills and larger vocabularies were expected to be more able to demonstrate a shift in narrative perspective on request. Moreover, variations in the bilingual language use the children experienced were expected to predict their perspective-taking skills. Extending the body of research that has identified a bilingual advantage in perspective taking, children who more often used their native language at home were expected to demonstrate more developed perspective-taking skills.

Exploring Narrative Perspective Taking: A Study of Bilingual Preschoolers

Participants

The study included 302 (171 girls and 131 boys) bilingual children living in Norway, aged three to five years (mean age in months = 54.46, *SD* = 9.02, range = 34–68). They were part of a larger sample of bilingual children whose parents and teachers had agreed to participate in a language intervention study addressing bilingual language learning. They all lived in highly multilingual neighborhoods with a majority of the children being second-language speakers of Norwegian, the common language in preschool. The subsample included all children who were assessable on a narrative perspective-taking task prior to the onset of the intervention.

Most parents agreed to a telephone interview that covered family language use and was conducted in the parents' preferred language. All children were identified as bilingual by their parents and spoke Norwegian as their second language. The children spoke a variety of native languages at home, with about half of them speaking one of the four languages that were most common in the sample: Urdu (20.53 percent), Somalian (14.90 per cent), Arabic (11.59 per cent), and Polish (8.28 percent). Most parents were born in their country of origin (92.62 per cent of mothers, $n = 271$, and 90.77 percent of fathers, $n = 260$), and most of them had moved to Norway as young adults. Parental education was assessed using one of six categories: 1 = zero to four years of schooling, 2 = five to seven years of schooling, 3 = eight to ten years of schooling, 4 = eleven to thirteen years of schooling (completed high school), 5 = completed bachelor's degree, or 6 = completed master's degree or more. Most mothers and fathers had a mean number of years in school equivalent to high school ($M = 4.01$, $SD = 1.26$, $n = 260$ for mothers; $M = 4.16$, $SD = 1.22$, $n = 245$ for fathers).

The parents were asked to describe family language use according to one of the following three categories: 1 = use mostly the native language, 2 = use a mixture of the native language and Norwegian, or 3 = use mostly Norwegian. The interviews confirmed that most parents spoke the native language with their child (maternal language use with child: $M = 1.41$, $SD = 0.68$, $n = 267$; paternal language use with child: $M = 1.45$, $SD = 0.72$, $n = 250$). For 77.81 percent of the families we had data on children's language use in relation to both parents. The children more often spoke a mixture of the native language and Norwegian to their parents (child language use with mother: $M = 2.11$, $SD = 0.88$, $n = 235$; child language use with father: $M = 2.03$, $SD = 0.91$, $n = 235$).

Procedures

Assessing second-language vocabulary skills. The children's receptive second-language vocabulary skills were assessed individually in the context of their preschools using a translated version of the British Picture Vocabulary Scale II (BPVS-II; Dunn, Dunn, Whetton, & Burley, 1997; Lyster, Horn, & Rygvold, 2010). The child was shown successive panels of four pictures and asked to point to the picture that matched the word said by the assessor. The Cronbach's alpha for the Norwegian translation of BPVS-II is 0.98 (Lyster et al., 2010).

The narrative skills and perspective-taking tasks. The children's narrative and perspective-taking skills were individually assessed in their second language in a two-step procedure using a wordless children's book (*Hug* by Alborough, 2002). The principal protagonist in the book was a little monkey searching for and finally reuniting with its parent. During the search, the monkey observed many different animals accompanied by and hugging their parents. A baby elephant and its parent, albeit more remote characters, were present on all pages except on one offering a close-up illustration of the monkey. The elephant witnessed the increasing sadness and despair of the monkey before it was reunited with its parent, ultimately making the monkey (and all the other animals) happy.

The child was first asked to 'tell the story as it is for the baby monkey' (the narrative skills task). No time limit was imposed. Some children did not produce a narrative but pointed to or labeled animals or colors without any attempt to make a story. When the child did use the picture book to make a story, the assessor pointed out to the child that there was a baby elephant on all pages (upon the child's completion of the story) and invited the child to retell the story 'as it is for the baby elephant' (the perspective-taking task). To support the shift in perspective, the child was offered a stuffed elephant to hold while narrating. If the child retold the story from the same perspective as during the first telling (about the monkey) or started out by taking the perspective of the elephant but then quickly returned to the monkey after the first couple of pages, the assessor thanked the child and terminated the assessment after four pages. The narrative skills task and the perspective-taking task were audiotaped and transcribed using the Child Language Data Exchange System (MacWhinney, 2000).

Coding narrative skills, internal state explanations, and perspective taking. Transcripts were coded for narrative components, internal state explanations, and perspective taking. The narrative skills task was coded using the coding conventions developed by Luo, Tamis-LeMonda, Kuchirko, Ng, and Liang (2014). In accordance with Luo et al., the narrative was divided into thirty-three possible story components addressing emotional behaviors and states. Children were credited for reference to each of them. The number of internal state explanations during the first telling was also coded; these were sequences in which the child spontaneously explained the monkey's internal state using an explanatory marker such as 'because', 'therefore', or 'so that' (e.g. 'He was sad because he did not have his mum'). Interrater reliability was 0.83 (Cohen's kappa).

Perspective taking was assessed as the child's skills in shifting the narrative perspective from the monkey to the elephant, using a coding scheme with eight categories linked to specific pages throughout the book. We developed these codes through repeated readings of the transcripts to capture ways in which a shift in narrative perspective from the monkey to the elephant appeared in the children's retellings. These categories were as follows: the elephant (1) hugged/was together with its parent; (2) saw that the monkey was feeling alone/missed its mother; (3) was sad because it saw that the monkey was sad; (4) talked with the monkey, asking why it was sad or offering company; (5) offered to help the monkey search for its parent; (6) noticed that the other animals had fun; (7) noticed that the monkey was becoming increasingly sad; and (8) was happy because the monkey was reunited with its parent. Children could demonstrate the shift to the elephant perspective either by taking the role of the elephant (narrating in first person as the elephant, typically in a high-pitched voice; 'I will help you find your mummy') or by applying the elephant's perspective on the monkey in the role of the narrator ('The elephant wanted to help the monkey find his mum'). The children were credited for each category appearing in their retelling (0–8). Cohen's kappa for the elephant coding was 0.82.

While 29.47 percent of the children included the first category in their retelling ('the elephant hugged/was together with its parent') and 6.62 percent included the second ('the elephant saw that the monkey was feeling alone/missed its mother'), the remaining categories appeared highly infrequently, a demonstration of how difficult this shift in perspective was.

Results

Table 13.1 offers descriptive statistics on vocabulary, narrative and perspective-taking skills, and bilingual language use. There was a huge variation in second-language vocabulary skills in the sample, with a mean of 29.82 points (based on raw scores). Similarly, the number of narrative components offered during the first telling varied from zero to fifteen per child. Internal state explanations were infrequent, varying between zero and three occurrences per child. Bilingual language use also varied in the sample. While some children spoke the native language to both parents, others used mostly Norwegian when they spoke to their parents; the sample mean suggested that most children used a mixture of their two languages with their parents. The children exhibited considerable variation in perspective-taking skills, with many children receiving a score of 0 and a few children demonstrating several of the categories identifying perspective taking (range of 0–6).

Vocabulary skills, narrative skills, internal state explanations, and perspective taking correlated highly with each other as well as with age. Vocabulary correlated more with narrative skills than with internal state explanations. This is not surprising, as children with larger vocabularies were typically more able to include more relevant emotion descriptions in their narratives, while internal

Table 13.1 *Descriptive Statistics and Correlations*

	1	2	3	4	5	6
Age in months	–					
BPVS-II	0.49***	–				
Narrative components	0.45***	0.44***	–			
Internal state explanations	0.16**	0.12*	0.28***	–		
Bilingual language use	−0.04	0.09	0.08	−0.01	–	
Perspective-taking skills	0.37***	0.39***	0.39***	0.31***	−0.07	–
Mean	54.46	29.82	4.43	0.11	4.14	0.51
SD	9.02	13.05	3.31	0.36	1.65	0.91
N	302	302	302	302	235	302

Note. BPVS-II = British Picture Vocabulary Scale II, Norwegian version. $*p < .05$. $**p < .01$. $***p < .001$.

state explanations additionally demanded the use of an explanatory marker when talking about emotions. On the other hand, the child's bilingual language use in relation to the parents did not correlate with vocabulary, narrative skills, or perspective taking. This suggests that the extent to which children spoke the native language to their parents at home did not influence the development of these competencies as assessed in the children's second language.

To predict which children would demonstrate perspective-taking skills when invited to shift perspective to the more remote protagonist, we ran multiple regressions with age, receptive vocabulary, narrative skills, internal state explanations, and bilingual language use. These regressions showed that after controlling for age in months and second-language vocabulary, narrative skills predicted the extent to which children demonstrated perspective taking during the retelling ($\beta = 0.23$, $SE = 0.02$, $p = 0.00$). Children who included more narrative components more often responded successfully in the perspective-taking task. Internal state explanations, when added in the model as the fourth step, significantly explained further variance in perspective-taking skills ($\beta = 0.21$, $SE = 0.13$, $p = 0.00$), implying that children who offered more internal state explanations in the first telling demonstrated more perspective-taking skills during the second. Finally, when the children's bilingual language use was added as the fifth step in the model, it predicted perspective taking in a marginally significant way ($\beta = -0.10$, $SE = 0.04$, $p = 0.08$). Children who more often used their native language at home tended to demonstrate more perspective-taking skills.

More girls than boys participated in the study, but gender did not show a relationship with any of the addressed dimensions. While maternal and paternal education correlated highly ($r = 0.48$, $p = 0.00$), the only correlation between parental education and second-language vocabulary, narrative skills, and perspective taking in this sample was between maternal education and BPVS-II ($r = 0.18$, $p = 0.01$). When maternal education was included in the regression as the fifth step before children's language use with the parents, children's language use still marginally predicted perspective taking ($\beta = -0.09$, $p = 0.10$). Parental language use with the child, added as the fifth step before the child's language use with the parents, did not explain variance in perspective taking, while children's language use with the parents remained a marginally significant predictor ($\beta = -0.12$, $p = 0.06$).

In conclusion, age, second-language vocabulary, narrative skills, and internal state explanations predicted the extent to which the children were able to retell a narrative from the perspective of a more distant protagonist. Controlling for these other factors bilingual language use predicted perspective taking in a marginally significant way, suggesting that children who more often used their native language when talking to their parents might have had a perspective-taking advantage.

Relevance to Education

This chapter reviewed perspective taking in bilingual children's second-language narratives. For young children, narratives are an important way of understanding the world; they offer a route to learning through language. The language skills needed to produce a narrative in early childhood may be precursors of the skills required to produce and comprehend texts in later school years. In addition to topic-relevant vocabulary and grammatical skills, producing and comprehending texts in school requires pragmatic competencies such as being able to identify multiple perspectives and positions embedded in the text (Snow & Uccelli, 2009).

Although perspective-taking skills correlate highly with age in the preschool years, some studies have suggested that variability in perspective taking may also be subject to qualities of exposure. Lohmann and Tomasello (2003) found that three-year-old children who participated in training improved their false-belief understanding in a condition involving perspective-shifting discourse about deceptive objects, while children did not improve in a condition in which they were exposed to such objects without accompanying language.

Evidence for the role of language in perspective taking has also come from correlational studies. For instance, Watson, Painter, and Bornstein (2002) suggested that language development and perspective-taking skills measured through theory-of-mind tasks are strongly correlated; this also applied to conditions when child language was assessed two years prior to children mastering theory-of-mind tasks. Moreover, Meins, Fernyhough, Arnott, Leekam, and Rosnay (2013) studied maternal mind-related comments and children's internal state vocabulary at twenty-six months and the children's theory of mind at fifty-one months; they found a direct link between maternal mind-related comments and children's theory of mind and an indirect link between such comments and theory of mind via the children's concurrent receptive vocabulary. These studies, all undertaken on monolingual children, suggested that children's skills in taking the perspective of others are subject to qualities of exposure.

Recent evidence indicating that perspective-taking skills are supported in bilingual environments further suggests that the development of this skill is sensitive to qualities of experience and exposure. Young bilingual learners who might have less developed vocabularies in either of their languages can use their perspective-taking skills as a resource in interpreting discourse meaning. Liberman et al. (2016) and Fan et al. (2015) suggested that young bilinguals or monolinguals living in multilingual contexts had more developed perspective-taking skills than children who were not exposed to two or more languages, but we do not yet know the level of exposure needed to attain that benefit. Children who interact with people who speak different languages within the same context (e.g. at home) might need to learn to address interlocutor concerns in a different way from children who only need to learn to discriminate based on context.

Challenges in identifying a bilingual advantage might have to do with the huge variability within the bilingual group. While all the children participating in this study were identified as bilingual by their parents, they still demonstrated much variation in their daily language use with their parents. We found that native language use with the parents had a marginally significant and positive effect on perspective taking when we controlled for the children's age, vocabulary, and narrative skills. Together with other studies, this marginally significant finding might indicate that the development of perspective-taking skills partly results from characteristics of bilingual exposure.

Future research should determine the extent to which children's perspective-taking skills could be subject to instruction in preschool and school. For example, we need to know whether teachers who encourage children to retell stories from the perspectives of different characters in a book could foster the children's development of perspective-taking skills. We also need to know more about whether children's different ways of being and living bilingually as they interact with people and contexts could affect the extent to which they are receptive to such instruction. Particularly for bilingual learners who may have less developed vocabularies in either language, it might be important to consider instructional strategies that invite them to use their discourse knowledge (potentially transferable across languages) and their perspective-taking skills in interpreting texts. Descriptive studies of relations between perspective taking, language skills, and bilingual language use in various settings, as well as experimental studies examining outcomes of instruction addressing these competencies, can further advance our understanding of the development of bilingual children's perspective-taking skills and how these skills influence their comprehension and production of narratives as well as other types of extended discourse.

Acknowledgements

I gratefully thank Veslemøy Rydland for collaboration on the project presented in this chapter. I also thank the PhD students and the research assistants who collected, transcribed, and coded data and the children and parents who participated in the study. The Norwegian Research Council, grant no 218280, funded the project.

14 How Does Vocabulary Instruction in Reading Help Chinese Young Minority Children Learn Vocabulary in Two Languages?

Si Chen

China has a great diversity of language groups. Millions of young children who speak a minority language acquire Chinese as their second language when they enter bilingual kindergarten or elementary school. Since most minority children living in China come from low-SES families, learning Chinese as a second language is a crucial milestone for them. However, little research has been conducted to explore how to support the bilingual development of young minority children in China.

Xinjiang: A Unique Bilingual Early Childhood Education Setting in China

Located on the northwestern border of China, neighboring Afghanistan, Tajikistan, and Mongolia, the Xinjiang Uyghur Autonomous Region is the biggest province in China. It is also the poorest. Xinjiang is the home to the Uyghur (more than 70 percent of the population in the Xinjiang region), a Turkic people who converted to Islam in the tenth century. Xinjiang has been subject to rapid modernization over the past decades, resulting in violence and restrictions on social and religious freedoms that have brought "China's most turbulent area" (Johnson, 2013) into the media spotlight.

Uyghur–Chinese Bilingualism

Today, Xinjiang has the greatest diversity of language groups in China. Officially there are seven languages used in formal education settings and textbooks: Uyghur, Mandarin Chinese, Kazakh, Mongolian, Kyrgyz, Xibe, and Russian (Wang & Meng, 2006). Except for Xibe and Russian, these languages have television broadcasts and newspapers (Statistic Bureau of Xinjiang Uyghur Autonomous Region, 2014a). Over 53 percent of the population (11 million people) in Xinjiang are Uyghur people (Statistic Bureau of Xinjiang Uyghur Autonomous Region, 2014b). As one of the largest language-minority groups, Uyghur people use Uyghur, a Turkic language, as their oral and written language. For them, Uyghur is also the language of home and community in most areas of the province.

Over 1.3 million Uyghur children aged zero to six (National Bureau of Statistics of the People's Republic of China, 2010) acquire Uyghur as their first language and learn Mandarin Chinese when they enter a bilingual kindergarten or elementary school. In most Chinese public kindergartens, children within the same class are the same age. Classes in Chinese kindergartens have three age cohorts: age four (Xiao Ban), age five (Zhong Ban), and age six (Da Ban). Since most Uyghur children living in Xinjiang come from low-SES families, as Xinjiang is one of the poorest regions in China, learning Chinese as a second language is a crucial milestone for them. To achieve academic success, young Uyghur children must become fluent in Chinese (reading, writing, and speaking), since most school instruction after first grade, especially in science, is in Mandarin Chinese (Li & Cai, 2012). Bilingualism is also a key economic outcome for education because being bilingual enables Uyghur young adults to pass the university entrance exam and be much more competitive for well-compensated jobs (Sun, 2012). Unfortunately, little empirical research has been conducted to determine the quality of bilingual education in Xinjiang or to explore how to support children's Mandarin Chinese and Uyghur development starting from a young age.

Bilingual Early Childhood Education in Xinjiang: Policy and Practice

The national Bilingual Education Experiment. In 1999, Xinjiang launched the Bilingual Education Experiment (BEE). This policy requested that elementary and middle schools teach science, mathematics, and English classes in Mandarin and other courses in Uyghur. In 2005, the Xinjiang government extended this policy to kindergartens by requesting that kindergartens teach more Mandarin (they had previously been teaching only in Uyghur), offer free lunch for Uyghur children, and offer pay incentives to teachers in bilingual kindergartens (Ma, 2008). By the end of 2014, 69.8 percent of Uyghur children were enrolled in BEE kindergartens (Statistic Bureau of Xinjiang, 2016), compared with 29.4 percent in 2006 (Ma, 2008).

Bilingual education quality. Although the number of children attending BEE kindergartens has increased remarkably, attention to the quality of the early bilingual curriculum in Xinjiang lags. The important role of Uyghur in bilingual education has long been underestimated. Neither the curriculum nor the teachers of the BEE schools are well-prepared for bilingual instruction.

The curriculum. During the early years of BEE, the curriculum and teaching in Xinjiang consisted of nothing more than immersive Chinese learning for Uyghur children. In 2009, a bilingual curriculum was introduced, with textbooks written in both Mandarin and Uyghur. But it wasn't even until 2012 that the first reference to the development of young children's home language in the national official Guidelines on Early Learning and Development occurred (China Ministry of Education, 2012). Finally, a new version of the bilingual kindergarten curriculum of Xinjiang formally required teachers to use both Mandarin and Uyghur in the Mandarin learning course starting in 2013.

The teachers. Although curricular materials emphasizing Uyghur are readily available, bilingual kindergarten teachers have had very few chances to develop efficient and high-quality bilingual teaching strategies. Native Chinese-speaking teachers are typically not able to speak Uyghur. Although many Uyghur bilingual kindergarten classrooms have two teachers, one Uyghur-speaking, most bilingual kindergarten teachers (both native Chinese or Uyghur-speaking) were instructed and trained to teach in Chinese only.

The teaching practice. According to the observations of researchers, language-learning classes in Xinjiang kindergartens emphasized simple decoding of Chinese words, Chinese character recognition, and writing, but paid little attention to the comprehension of language and text (Sun, 2012). In a typical bilingual kindergarten classroom, there were few picture books, reading materials, or shared book reading activities, in either Mandarin Chinese or Uyghur (Zhou et al., 2014).

The learning outcomes of children. Case studies and theoretical work focusing on the Xinjiang bilingual education system report contradictory findings. Tsung and Cruickshank (2009) observed classroom teaching in two Xinjiang primary schools and concluded that the Xinjiang bilingual school system failed to provide sufficient access for language-minority children to learn Uyghur, Chinese, or a third language (English). They claimed the education *delayed* children's language learning, thereby impeding access to higher education. In contrast, Huang's (2011) case study observed Xinjiang kindergarten classes and students' home literacy environment found that kindergarten students' bilingual development was not delayed if they had a rich second-language input (i.e., read Mandarin books and watched Mandarin television). However, according to other researchers comparing the vocabulary development of four- to six-year-old monolingual Mandarin children and Mandarin–Uyghur bilingual children with similar maternal education level, on average, Uyghur children scored 1.58 standard deviations lower on Chinese receptive vocabulary and 1.87 standard deviations lower on Chinese expressive vocabulary (Li, 2013; Chen, 2014).

So far the findings do not agree on a common narrative, but it is likely that bilingual education in Xinjiang needs to be improved. Beyond these studies, there is little empirical evidence on the state of Uyghur children's bilingual learning. In the present study, we test the effectiveness of an intervention intended to support kindergarten children's development of Mandarin Chinese and Uyghur language skills through the introduction of bilingual reading materials in the context of ongoing professional development for teachers. In the literature review that follows we provide a rationale for our focus on expressive and receptive vocabulary (in L1 and L2) and then describe the materials and the procedure in the intervention.

Helping Young Minority Children: Evidence from Previous Interventions

For young children, learning the meaning of words is a foundational skill for language and literacy development (Muter, Hulme, Snowling, & Stevenson, 2004; Sénéchal, Ouellette, & Rodney, 2006). On average, children from a low-SES and/or language-minority background face challenges when they enter school with comparatively limited vocabulary (Hart & Risley, 1995; Snow, Burns, & Griffin, 1998). Language-minority children, who usually also come from low-SES families, globally have lagged behind in L2 language skills when compared with their monolingual peers (August & Shanahan, 2006; Lesaux, Rupp, & Siegel, 2007; Patterson, 2004; Reese, Sparks, & Leyva, 2010; Uccelli & Páez, 2007).

Focusing on Vocabulary

Researchers show that several essential intervention components improve vocabulary for young language-minority children efficiently: (1) providing students with multiple exposures to words (Loftus, Coyne, McCoach, Zipoli, & Pullen, 2010; Silverman & Hines, 2009; Uchikoshi, 2005); (2) encouraging in-class discussion (Silverman, 2007; Ruston & Schwanenflugel, 2010); and (3) providing professional development to prepare teachers to help young bilingual children (Cheung & Slavin, 2005; Kohnert, Yim, Nett, Kan, & Duran, 2005). A meta-analysis reveals that the effect size of vocabulary interventions with these components in kindergarten and kindergarten is relatively large; on average, such interventions can help young children score nearly one standard deviation higher than controls on measures of target words (Marulis & Neuman, 2010).

Using Picture Books

Shared book reading in the classroom has proven an efficient and reliable method to help young children develop language proficiency. The effect size of interventions with picture book reading as the essential components varies from 0.1 to 1.0 standard deviation (Wasik, Hindman, & Snell, 2016). Well-designed experiments show that picture books provide valuable opportunities for young children to learn unfamiliar yet essential vocabulary that they may not encounter in daily life (Mol, Bus & de Jong, 2009; Weizman & Snow, 2001). Researchers emphasize that shared book reading and extended activities related to the books bring questions and discussions that prompt children to practice vocabulary and sentences they have learned in reading (De Temple & Snow, 2003; Lever & Sénéchal, 2011; Sim & Berthelsen, 2014).

The Xinjiang Project: Helping Young Uyghur Children Learn Two Languages

The Xinjiang Project Book Reading Intervention

Learning from previous interventions, the XJP intervention was designed to help young Uyghur children improve vocabulary and language skills.

There are three main elements of the XJP:

1 Enriching the classroom literacy environment for Uyghur students. The XJP provided each class with ten copies of thirty different Mandarin–Uyghur picture books that included related posters and word cards. These books were chosen based on (1) recommendations from early childhood education experts, (2) the books' rich vocabulary, and (3) the presence of interesting stories or topics that can be easily discussed (e.g., music, animals).

2 Implementing a new curriculum that promotes language exposure and practice via classroom discussions. The teachers received training and lesson plans containing methods for utilizing the curriculum for twenty minutes each day. Each week, teachers introduced four topics (related to the picture books) for small-group discussion and one whole-class activity (e.g., a field trip). The key goal of the curriculum was to enable children to encounter and utilize vocabulary and then to reinforce their learning by probing with open-ended questions. The XJP gave teachers flexibility in incorporating the Project's language books into their teaching agenda.

3 Providing teachers with a thorough understanding of the theories behind the intervention and introducing practical strategies to integrate these materials and principles into their curricula (e.g., concepts of early literacy education, methods for using picture books to improve language learning, and class-room teacher–child interaction strategies). The XJP provided three types of

teacher training, including a one-on-one training session in the classroom, two group meetings, and three sessions of online long-distance training.

Evaluation of the Xinjiang Project

We developed two studies to investigate the impact of the XJP on the teachers' vocabulary instruction and on Uyghur children's vocabulary development. To measure the effects of this intervention, we employed a randomized controlled trial (RCT) that sampled thirty-one Uyghur–Chinese bilingual classes from twelve kindergartens in two cities in Xinjiang (Urumqi and Turpan). Depending on the children's age when the XJP started, we recruited classes from two age cohorts: entry age four and entry age five. The treatment group (sixteen classes and their teachers) received the XJP intervention while the control group (fifteen classes and teachers) received no intervention and maintained their existing curriculum and schedule.

Modeling the changes in teachers. The first study focused on evaluating how the XJP impacted teachers' vocabulary instruction. Specifically, we asked two questions: first, in the classroom, does the XJP stimulate the teacher to provide more information about the meanings of vocabulary words? Second, does the XJP training help the teacher apply more vocabulary teaching strategies?

Data collection. We videotaped all thirty-one teachers for a week before the XJP intervention. Before the filming, each teacher had three days to prepare a thirty-minute group activity (e.g., group discussion and field trip) related to language learning. After the one-year XJP intervention, all teachers were asked to develop another thirty-minute group activity related to language learning. We also videotaped this activity. Recordings were transcribed using a standardized format, CHAT (Codes for the Human Analysis of Transcripts; MacWhinney, 2000).

Video coding. Adopting the video coding system of Bowne, Yoshikawa, and Snow (2016), we first identified all the explicit vocabulary instruction episodes that met two standards. First, they drew children's attention to a particular word; and second, they provided some information (e.g., explaining the meaning, or repeating a word) about the meaning.

After identifying all the episodes of vocabulary instruction, we applied a set of codes to identify: (1) the *information* that the teacher provided and (2) the *strategy* that they used in vocabulary instruction. The coding of *information* captured all new references to conceptual information about a word's meaning that the teacher provided to children. There were twelve types of information codes, including "elaborating details," "usage," and "meta-cognitive information of the target word." The coding of *strategy* counted the number of different ways in which the teacher presented the conceptual meaning of the target word, including using objects or pictures, indicating children's prior experience, and explaining in two languages. There were twelve types of strategy codes as well.

We used multiple regression models to detect the treatment effects on the *information* and *strategy* of the teachers' vocabulary instruction.

Modeling the change of children. By modeling the children's individual growth trajectories in Chinese and Uyghur, using standardized tasks translated from Chinese to Uyghur, we addressed the following two research questions: Does participation in the XJP improve Uyghur children's (1) Chinese vocabulary and (2) Uyghur vocabulary?

Participants. Children entered the evaluation in prekindergarten and kindergarten and were followed for one year. The same classes were followed in this evaluation as in the instructor evaluation. To summarize, thirty-one classes from twelve kindergartens in two cities in Xinjiang were randomly assigned to treatment (sixteen classes) and control (fifteen classes) conditions. Within each class, seven to nine Uyghur children were randomly selected to take vocabulary tests. In total, 256 children participated in this study.

Data collection and instruments. Children were tested in both Chinese and Uyghur vocabulary three times: right before the XJP (the pretest), a half-year after the start of the XJP (the first test), and one year after the start of the XJP (the second test, or posttest). We tested four outcomes: Chinese receptive vocabulary, using the Chinese Peabody Picture Vocabulary Test (PPVT; Lu & Liu, 1998); Chinese expressive vocabulary, using the Expressive Vocabulary Test (translated and adapted from the English Expressive Vocabulary Test, EVT; Williams, 1997); Uyghur receptive vocabulary, using the Uyghur PPVT (translated and adapted from the Chinese version); and Uyghur expressive vocabulary, using the Uyghur EVT (translated and adapted from the Chinese version).

Data analytic plan. We used individual growth models with a generalized linear mixed model (Rabe-Hesketh, Skrondal, & Pickles, 2005; Singer & Willett, 2003) to estimate the treatment effects of the XJP on children's vocabulary growth.

Efficacy of the Xinjiang Project Intervention

Improving teaching performance in the classroom. The instruction evaluation study focused on the teachers' vocabulary instruction performance in the classroom. We found that after attending the XJP teacher training and applying the new curriculum with shared book reading, teachers improved their vocabulary instruction performance by providing more information on vocabulary meaning and employing more diverse ways to explain words than control teachers.

Providing more information on vocabulary meanings. Subtracting the total number of details about vocabulary that the teachers provided in the first video from the last video, we found that the treatment group taught significantly more details by the year's end than the control. Multiple regression showed that after controlling for the teachers' pretest performance (in both information and strategy of vocabulary instruction) and demographic factors (e.g., age, teaching experience, education), in each twenty-minute class, the XJP teachers introduced half a standard deviation more information concerning vocabulary meanings than control teachers ($\beta = 0.58$, SE $= 58.66$, $p = 0.03$). Specifically, XJP teachers provided significantly more bilingual explanations, more information on the usage of the target word, and more phonological details.

Applying more vocabulary teaching strategies. The results of multiple regression models also showed that after controlling for the teacher's pretest performance and demographic factors, the XJP helped treatment teachers to use half a standard deviation more teaching strategies in vocabulary instruction ($\beta = 0.51$, SE $= 57.43$, $p = 0.02$) than control teachers. The XJP teachers used significantly more pictures and actions to present target words. They also use more strategies like repeating words and recalling children's prior experiences to help them understand the words.

Helping Uyghur children to learn more vocabulary. After collecting three waves of vocabulary test scores from the treatment and control groups, we also investigated the impact of the XJP on Uyghur children's first and second-language vocabulary growth. We found that the XJP improved children's Chinese receptive and Uyghur expressive vocabulary development, though not Chinese expressive and Uyghur receptive vocabulary.

Chinese vocabulary development. The individual growth modeling revealed that the XJP increased the growth rate of Chinese receptive vocabulary. Compared to the control group, after controlling for the children's demographic features (gender, age, school) and baseline language skills (Chinese and Uyghur), children in the XJP classes had a significantly faster Chinese receptive vocabulary growth: 9.17 PPVT points per year (SE $= 3.07$, $p = 0.003$), which corresponded to an effect size of 68 percent of a standard deviation per year. In addition, we found interaction effects of the XJP with children's cohort (young or old), and with school ranking (high or low). In Xinjiang, every public kindergarten has a ranking that indicates their education quality and directly relates to the funding from the government. The ranking standard was designed by the Commission of Education of Xinjiang (CoE). This official kindergarten ranking considered three characteristics of the kindergarten: (1) the physical environment; (2) the teacher background (e.g., education level; years of teaching experience); and (3) the teaching quality. The CoE conducts school and classroom observation and re-evaluates the ranking yearly. There were two levels of ranking in this study: excellent (the higher ranking) and normal (the lower ranking). Specifically, older children benefited more than their younger peers, and children from high-ranking kindergartens showed faster growth than children in low-ranking kindergartens. Researchers did not find differences between the XJP and control children on Chinese expressive vocabulary development growth (see Figure 14.1).

Uyghur vocabulary development. Though only 30 percent of teachers in the XJP can speak Uyghur, interestingly, we detected growth in children's Uyghur expressive vocabulary. After controlling for children's gender, age, school, and baseline language skills, models revealed that the XJP significantly improved the growth of Uyghur children's Uyghur expressive vocabulary growth, by 3.29 EVT points per year (SE = 1.35, p = 0.02). The effect size was 38 percent of a standard deviation per year. There were no statistically significant interaction effects found between age cohorts and differently ranked schools. No significant differences between the XJP and control children were observed in the matter of Uyghur receptive vocabulary development (see Figure 14.2).

Threats to validity. We report a missing data issue of seventeen children's posttest scores, which may lead bias in the estimation of treatment effects. Additionally, the vocabulary test instruments in this study have not been standardized for Uyghur children. Therefore, the effect sizes of the XJP were calculated based on the raw score and standard deviation of the current sample. Caution should be taken when generalizing the results of this study to other populations of minority children in China.

Unpacking the Effectiveness: Why Does the XJP Work?

The purpose of the two studies was to understand how a book-reading intervention could help teachers improve vocabulary instruction, as well as help language-minority children develop vocabulary skills. As the first randomized controlled early literacy intervention conducted in Xinjiang kindergartens, the XJP intervention contributes empirical evidence to illustrate that an intervention focusing on shared book reading can efficiently help teachers and children in a disadvantaged language-minority area.

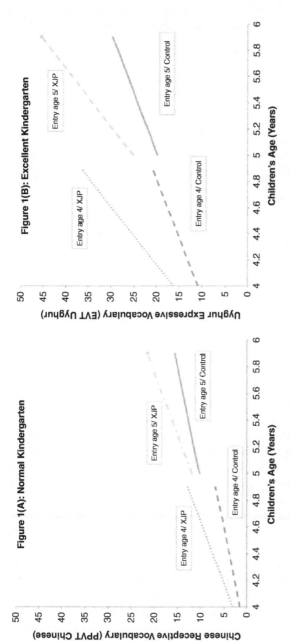

Figure 14.1 Average fitted growth trajectories for Uyghur children in low government ranking (Excellent = 0) and high government ranking (Excellent = 1) kindergartens that describe the effect of Xinjiang Project intervention and entry age cohort on the change in the Chinese receptive vocabulary.

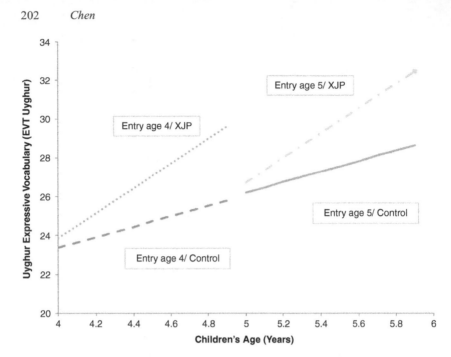

Figure 14.2   Average fitted growth trajectories for Uyghur children describing the effect of Xinjiang Project intervention and entry age cohort on the change in Uyghur expressive vocabulary.

Book Reading as a Powerful Scaffolding

As previous researchers have suggested, book reading is a significant way to provide vocabulary rarely found in daily life (Weizman & Snow, 2001). In the XJP, picture books with diverse topics provided teachers with abundant opportunities to develop language education curriculum and class activities. With the help of picture books, the XJP teachers conducted interesting discussions of diverse topics (e.g., animals, traditional festivals, music, and dance). Book reading not only provided content but also could easily be related to children's daily experiences. Teachers used the pictures in the books to create scaffolded memories and imagined experiences outside of schools, which were likely crucial to language learning.

We also suggest that the varied contents and stories of picture books could be the source of the development of children's Uyghur expressive vocabulary. The topics of the shared reading may encourage children to expand the discussion outside the school. It is possible that children get more opportunity to practice Uyghur expressive vocabulary when they retell stories and share knowledge in Uyghur with parents and peers in their communities.

Reading accelerates meaningful changes in classrooms. We found that in each twenty-minute class session, on average, the XJP teachers introduced about half a standard deviation more information on vocabulary meaning than control teachers, equal to approximately twenty more instances of vocabulary teaching. The number means that after a one-year intervention, each XJP teacher explained vocabulary in thirty-six hundred more instances (5 classes/ week × 18 weeks/semester × 2 semesters/year) than control teachers. These vocabulary learning opportunities are important for second-language learners to conceptualize words and their context. We believe this aspect of the XJP intervention is behind the growth of the children's receptive vocabulary in Chinese. Discussion in the classroom may also provoke an active connection between words and knowledge in the real world (Lonigan & Shanahan, 2009). Real-world knowledge serves as the basis of vocabulary learning for both L1 and L2 (Carlo et al., 2004; Slavin & Chueng, 2005). In the XJP, vocabulary instruction provided a solid base for Uyghur children's understanding. A growth in real-world knowledge may have helped Uyghur children to improve both L1 and L2 vocabulary.

Impacts on Bilingual Education Policy

Given the shift from the BEE to the new kindergarten bilingual curriculum, we note that the early bilingual education policy in Xinjiang has not been static. However, achieving successful bilingual education in Xinjiang is still a serious challenge. According to the Bilingual Education Development Plan for Xinjiang Kindergartens, by 2020, 85 percent of language-minority children in Xinjiang should enjoy two-year kindergarten bilingual education before they enter elementary school. When this goal is achieved everywhere except several remote rural areas, all schools (from elementary to high school) will only provide immersion in Chinese curriculum for all courses (Xinjiang Department of Education, 2013), which means Chinese will be the only academic language in formal school settings. This policy places great emphasis on early bilingual education. Since the two-year bilingual education in kindergartens will be the only opportunity for Uyghur and other language-minority children to prepare for Chinese immersion, this window should be exploited to the utmost. The XJP study is the first and, so far, the only empirical evidence that it is possible to enrich language learning in this context through shared book-reading activities in the classroom, fostering class discussion, and preparing teachers to promote bilingual development. For policy makers, this study suggests the feasibility and promise of the new early bilingual education curriculum.

Acknowledgments

The author thanks funding from the Chinese Ministry of Education. The author gratefully thanks Jing Zhou, Joshua F. Lawrence, Lanbin Min, John Willett, and Catherine E. Snow for valuable feedback and the research assistants and participants of the Xinjiang Project intervention.

15 Young Monolingual and Bilingual Children's Exposure to Academic Language as Related to Language Development and School Achievement

The DASH Project

Paul P. M. Leseman, Lotte F. Henrichs, Elma Blom, and Josje Verhagen

As in many other countries across the world, the Netherlands is becoming increasingly culturally diverse. As a consequence, many elementary school classrooms – especially in urban areas – are characterized by a highly diverse student population (CBS [Statistics Netherlands], 2015). Although research into school careers shows considerable upward mobility among non-Western immigrant groups in the past decades (Ledoux, Roeleveld, Mulder et al., 2015), the education gap between these groups and the native Dutch is significant and persistent, arises already in the preschool period, and becomes hardly smaller after the preschool years. This concerns in particular Turkish Dutch and Moroccan Dutch children who are often exposed to another language than Dutch at home in their early years.

The present chapter focuses on the role of the early home language environment in the development of language skills that are relevant for school learning, in both monolingual and bilingual preschool children, and examines the relations between home language practices and family socioeconomic status. We first review research on the early arising gaps in language skills between mono- and bilingual children and examine how these gaps relate to the home language environment. We then present findings of the DASH project, a longitudinal study in the Netherlands among monolingual Dutch and bilingual Moroccan Dutch and Turkish Dutch preschool children.

Academic Language Development in Mono- and Bilingual Children

The concept of academic language, as used in this chapter, is derived from the theory of Systemic Functional Linguistics and refers to the specific lexical, grammatical, and textual choices that a speaker normally makes in the formal context of school when communicating about school subjects (Halliday & Matthiessen, 2004; Schleppegrell, 2004; Snow & Uccelli, 2009). The language choices of speakers in school contexts realize a specific register of the language (cf. Biber & Conrad, 2009), the *academic language register*, that differs in several respects from other registers of the language, especially the register of informal communication (Schleppegrell, 2004). At the lexical level, academic language typically contains specific, technical words (e.g. 'the industrial revolution'), lexical and grammatical strategies of condensing information ('the old, worried history teacher'), and explicit and specific references to time and space ('In the 18th century, in the capital of France, the guillotine ... ') in order to establish a shared frame of reference with the audience. As a result, academic discourse consists of relatively information-dense sentences that contain many content words compared with sentences in informal talk.

Early Exposure to Academic Language

For young children starting in elementary school, the academic register appears as an already existing code that needs to be mastered. Already in kindergarten, teachers expect children to use language that displays many features of the academic language register. For instance, during sharing time, children are assumed to take up the role of an expert when sharing their personal experiences with others who did not take part in these events, and to express themselves accordingly by using particular lexical and grammatical structures that code for 'authority' and 'truthfulness' (Christie, 2002; Henrichs, 2010; Schleppegrell, 2004). Several studies indicate that preschool children differ considerably in their receptive and productive knowledge of academic vocabulary, complex grammatical constructions, and discourse structuring skills (cf. Hoff, 2006). Children's early ability to understand and produce academic language predicts their understanding of different genres of oral discourse and, at a later stage, also their reading comprehension and achievement in several subject matter areas in elementary school (Chang, 2006; Fang, Schleppegrell, & Cox, 2006; Nagy & Townsend, 2012; Snow & Ucelli, 2009).

Although children below school age are usually not yet confronted with academic language use in formal instruction situations, several genres of informal oral and literate language use in daily family routines are presupposed to support the initial acquisition of academic language. Frequently occurring activities at home, such as talking about children's experiences, sharing memories, explaining and discussing topics of general interest to children (for example about animals or plants), possess linguistic features that resemble academic language use in school settings (Curenton, Craig, & Flanigan, 2008; Snow & Beals, 2006; Weizman & Snow, 2001). Talking about topics of interest elicits the use of technical vocabulary, conventional definitions, and complex sentences that express abstract relationships and processes (Weizman & Snow, 2001). Shared book reading presents children with coherently interrelated sentences that usually contain many new, often specific and rare words in a semantically rich context which helps children grasping the sophisticated meaning of these words (Hammett, Van Kleeck, & Huberty, 2003). However, the frequency of occurrence of these precursor forms of academic language in the home environment differs strongly by socioeconomic status of the family, the education level of the parents and their own literacy practices (e.g., Hoff, 2013; Leseman, Scheele, Messer, & Mayo, 2007).

Bilingual Development

Studies have repeatedly shown that young bilingual children's language proficiency in each language lags behind that of their monolingual peers (Bialystok, Luk, Peets, & Yang, 2010; Hammer et al., 2014; Uccelli & Páez, 2007). This disadvantage cannot be attributed to generally lower language learning abilities of bilingual children. Research has shown that bilinguals' conceptual knowledge that underlies their vocabulary in both of their languages equals that of monolinguals (Pearson, Fernandez, Ledeweg, & Oller, 1997). Previous work has also shown that bilinguals, on average, have equal learning potential as monolinguals of the same socioeconomic background (Scheele, Leseman, & Mayo, 2010). In fact, being bilingual can bring cognitive advantages such as enhanced metalinguistic awareness (Bialystok, 1987), executive control (Calvo & Bialystok, 2014), and working memory (Blom, Küntay, Messer, Verhagen, & Leseman, 2014). Therefore, a more plausible explanation of the vocabulary disadvantage is that bilinguals receive less input in each of their languages due to the fact that exposure to language has to be divided between two languages.

Cross-Language Facilitative Effects

A number of studies have pointed to possible facilitative effects of L1 skills on L2 learning (Cummins, 1991; Genesee, Paradis, & Crago, 2004). According to the linguistic interdependence hypothesis (Cummins, 1991, 2012), bilingual children can use the knowledge and skills acquired in L1 for acquiring L2 and for learning at school in L2. The expected negative effect that bilingual children experience of reduced input per language may be counteracted, at least partly, by a *positive* facilitating effect of L1 knowledge. Although it takes children longer to acquire two languages than it takes them to acquire one, it probably does not take twice as long (Hoff, 2013). Two languages may differ in several features but may also share particular grammatical rules, semantic-conceptual knowledge, and pragmatic uses, constituting a common proficiency that, when first acquired in L1, can be transferred to L2.

The question to what extent L1 knowledge facilitates L2 acquisition and school learning in L2, however, still lacks a clear answer. Contrasting findings have been reported regarding cross-language facilitation at the conceptual level, with either no indication of facilitation (Kan & Kohnert, 2008; Uccelli & Páez, 2007) or an indication of significant positive facilitation (Atwill, Blanchard, Gorin, & Burstein, 2007; Conboy & Thal, 2006; Leseman, 2000). Also with regard to facilitating effects of bilinguals' L1 proficiency on their academic achievement in the majority language, mixed results have been reported. Davison, Hammer, and Lawrence (2011) found a positive effect of bilinguals' L1 (Spanish) receptive vocabulary on L2 (English) reading outcomes in grade 1, but Lervåg and Grøver Aukrust (2010) found only a marginal contribution of L1 (Urdu) vocabulary on L2 (Norwegian) reading comprehension.

Bilingualism, Academic Language, and Academic Achievement

The mixed findings regarding facilitative effects of L1 on L2 and on academic achievement in L2 may point to the role of other factors, in particular the linguistic distance of L1 to L2 and the ways in which L1 is predominantly used in the child's home environment. There are several indications for linguistic distance moderating the potential facilitative effects of L1 on both L2 learning and L2 school achievement (Guglielmi, 2008; Blom, Paradis, & Duncan, 2012). Regarding L1 use, several studies indicate that due to the confound of bilingualism with low socioeconomic status and low parental literacy levels, especially in immigration contexts, the quality of exposure to L1 may not provide adequate support to L2 learning or academic performance in L2. Activities such as shared book reading and decontextualized conversations in L1 occur less frequently on average in bilingual immigrant families, but this is strongly linked to family socioeconomic status (Hoff, 2013). Several studies have demonstrated that, on average, bilingual children have lower proficiency in academic language in both L1 and L2 upon their start in primary school (Leseman, 2000; Limbird, Maluch, Rjosk, Stanat, & Merkens, 2013). In addition, although studies have shown sometimes catching-up of bilingual children in L2 within a few years (Paradis & Jia, 2017), this effect may be less strong with regard to rare and specialized academic vocabulary and to grammatical features that characterize academic discourse in school, with consequences for achievement in school subjects that strongly involve the use of academic language. For example, De Jong and Leseman (2001) found that bilingual Turkish Dutch children, compared to monolingual Dutch children, had initial delays in both word decoding and listening comprehension (seen as oral precursor of reading comprehension), assessed in L2. During the first three grades of primary school, the gap in word decoding closed completely, but the gap in reading comprehension remained substantial and showed lasting effects of the home language environment.

The DASH Project

The DASH project[1] was initiated to investigate the early arising linguistic and educational disadvantages of bilingual Turkish Dutch and Moroccan Dutch children. The Moroccan Dutch children in the study were of Berber descent (which holds for about 70 percent of the Moroccans in the Netherlands) and had Tarifit-Berber as their L1. We specifically aimed at disentangling the effects of the use of L1 versus Dutch as L2 from the academic use of language across first and second language in the preschool home environment. The comparison of Turkish and Tarifit as L1s was especially interesting as the two languages differ in social status and in the access parents have to academic and formal uses of L1 in the wider social context. Turkish is a written language with a rich literary and academic tradition, available to Turkish immigrants through books, newspapers, television, and new media. Tarifit, in contrast, was until recently not written and not instructed in schools in Morocco and is currently still hardly available in written form or through media to Moroccan immigrants. Moreover, Tarifit-Berber actually refers to a variety of dialects and speakers of different dialects have been reported to have difficulties with understanding each other (Laghzaoui, 2011), which enhances the likelihood that the society's majority language will be used. Monolingual Dutch children with varying socioeconomic backgrounds were involved as a comparison group. Below we report the main findings of DASH for the two phases of the study: the preschool age from three to six years and the follow-up of the sample in elementary school from age six to eleven years.

---

[1] The DASH (Development of Academic language in School and at Home) project was a joint research project of the Universities of Utrecht, Amsterdam, and Tilburg. The project was coordinated by Paul Leseman (Utrecht University) and funded by the Netherlands Organization for Scientific Research (file number 411-03-060). The project comprised of a longitudinal whole sample study with three- to six-year-old Dutch, Turkish Dutch and Moroccan Dutch children ($N = 165$ at the start), three longitudinal in-depth studies in small nested sub-samples of the three groups and a follow-up study, following part of the original DASH sample of children through elementary school ($N = 111$). Note that bilingual children were included only if, at the start of the study, their L1 was used in the majority of everyday communicative situations at home.

Early Exposure to Academic Language

Exposure to academic language in children's home environment was examined in two ways. First, we interviewed children's main caregivers using a structured questionnaire in the whole sample, in order to gain insight in the occurrence of particular language practices in the home context. We focused specifically on language practices that would elicit (precursor forms of) school-relevant academic language, such as shared book reading, personal conversations, conversations about topics of interest (e.g., dinosaurs), and story-telling. This revealed large differences between families and, in case of the immigrant families, different patterns of L1 and L2 use across these language practices (Leseman, Mayo, & Scheele, 2009; Scheele et al., 2010). The reported mean frequency of reading with children, regardless of the language in which this was done, was highest in Dutch families, followed by Turkish Dutch families and then the Moroccan Dutch families. Dutch and Turkish Dutch families did not differ significantly in the reported mean frequencies of story-telling and conversations. The Moroccan Dutch families reported a significantly lower frequency of most language practices. Regarding the use of L1 and L2, Turkish Dutch families reported to use L1 more often in all activities than Moroccan Dutch families. Moroccan Dutch families, in contrast, used L2 more often, except in conversations where they, just as the Turkish Dutch families, mainly used L1. Importantly, reading to children in L1 did virtually not occur in Moroccan Dutch families due to the fact that parents could not read in Tarifit and the lack of children's books in this language (a few parents reported to use picture books to tell stories in L1 occasionally). In both groups, overall L1 use was much higher than L2 use.

To obtain an in-depth measure of the use of academic language in children's families, we visited small sub-samples of the participating families at home and videotaped them in a range of semi-standardized conversational settings (Aarts, Demir-Vegter, Kurvers, & Henrichs, 2016). We presented the parents with an age-appropriate picture book, a set of wooden blocks to build a marble slide and a large picture with complex scenery to elicit narrative and explanatory talk. In all three groups, parents sometimes did create linguistic contexts that resembled those of the preschool setting. This typically occurred when parents used a particular conversational situation as an opportunity to teach the children something. Parents then more often asked open-ended questions, expanded on children's utterances, added new information to the conversation, and engaged their children in extended discourse. In doing so, they familiarized their children with the communicative expectations of (pre)school settings and created opportunities for their children to practice academic language. However, most children were not made familiar with the academic register at home (Aarts et al., 2016; Henrichs, 2010; Laghzaoui, 2011).

The variability in academic language input found in both the whole sample questionnaire study and in the sub-sample observational studies could to a large extent be explained by parents' educational levels and jobs, the presence of more than one language at home, parents' literacy levels, and the family constellation (Leseman, Scheele, Messer, & Mayo, 2009). In the in-depth study, in all three groups, higher educated parents were more likely to use features of academic language than lower educated parents (Aarts et al., 2016; Henrichs, 2010; Laghzaoui, 2011). The Moroccan Dutch families participating in the DASH project had on average a lower socioeconomic status than the families in the other two groups, more children per family, and they reported higher levels of parenting stress, which all appeared to be related to the lower reported frequencies of school-related academic language activities (Leseman, Mayo et al., 2009).

Home Language Input and Academic Language Skills

The full DASH sample of monolingual Dutch and bilingual Turkish Dutch and Moroccan Dutch children was followed from age three to age six to examine the relationships between parental language input and children's academic vocabulary development. A test of vocabulary was used that was based on a corpus of words deemed relevant by kindergarten and elementary school teachers for learning in preschool and elementary school. For the purpose of research into bilingual development, equivalent parallel forms of the test were available in Dutch, Turkish, and Tarifit. The questionnaire on language practices at home was administered in personal interviews at four measurement times with a final measurement when children were about six years of age, shortly before their start in grade 1 of elementary school. The reported occurrence of academic language use (a composite of book reading, conversations on topics of interest and story-telling) slightly increased in both the native Dutch and immigrant families over the years. Moreover, in the Turkish Dutch and Moroccan Dutch families, there was a shift from using L1 most in all situations (Turkish Dutch families) or in conversations and story-telling (Moroccan Dutch families) at time 1 to increased use of L2 and decreased use of L1 at later times. More frequent use of L1 was associated with less use of L2 in these families. We termed this pattern 'competition between L1 and L2 for scarce family interaction time' (Leseman, Scheele et al., 2009; Van Dijk, Blom, & Leseman, 2015), a phenomenon that has also been reported by Place and Hoff (2011) regarding Spanish–English bilingual families in the United States.

Table 15.1 *Developmental Relations between L1 and L2 Exposure and Vocabulary Development from Age Three to Age Six Based on Multi-Group Latent Growth Models*

	Moroccan Dutch	Turkish Dutch
Direct transfer		
Intercept L1 vocabulary → intercept L2 vocabulary	.52**	.48**
Competition for exposure time		
Intercept L1 exposure ↔ intercept L2 exposure	−.44**	−.41**
Slope L1 exposure ↔ slope L2 exposure	−.66**	−.66**
Within-language exposure effects		
Intercept L1 exposure → intercept L1 vocabulary	.45**	.37*
Slope L1 exposure → slope L1 vocabulary	.53**	.36*
Intercept L2 exposure → intercept L2 vocabulary	.49**	.50**
Slope L2 exposure → slope L2 vocabulary	.44**	.44***
Cross-language exposure effects		
Intercept L1 exposure → intercept L2 vocabulary	.30+	.34*
Slope L1 exposure → slope L2 vocabulary	.57**	.57**

Note. Significant regressions (→) and covariances (↔) are presented as standardized values.
+$p < .10$. *$p < .05$. **$p < .01$. ***$p < .001$.

Latent growth modelling was applied to relate the changes in the language input that children received to their vocabulary development. The main results are summarized in Table 15.1. The results for the immigrant children, first of all, confirmed the competition hypothesis. Both the overall level (intercept) and the changes (slope) in L1 and L2 input over time were significantly negatively correlated. The results, secondly, provided indications of two types of facilitating effects of L1 on L2. First, both the overall level and growth in L1 vocabulary were substantially positively related to the overall level and growth of L2 vocabulary. Second, *L1 input* was also positively related to *L2 vocabulary*. L2 input, however, was not related to L1 vocabulary. These results suggest that a higher level of academic language input in L1, the language parents are likely most proficient in, can contribute to children's L2 academic vocabulary development in the preschool period (Van Dijk et al., 2015).

L2 Academic Achievement as Related to Academic Language at Age Six

A follow-up study of the DASH project was conducted when the children of the original DASH sample were eleven years old. The guiding question of the follow-up study was to what extent academic language skills at age six, the final measurement time of the first stage of the DASH project, predicted children's academic achievement from age seven to eleven years. Academic language skills at age six were indexed by a composite measure of academic L2 vocabulary and L2 conceptual knowledge (e.g., knowledge of superordinate semantic categories and logo-mathematical concepts such as 'more', 'smaller', 'equal'), on the one hand, and a composite measure of L2 academic discourse comprehension, on the other, as assessed with a narrative task and an instruction task (for details, see Scheele, Leseman, Mayo, & Elbers, 2012). In addition, for the Turkish Dutch and Moroccan Dutch children, we had parallel composite measures of academic vocabulary and discourse skills in their L1.[2]

The analyses proceeded in two steps. First, latent growth models of children's achievement in reading comprehension and mathematics over five measurement waves from grade 1 to grade 5 were estimated in a multi-group design. Figure 15.1 shows the average growth trajectories of the three groups. The results showed that growth in both reading comprehension and math was nearly linear (with a slight acceleration in the early grades). Factor loadings could be constrained to be equal across the three groups. The intercepts, however, differed significantly. Specifically, for reading, the Dutch children outperformed the Turkish Dutch children (with strong effect sizes according to Cohen's criteria) and the Turkish Dutch children outperformed the Moroccan Dutch children. For mathematics, the Dutch children outperformed both immigrant groups as well (again strong effects), but there were no differences between these groups. Our analyses did not show differences in slopes across the groups for reading comprehension, indicating that the initial gaps between the Dutch, Turkish Dutch, and Moroccan Dutch children remained the same over time and that children grew at similar rates. For mathematics, the two immigrant groups showed significantly *faster* growth than the Dutch group, indicating that the immigrant children significantly and substantially caught up in mathematics during elementary school, with the initial gap in mathematics achievement at age seven being about halved at age eleven.

In the second step, we analysed the relationships of age six academic language proficiency in L1 and L2 with the overall level (intercept) and growth (slope) of reading comprehension and math during elementary school. The main results are presented in Table 15.2. The composite measures of academic language skills in L2 at age six were strong significant predictors of the overall level in reading comprehension in all groups and slightly less so, but still significantly, of mathematics. There were no significant relations between children's proficiency in academic language at age six, on the one

---

[2] Productive academic discourse skills could not be used in these analyses as the vast majority of the Moroccan Dutch children were no longer able or willing to use their L1 in the productive narrative and instruction tasks.

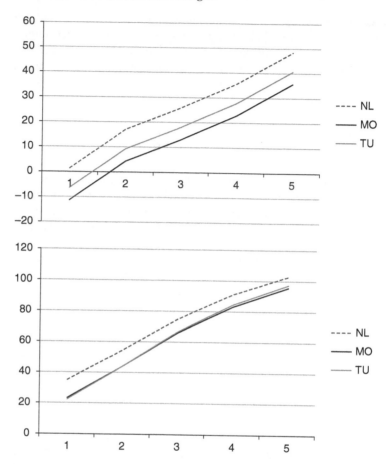

Figure 15.1 Development of reading comprehension and mathematical achievement from first to fifth grade of elementary school, based on latent growth modelling.

hand, and the growth of reading comprehension and math thereafter, on the other hand. Taken together, these findings provide evidence that differences in early Dutch academic language skills are related to subsequent academic achievement. Note that the intercept in growth modelling is not merely the first measurement of an ability but present as a component in all subsequent measurements of this ability.

In a separate analysis, we examined the relationships between L1 academic language proficiency and L2 academic achievement of the Turkish Dutch and Moroccan Dutch children (see Table 15.2). L1 academic language skill was significantly and positively related to the intercept of

Table 15.2 *Academic Language Skills in Dutch and L1 Predicting the Intercept and Slope of Reading Comprehension and Mathematical Achievement through Elementary School (Standardized Regression Coefficients)*

	Dutch		Moroccan Dutch		Turkish Dutch	
Reading comprehension	Intercept	Slope	Intercept	Slope	Intercept	Slope
Dutch academic vocabulary	.54**	.25	.50**	.03	.61**	.15
Dutch academic discourse	.59**	.25	.54**	−.09	.60**	.08
L1 academic vocabulary			−.39*	.32$^+$	.33*	.21
L1 academic discourse			.25	.01	.30$^+$	.25
Mathematical achievement						
Dutch academic vocabulary	.30*	−.17	.48**	−.26	.55**	−.21
Dutch academic discourse	.36*	−.01	.41*	−.27	.47**	−.32$^+$
L1 academic vocabulary			−.13	.01	.39*	−.36*
L1 academic discourse			.27	.03	.39*	−.28

Note. Separate analyses were conducted with Dutch, respectively, L1 academic skills as predictors.
$^+p < .10$. $^*p < .05$. $^{**}p < .01$.

reading comprehension and math in the Turkish Dutch group, but not (composite of L1 academic discourse skills) or significantly negatively (composite of L1 academic vocabulary and concept knowledge) in the Moroccan Dutch group. These findings suggest a facilitating effect of L1 academic language skills on L2 academic achievement for the Turkish Dutch group, supporting Cummins' interdependency hypothesis, but not for the Moroccan Dutch group. It is likely that the aforementioned difference in social prestige between Turkish and Tarafit-Berber plays a role. The findings suggest that a facilitating effect of L1 on L2 is limited in situations in which academic use of L1 is not supported in the wider social-cultural context, and examples of formal academic use of L1 are not easily accessible through, for example, books, newspapers, television, and new media (Leseman, Mayo et al., 2009).

Conclusions and Implications

The studies of the DASH project described in this chapter show that the experience young children have with school-relevant academic language use at home before they start elementary education differs greatly depending on socioeconomic status and immigrant background. These differences are related to differences in the development of academic language skills in the preschool years, and are likely to explain, at least in part, the early education gap of children from low socioeconomic and immigrant backgrounds. These findings are fully in line with the literature reviewed in the first part of this chapter. For bilingual children in the Netherlands, the lower amount of exposure and overall lower degree of academic use of Dutch is an additional explanation of the early education gap. Yet, regarding academic achievement in elementary school, at least for the Turkish Dutch children investigated, exposure to academic Turkish language was found to partly compensate for this disadvantage. For the Moroccan Dutch group, no compensatory effect of L1 on academic achievement was found, which was likely due to the lower social status of their L1, the lack of literacy materials in L1 and the lower maintenance of L1 compared to the Turkish group, as was argued above. In both the Turkish Dutch and Moroccan Dutch group, during the preschool period, L1 academic vocabulary was positively related to L2 academic language skills, and L1 academic language exposure was positively related to L2 academic vocabulary, suggesting facilitating effects of L1 on L2 in both groups, at least in the preschool period.

Although exposure to Dutch academic language at home was found beneficial for the immigrant children in the current studies, immigrant parents may lack the proficiency to provide the linguistic structures and vocabulary of Dutch academic language to their children. In these cases, it is recommendable to provide Dutch language education to children from these groups through high-quality centre-based programmes at an early age, as is currently the case on a large scale in the Netherlands. In addition, non-Dutch speaking parents can be effectively involved in familiarizing their children with academic language in their L1, which may contribute to L2 development in the preschool period as well as subsequent academic achievement in elementary school, via facilitating effects of L1 on L2. Supporting parents by providing home-based programmes that can increase the occurrence of academic language use in L1 is recommendable. Regarding languages such as Tarifit, contextual resources that can support academic use of these languages in families should be made available.

In the above-reviewed research, early academic language skills were not related to the *growth* of academic skills in elementary school. This suggests that further development of these skills during elementary school depends on other factors than the preschool home environment and the language skills acquired in that period. Instruction in school is a likely candidate. Especially in the case of mathematics, the substantial catching-up effect that was found for the immigrant children is likely to be attributable to effective instruction in a domain that is relatively new for all children. The lack of such catching-up effect for reading comprehension is a worrying finding of the current study, because it suggests that instruction in school may not reduce early gaps in this domain. We recommend a stronger focus in the early grades of elementary school on explicit academic language instruction as a new subject domain, much like mathematics, both at the lexical, syntactic and pragmatic level, instead of academic language skills being merely presupposed.

16   Cross-Linguistic Relations among Bilingual and Biliterate Learners

C. Patrick Proctor and Qianqian Zhang-Wu

It is possible that the idea of "learning through language" evokes a monolingual perspective since the word *language* is in fact singular. Too often, this is the case, and more specifically, we too often assume that learning through language reflects learning through the *English language*. In this chapter, we consider the plural, *languages*, and conceptualize the notion of "learning through languages" from a bilingual[1] perspective. We operationalize learning by focusing on cross-linguistic relations among well-studied language and literacy variables, and target specific bilingual populations for whom relatively large bodies of empirical data exist. Our goal here is to provide an overview of how applied researchers study cross-linguistic associations and what they have found with respect to associations between language and literacy variables.

This chapter is structured in three sections. In the first section, we present results from a review of the extant cross-linguistic research on four bilingual pairs: Spanish–English, Chinese[2]–English, French–English, and Korean–English. We summarize our review methods, the contexts in which the studies took place, and the nature of cross-linguistic associations between five language and literacy components: phonological and phonemic awareness, morphological awareness, vocabulary, reading comprehension, and orthographic skills. In the second section, we provide a cross-linguistic analysis of data collected from Spanish–English bilingual and biliterate children in grades K–4 from three dual-language immersion[3] programs in the United States. The analysis sheds light on

---

[1] In using the term *bilingual*, we defer to Grosjean's (2010) argument that "there is a long tradition in the field of extending the notion of bilingualism to those who use two or more languages on a regular basis" (p. 4).

[2] Given the complexity and diversity among Chinese language, "Chinese" was used throughout the paper as an umbrella term for Cantonese and Mandarin.

[3] Dual language programs bring native speakers of English and, in this case, Spanish, together to learn content and language simultaneously.

the findings from the first section. Finally, we provide a set of cautions and recommendations for cross-linguistic researchers given the state of the field.

Literature Review

Method

We searched three databases: ERIC, Linguistics and Language Behavior Abstracts, and PsycInfo. We identified studies that assessed cross-linguistic relations among English and other language pairings (e.g., Spanish–English, Arabic–English) that were written in the twenty-first century. We limited our focus to peer reviewed scholarly journal articles. While we recognize the irony, only studies written in English were included in this review.

The study of bilingualism between English and other languages is broad. We first used the key word *bilingual**, which resulted in 33,580 results, and in language pairings (with English), including Chichewa, Chinese, Farsi, French, Greek, Italian, Korean, Malay, Nahuatl, Oriya, Russian, Spanish, Tamil, Urdu, and Zulu. We excluded language pairs that appeared in a single study, which left four major languages paired with English: Spanish, Chinese, French, and Korean. We narrowed the parameters to specific literacy constructs – *vocabulary, reading, language, literacy* – and matched those with the terms *cross-linguistic* or *transfer*, trimming to a pool of sixty-eight studies. Two studies (Bialystok, Luk, & Kwan, 2005; Wang, Anderson, Cheng, & Park, 2008) covered two of the four language pairings simultaneously and were counted twice.

We included English as a second language (ESL; i.e., studies conducted among language learners in English-speaking countries) and English as a foreign language (EFL; i.e., studies conducted among language learners in non-English-speaking countries) contexts in a search for commonalities. After deletion for duplicates, the final sample was comprised of forty-three total studies. See Table 16.1 for an overview.

Fully forty-one of the forty-three studies used quantitative methods such as multiple regression, hierarchical linear modeling, structural equation modeling/path analysis, and factor analysis. Only one study (Gort, 2006) adopted qualitative methods (cross-case analysis), and another (Soto Huerta, 2012) employed mixed-methods techniques (mixed-sequential). While most research was cross-sectional, twelve studies were longitudinal. One study (Gort, 2006) reported a sample size of less than ten. The majority included samples ranging between fifty and two hundred students, and three studies reported results from analyses with samples comprised by greater than one thousand participants

Table 16.1 *Summary of Studies*

Article	Languages	Sample/location	Ages/grades	Focus
Anthony et al. (2009)	Spanish–English	Bilingual preschoolers/Head Start	3–4 years old	Vocabulary, letter knowledge, phonological awareness
Atwill et al. (2007)	Spanish–English	Bilinguals qualified for free/reduced-price lunch/US	Kindergarteners	Phonemic awareness, vocabulary
Bialystok, Luk, and Kwan (2005)	Chinese–English; Spanish–English; Hebrew–English	Children living in the same metropolitan area/Canada	first graders	Literacy, orthographic differences, reading
Cardenas-Hagan, Carlson, and Pollard-Durodola (2007)	Spanish–English	Children of immigrants/US	Kindergarteners	Literacy skills, phonological awareness
Chuang et al. (2011)	Chinese–English	EFL students/Taiwan	ninth graders	Reading
Chung et al. (2013)	Chinese–English	EFL students/Hong Kong	Kindergarteners, second and fourth graders	Phonological awareness, word reading, auditory processing
Deacon et al. (2007)	French–English	Canadian bilingual children/French immersion programs in Canada	three-year study starting from first graders	Morphological awareness, reading
Deacon et al. (2013)	French–English	Canadian bilingual children/French immersion programs in Canada	First graders	Orthographic processing, reading
Dickinson et al. (2004)	Spanish–English	Low-SES bilinguals/Head Start	Preschoolers	Phonological awareness
Dixon et al. (2012)	Chinese–English; Malay–English; Tamil–English	EFL students/Singapore	Kindergarteners	Vocabulary, phonological awareness

Study	Languages	Participants/Program	Grade/Age	Focus
Freinauer et al. (2013)	Spanish–English	Bilingual children/two-way immersion programs in US	Kindergarten to second graders	Literacy skills, reading
Gort (2006)	Spanish–English	Emergent bilinguals/two-way Bilingual Education program in America	Second graders	Writing, vocabulary, interliteracy
Gottardo et al. (2014)	Spanish–English	Bilingual children/Canada	Fourth to sixth graders	Word reading, reading
Hipfner-Boucher, Lam, and Chen (2014)	Chinese–English; French–English English	Chinese-speaking Canadian children in three programs/ Canada	First graders	Phonological and morphological awareness, word reading, vocabulary
Howard et al. (2012)	Spanish–English	Bilingual children/two-way immersion programs in US	Three-year study starting from second graders	Spelling errors
Hu (2013)	Chinese–English	EFL students/Taiwan	Third graders	Phonological and morphological awareness
Jared, Cormier, Levy, and Wade-Woolley (2011)	French–English	Canadian bilingual children/French immersion programs in Canada	Kindergarteners	Reading, vocabulary, phonological awareness
Kang (2013)	Korean–English	Bilingual children/English immersion school in Korea	Kindergarteners	Word reading, vocabulary, phonological awareness
Kim (2009)	Korean–English	Bilingual children/bilingual programs in America	Kindergarteners	Phonological awareness, literacy skills
Leider et al. (2013)	Spanish–English	Latino students/US	Third, fourth, and fifth graders	Reading, vocabulary, morphology
Lesaux et al. (2010)	Spanish–English	Latino students/US	Fourth and fifth graders	Reading, language, decoding
Lindsey et al. (2003)	Spanish–English	Low-SES Latino students/early transition bilingual program in Texas	Kindergarteners	Phonological awareness, vocabulary, reading
Lopez and Greenfield (2004)	Spanish–English	Bilingual children/Head Start	48–66 months old	Phonological awareness
Lopez (2012)	Spanish–English	Bilinguals/84% in Head Start	Preschoolers	Phonological awareness

Table 16.1 (*cont.*)

Article	Languages	Sample/location	Ages/grades	Focus
Luo, Chen, and Geva (2014)	Chinese–English	Children of immigrants/ Canada	Kindergarteners and first graders	Phonological and morphological awareness
Miller et al. (2006)	Spanish–English	Latino ELLs/US	Kindergarten to third graders	Reading, oral language skills
Nakamoto et al. (2008)	Spanish–English	Low-SES Latino students/US	Third to sixth graders	Word reading, passage comprehension, listening comprehension, vocabulary
Pasquarella et al. (2011)	Chinese–English	Children of immigrants/Canada	First, second, and fourth graders	Morphological awareness
Pasquarella et al. (2014)	French–English	Canadian bilingual children/ French immersion programs in Canada	First and second graders	Word reading, orthographic processing
Proctor et al. (2006)	Spanish–English	Bilingual children/ U.S.	Fourth graders	Reading, literacy skills, vocabulary
Proctor et al. (2010)	Spanish–English	Bilingual children/ U.S.	Fourth graders	Reading, alphabetic knowledge
Ramírez, Chen, and Pasquarella (2013)	Spanish–English	Spanish-speaking ELLs/ Canada	Fourth and seventh graders	Vocabulary, reading
Siu and Ho (2015)	Chinese–English	EFL students/ Hong Kong	First and third graders	Reading, syntactic skills
Soto Huerta (2012)	Spanish–English	Emergent bilinguals/ U.S.	Fourth graders	Reading
Sun-Alperin and Wang (2011)	Spanish–English	Latino students/ U.S.	Second and third graders	phonological and orthographic processing skills
Uccelli and Páez (2007)	Spanish–English	Low-SES bilingual children/ U.S.	Kindergarteners and first graders	Oral language proficiency, literacy skills
Wang et al. (2008)	Chinese–English; Korean–English	Immigrant children/U.S.	8 years old	Auditory processing, phonemic awareness, reading

Study	Languages	Population/Context	Age/Grade	Measures
Wang, Cheng, and Chen (2006)	Chinese–English	immigrant children/U.S.	8 years old	Morphological awareness, reading, biliteracy
Wang, Ko, and Choi (2009)	Korean–English	Children of immigrants/ Korean language school in America	Second, third, and fourth graders	Morphological awareness, reading, word reading
Wang, Park, and Lee (2006)	Korean–English	Children of immigrants/ Korean language school in America	First, second, and third graders	Phonological and orthographic skills, reading, word reading
Yeong and Liow (2012)	Chinese–English	EFL students/Singapore	Kindergarteners	Phonological awareness, phonemic awareness
Yeong, Fletcher, and Bayliss (2014)	Chinses–English; English	EFL students/ Singapore Monolinguals/Australia	8–9 years old; 11–12 years old	Phonological and orthographic skills, word reading, spelling
Zhao et al. (2015)	Spanish–English	Bilingual children/Head Start	4–5 years old	Vocabulary, reading, phonological awareness

(Cardenas-Hagan, Carlson, & Pollard-Durodola, 2007; Chuang, Joshi, & Dixon, 2011; Miller, Heilmann, Nockerts, Iglesias, Fabiano, & Francis, 2006).

Geographic and Socioeconomic Contexts

The research contexts of the collected studies varied with respect to location and socioeconomic status (SES) of participants. For example, while all twenty identified studies on Spanish–English associations were conducted with Latinx students in North America, the four studies on French–English associations were conducted among English-speaking children enrolled in French immersion programs in Canada. Conversely, studies on Korean–English and Chinese–English cross-linguistic relations had more diverse contexts, including not only immigrant descendants participating in bilingual immersion programs in the United States and Canada (e.g., Hipfner-Boucher et al., 2014; Kim, 2009) or learning ESL in public schools and heritage language in weekend language schools (e.g., Luo, Chen, & Geva, 2014; Wang et al., 2008), but also Chinese or Korean students in EFL contexts either through public school education (e.g., Chuang, Joshi, & Dixon, 2011; Pasquarella, Chen, Lam, & Luo, 2011; Siu & Ho, 2015) or private English immersion schools (Kang, 2013).

The role of SES was distinctive by language pairs. A number of Spanish–English studies recruited participants from Head Start, a US Department of Health and Human Services program which supports early childhood education for low-income children (e.g., Anthony et al., 2009; Lopez & Greenfield, 2004; Zhao, Dixon, Quiroz, & Chen, 2015). By contrast, all four French–English studies reported on middle- or upper-class Canadian children enrolled in "an optional program" to acquire "a second, socially valued language" (Jared et al., 2011, p. 2). As children from higher SES families often have access to better educational and parental resources, they are more likely to be advantaged, particularly with respect to performance on the types of standardized measures of language and literacy used in many of the reviewed studies (see, e.g., Valdés & Figueroa, 1994). Thus any comparisons relating to children's bilingualism and biliteracy development patterns across contexts should be made with caution.

Nature of Cross-Linguistic Associations

Phonological, phonemic awareness, and word reading. Constructs in this domain represent the ability to understand, analyze, identify, and decode the phonological structures of language. Twenty-one studies were found in this category, representing an area of interest across all four language pairs, with positive cross-linguistic correlations reported. While research exploring Chinese–English associations targeted Chinese phonological awareness and English word reading (e.g., Chung et al., 2013; Hipfner-Boucher et al., 2014; Hu, 2013), research on Spanish–English associations was somewhat broader, exploring correlations between Spanish and English phonological awareness (e.g., Anthony et al., 2009; Lopez & Greenfield, 2004) as well as phonemic awareness (Atwill et al., 2007). Among French–English and Korean–English studies, phonological awareness of one language (French/Korean) was found to be predictive of decoding (Jared et al., 2011; Kim, 2009) and comprehension (Jared et al., 2011) in the other (English). Comparing children from four different language groups, including Spanish–English and Chinese–English bilinguals, Bialystok et al. (2005) reported cross-linguistic associations between code-based skills were more likely to occur when languages were similar (e.g., Indo-European with Spanish–English) and shared a common writing system (e.g., alphabetic vs. logographic).

Morphological awareness. Morphological awareness represents the ability to interpret and manipulate word structures in the language. There are three types of morphology generally recognized in this literature: inflectional (e.g., *type* begets *typed, typing, types*), derivational (e.g., *happy* begets *unhappy, happily, happiness*), and compound (e.g., *snow + man = snowman*). Languages differ regarding morphological structures. Inflectional and derivational words make up a significant proportion among alphabetic languages such as English and Spanish. Conversely, compound words are proportionally more common in logographic languages such as Chinese (Kuo & Anderson, 2006).

Seven morphology studies were reviewed, and despite varying morphological structures across languages, research in all four language pairings showed positive cross-linguistic correlations, suggesting morphological awareness in one language may facilitate literacy development in the other. For instance, Deacon, Wade-Woolley, and Kirby (2007) found that, for French–English bilinguals, early performance on French morphological awareness correlated with only French but not English reading. As children aged, however, French morphological awareness was associated with English reading as well. This points to the potential possibility that cross-language influences may change over time. Focusing specifically on the cross-language influences of derivational awareness between Spanish and English, Ramírez et al. (2013) found that Spanish derivational awareness was associated with English cognate vocabulary, but not with noncognates. Pasquarella et al. (2011) identified associations between English compound awareness and Chinese vocabulary and reading comprehension.

Vocabulary. Only studies with Spanish–English bilinguals constituted the sixteen cross-linguistic vocabulary studies. Vocabulary knowledge in Spanish was associated with English cognate vocabulary (Ramírez et al., 2013), reading comprehension (Proctor, August, Carlo, & Snow, 2006), word reading (Zhao et al., 2015), phonemic awareness (Atwill et al., 2007), and phonological awareness (Anthony et al., 2009; Uccelli & Páez, 2007). Spanish vocabulary knowledge was also found to interact with English word reading, such that students with stronger English decoding skills were more likely to benefit from Spanish vocabulary knowledge on their English reading (Nakamoto, Lindsey, & Manis, 2008; Proctor et al., 2006). Thus, as articulated by Cummins (1979), children may have to achieve a certain level of proficiency in the L2 before effects of L1 vocabulary become manifest.

Reading comprehension. Twenty-six studies across all four language pairs were found for reading comprehension, and all reported evidence for positive cross-linguistic associations. Feinauer et al. (2013), Nakamoto et al. (2008), and Proctor et al. (2006) found that cross-language associations in reading occurred not only with code-based skills (e.g., letter knowledge), but also with meaning-based (e.g., vocabulary) skills for Spanish–English bilinguals. Based on longitudinal data of thirty thousand Chinese–English bilinguals' reading performance in Taiwan, Chuang et al. (2011) further identified that, in addition to Chinese reading proficiency, gender and school type (i.e., urban, rural) also correlated with English reading performance, implying that cross-linguistic associations may vary depending on the environmental conditions in which bilingual children are raised. Of note in this study is the unusually large sample size.

Orthographic skills. While areas such as phonological and phonemic awareness, or reading comprehension, have been given relatively broad attention, there has been less focus on cross-language associations among orthographic skills (Sun-Alperin & Wang, 2011), which refers to children's ability to develop awareness toward patterns of printed languages. Five studies across three language pairs addressed orthographic skills, including Spanish–English (Sun-Alperin & Wang, 2011), French–English (Deacon et al., 2013; Pasquarella et al., 2014), and Korean–English (Wang et al., 2006).

Sun-Alperin and Wang (2011) and Wang et al. (2006) found that despite evidence of associations in L1 phonological awareness and L2 reading, orthographic skills tended toward intralinguistic, rather than cross-linguistic, associations. Deacon et al. (2013) explored orthographic processing and word reading among French–English bilinguals in Canadian immersion programs, noting associations between French orthographic processing and English reading only when orthographic features were common across languages.

Directionality of Cross-Linguistic Associations

While a great many of the published studies show evidence of cross-linguistic associations across language pairs, relatively few sought to disentangle nuances of "the direction of transfer of the skill between the two languages" (Yeong & Liow, 2012, p. 114). While most research explored one-way relationships via regression modeling, other researchers have questioned the degree to which cross-linguistic associations are bidirectional such that L1 skills predict L2, but L2 in turn predicts L1 (e.g., Bialystok, Luk, & Kwan, 2005; Cook, 2003; Deacon, Wade-Woolley, & Kirby, 2007; Pasquarella et al., 2011).

Using parallel measures of English and Chinese morphological awareness, Pasquarella et al. (2011) showed evidence of bidirectionality between English compound morphological awareness and Chinese vocabulary. This finding might relate to the unique morphological features of Chinese vocabulary, in which 80 percent of the lexicon is comprised by compound words (Kuo & Anderson, 2006). Deacon et al. (2007) also identified evidence of bidirectionality between English-French bilingual children's morphological awareness and reading performance from grades 1 to 3. However, reciprocity was found only in later performance, suggesting perhaps that directionality interacts with age and/or language proficiencies.

Other findings were inconsistent. In examining Chinese–English biliteracy, Wang et al. (2006) provided evidence of morphological awareness predicting unidirectionally from L2 (English) compound awareness to L1 (Chinese) character reading and reading comprehension. Directionality did not move from L1 to L2. In contrast, Chung et al. (2013) found evidence only for cross-linguistic associations between Chinese (L1) phonological awareness and English (L2) word reading, indicating that children in EFL contexts may rely on L1 strategies to acquire L2 literacy, but not the reverse. Similarly, Gottardo et al. (2014) found evidence only for unidirectional associations from Spanish word reading to English reading comprehension among Latino children ten to twelve years of age in Canada.

A Cross-Linguistic Exploration

Given the associations established in the "Literature Review" section, we present some cross-sectional data to model some of the approaches that characterize those taken in many of the studies reviewed above. Specifically, we examine cross-linguistic associations between word reading, vocabulary, semantics, and reading comprehension among a cross-sectional sample of 117 Spanish–English bilingual students in kindergarten through fourth grade in three dual-language immersion schools in the United States.

Table 16.2 *Overview of Sample*

Gender		Grade					Totals
Male	Female	K	1	2	3	4	
44	73	60	17	10	12	18	117

Method

Participants and setting. Participants were students who attended schools that were part of an ongoing research and development project for a network of dual-language immersion programs across the United States. Students came from both native English, native Spanish, and Spanish–English bilingual backgrounds. For the purposes of illustration, and due to sample size restrictions, we include them together.

Measures. Participating schools assessed their students using subtests from the Spanish and English versions of the Woodcock–Muñoz Language Proficiency Battery – Revised (WLPB-R; Woodcock, Muñoz, & Sandoval, 2005). **Word reading** was assessed using the Letter-Word Identification subtest in which students read a list of words, ordered in increasing difficulty, until reaching a ceiling of six incorrect items in a row. **Vocabulary** was assessed using the Picture Vocabulary subtest in which students were presented a series of pictured objects ordered by increasing difficulty and named the object to the assessor. Ceiling for Picture Vocabulary is set at six incorrect items in a row. **Semantics** was assessed with the Verbal Analogies subtest in which students provided a verbal response to a cloze analogy (e.g., *Up is to down, as left is to* _____) until six consecutive incorrect items were recorded. **Reading comprehension** was assessed using the Passage Comprehension subtest in which students read cloze passages of increasing difficulty and provided a verbal response to the missing item, until five consecutive incorrect responses were recorded. For the straightforward purpose of exploring cross-linguistic associations, raw scores were used in all analyses.

Analyses and results. Table 16.2 presents the distribution of students. Thirty-eight percent of the sample was male, the majority of students (51 percent) were in kindergarten, while the remainder was spread evenly across grades 1–4.

Table 16.3 presents correlations between the English and Spanish variables. Not surprisingly, intralinguistic correlations were strong for both Spanish and English, ranging between .542 and .891 for English, and between .344 and .737 for Spanish (all $ps < .01$). Cross-linguistically, the strongest associations

Table 16.3 *Descriptive Statistics and Correlations*

	1	2	3	4	5	6	7	8
1. EWR	1							
2. EPV	.542**	1						
3. EVA	.543**	.772**	1					
4. EPC	.891**	.604**	.649**	1				
5. SWR	.793**	.309**	.363**	.633**	1			
6. SPV	.055	-.331**	-.241*	-.122	.391**	1		
7. SVA	-.029	-.162	-.043	-.054	.344**	.737**	1	
8. SPC	.678**	.179	.304**	.489**	.760**	.518**	.423**	1
Mean (SD)	22.36	24.84	12.00	7.96	24.24	16.48	10.06	5.79
	(16.52)	(7.31)	(4.78)	(6.39)	(12.58)	(9.37)	(6.89)	(4.16)

Note. E = English; S = Spanish; WR = Word Reading; PV = Picture Vocabulary; VA = Verbal Analogies; PC = Passage Comprehension. *Correlation is significant at the 0.05 level (2-tailed). **Correlation is significant at the 0.01 level (2-tailed).

occurred between English and Spanish word reading (.793, $p < .01$) and English word reading and Spanish reading (.678, $p < .01$). Spanish word reading and English reading were also highly and significantly correlated (.633, $p < .01$). Spanish and English reading correlated at .489 ($p < .01$). Interestingly, English verbal analogies correlated significantly with both Spanish word reading and reading comprehension (.363 and .304, respectively, $p < .01$), but Spanish verbal analogies were not significantly associated with any English variables. Spanish vocabulary was negatively associated with both English vocabulary and verbal analogies ($-.331$ and $-.241$, $p < .01$).

We next ran regression models predicting English and Spanish reading (Tables 16.4 and 16.5, respectively). Both tables display the same model-building process that begins with a baseline controlling for grade, followed by an uncontrolled intralinguistic, an uncontrolled cross-linguistic, and a controlled cross-linguistic model. In taking this approach, we examine cross-linguistic effects with and without variance explained by intralinguistic factors.

Predicting English, the intralinguistic model shows word reading and language (in this case, verbal analogies) predicting English reading comprehension. The uncontrolled cross-linguistic model shows Spanish word reading predicting English comprehension (note correlation between English and Spanish word reading in Table 16.3 was .793, $p < .01$), with a significant negative association between Spanish vocabulary and English reading (note correlation between English and Spanish vocabulary in Table 16.3 was $-.331$, $p < .01$). When English variables are controlled in the second cross-linguistic model (Model 3), unique positive effects of Spanish word reading and negative effects of Spanish picture vocabulary are washed out and only the English predictors are significant. A similar phenomenon is noted in predicting Spanish. Similar to the intralinguistic English model, Spanish word reading and language (picture vocabulary) were the significant predictors of Spanish reading. In the uncontrolled cross-linguistic model (Model 2), English word reading predicts Spanish reading, and English and Spanish reading are negatively associated, which is eliminated when Spanish controls are entered into the cross-linguistic model (Model 3).

Discussion and Directions

The purpose of this brief overview of data was to provide an example of cross-linguistic analysis with a focus on bidirectionality, which highlights some inherent challenges in quantitative cross-linguistic research. First, it has become clear that phonemic and phonological awareness (including later instantiations of these as word reading) are robust to cross-language associations. This is not a novel finding (see Genesee, Dressler, Geva, & Kamil, 2006 for an early preview), and there is good research that suggests these phonemic

Table 16.4 *English Reading Model: Grade-Controlled Spanish Language and Literacy Predicting English Reading, with and without Covariates*

	Model 1		Model 2		Model 3	
	Intralinguistic		Uncontrolled cross-linguistic		Controlled cross-linguistic	
Variable	*B*	*SE*	*B*	*SE*	*B*	SE
Intercept	−2.56**	1.0	5.5**	1.1	−.04	1.4
Grade	.92*	.443	3.1**	.46	1.6**	.49
English variables						
EWR	.28**	.04			.28**	.05
EVA	.22*	.11			.22*	.09
EPV	.04	.06				
Spanish variables						
SWR			.2**	06	.01	.06
SVA			.06	.1	−.07	.09
SPV			−.28**	.07	−.01	.08
SPC			−.28	.2	−.29	.19
R^2	.85		.71		.89	
df	73		73		61	

Note. E = English; S − Spanish; WR = Word Reading; PV = Picture Vocabulary; VA = Verbal Analogies; PC − Passage Comprehension.
*Correlation is significant at the 0.05 level (2-tailed). **Correlation is significant at the 0.01 level (2-tailed).

associations are often driven by the orthographic distance between the languages in question. That is, Spanish and English share an alphabet, while Chinese and English do not. As such, phonemic awareness and word reading in the two orthographically closer languages (Spanish and English) are more likely to be cross-linguistically associated than are two orthographically distant languages like Chinese and English. These code-based outcomes are more robust to cross-linguistic associations when the systems (e.g. alphabetic vs. logographic) and scripts (Roman, Cyrillic, Hànzì) of two languages are common (Bialystok et al., 2005). Thus, one recommendation for cross-linguistic researchers is to move exploratory analyses beyond phonology, phonemics, and word reading into the much more elusive and multiply determined domains of language proficiency.

Interestingly, however, some newer research reviewed here with orthographically distinctive languages shows evidence of cross-linguistic associations, suggesting that phonology (and phonological awareness) reflects a commonality to the species relative to sound symbolism (Blasi, Wichmann,

Table 16.5 *Spanish Reading Model: Grade-Controlled English Language and Literacy Predicting Spanish Reading, with and without Covariates*

	Model 1		Model 2		Model 3	
	Intralinguistic		Uncontrolled cross-linguistic		Controlled cross-linguistic	
Variable	*B*	*SE*	*B*	*SE*	*B*	SE
Intercept	.01	.75	3.98**	.87	.57	1.1
Grade	1.1**	.28	1.69**	.37	.92*	.36
Spanish variables						
SWR	.1**	.04			.15**	.04
SVA	.03	.06				
SPV	.09*	.04			.05	.03
English variables						
EWR			.1*	.04	.02	.04
EVA			.05	.09	.07	.08
EPV			−.05	.05	−.03	.05
EPC			−.23*	.1	−.13	.1
R^2	.64		.54		.72	
df	75		67		60	

Note. E = English; S = Spanish; WR = Word Reading; PV = Picture Vocabulary; VA = Verbal Analogies; PC = Passage Comprehension.
* = Correlation is significant at the 0.05 level (2-tailed). ** = Correlation is significant at the 0.01 level (2-tailed).

Hammarström, Stadler, & Christiansen, in press). Thus, phonological awareness in one language might be reasonably assumed to "transfer" to another irrespective of orthographic distance. Relatedly, to date, most research has focused on the early years, which caters to analyses of early reading skills (e.g., phonological/phonemic awareness) and their cross-linguistic associations. Far less frequent are longitudinal studies that follow fluent biliterate dual-language learners into the later years of middle school while also examining crucial contextual variables more systematically. More studies that target these less-explored dimensions of cross-linguistics are needed and would make even stronger contributions if they were mixed in their methodological approaches.

Quantitative researchers also need to address what it means to find cross-linguistic effects in uncontrolled cross-linguistic models, which are then washed away when intralinguistic variables are added (Tables 16.4 and 16.5). The determination is that a Language X variable may predict a Language Y outcome, but not uniquely, once analogue Language Y predictors are entered into the regression model (see Kieffer, 2012). The question is whether and how that matters. The statistical interpretation of cross-linguistic findings being washed away by intralinguistic controls is that the "true" variance in an outcome is explained intralinguistically. Any unique cross-linguistic effects are artifacts of shared variance between predictors. But practically, this means little for the kindergarten teacher of a Spanish-speaking child who speaks no English but is proficient in Spanish. Thus we recommend that more cross-linguistic research engage qualitative approaches that might serve as explanatory mechanisms for questions such as these that arise from quantitative research. There is a growing qualitative research movement that revolves around the study of *translanguaging* (García, 2014), which seeks to understand how bilinguals dynamically navigate the use of their two (or more) languages in varied social and educational contexts (see, e.g., Gort & Sembiante, 2015; Marínez-Roldán, 2015; Martínez, Hikida, & Durán, 2015).

While most of these studies do not attempt to directly explain the qualitative nature of cross-linguistic associations, two of the studies in the current review did. Gort (2006) focused on the cross-linguistic development of eight first-grade Spanish–English emergent bilinguals attending a writing workshop in a US-based dual-language program. She spent six months examining focal students' writing performances, behaviors, strategies, and thoughts through observations and interviews. Situating each individual learner's bilingual writing profile as a case, Gort (2006) conducted cross-case analyses and found patterns of intentional code-switching and literacy transfer across languages. Based on evidence collected, Gort (2006) proposed a preliminary model capturing the bilingual literacy development among emergent bilinguals with different degrees of language dominance. Gort's (2006) findings shed light on how language dominance plays a role in cross-language associations, that language production is messy and dynamic, and that cross-linguistic development should be regarded as a positive trajectory of bilingual progress rather than anything disadvantaged. Soto Huerta (2012) investigated the English reading development among forty-five Spanish–English bilingual fourth graders through a sequential mixed-methods study. Quantitative analysis of students' reading performance revealed cross-linguistic associations, which were followed by an in-depth qualitative exploration of emergent bilinguals' reading strategies and behaviors. Soto Huerta (2012) found that despite the various English proficiency levels among the focal students, all of them drew upon cross-linguistic and cross-cultural knowledge as reading comprehension strategies.

These two unique cross-linguistic studies underscore new developments in the field of cross-linguistic research, and findings from across the spectrum of research indicate that bilingual theory and research continue to advance in the twenty-first century. As it does, more attention needs to be paid to dimensions of language and literacy that are not clear candidates for associations that are obviated by construct universality or orthographic overlap. The field should work to adopt mixed-methods approaches that use qualitative research to provide explanatory frameworks for quantitative findings, which will push both method and theory in the direction of improved understanding of language acquisition and learning for bilingual populations.

17   Pushing the Limits
Dual-Language Proficiency and Reading Development in the United States and Canada

Yuuko Uchikoshi and Stefka H. Marinova-Todd

The limits of my language means the limits of my world. – Ludwig Wittgenstein

On an abstract level language is limitless. It comprises of a limited set of words that can be combined with an even more limited set of grammatical rules, to form an unlimited number of sentences – a representation of the boundless nature of human thought. On a practical level, however, language is limited by how much we know – some people have immense vocabularies and some have very limited, some people know more grammatical rules and apply them appropriately, than others. This second more limiting view of language is what Wittgenstein referred to in the quote above, or in other words, how much language we know and how well we are able to apply it shapes our experience, thought, and worldview.

And what if we are to add another language, which brings yet new words and grammatical rules? It inevitably enriches our experience and ability to communicate. Having read Shakespeare and Goethe in three languages, we find that nothing compares to reading them in the original English and German, respectively. But fancy literature aside, in the modern day of globalization and free movement of people, and the ubiquitous presence of the Internet in our daily lives, we find the necessity to speak more than one language constantly increasing. And while some of us choose to learn new languages, some are required to learn them by necessity, whether adults who immigrate to new countries in search of prosperity or refugees escaping the horrors of wars. And inevitably, these adults bring their children along, who then have to learn a new language in order to do well in school, meet new friends, and adapt successfully to a whole new world. Comparing the language and literacy abilities of these children in the United States and Canada is the main focus of this chapter. As a result of their sociolinguistic circumstances (likely belonging to language-minority communities), these children are emerging bilinguals (and in some cases multilinguals), but we will use the term "bilingual" to refer to them, since we do not review any of the research on bilingual children from a language-majority background who are often learning an additional language by choice rather than by necessity.

Evidence from the educational research overwhelmingly supports a positive relationship between oral proficiency and reading achievement for monolinguals (e.g., Dickinson & Tabors, 2001; Pearson, Hiebert, & Kamil, 2007), confirming that children with better oral language skills make earlier and faster progress in acquiring literacy skills through the elementary school years. Recently, this has also been supported for bilinguals, mainly those with Spanish–English language combinations (e.g., August & Shanahan, 2006; Leider, Proctor, Silverman, & Harring, 2013). Yet, although studies have examined the oral proficiency of both the native language (L1) and second language (English) of emerging bilinguals, only more recently have studies begun to examine how and whether the two languages are contributing to their later reading abilities (e.g., Davison, Hammer, & Lawrence, 2011). Moreover, relatively little work has been done examining the interactions of the two languages and how this applies to bilinguals with varying language backgrounds. Although there appears to be wide within-group diversity among bilinguals (Hammer et al., 2014), how this influences their literacy acquisition also remains a question.

Examining the relationships between oral language and reading is more complex with bilinguals when compared to monolinguals because of the former's developing knowledge of two languages. Some theories, such as the Separate Underlying Proficiency (Cummins, 1981), support a model where oral proficiency in one language influences the reading development in only that language. This model assumes that the two languages of bilinguals are separate and do not influence each other. On the contrary is the Common Underlying Proficiency (Cummins, 1981), where children's experience and oral proficiency in either language affects reading development in both languages. Much of the studies stemming from these theories study the transfer of abilities from one language to the other. The populations of bilingual children learning English as a second language in both the United States and Canada comprise a large portion of the general population and are similarly diverse. However, past research has been largely conducted independently in the United States and Canada. Moreover, previous studies have not made specific comparison between bilinguals with the same first languages between the two countries.

In this chapter, we review the research evidence accumulated over the past ten years from both the United States and Canada in order to examine the oral language proficiency in each language of bilinguals and how it influences their later reading development. We first present a review of the literature from each country separately, followed by empirical evidence that makes explicit comparisons between the two countries, and conclude with potential educational implications and directions for future research investigations.

Literature Review

Past research has examined bilinguals in various contexts across the United States and Canada. The majority of the studies focus on Spanish–English bilinguals, and a few examined other language combinations, such as Chinese–English bilinguals. The bulk of the studies were empirical, and only a few used existing databases such as the National Educational Longitudinal Study database (Guglielmi, 2008) and the Early Childhood Longitudinal Study-Kindergarten Cohort (ECLS-K; Kieffer, 2008). Many of the studies were longitudinal, varying in years from one year to ten years, with the majority being between one and three years.

Within-Language Relationships between Oral Proficiency and Reading

United States. Among the studies conducted in the United States, the majority found within-language relationships between oral proficiency and reading. Using the ECLS-K data, Kieffer (2008) found that bilinguals who enter kindergarten proficient in English attain English reading levels that are equivalent to or higher than those reached by English speakers by grade 5. On the other hand, emergent bilinguals who entered kindergarten with limited English proficiency performed poorly on English reading achievement.

This relationship was also seen with specific bilingual groups. For Spanish–English bilinguals at various ages from preschool to end of grade 5, English vocabulary was a significant predictor of English word-reading skills and reading comprehension both concurrently (Howard et al., 2014; Lesaux, Crosson, Keiffer, & Pierce, 2010; Mahon, 2006; Miller et al., 2006; Rinaldi & Páez, 2008; Swanson, Rosston, Gerber, & Solari, 2008) and longitudinally (Davison et al., 2011; Fitzgerald, Amendum, Relyea, & Garcia, 2015; Nakamoto, Lindsey, & Manis, 2012). In fact, oral language emerged as a strong, significant predictor of reading comprehension, over English word reading, especially when reading comprehension was measured with text passages and corresponding questions with Spanish–English bilinguals (Lesaux et al., 2010). In the case of Chinese–English bilinguals, Uchikoshi (2013) also found a within-language relationship between oral vocabulary and English reading with children in grade 2.

Two studies found that it was the children's *growth* in English abilities during Head Start that predicted children's early English reading outcomes with Spanish–English bilinguals (Davison et al., 2011; Hammer, Lawrence, & Miccio, 2007). Additionally, although a majority of studies assessed children's oral proficiency, one study reported that self-reported English proficiency predicted initial reading but not reading trajectories (Guglielmi, 2008).

This relationship between oral language and reading held for the L1 as well. Spanish oral proficiency predicted Spanish reading with both cross-sectional data (Miller et al., 2006; Proctor, August, Snow, & Barr, 2010; Swanson et al., 2008) and longitudinal data with Spanish–English bilinguals attending transitional bilingual, dual-language immersion, and English immersion programs (Nakamoto et al., 2012). Growth in Spanish oral proficiency during Head Start years also predicted grade 1 Spanish word reading and reading comprehension (Davison et al., 2011).

Canada. Similar to the United States, the majority of studies conducted in Canada found a within-language transfer of English oral proficiency to English reading. Specifically, English vocabulary size predicted reading comprehension for bilinguals and English monolinguals (Farnia & Geva, 2013; Geva & Farnia, 2012; Jean & Geva, 2009). Moreover, in addition to vocabulary and listening comprehension, English syntax predicted reading comprehension in English for bilinguals only (Farnia & Geva, 2013; Geva & Farnia, 2012; Gottardo & Mueller, 2009). In the longitudinal study by Geva and Farnia (2012), they examined the literacy development of bilinguals from various L1 backgrounds and English monolingual children between grades 2 and 5. Their results revealed that in grade 5 phonological awareness, vocabulary, and text reading fluency predicted English reading comprehension in both groups, but there was an added effect of English syntax and listening comprehension only for the bilingual group. The authors concluded that the developmental trajectories between the two groups were similar, but not identical, indicating that oral proficiency may be still developing even when children are in grade 5. In a subsequent study, however, Farnia and Geva (2013) found that for grade 6 students, English syntax predicted English reading comprehension both for the bilingual and monolingual groups, although the growth trajectories of the two groups were different (nonlinear for the former and linear for the latter group).

In addition to oral proficiency measures, studies in Canada also examined the effect of various metalinguistic skills on the reading abilities of bilinguals. In particular, a study by Lipka and Siegel (2012) examined the effect of phonological awareness, morphological awareness and syntactic awareness on English reading comprehension and found that by grade 7 all three factors were important in predicting reading comprehension abilities of bilinguals. Similar relationship between English morphological awareness and English reading was observed in a study with grades 4 and 6 Spanish–English bilinguals (Ramirez, Chen, Geva, & Kiefer, 2010) as well as grade 6 bilinguals from various L1 backgrounds (Marinova-Todd, Siegel, & Mazabel, 2013).

While many of the studies conducted in Canada included bilinguals from various L1 backgrounds, several focused their examination specifically on Chinese–English bilinguals. Due to the specific characteristics of Chinese orthography as a morphosyllabic language, most studies examined the effect of morphological awareness on reading and found that morphological awareness in English was a significant predictor of English reading comprehension (Lam, Chen, Geva, Luo, & Li, 2012; Ramirez, Chen, Geva, & Luo, 2011). Moreover, English phonological processing also predicted English reading in Chinese-speaking bilinguals in grades 1 through 8.

Finally, similar to the research findings from the United States, the relationship between oral language and reading held for the L1 as well. Ramirez and colleagues (2010) found that morphological awareness in Spanish predicted word reading in Spanish, and Gottardo, Chiappe, Yan, Siegel, and Gu (2006) found that syntactic awareness in Chinese measured with an oral close task predicted character reading in Chinese in their groups of bilinguals between grades 1 and 8.

Cross-Language Relationships between Oral Proficiency and Reading

United States. The evidence whether there is a cross-language relationship between oral language in one language and reading in the other appears to be mixed. Several studies showed positive effects, but some – negative or null effects. The mixed results seem to suggest that bilinguals may need to reach a certain threshold in language proficiency and literacy skills in the L1 and L2 in order for a cross-language effect to be observed.

Miller and colleagues (2006) found that oral language in one language predicted reading scores in the other language with a cross-sectional group of Spanish–English bilinguals in kindergarten through grade 3. This was a bidirectional relationship. Rinaldi and Páez (2008) also found that Spanish vocabulary and word-reading skills accounted for additional variation in English word-reading skills over and above the contributions of similar English predictors with grade 1 Spanish–English bilinguals. Proctor and colleagues (2010) also show that Spanish oral language predicted Spanish reading comprehension, which also had a small but significant effect on English reading comprehension with a group of Spanish–English bilinguals in grade 4.

Similar to the research that found within-language transfer, past research shows that *growth* in one language also predicts later reading outcomes in the other with Spanish–English bilinguals (Davison et al., 2011; Hammer et al., 2007). This relationship found in the early years with Spanish–English bilinguals was bidirectional.

With bilinguals who have a nonalphabetic language as L1, such as Cantonese–English, Uchikoshi, Yang, Lohr, and Leung (2016) found a cross-language relationship when oral proficiency was measured with a nonstandardized narrative assessment, using *Frog, Where Are You?*, a wordless picture book. They found evidence of cross-language transfer with Grade 1 L1 narrative skills predicting grade 2 L2 reading comprehension in both Cantonese– and Spanish–English bilinguals. However, Uchikoshi (2013) did not see this cross-language relationship between L1 Cantonese oral proficiency and L2 English reading comprehension in an earlier study when oral proficiency was measured by a standardized vocabulary assessment. The authors discuss that a nonstandardized narrative measure may have been a more valid measure of the bilinguals' L1 oral proficiency than a standardized vocabulary test.

Some studies have found that it is the combination or interaction of L1 and L2 that predict reading achievement. Mahon (2006) found that Spanish achievement, when combined with English proficiency, predicted English achievement for a group of grade 4 and 5 Spanish–English bilinguals. Additionally, Proctor and colleagues (2006) found a significant main effect of Spanish vocabulary knowledge and an interaction between Spanish vocabulary and English fluency with a group of Spanish–English bilinguals in grade 4. Fluent English readers benefited more from Spanish vocabulary knowledge than their less fluent peers.

Not all cross-language relationships have been positive. With a group of Spanish–English bilinguals in grades 3–5 who did not receive any academic instruction in Spanish, Leider and colleagues (2013) found that Spanish language proficiency had a negative effect on English reading comprehension. Additionally, Davison and colleagues (2011) found cross-language relationships only for children whose sole home language was Spanish and had an early English exposure. These results suggest that bilinguals' Spanish proficiency may need to reach a certain threshold in order to exert an effect on English reading outcomes. This difference based on exposure to L1 and levels of L1 was also seen with Spanish–English bilinguals in Kovelman, Baker, and Petitto's (2008) work. Early bilinguals, who were exposed to both languages before age 3 tended to have high reading performance in both of their languages in grades 2–3 when compared to bilinguals who were exposed to the L2 at a later time, suggesting that age of bilingual language exposure affects bilinguals' reading development.

The amount of L1 exposure may be further determined by the language(s) of instruction in school. Uchikoshi (2013) found that the relationship between Cantonese expressive vocabulary and English reading comprehension differed between the Cantonese–English bilinguals enrolled in bilingual programs and their peers enrolled in mainstream classrooms. For children in bilingual programs, who were receiving language and literacy instruction in both languages, the two variables were positively and significantly correlated with each other, while for the mainstream group, although not significant, there was a trend for negative correlation. Similarly, Carlo and colleagues (2014) found that while all three Spanish–English groups (mainstream, early-exit bilingual, late-exit bilingual) showed growth in reading comprehension, those in the early-exit bilingual group who had a strong foundation in Spanish as well as formal literacy instruction in English had the fastest rates of growth between grades 3 and 5. Bilinguals who have the requisite levels of L1 and English literacy may be able to readily apply knowledge and skills learned in the L1 to the L2.

Canada. The evidence for cross-language transfer appears to be more limited in Canada when compared to the United States, which is not surprising considering the demographic characteristics of each country. In order to study cross-language transfer, participants from particular language combinations have to be included in the study. While the largest proportion of the language-minority speakers are Spanish speakers in the United States, in Canada there is no equivalent population, and instead language-minority speakers come from various L1 backgrounds, with Chinese speakers being among the largest, but still a much smaller proportion of the language-minority population in Canada. Therefore, many of the studies in Canada have been conducted on mixed populations of bilinguals, with some studies focused on Spanish and Chinese speakers.

Studies with Spanish-speaking bilinguals consistently found unidirectional transfer from Spanish to English only. Chen, Ramirez, Luo, Geva, and Ku (2012) studied lexical transfer (particularly the ability to recognize Spanish–English cognates) and found that both cognates and noncognates transferred from Spanish to English, however, the transfer of noncognates was related to the participants' length of residence in Canada. In other words, Spanish-speaking children were able to learn cognates well due to transfer of lexical knowledge from their home language, and it was not affected by their length of residence in Canada. Morphological awareness in Spanish also transferred to English word reading for bilinguals in grades 4 and 7 (Ramirez et al., 2010), and also Spanish word reading predicted English reading comprehension in bilinguals between grades 4 and 6 (Gottardo, Javier, Farnia, Mak, & Geva, 2014). Similar to the findings by Chen and colleagues (2012), Ramirez and colleagues (2010; Ramirez, Chen, & Pasquarella, 2013) found that cognates facilitated the transfer of Spanish derivational awareness to English reading comprehension in two groups of bilinguals, one in grade 4 and one in grade 7. The presence of this unidirectional transfer from the L1 to the L2 observed in Spanish–English bilinguals in Canada was explained with similar unidirectional transfer observed in previous research with bilingual children in the United States (Durgunoğlu, 2002; Kroll & de Groot, 1997), as well as with MacWhinney's Competition Model (MacWhinney, 2004b), which states that L2 skills tend to interfere (i.e., compete) with L1 skills.

Studies with Chinese–English bilinguals in Canada revealed a mild support for the presence of a bidirectional transfer. A longitudinal study of children in kindergarten and grade 1 examined the presence of transfer effects of phonological and morphological awareness in English and Chinese, as well as between phonological and morphological awareness in one language and word reading in the other (Luo, Chen, & Geva, 2014). Results showed a bidirectional transfer of phonological and morphological awareness skills between the two languages after controlling for nonverbal reasoning, vocabulary, and either phonological or morphological awareness, respectively, in each language. However, only Chinese phonological awareness uniquely predicted English word reading, while morphological awareness in English had an indirect effect on Chinese character reading which was mediated by Chinese morphological awareness. The authors explained these transfer effects with the specific demands of reading in each language: on one hand, English as an alphabetic language requires more phonological awareness for reading, thus phonological awareness skills from Chinese transfer to support English reading; on the other hand, Chinese requires more morphological awareness (specifically compound morphology), and thus compound awareness in English predicts character reading in Chinese. A different study also found similar transfer effect of English compound awareness to Chinese character reading in a group of bilinguals between grades 1 and 4 (Pasquarella, Chen, Lam, Luo, & Ramirez, 2011).

In summary, across both countries, the within-language transfer between oral proficiency and reading was present and common. Also, as reported elsewhere (Prevoo et al., 2015), more studies across both countries reported on within-language transfer in the L2 (i.e., English) than the L1 (i.e., either Spanish or Chinese). In terms of cross-language transfer, the positive cross-language associations found between L1 oral proficiency and L2 early literacy and reading are in line with the *interdependence hypothesis* (Cummins, 1979), according to which competence in L2 is partly based on competence in L1. However, the few studies in the United States that reported negative transfer across language highlight the importance of formally examining the degrees of proficiency in each language of bilinguals and the effect that they have on the children's reading development, especially reading comprehension in the upper grades.

Direct Comparisons between the United States and Canada

In the United States, although bilinguals in early elementary grades scored at or above average on English decoding and English passage comprehension when compared to monolinguals (e.g., Uchikoshi, 2013), research has shown that by grade 4, bilinguals tend to fall behind in their English reading comprehension relative to their English-speaking classmates (e.g. Lesaux et al., 2010; Proctor et al., 2006). This is the time when reading comprehension begins to require larger vocabulary and richer general knowledge. Yet, longitudinal research with Canadian children enrolled in balanced literacy programs, as well as French immersion programs, spanning kindergarten to grade 7, has shown that bilinguals can eventually develop strong reading skills and their emerging bilingual status did not put them at any risk for reading difficulties. As in the United States, bilinguals in Canada performed just as well or even better on simple reading (decoding) tasks (Chiappe & Siegel, 2006; Geva, 2006; Marinova-Todd & Hall, 2013; Marinova-Todd et al., 2013), or if they trailed behind the monolinguals in kindergarten, then managed to catch up to them as early as in grade 2 (Lesaux & Siegel, 2003), and maintain equivalent performance in subsequent grades (Lesaux, Rupp, & Siegel, 2007). Across the elementary school grades, bilingual children were consistently reported to have equivalent or even better performance in multiple studies on reading comprehension conducted in different research labs across the country (Grant, Gottardo, & Geva, 2011; Geva et al., 2012; Lesaux, Lipka, & Siegel, 2006; Lesaux et al., 2007; Lipka & Siegel, 2007, 2010, 2012). Notably, the reported strength of bilingual children in English reading comprehension was despite their generally lower oral English proficiency relative to that of their monolingual counterparts, mainly in terms of vocabulary size (Geva et al., 2012; Marinova-Todd & Hall, 2013) or syntax (Lesaux et al., 2006, 2007). Finally, in the context of French immersion programs, children who came from homes where neither English nor French was spoken performed equivalently to children from English-speaking homes on reading comprehension in English and in French in the early (Au-Yeung et al., 2014) and the later elementary school grades (Bérubé & Marinova-Todd, 2012), despite some having lower vocabulary scores in English compared to their monolingual counterparts.

Only two studies from the same lab in Canada reported that the bilingual children in the upper elementary grades had lower English oral proficiency scores and English reading comprehension scores when compared to monolingual counterparts (Farnia & Geva, 2013; Geva & Farnia, 2012). Moreover, the growth trajectories of reading comprehension of the two groups also differed, whereby the trajectory of the bilingual children was nonlinear and the gap between the performance of bilinguals and monolinguals increased between grades 4 and 6 (Farnia & Geva, 2013). The authors identified the type of classroom instruction, the age of exposure to English (the L2), and the measures of reading comprehension used as possible factors that could explain their results.

The observed differences in English reading comprehension between Canada and the United States can be attributed to the diversity of the bilingual populations and the influence of sociocultural factors such as the children's age of exposure to English, amount and quality of L1 and L2 exposure, school instruction, language proficiency, parental education, and socioeconomic status of the family, among others (Goldberg, Paradis, & Crago, 2008; Lesaux & Geva, 2006). However, there is a paucity of any direct comparison of bilingual groups in the United States and Canada, and it is impossible to explain whether differences in samples, in social contexts, or in instruction account for their greater success in Canada.

In order to understand the similarities and differences in the American and Canadian samples better and to obtain a larger sample size, Uchikoshi and Marinova-Todd (2012) conducted a joint study with total of 113 Cantonese-speaking kindergarteners in Western Canada and in the West Coast of the United States. Two-thirds of the US children were enrolled in early-exit transitional bilingual programs, while the remaining children were in mainstream classrooms from the same district. Canadian children were enrolled in mainstream classrooms. Children in both countries attended schools in working-class neighborhoods and came from homes with equivalent socioeconomic status.

Results showed that Cantonese–English bilinguals in both Canada and the United States appear to be more similar than different in their English language skills. There were no differences in their English vocabulary and alphabetic knowledge/decoding scores. Additionally, although there were some significant group differences on phonological awareness, on average, all three groups scored within the norm compared to monolingual English-speaking published norms. However, there were significant differences in the levels of Cantonese. Children who attended bilingual programs in the United States and children who lived in Canada tended to have higher scores on the Cantonese measures than US children who attended mainstream classrooms with no formal L1 exposure.

The variation among the bilinguals' language and reading scores appeared not to be due to location, but rather based on school environment and opportunity for L1 support. Multiple regression results revealed a possible transfer of phonological awareness skills even between two languages with different writing systems, and particularly the effect of English phonological awareness skills on the early literacy skills in Chinese. The transfer observed in the present study was seen only from L2 to L1. This may be due to the fact that the children in our study were attending schools that emphasize mastery of the English language and literacy, true even in the bilingual programs in the United States, which main goal is quick and efficient transition to English-only instruction. So far, we have only examined the children's performance in kindergarten and, thus, we studied only their alphabetic knowledge/decoding skills. Our results, therefore, are in line with previous studies in both countries showing equivalent performance between groups on word-reading tasks. However, published studies on children in grade 4 and above tend to reveal country differences especially in the domain of reading comprehension, as well as some disparity in findings between different labs. Therefore, it would be important for us to continue our comparative research with older children and to focus on their reading comprehension skills, as well as trajectory of growth. This type of research would allow us to study more formally the effect of L1 and L2 proficiency on reading comprehension over time, the role of the educational experience and educational policy in each country, and to reveal aspects of the language and literacy development of bilingual children that are similar and different between the two countries.

Conclusion

The findings from our review are relevant to education policies and practices aimed at bilingual children's reading development. The positive cross-language transfer observed in both countries reveals that a focus on improving both L1 and L2 can be beneficial for emerging bilingual's reading achievement. This is particularly relevant in the context of the United States, where the achievement gap between the bilingual and monolingual children tends to be greater, but has also been reported in Canada. Moreover, the positive cross-language transfer especially from the L1 oral language to the L2 reading skills suggests that maintaining strong L1 proficiency is not detrimental to reading development in the L2, and this is true for both countries. Among bilingual children with an immigrant background, children who are more proficient in oral language generally have better school outcomes. This observation is supported by research that reported an association between oral language and reading comprehension skills, which appears to be stronger in emerging bilingual children than in monolingual children (Gottardo & Mueller, 2009; Verhoeven & van Leeuwe, 2012). Overall, it is apparent that oral language skills in both L1 and L2 tend to be beneficial for bilingual children's reading development, even in languages that are not closely related, such as English and Chinese. In addition, age of L2 exposure, home language environment and exposure, family characteristics (such as parent level of education, socioeconomic status, or literacy practices), and educational context (such as language of instruction or language program) all play a role in the academic outcomes for bilingual children. Although more research is needed to further examine the relationships between L1 and L2, the findings from the literature suggest that sufficient skills and knowledge in both L1 and L2 are needed for the benefits of cross-language transfer to occur. Parents and schools in both countries should be encouraged to support bilingual children's L1, thereby allowing for home language growth to occur alongside English language acquisition.

We encourage bilingual children to continue to push the limits in order to benefit from the enriching experience of knowing more than one language. In addition to the academic benefits described in this chapter, bilingual children are likely to experience sociocultural and possibly economic advantages, which should not be denied to them. And those of our readers who are monolingual, we suggest that no matter what age you are, you can still expand your world by learning another language. You are already halfway there!

Discussion 1
Bilingualism as Action

Sara Rutherford-Quach and Kenji Hakuta

The purposes of this volume are to offer a series of empirically robust and innovative studies that synthesize accumulated knowledge informing a pedagogically relevant theory of language learning and to highlight areas of study that advance this research program. The five papers in this section (Chen; Grøver; Leseman, Henrichs, Blom, & Verhagen; Proctor & Zhang-Wu; and Uchikoshi & Marina-Todd) offer helpful reviews of the literature and preliminary analyses of their own empirical efforts to make advances in the area of what is currently called "academic language." The field has progressed significantly since the seminal work of Jim Cummins (1981), who articulated a distinction between BICS (Basic Interpersonal Communication Skills) and CALP (Cognitive Academic Language Proficiency) and the associated theories of a Common Underlying Proficiency (CUP) and its strawman alternative – Separate Underlying Proficiency (SUP) – to describe the complexities of language and learning for bilingual students.

The value of a strong theory and research base in the area of student academic use of language ("academic language" for shorthand, but resisted by those who conceptualize language as an activity rather than a cognitive construct) is underscored by the turbulent political history of bilingual education in the United States. The "b" word has often been considered a political wedge. So much so that Congressional staffers scrubbed any reference to bilingual education out of the 2001 reauthorization of the Elementary and Secondary Education Act (as No Child Left Behind), and renamed "the Bilingual Education Act" as the "English Language Acquisition, Language Enhancement, and Academic Achievement Act" (Hakuta, 2011).

Rather than debate the pros and cons of bilingual education from a political base, the notion of focusing the field on academic language development (and for teachers, facilitating the academic uses of language by their students) provided a bridge to the academic aspirations for all students. In recent years this has become a foundational concept for providing all students in the United States with access to the Common Core State Standards, the Next Generation Science Standards, and their supporting practice standards. In addition, English Language Proficiency standards – the attainment of which is required by the

Office for Civil Rights of the US Department of Education – further shifted from structural considerations to the *language practices* required for the attainment of the new academic standards. (More on this shift will be discussed later.)

Across these papers, the main dependent factors being considered are conventional aspects of language and reading: phonemic, phonological, and morphological awareness, vocabulary, reading comprehension, and orthographic skills. (Grøver's investigation into *perspective taking* is a notable exception.) These dependent factors are examined across multiple languages, both within individuals as well as between individuals and groups. Considerations of groups include characteristics associated with language structure and orthography, settings (the Uyghur region of China; Norway; the Netherlands; Canada, United States) and educational settings with differing goals toward bilingualism.

Proctor and Zhang-Wu reference a useful list of studies that provides a wide-lens view of the phenomenon of cross-linguistic relationships. They explore correlations of language pairs (English, paired with Spanish, Chinese, French, and Korean) on a variety of aspects of language and reading. While the details of the meta-analysis are not provided in the chapter write-up, the authors note that there is consistent and positive cross-linguistic association in reading comprehension/literacy measures, but also a set of more specific relationships for the other skills, including asymmetrical relationships between the languages. What accounts for this variability is not clear, but the variances are likely due to (1) structural aspects of the languages and how the particular measures are implemented; (2) developmental aspects of the student population, including their grade level and age of initial bilingualism; (3) the sociolinguistic and educational characteristics of the study context; and (4) random error. The review alludes to, but is not specific about, the role of particular structural language characteristics. It also points to the importance of appreciating the sociolinguistic setting. There is clearly a lot of exploration to do in this area.

Leseman, Henrichs, Blom and Verhagen ground their work in this suggestion that the sociolinguistic setting, and in particular, the home language environment, has an influence on students' academic language skills, across monolingual and bilingual contexts in the Netherlands. This paper provides an analysis of children's academic language[1] as well as academic and linguistic growth patterns, and relates these to the language practices in which families

---

[1] The definition of "academic language" used by Leseman and colleagues is distinct from ours above in that it is closely derived from Systemic Functional Linguistics and focuses specifically on the structural, semantic, and textual choices a student typically makes in a school setting. Their measure of academic language is also bifurcated into separate vocabulary and discourse categories.

from three different sociolinguistic groups engaged. These sociolinguistic groups, which included the families of monolingual Dutch speakers, bilingual Turkish/Dutch speakers of Turkish heritage, and bilingual Tarifit-Berber/Dutch speakers of Moroccan heritage, were chosen strategically; the articulated purpose of the DASH project in which this study was embedded was to interrogate the "linguistic and educational disadvantages" of children from the latter two immigrant groups. Unsurprisingly, the authors find that the variability of that deemed academic language input (i.e., talk including linguistic features similar to what would be found in a classroom) is correlated with parental education level, socioeconomic status, and unequal status of the home language. More unexpected are the findings that across both bilingual groups L1 exposure and knowledge appears to facilitate L2 skills *and* that children's early measures of academic language were not related to their later academic growth with respect to mathematics. The authors' discussion suggests that the latter finding may be due to effective instruction in this content area, which allows emergent bilinguals to "catch up." Future work could investigate this hypothesis, as well examine the ways in which students and teachers are actually using language during mathematical learning.

Grøver's study is unique in that its dependent variable, perspective taking, is a dynamic measure of a particular type of discursive competence. This study provides the most in-depth description of *how* bilingual children navigate language in a particular context. Specifically, it examines how preschoolers in Norway, all of whom speak Norwegian as a second language, use language to step outside a particular role or perspective. In this study, perspective taking is operationalized and examined as the capacity to switch narrative perspectives. Grounding her investigation in literature that explores a potential bilingual advantage in perspective taking, Grøver examines the relationships between age, other academic language skills, native language use, and perspective taking. Yet the findings indicate that while age and all other academic language skills included in the study – second-language vocabulary, narrative skills, and internal state explanations – predicted perspective taking at a statistically significant level, increased native language use at home was only marginally predictive. In the discussion, the author suggests that it may have been difficult to identify a 'bilingual advantage' because of the great variability in bilingual language use among participants. Future work could expand upon how perspective taking is operationalized as well as look more closely at this bilingual variability, examining the ways in which children are using their two languages and incorporating perspective taking across contexts.

Chen offers an analysis of receptive and expressive vocabulary as a result of a complex intervention that utilizes bilingual reading materials and professional development for teachers. The intervention involves teachers conducting classroom discussions, and developing awareness about language. The study is equally fascinating because of its novel context: bilingual education in the Uyghur province of China. A robust finding is that the intervention produced positive outcomes in receptive vocabulary in Chinese and in expressive vocabulary in Uygur, but not in the other outcomes (i.e., expressive Chinese, receptive Uyghur). It is worth noting that the reported effect size is large for the significant differences. Although a power analysis is not reported, it is likely that there would have been sufficient statistical power to find effects for these outcomes and therefore the null findings are equally compelling. While the author does not offer explanations for this asymmetry, future research could usefully explore individual characteristics that might interact with these findings. Future work could also explore how this pattern of growth in these four domains of receptive/expressive and Chinese/Uyghur might interact with the sociolinguistic and educational program goals for the students, particularly given the status differences between Chinese and Uyghur and how these are reflected in the curriculum.

Uchikoshi and Marina-Todd make the case for the connections between oral language, language awareness (phonological and morphological), reading comprehension, and the claim that children with better oral language skills make earlier and faster progress in acquiring literacy skills. They then examine the literature on the cross-language relationships between oral language and reading comprehension across the two languages of the bilinguals, and compare results from the US and Canadian contexts. Across the two countries, there is consistent evidence regarding the relationship between oral language and literacy measures; "positive cross-language transfer" suggests that focusing on language development in *both* languages, such as that which occurs in dual-language programs, could be helpful for bilingual students' literacy development. However, even within country (United States) there is evidence that some of the relationships are modulated by the educational program – with a positive relationship in bilingual education programs but not in English-only programs. The discussion alludes to the significant sociolinguistic differences between Canada and the United States with respect to the language and educational backgrounds represented among bilingual students.

According to these chapters, measures of oral language and broader measures of literacy are frequently correlated across languages, some of which is predictable on the basis of the structural characteristics of the languages involved, and some of which is probably modulated by the sociolinguistic or educational context. That said, it is difficult to separate signal from noise, because there are multiple permutations of factors, sampling is sporadic and mostly driven by convenience, and research resources are limited. Actually, in the absence of a strong theory that predicts how different measures of language and learning play out depending upon the linguistic, social, and educational structures within which instruction and learning are embedded, perhaps no amount of research activity will ever start separating the signal from the noise. A summary of the relationship between language and its various manifestations, the particulars of the language, and the learning context in which they are manifested might be captured by the often-repeated observation that "everything was intertwined" but with the important caveat that "and yet they appear different depending on the conditions."

In the remainder of this discussion, we will adopt two distinct perspectives to suggest different ways to distinguish signal from noise. Our hope is that these perspectives allow all of us to investigate language in a more dynamic and connected fashion as well as untangle and eventually affect the sociolinguistic and educational contexts. One is through a lens of language as a sociolinguistic activity – what van Lier and Walqui (2012) have labeled "language as action." While the components of language examined in these papers are mostly treated as cognitive or metacognitive constructs, we consider how language viewed as a set of user practices around learning activities could reveal new avenues for research. The second perspective addresses what research can do to examine and enable bilingual development in educational contexts. Chen's effort to conduct teacher training around language support and to examine the effects is a great start toward a better understanding and operationalization of this perspective – while the measures of student language growth are quite static (receptive and expressive vocabulary), the independent variable manipulated in this study is quite dynamic and can lead to important insights about teacher learning in support of student language development. This effort would be even more robust if the dependent measures could be better aligned to the training. For example, the training included engaging students in conversations, so measuring language development in terms of ability to engage in meaningful conversations would be a better-aligned measure.

This first perspective, which posits language as action, pushes back against the historic trend to examine and measure language as structural or functional "units in isolation and in abstraction" (Widdowson, 1979, p. 247). As van Lier and Walqui (2012) have articulated, to treat language as action is to expand upon a functional perspective of language, which falls short with respect to students developing discursive or interactive competence within content areas such as mathematics or history. This perspective intersects with sociocultural theory in that language is treated as a "fundamentally social phenomenon, acquired and used interactively, in a variety of contexts for myriad practical purposes" (Firth & Wagner, 1997, p. 296). According to this perspective, learning is a social phenomenon, and language is acquired primarily through meaningful interaction – through action – and the co-construction of knowledge (Mercer & Howe, 2012; Vygotsky, 1978). Participation is therefore both the goal and the means of language development (Dewey, 1916; Kong & Pearson, 2003).

Teachers and school communities that embrace a language as action perspective engage emergent bilinguals in activities that require them to interact, converse, discuss, argue, question, research, and explain. Language development thus does not occur separately from content-area learning, but rather occurs during carefully scaffolded processes of meaning-making (van Lier & Walqui, 2012; Vygotsky, 1978). Chen's study provides an example of an instructional intervention that potentially could be posed to embrace this perspective: shared book reading about relevant topics and related classroom discussions in bilingual kindergarten classes. Whether or not this intervention actually embraced language as action, however, is unclear as it depends on the details related to purpose and implementation. How were the books related to a relevant curriculum? In what ways were students able to participate in discussions? (How) did teachers scaffold lessons and students participate? These questions would need to be addressed in order to make that determination.

Research conducted through this first lens can take many forms. It can attempt to answer questions about instruction interventions and practices like that described above. Or, like Grøver has proposed, research could take on even more basic questions such as: what are the different ways of living and being bilingual? And how might these different ways of living and being bilingual intersect with what happens in the classroom? Or building on the work that Leseman and colleagues conducted, studies may examine the different ways that bilingual families navigate and act through languages, even if these practices do not completely line up with classroom-relevant "academic language practices." Especially needed are qualitative or mixed-method studies that investigate *how* children and families live and learn through more than one language, not only the extent to which they do or do not meet already established parameters measuring language or literacy. Proctor and Zhang-Wu call for this type of research, particularly as it relates to *translanguaging,* in their discussion and we echo that appeal here.

The research possibilities addressing instructional practices and classroom activity mentioned above also relate to our second perspective. Central to this perspective is the following question: How can researchers help uncover what teachers and students need to DO with language in order to support students' bilingual development? This question is an extension of that asked by Wong Fillmore and Snow (2000) nearly twenty years ago in their seminal work "What Teachers Need to Know about Language." Yet shifting the focus from *knowing* to *doing* and from *teachers* to *teachers and students* moves language out of the metacognitive realm and into the language-as-action arena.

There is an urgent need for different types of research that will support teachers to enable bilingual development, as more and more students are learning through more than one language. Content-area specific research is necessary, both to examine how content knowledge is structured with regards to language and how language is implicated during the learning of content (Greene & Hakuta, 2015). More investigations regarding linguistic and analytical practices that are important across content areas and grade levels, such as argumentation, explanation, and reasoning, also need to be conducted. Finally, in order to complete this research and affect positive change with respect to students learning through more than one language, researchers need to align themselves and collaborate with other educational professionals concerned with both bilingual development and content learning. Chen's intervention provides an example of this type of collaboration, which resulted in the development and evaluation of a successful bilingual language and literacy intervention.

Interventions like Chen's, however, should just be a beginning. If uncovering what teachers and students should *do* with language to support bilingual development is the *first* goal, then much more research needs to be conducted in this area. Moreover, if actually facilitating the implementation of instructional suggestions that result from this research is the *second* goal, then the research community will need to provide a tremendous amount of support in the form of resources and training to teachers, administrators, and policy makers. Then the question becomes, are we ready for this challenge?

Discussion 2
Multilingualism and Socioeconomic Development

Robert A. LeVine

Multilingualism has been prevalent in many parts of the world for a long time and is prevalent today, although the institutional conditions for its development have changed over time. In Africa and much of Asia, nation building during the nineteenth and twentieth centuries created nation-states in parts of the world like Nigeria, with hundreds of distinct languages, and Nepal, with forty-five languages, spoken by localized and formerly autonomous ethnic groups. Trade between ethnic groups in the colonial era often made it advantageous to speak at least two languages, and the spread of schooling usually required children to learn a national language like Mandarin Chinese in school even if they use an ethnic or regional vernacular like Cantonese at home. In addition, the migration of peoples from one country to another has created a multitude of multilingual situations.

Americans, unlike the residents of India, Thailand, Scandinavia, or the Netherlands, do not take multilingualism for granted but tend to see it as a personal inadequacy to be corrected by learning standard English. Japan is another country like the United States, where monolingualism is the norm. Yet monolingualism in a country or region may be relatively rare worldwide, particularly at a time when more than 90 percent of the world's children are growing up outside the West. If being multilingual confers cognitive or communicative advantages, then many children are thus advantaged.

My first encounter with the idea that children who grow up multilingual might have cognitive advantages came from Sandra Ben-Zeev, a student I supervised at the University of Chicago. The article based on her dissertation, published in *Child Development* in 1977, showed that Chicago-area children growing up speaking Hebrew and English did better on cognitive tests than their English-only counterparts; children who learned to speak both languages in Israel did better than their Hebrew-only counterparts. This was the same period that Wallace Lambert and his group at McGill University in Montreal were demonstrating that children bilingual in French and English had better communication skills than their monolingual counterparts (Genesee, Tucker, &

Lambert, 1975; Peal & Lambert, 1962). The better performances by bilinguals, *other things being equal*, having been replicated many times, is by now a well-established phenomenon (Bialystok, 1987).

But what about the fact that many bilingual children score lower in vocabulary as well as cognitive and communication skills? The answer is that, though the studies showing bilingual children with cognitive advantages also show that they lag in vocabulary, many bilingual children are more generally disadvantaged: by immigration, low socioeconomic status, low parental education. The French–English speaking children in Canada and the Hebrew–English speaking children in Chicago and Israel had middle-class parents with high levels of education. Multivariate analysis is necessary to disentangle the advantages and disadvantages the bilingual children might have.

The chapters in this section use multivariate analysis in a variety of contexts: in Xinjiang, China, near the border of Afghanistan, where Uyghur children, who speak a Turkic language and are mostly of low SES, learn Mandarin Chinese in school (Chen); in western Canada, where immigrant bilingual children who speak Cantonese learn English in school (Uchikoshi and Marinova-Todd); in the Netherlands, where monolingual Dutch children can be compared with their Moroccan Dutch and Turkish Dutch immigrant counterparts (Leseman et al.); and in the United States, where the focus is on Spanish-speaking children who learn English in school (Proctor and Zhang-Wu). In these diverse contexts, the authors use multivariate analysis to disentangle the impact of bilingualism and socioeconomic status on language variables such as reading comprehension, vocabulary, and phonemic awareness. Without a multivariate approach, the researchers might mistakenly attribute child language variations to the child's bilingualism or to advantages in his or her environment. And without a far-reaching approach, the researchers might mistakenly assume a uniformity of the situations in the world in which bilingual children find themselves. A multiple-replication strategy is necessary to analyze how the language environment of schools affects the skills of children.

In our four-country study of women's schooling (LeVine et al., 2012), we sought to solve a problem that had long puzzled demographers: what processes mediate the consistent associations of female school attainment with health and other beneficial outcomes? The demographers had speculated that schooling made girls more autonomous, assertive, or self-confident; they ignored or discounted the possibility that girls might actually acquire skills in school that affected their behavior as mothers. At the suggestion of students at the Harvard Graduate School of Education, Patricia Velasco and Medardo Tapia-Uribe, we turned to literacy skills as assessed by our colleagues Catherine Snow and the late Jeanne Chall, through decontextualized (or academic) language and reading comprehension, respectively (Chall, 1996; Snow, 1990, 2010; Snow & Uccelli, 2009). A pilot study in Mexico showed the promise of these skills as mediators of the impact of schooling on maternal health behavior and other outcomes. These skills, we found, were highly correlated with years of schooling, suggesting that they might be tapping the proximate processes through which schooling affects learning.

But while the growth of reading comprehension may seem a straightforward index of literacy acquisition, what made us think that the Noun Definitions test, a component of the Wechsler intelligence test for adults, was a test of academic language? It was Catherine Snow's demonstration that children's performance depends on "experience in classrooms where definitions are requested, read, given and discussed" (Snow, 1990, p. 13). She argued that definitions in the Aristotelian, deductive sense, linking superordinate terms with particulars, are central to the content of instruction in primary (elementary) schools, qualifying their measurement as an index of school experience.

Sarah LeVine and I decided to assess the two skills, reading comprehension and noun definitions, in samples of mothers comparatively, adding other students of Catherine Snow – Beatrice Schnell-Anzola, Meredith Rowe, and Emily Dexter – to our team as we expanded the study to Venezuela, Nepal, and Zambia. We found through multivariate analysis in each of the four countries, and in urban and rural contexts, that a process involving retention of the two skills was involved. Our findings strongly suggest that this is more than a simple literacy effect, affecting comprehension of oral messages, frequency of talking to children, and other behaviors that we interpret in the book. The acquisition of academic language in school (Snow, 2010) has a broad range of psychosocial effects that call for further research.

Our studies were cross-sectional; without longitudinal research, our findings remain provisional. Leseman et al.'s DASH project in the Netherlands, however, is longitudinal, so its findings, reported in their chapter in this volume, are more robust and point to a future standard for language research.

Afterword
So Much Progress, So Much Left to Do

Catherine E. Snow

A little over forty years ago, Charles Ferguson and I edited a volume, published by Cambridge University Press, called *Talking to Children: Language Input and Acquisition* (Snow & Ferguson, 1977). The volume emerged from a conference held in 1974 (sponsored by the Sociolinguistics Committee of the Social Science Research Council), which itself had been organized as an acknowledgment of the emergence of a new field of study – the systematic analysis of how adults talked to language-learning children. The first studies in that field of research had been motivated by a desire to test nativists' claims that the primary linguistic data were degraded and ungrammatical, thus not in any sense useful to children trying to figure out the structure of language. The precocious state of the field was signaled by the difficulty we had in filling up the conference program with researchers interested in the topic of input as related to language acquisition. We included contributions from sociologists, from anthropologists studying cross-linguistic convergences in the baby talk register, and from researchers analyzing other simplified registers (e.g., foreigner talk). In 1977, only a handful of empirical studies had focused directly on understanding input as it might relate to children's language learning, and no one had demonstrated clear relationships. How the field has changed!

The papers in the current volume are all inspired by the notion that understanding language development, from infancy to adolescence, among monolinguals and bilinguals, across the full variety of local environments and of national/cultural macrosystems (Bronfenbrenner & Morris, 2007), requires studying children in their natural settings and with attention to the interactions they engage in. These papers also reflect the view that understanding how children learn language is not just a worthy end in itself but also a crucial contribution to understanding how children learn about the world. Learning about the world takes place as children hear narratives that reveal others' psychological realities, as they participate in pretend play scenarios about infant care or superhero conflict, as they are inducted into conversations about the past and the future, and of course, as they participate in structured learning opportunities in school. The medium is language, but the learning far transcends language.

P. David Pearson, in his commentary in this volume, reminds us of Halliday's (1993) language learning triad: *learning language, learning through* language, and *learning about* language. One urgent question for educational practitioners, and for those of us who work with and learn from classroom teachers, is how we should distribute learning opportunities over those three activities. Several of the chapters in this book demonstrate how educational systems and innovative interventions vacillate between teaching language and teaching content that brings language with it. For example, we have examples of vocabulary programs in preschool classrooms where the target words are determined by frequency in the language – letting facts about language guide what children should learn. Similarly, many programs for second language speakers focus on target-language vocabulary and grammar divorced from content. Teaching reading comprehension has too often been conceptualized as teaching strategies for reading rather than grappling with passage content (see Silverman and Hartranft, this volume).

In other cases, the organizing educational principle is the content to be taught – giving decontextualized explanations, resolving social conflicts, taking perspective, learning about science or about abstract phenomena from a combination of talk and text. In these cases of learning through language, it is assumed that the relevant language forms come along for free with the content, for some students at least. Selman articulates a particular and powerful version of this view, putting learning about identity and social relations at the center of opportunities to learn about language. One research challenge for the next era is to determine for which learners and under what circumstances focusing on the content is sufficient to ensure language learning and how to supplement learning through language with explicit language-learning opportunities for other learners in other circumstances.

Observations and AHA Experiences

My reading of the chapters and the commentaries in this volume has recurrently resulted in AHA experiences; in some cases I was reminded of things known but forgotten, but I also encountered some entirely new facts and principles, and in many cases, an inchoate understanding was crystallized and clarified. I list a few of these various AHA experiences here.

Amount of input matters. First, it is striking, as documented in the chapters by Lieven and by Rowe, how recent much of the work on patterns and consequences of mother–child interaction is. When an article based on my doctoral dissertation (Snow, 1972) argued that maternal input to young children was potentially useful to children trying to figure out something about the structure of their language, no one showed much interest. For some years, questions about the utility or consequences of input were hard to address, in part because the data base was too limited and in part because the very question clashed with the dominant nativist view. The vast expansion of the knowledge base, made possible by new data collection and analysis tools, has allowed for great advances and has brought interaction studies (back) into fashion.

Quality of input matters. In addition to quantity, it is now clear that quality of the input matters. There is still, though, some lack of clarity about how to define the quality dimension in language – does it consist of diverse vocabulary, complex syntax, decontextualized language, academic language, extended discourse, or abstract topics? Are these dimensions distinct, or do we need a notion of input quality that incorporates all of these, while including a dimension of developmental sensitivity? Is it perhaps even possible that quality is defined, not by features of the language itself, but by features of the content being talked about? Conversations about past and future events, hypothetical and counterfactual claims, explanations about complex processes, and other such content require certain language features and create contexts in which learning language and learning through language are inextricable.

The role of intentional teaching remains contested. Attention to the role of explicit teaching for language and for literacy has waxed and waned over the last fifty years. In early childhood circles the debate about the right mix of curricular planning and free play or child-determined activity remains unre-solved, with many deploring the incursion of math and literacy instruction into kindergarten and early childhood classrooms, whereas others point out the value of such approaches in shrinking the SES achievement gap (see chapters by Leyva and Skorb, this volume, and by Rolla et al., this volume). In the primary grades, formal instruction in math and literacy are now essentially universal, but the right balance of explicit attention to decoding versus practice with taught patterns versus reading for fun remains contested territory. Ford-Connors and O'Connor (this volume) provide useful guidelines for intentional teaching, and Hemphill, Kim, and Troyer (this volume) describe a set of practices that, if implemented with struggling middle-grades readers, provides them access to sophisticated literacy skills. It is crucial to point out, though, that in all these cases, formal instruction in language or literacy occurs only after student engagement is ensured, by making the content relevant to student concerns.

We have a new sense of how interaction works. The simplistic notion of language input that characterized the early analyses of mothers' speech to children has been elaborated and complexified. We now conceptualize adult–child interaction as a Vygotskian envelope for learning, in which under-standing the social mind, i.e., others' communicative intentions, becomes the source of knowledge about language. The design of language could be much simpler if we didn't need to use language to represent differing perspectives, to convey sensitivity to others' perspectives, and to commit complex social acts with deniability. Adult–child interaction presents the complexities of the social world in miniature, so that children can learn how to function in it.

We need better assessments. Though we think of assessments as evaluating students or programs, in fact assessment is primarily a mechanism for defining a construct. Academic language and reading comprehension are prime, though contrasting, examples. Academic language was a relatively fuzzy construct – widely acknowledged but minimally understood – until Uccelli and her colleagues (see Uccelli, this volume) produced an assessment that concretized the concept. Reading comprehension, on the other hand, is assumed to mean something specific but in fact covers a wide territory and has a very different character as reflected in different assessments. Biancarosa (this volume) argues convincingly that reading comprehension assessments in general focus too much on outcomes and not enough on process. The distinction between process and outcome is equally relevant to language assessment: should we be measuring language knowledge or language use? Knowledge about forms or achievement of functions?

Bilingualism is becoming a default, not an exoticism. All the chapters in Part III of this volume reveal the extent to which research on language development must accept bilingual individuals, multilingual classrooms, and multicultural societies as the default. The ubiquity of bilingualism generates social and educational tensions but also opens up rich new approaches to understanding the full array of linguistic, social, societal, and educational forces that influence language and literacy acquisition. The programs described in Part III reflect the sophisticated application, adaptation, and evaluation for bilinguals of principles derived from careful studies of language learning and language interaction with monolinguals.

Considering implications for practice is informative about developmental processes. Someone once said "there is nothing so practical as a good theory." It is equally true, though, that there is nothing so theoretical as good practice. Attentive parents and responsive early childhood educators have long been experts in the details of promoting language learning, in the context of warm and responsive relationships with their children and their charges. Researchers could well take advice from effective practitioners about what elements to integrate into our experimental interventions or what features of talk to isolate in our predictive studies. Kim and Yun (this volume) reflect the value of practice by offering us four eminently practical principles

(E^5: exploration, elicitation, extension, and emotional engagement), each of which can be seen as a claim about how learning happens.

Unfortunately, as children progress through school, they may risk moving out of environments in which adults are optimally responsive to their interests and focused on interaction. As the skill and content learning demands of school increase, as teachers become increasingly focused on preparing students for high-stakes assessments, and as the curriculum is increasingly constrained by efforts to meet global standards, educational practice comes to reflect forces disconnected from authentic learning. An excellent early childhood classroom has many features that could and should be replicated in classrooms designed for older students: centers that offer students choice, opportunities for peer collaboration, freedom to move around and to sit in soft chairs or on the floor, engaging activities, authentic reading and writing tasks, and loving teachers. If we could reshape elementary and secondary classrooms to incorporate more of these features, we might find that older students retain the curiosity, motivation, and joyfulness of preschool learners.

References

Aarts, R., Demir-Vegter, S., Kurvers, J., & Henrichs, L. F. (2016). Academic language in shared book reading: Parent and teacher input to mono- and bilingual preschoolers. *Language Learning, 66*, 263–295.

Adams, M. J., & Bruck, M. (1995). Resolving the great debate. *American Educator, 19* (7), 10–20.

Akhtar, N., & Menjivar, J. A. (2012). Cognitive and linguistic correlates of early exposure to more than one language. *Advances in Child Development and Behavior, 42*, 41–78.

Akhtar, N., & Tomasello, M. (2000). The social nature of words and word learning. In R. M. Golinkoff & K. Hirsh-Patek (Eds.), *Becoming a word learner: A debate on lexical acquisition* (pp. 115–135). New York, NY: Oxford University Press.

Alborough, J. (2002). *Hug*. Cambridge, MA: Candlewick Press.

Aldrich, N. J., Tenenbaum, H. R., Brooks, P. J., Harrison, K., & Sines, J. (2011). Perspective taking in children's narratives about jealousy. *British Journal of Developmental Psychology, 29*, 86–109.

Allen, A. (2002). Power, subjectivity, and agency: Between Arendt and Foucault. *International Journal of Philosophical Studies, 10*(2), 131–149.

Ambridge, B., Kidd, E., Rowland, C. F., & Theakston, A. L. (2015). The ubiquity of frequency effects in first language acquisition. *Journal of Child Language, 42*(2), 239–273.

Ambridge, B., Pine, J. M., Rowland, C. F., Chang, F., & Bidgood, A. (2013). The retreat from overgeneralization in child language acquisition: Word learning, morphology, and verb argument structure. *Wiley Interdisciplinary Reviews: Cognitive Science, 4*(1), 47–62.

Anthony, A. R. B. (2008). Output strategies for English-language learners: Theory to practice. *The Reading Teacher, 61*(6), 472–482

Anthony, J. L., & Francis, D.J. (2005). Development of phonological awareness. *Current Directions in Psychological Science, 14*(5), 255–259.

Anthony, J. L., Solari, E. J., Williams, J. M., Schoger, K. D., Zhang, Z., Branum-Martin, L., & Francis, D. J. (2009). Development of bilingual phonological awareness in Spanish-speaking English language learners: The roles of vocabulary, letter knowledge, and prior phonological awareness. *Scientific Studies of Reading, 13*(6), 535–564.

Applebee, A. N. (1996). *Curriculum as conversation: Transforming traditions of teaching and learning*. Chicago, IL: University of Chicago Press.

Aram, D., & Levin, I. (2001). Mother-child joint writing in low SES: Sociocultural factors, maternal mediation, and emergency literacy. *Cognitive Development, 16,* 831–852.

(2004). The role of maternal mediation of writing to kindergartners in promoting literacy in school: A longitudinal perspective. *Reading and Writing, 17,* 387–409.

Arbour, M., Yoshikawa, H., Atwood, S., Duran, F. R., Godoy, F., Trevino, E., & Snow, C. E. (2015). Quasi-experimental study of a learning collaborative to improve public preschool quality and children's language outcomes in Chile. *BMJ Quality & Safety, 24*(11).

Ardoin, S. P., Christ, T. J., Morena, L. S., Cormier, D. C., & Klingbeil, D. A. (2013). A systematic review and summarization of the recommendations and research surrounding curriculum-based measurement of oral reading fluency (CBM-R) decision rules. *Journal of School Psychology, 51*(1), 1–18.

Armbruster, B. B., & Anderson, T. H. (1988). On selecting "considerate" content area textbooks. *Remedial and Special Education, 9*(1), 47–52.

Armbruster, B. B., Lehr, F., Osborn, J. (2001). *Put reading first: The research building blocks for teaching children to read.* Washington, DC: US Government Printing Office.

Arriaga, R. I., Fenson, L., Cronan, T., & Pethick, S. J. (1998). Scores on the MacArthur Communicative Development Inventory of children from low and middle-income families. *Applied Psycholinguistics, 19*(2), 209–223.

Atance, C. M. (2015). Young children's thinking about the future. *Child Development Perspectives, 9,* 178–182.

Atance, C. M., & O'Neill, D. K. (2001). Episodic future thinking. *Trends in Cognitive Sciences, 5,* 533–539.

Atwill, K., Blanchard, J., Gorin, J. S., & Burstein, K. (2007). Receptive vocabulary and cross-language transfer of phonemic awareness in kindergarten children. *Journal of Educational Research, 100*(6), 336–345.

August, D., & Shanahan, T. (Eds.). (2006) *Developing literacy in second-language learners. Report of the National Literacy Panel on language-minority children and youth.* Mahwah, NJ: Lawrence Erlbaum Associates.

Au-Yeung, K., Hipfner-Boucher, K., Chen, X., Pasquarella, A., D'Angelo, N., & Deacon, H. (2014). Development of English and French language and literacy skills in EL1 and ELL French immersion students in the early grades. *Reading Research Quarterly, 50,* 233–254.

Bailey, A. L. (2007). *The language demands of school: Putting academic English to the test.* New Haven, CT: Yale University Press.

Baker, D. L., Biancarosa, G., Park, B. J., Bousselot, T., Smith. J., Baker, S. K., Kame'enui, E. J., . . . Tindal, G. (2015). Validity of CBM measures of oral reading fluency and reading comprehension on high-stakes reading assessments in Grades 7 and 8. *Reading & Writing, 28*(1), 57–104.

Baldwin, D. A. (1991). Infants' contribution to the achievement of joint reference. *Child Development, 62,* 875–890.

Bandura, A. (2008).Toward an agentic theory of the self. In H. Marsh, R. G. Craven, & D. M. McInerney (Eds.), *Advances in self research: Vol. 3. Self-processes, learning, and enabling human potential* (pp. 15–49). Charlotte, NC: Information Age.

Barr, C. D., & Uccelli, P. (2016). CALS-I psychometric report. Unpublished internal report prepared for the IES-funded Catalyzing Comprehension through Discussion and Debate research project.

Barth, A. E., Barnes, M., Francis, D., Vaughn, S., & York, M. (2015). Inferential processing among adequate and struggling adolescent comprehenders and relations to reading comprehension. *Reading and Writing, 28*(5), 587–609.

Barth, A. E., Catts, H. W., & Anthony, J. L. (2009). The component skills underlying reading fluency in adolescent readers: A latent variable analysis. *Reading and Writing, 22*(5), 567–590.

Beals, D. E. (1993). Explanatory talk in low-income families' mealtime conversations. *Applied Psycholinguistics, 14*, 489–513.

(2001). Eating and reading: Links between family conversations with preschoolers and later language and literacy. In D. K. Dickinson & P. O. Tabors (Eds.), *Beginning literacy with language: Young children learning at home and school* (pp. 75–92). Baltimore, MD: Paul H. Brookes.

Beck, I. L., & McKeown, M. G. (1999). Comprehension: The sine qua non of reading. *Teaching and Change, 6*(2), 197–211.

Beck, I. L., McKeown, M. G., & Kucan, L. (2008). *Creating robust vocabulary: Frequently asked questions and extended examples.* New York, NY: Guilford Press.

(2013). *Bringing words to life: Robust vocabulary instruction* (2nd ed.). New York, NY: Guilford Press.

Begus, K., Gliga, T., & Southgate, V. (2014). Infants learn what they want to learn: Responding to infant pointing leads to superior learning. *PloS ONE, 9*, e108817.

(2016). Infants' preferences for native speakers are associated with an expectation of information. *PNAS, 113*, 12397–12402.

Begus, K., & Southgate, V. (2012). Infant pointing serves an interrogative function. *Developmental Science, 15*, 611–677.

Ben-Zeev, S. (1977). The influence of bilingualism on cognitive strategy and cognitive development. *Child Development, 48*, 1009–1018.

Bergelson, E., & Swingley, D. (2012). At 6–9 months, human infants know the meanings of many common nouns. *Proceedings of the National Academy of Sciences, 109*(9), 3253–3258.

Berlinski, S., & Schady, N. R. (2015). *The early years: Child well-being and the role of public policy.* New York, NY: Palgrave Macmillan.

Berman, R. A., & Ravid, D. (2009). Becoming a literate language user: Oral and written text construction across adolescence. In D. R. Olson & N. Torrance (Eds.), *Cambridge handbook of literacy* (pp. 92–111). Cambridge, England: Cambridge University Press.

Berninger, V. W., & Abbott, R. D. (2010). Listening comprehension, oral expression, reading comprehension, and written expression: Related yet unique language systems in grades 1, 3, 5, and 7. *Journal of Educational Psychology, 102*, 635–651.

Bérubé, D., & Marinova-Todd, S. H. (2012). The development of language and reading skills in the second and third languages of multilingual children. *International Journal of Multilingualism, 9*(3), 272–293.

Bialystok, E. (1987). Influences of bilingualism on metalinguistic development. *Second Language Research, 3*, 154–166.

Bialystok, E., Luk, G., & Kwan, E. (2005). Bilingualism, biliteracy, and learning to read: Interactions among languages and writing systems. *Scientific Studies of Reading, 9*(1), 43–61.

Bialystok, E., Luk, G., Peets, K. F., & Yang, S. (2010). Receptive vocabulary differences in monolingual and bilingual children. *Bilingualism: Language and Cognition, 13* (4), 525–531.

Biancarosa, G., Davison, M. L., Carlson, S. E., & Seipel, B. (2016, July). *Diagnosing the reading comprehension processes of poor comprehenders: Year 2 results of the Multiple-choice Online Causal Comprehension Assessment.* Paper presented at Society for Scientific Studies of Reading, Porto, Portugal.

Biancarosa, G., & Snow, C. E. (2003). *Adolescent literacy and the achievement gap: What do we know and where do we go from here?* New York, NY: Carnegie Corporation.

Bianco, M., Bressoux, P., Doyen, A.-L., Lambert, E., Lima, L., Pellenq, C., & Zorman, M. (2010). Early training in oral comprehension and phonological skills: Results of a three-year longitudinal study. *Scientific Studies of Reading, 14*, 211–246.

Biber, D., & Conrad, S. (2009). *Register, genre, and style.* Cambridge, MA: Cambridge University Press.

Biemiller, A., & Slonim, N. (2001). Estimating root word vocabulary growth in normative and advantaged populations: Evidence for a common sequence of vocabulary acquisition. *Journal of Educational Psychology, 93*, 498–520.

Bindman, S. W., Skibbe, L. E., Hindman, A. H., Aram, D., & Morrison, F. J. (2014). Parental writing support and preschoolers' early literacy, language, and fine motor skills. *Early Childhood Research Quarterly, 29*, 614–624.

Bishop, D. V., Holt, G., Line, E., McDonald, D., McDonald, S., & Watt, H. (2012). Parental phonological memory contributes to prediction of outcome of late talkers from 20 months to 4 years: A longitudinal study of precursors of specific language impairment. *Journal of Neurodevelopmental Disorders, 4*(3).

Blachowicz, C. L. Z., Fisher, P. J., Ogle, D., & Watts-Taffe, S. (2006). Vocabulary: Questions from the classroom. *Reading Research Quarterly, 41*, 524–539.

Blachowicz, C. L. Z., Ogle, D., Fisher, P., & Taffe, S. W. (2013). *Teaching academic vocabulary K–8: Effective practices across the curriculum.* New York, NY: Guilford Press.

Blasi, D. E., Wichmann, S., Hammarström, H., Stadler, P. F., & Christiansen, M. H. (in press). Sound-meaning association biases evidenced across thousands of languages. Proceedings of the National Academy of Sciences.

Block, C. C., & Johnson, R. B. (2002). The thinking process approach to comprehension development: Preparing students for their future comprehension challenges. In C. C. Block, L. B. Gambrell, & M. Pressley (Eds.), *Improving reading comprehension instruction: Rethinking research, theory, and classroom practice* (pp. 54–79). San Francisco, CA: Jossey-Bass.

Blom, E., Küntay, A. C., Messer, M., Verhagen, J., & Leseman, P. P. M. (2014). The benefits of being bilingual: Working memory in bilingual Turkish-Dutch children. *Journal of Experimental Child Psychology, 128*, 105–119.

Blom, E., Paradis, J., & Duncan, T. S. (2012). Effects of input properties, vocabulary size, and L1 on the development of third person singular – *s* in child L2 English. *Language Learning, 62*(3), 965–994.

Bloom, H. S., Hill, C. J., Black, A. R., & Lipsey, M.W. (2008). Performance trajectories and performance gaps as achievement effect-size benchmarks for educational interventions. *Journal on Research of Educational Effectiveness, 1*(4), 289–328.

Blum-Kulka, S. (2008). Language, communication and literacy: Major steps in the development of literate discourse. In P. Klein & Y. Yablon (Eds.), *From research to practice in early education* (pp. 117–154). Jerusalem: Israeli Academy of Science.

Blum-Kulka, S., & Snow, C. E. (Eds.). (2002). *Talking to adults: The contribution of multiparty discourse to language acquisition.* Mahwah, NJ: Lawrence Erlbaum Associates.

Boals, T., Kenyon, D. M., Blair, A., Cranley, M. E., Wilmes, C., & Wright, L. J. (2015). Transformation in K–12 English language proficiency assessment: Changing contexts, changing constructs. *Review of Research in Education, 39*(1), 122–164.

Bornstein, M. H., Hahn, C. S., Putnick, D. L., & Suwalsky, J. T. (2014). Stability of core language skill from early childhood to adolescence: A latent variable approach. *Child Development, 85*(4), 1346–1356.

Bornstein, M. H., Putnick, D. L., Cote, L. R., Haynes, O. M., & Suwalsky, J. T. (2015). Mother-infant contingent vocalizations in 11 countries. *Psychological Science, 26* (8), 1272–1284.

Boundy, L., Cameron-Faulkner, T., & Theakston, A. (2016). Exploring early communicative behaviours: A fine-grained analysis of infant shows and gives. *Infant Behavior and Development, 44*, 86–97.

Bowerman, M. (1988). The "no negative evidence" problem: How do children avoid constructing an overly general grammar? In J. A. Hawkins (Ed.), *Explaining language universals* (pp. 73–101). Oxford, England: Blackwell.

Bowers, E. P., & Vasilyeva, M. (2011). The relation between teacher input and lexical growth of preschoolers. *Applied Psycholinguistics, 32*(1), 221–241.

Bowlby, J. (1969). *Attachment.* New York, NY: Basic Books.

Bowne, J. B., Yoshikawa, H., & Snow, C. E. (2016). Experimental impacts of a teacher professional development program in early childhood on explicit vocabulary instruction across the curriculum. *Early Childhood Research Quarterly, 34*, 27–39.

Boyd, M. P. (2012). Planning and realigning a lesson in response to student needs: Intentions and decision making. *Elementary School Journal, 113*(1), 25–51.

Brandt, S., Kidd, E., Lieven, E., & Tomasello, M. (2009). The discourse bases of relativization: An investigation of young German and English-speaking children's comprehension of relative clauses. *Cognitive Linguistics, 20*(3), 539–570.

Brandt, S., Lieven, E., & Tomasello, M. (2010). Development of word order in German complement-clause constructions: Effects of input frequencies, lexical items, and discourse function. *Language, 86*(3), 583–610.

Bransford, J. D., Brown, A. L., & Cocking, R. R. (Eds.). (2000). *How people learn: Brain, mind, experience, and school.* Washington, DC: National Academy Press.

Brasseur-Hock, I. F., Hock, M., Kieffer, M., Biancarosa, G., & Deshler, D. D. (2011). Adolescent struggling readers in urban schools: Results of a latent class analysis. *Learning and Individual Differences, 21*(4), 438–452.

Bråten, S. (Ed.). (1998). *Intersubjective communication and emotion in early ontogeny.* Cambridge, England: Cambridge University Press.

Bronfenbrenner, U., & Morris, P. A. (2007). The bioecological model of human development. In R. M. Lerner & W. Damon (Eds.), *Handbook of child psychology: Theoretical models of human development* (pp. 793–823). Hoboken, NJ: John Wiley.

Brown, P. (2011). The cultural organization of attention. In A. Duranti, E. Ochs, & B. B. Schieffelin (Eds.), *The handbook of language socialization* (pp. 29–55). Malden, MA: Wiley-Blackwell.

Brown, R. (1973). *A first language: The early stages.* Cambridge, MA: Harvard University Press.

Bruner, J. (1981). The pragmatics of acquisition. In W. Deutsch (Ed.), *The child's construction of language* (pp. 39–55). New York, NY: Academic Press.

(1983). *Children's talk: Learning to use language.* New York, NY: W. W. Norton.

(1990). *Acts of meaning.* Cambridge, MA: Harvard University Press.

Bunce, B. H. (1995). *Building a language-focused curriculum for the preschool classroom* (Vol. 2). Baltimore, MD: Paul H. Brookes.

Burchinal, M. R., Howes, C., Pianta, R., Bryant, D., Early, D., Clifford, R., & Barbarin, O. (2008). Predicting child outcomes at the end of kindergarten from the quality of pre-kindergarten teacher–child interactions and instruction. *Applied Development Science, 12*(3), 140–153.

Burchinal, M. R., Peisner-Feinberg, E., Pianta, R., & Howes, C. (2002). Development of academic skills from preschool through second grade: Family and classroom predictors of developmental trajectories. *Journal of School Psychology, 40*(5), 415–436.

Burchinal, M. R., Vandergrift, N., Pianta, R., & Mashburn, A. (2010). Threshold analysis of association between child care quality and child outcomes for low-income children in pre-kindergarten programs. *Early Childhood Research Quarterly, 25*(2), 166–176.

Bus, A., van Ijzendoorn, M., & Pellegrini, A. (1995). Joint book reading makes for success in learning to read: A meta-analysis on intergenerational transmission of literacy. *Review of Educational Research, 65*, 1–21.

Buttelmann, D., Carpenter, M., & Tomasello, M. (2009). Eighteen-month-old infants show false belief understanding in an active helping paradigm. *Cognition, 112*, 337–342.

Cabell, S. Q., Justice, L. M., McGinty, A. S., DeCoster, J., & Forston, L. D. (2015). Teacher–child conversations in preschool classrooms: Contributions to children's vocabulary development. *Early Childhood Research Quarterly, 30*, 80–92.

Cabell, S. Q., Justice, L. M., Piasta, S. B., Curenton, S. M., Wiggins, A., Turnbull, K. P., & Petscher, Y. (2011). The impact of teacher responsivity education on preschoolers' language and literacy skills. *American Journal of Speech-Language Pathology, 20*(4), 315–330.

Cadima, J., Gamelas, A., Mcclelland, M., & Peixoto, C. (2015). Associations between early family risk, children's behavioral regulation, and academic achievement in Portugal. *Early Education and Development, 26*, 708–728.

Cain, K., & Catts, H. (2016). *Predictors of reading and listening comprehension from prekindergarten to grade 3.* Paper presented at the 23rd annual meeting of the Society of Scientific Studies of Reading, Porto, Portugal.

Cain, K., & Oakhill, J. (2006). Assessment matters: Issues in the measurement of reading comprehension. *British Journal of Educational Psychology, 76*(4), 697–708.

(2011). Matthew effects in young readers: Reading comprehension and reading experience aid vocabulary development. *Journal of Learning Disabilities, 44*(5), 431–443.

Callaghan, T., Moll, H., Rakoczy, H., Warneken, F., Liszkowski, U., Behne, T., & Tomasello, M. (2011). Early social cognition in three cultural contexts. *Monographs of the Society for Research in Child Development, 76*, 1–142.

Calvo, A., & Bialystok, E. (2014). Independent effects of bilingualism and socioeconomic status on language ability and executive functioning. *Cognition, 130*(3), 278–288.

Cameron-Faulkner, T., Theakston, A., Lieven, E., & Tomasello, M. (2015). The relationship between infant holdout and gives, and pointing. *Infancy, 20*(5), 576–586.

Cárdenas-Hagan, E., Carlson, C. D., & Pollard-Durodola, S. D. (2007). The cross-linguistic transfer of early literacy skills: The role of initial L1 and L2 skills and language of instruction. *Language, Speech, and Hearing Services in Schools, 38*(3), 249–259.

Carlisle, J. F., Kelcey, B., & Berebitsky, D. (2013). Teachers' support of students' vocabulary learning during literacy instruction in high poverty elementary schools. *American Educational Research Journal, 50*, 1360–1371.

Carlisle, J., Kelcey, B., Berebitsky, D., & Phelps, G. (2011). Embracing the complexity of instruction: A study of the effects of teachers' instruction on students' reading comprehension. *Scientific Studies of Reading, 15*, 409–439.

Carlo, M. S., August, D., McLaughlin, B., Snow, C. E., Dressler, C., Lippman, D. N., . . . White, C. E. (2004). Closing the gap: Addressing the vocabulary needs of English-language learners in bilingual and mainstream classrooms. *Reading Research Quarterly, 39*(2), 188–215.

Carlo, M. S., Barr, C. D., August, D., Calderón, C., & Artzi, L. (2014). Language of instruction as a moderator for transfer of reading comprehension skills among Spanish-speaking English language learners. *Bilingual Research Journal, 37*(3), 287–310.

Carlson, S. E., Seipel, B., & McMaster, K. (2014). Development of a new reading comprehension assessment: Identifying comprehension differences among readers. *Learning and Individual Differences, 32*, 40–53.

Carpenter, M., Nagell, K., Tomasello, M., Butterworth, G., & Moore, C. (1998). Social cognition, joint attention, and communicative competence from 9 to 15 months of age. *Monographs of the Society for Research in Child Development, 63*(4), 1–143.

Cartmill, E. A., Armstrong, B. F., Gleitman, L. R., Goldin-Meadow, S., Medina, T. N., & Trueswell, J. C. (2013). Quality of early parent input predicts child vocabulary 3 years later. *Proceedings of the National Academy of Sciences*, *110*(28), 11278–11283.

Catts, H. W., Adlof, S., & Ellis Weismer, S. (2006). Language deficits in poor comprehenders: A case for the simple view of reading. *Journal of Speech, Language, and Hearing Research*, *49*, 278–293.

Catts, H. W., Compton, D., Tomblin, J. B., & Bridges, M. S. (2012). Prevalence and nature of late-emerging poor readers. *Journal of Educational Psychology*, *104*, 166–181.

Catts, H. W., Hogan, T. P., & Adlof, S. M. (2005). Developmental changes in reading and reading disabilities. In H. W. Catts & A. G. Kamhi (Eds.), *The connections between language and reading disabilities* (pp. 23–36). Mahwah, NJ: Lawrence Erlbaum Associates.

Cazden, C. B. (2002). *Classroom discourse: The language of teaching and learning* (2nd ed.). Portsmouth, NH: Heinemann.

Centro de Estudios, Ministerio de Educación. (2013). *Estado del arte de la Educación Parvularia*. Santiago, Chile: Ministerio de Educación.

Cervetti, G. N., Tilson, J., Goss, M., Castek, J., & Jaynes, C. (2008, October). Teaching and learning vocabulary in the context of science. Presentation at the annual meeting of the California Reading Association, Sacramento, CA.

Chall, J. (1967). *Learning to read: The great debate*. New York: McGraw-Hill.

(1996). *Stages of reading development* (2nd ed.). Fort Worth, TX: Harcourt Brace.

Chang, C. (2006). Linking early narrative skill to later language and reading ability in Mandarin-speaking children: A longitudinal study over eight years. *Narrative Inquiry*, *16*(2), 275–293.

Chernyk, N., Leech, K. A., & Rowe, M. L. (2017). Training prospective abilities through conversation about the extended self. *Developmental Psychology*, *53*(4), 652–661.

Chen, S. (2014). *The effectiveness of a Chinese literacy intervention for Uyghur young children: A randomized controlled trial* (Unpublished doctoral dissertation). East China Normal University, Shanghai, China.

Chen, X., Ramirez, G., Luo, Y., Geva, E., & Ku, Y.-M. (2012). Comparing vocabulary development in Spanish- and Chinese-speaking ELLs: The effects of metalinguistic and sociocultural factors. *Reading and Writing*, *25*, 1991–2020.

Cheung, A., & Slavin, R. E. (2005). Effective reading programs for English language learners and other language-minority students. *Bilingual Research Journal*, *29*(2), 241–267.

Chiappe, P., & Siegel, L. S. (2006). The development of reading for Canadian children from diverse linguistic backgrounds: A longitudinal study. *Elementary School Journal*, *107*, 135–152.

China Ministry of Education. (2012). *Early Learning and Development Guideline*. Retrieved from www.moe.gov.cn/publicfiles/business/htmlfiles/moe/s7371/20130 5/152136.html.

Chomsky, N. (1957). *Syntactic structures*. The Hague, Netherlands: Mouton.

(1959). A review of B. F. Skinner's Verbal Behavior. *Language*, *35*(1), 26–58.

(1965). *Aspects of the theory of syntax*. Cambridge, MA: MIT Press.

Chouinard, M. M., & Clark, E. V. (2003). Adult reformulations of child errors as negative evidence. *Journal of Child Language*, *30*(3), 637–669.

Christie, F. (2002). *Classroom discourse analysis: A functional perspective.* London, England: Continuum.

Chuang, H. K., Joshi, R. M., & Dixon, L. Q. (2011). Cross-language transfer of reading ability: Evidence from Taiwanese ninth grade adolescents. *Journal of Literacy Research, 44*(1), 97–119.

Chung, K. K., McBride-Chang, C., Cheung, H., & Wong, S. W. (2013). General auditory processing, speech perception and phonological awareness skills in Chinese–English biliteracy. *Journal of Research in Reading, 36*(2), 202–222.

Claessens, A., Duncan, G., & Engel, M. (2009). Kindergarten skills and fifth-grade achievement: Evidence from the ECLS-K. *Economics of Education Review, 28,* 415–427.

Clark, C., Pritchard, V., & Woodward, L. (2010). Preschool executive functioning abilities predict early mathematics achievement. *Developmental Psychology, 46* (5), 1176–1191.

Cleave, P. L., Becker, S. D., Curran, M. K., Van Horne, A. J. O., & Fey, M. E. (2015). The efficacy of recasts in language intervention: A systematic review and meta-analysis. *American Journal of Speech-Language Pathology, 24*(2), 237–255.

Collins, M. F. (2012). Sagacious, sophisticated, and sedulous: The importance of discussing 50-cent words with preschoolers. *Young Children, 67*(5), 66–71.

(in press). Supporting inferential thinking in preschoolers: Effects of discussion on children's story comprehension. Early Education and Development.

Colonnesi, C., Stams, G. J. J. M., Koster, I., & Noom, M. J. (2010). The relation between pointing and language development: A meta-analysis. *Developmental Review, 30,* 352–366.

Comeau, L., Genesee, F., & Mendelson, M. (2007). Bilingual children's repairs of breakdown in communication. *Journal of Child Language, 34,* 159–174.

Conboy, B. T., & Thal, D. J. (2006). Ties between the lexicon and grammar: Cross-sectional and longitudinal studies of bilingual toddlers. *Child Development, 77*(3), 712–735.

Connor, C. M., Morrison, F. J., & Petrella, J. (2004). Effective reading comprehension instruction: Examining Child × Instruction interactions. *Journal of Educational Psychology, 96,* 682–698.

Connor, C. M., Morrison, F. J., & Slominski, L. (2006). Preschool instruction and children's emergent literacy growth. *Journal of Educational Psychology, 98,* 665–689.

Connor, C. M., Son, S. H., Hindman, A. H., & Morrison, F. J. (2005). Teacher qualifications, classroom practices, family characteristics, and preschool experience: Complex effects on first graders' vocabulary and early reading outcomes. *Journal of School Psychology, 43*(4), 343–375.

Connor, C. M., Spencer, M., Day, S. L., Guiliani, S., Ingebrand, S. W., McLean, L., & Morrison, F. J. (2014). Capturing the complexity: Content, type, and amount of instruction and quality of the classroom learning environment synergistically predict third graders' vocabulary and reading comprehension outcomes. *Journal of Educational Psychology, 106,* 762–778.

Cook, A. E., & Guéraud, S. (2005). What have we been missing? The role of general world knowledge in discourse processing. *Discourse Processes, 39,* 265–278.

Cook, V. (Ed.). (2003). *Effects of the second language on the first* (Vol. 3). XXXX: Multilingual Matters.

Coulmas, F. (1989). *The writing systems of the world*. Oxford, England: Blackwell.

Council of Chief School Officers. (2010). *Common Core State Standards for English language arts and literacy in history/social studies, science, and technical subjects*. Washington, DC: CCSO.

Coxhead, A. (2000). A new academic word list. *TESOL Quarterly, 34*, 213–238.

Crain-Thorenson, C., Lippman, M. Z., & McClendon-Magnuson, D. (1997). Windows on comprehension: Reading comprehension processes as revealed by two think-aloud procedures. *Journal of Educational Psychology, 89*(4), 579–591.

Cristofaro, T. N., & Tamis-LeMonda, C. S. (2012). Mother-child conversations at 36 months and at pre-kindergarten: Relations to children's school readiness. *Journal of Early Childhood Literacy, 12*, 68–97.

Crookes, G. (1990). The utterance, and other basic units for second language discourse analysis. *Applied Linguistics, 11*, 183–99.

Cummins, J. (1979). Linguistic interdependence and the educational development of bilingual children. *Review of Educational Research, 49*(2), 222–251.

(1981). The role of primary language development in promoting Educational success for language minority students. In *Schooling and language minority students: A theoretical framework* (pp. 3–49). Los Angeles, CA: California State University, Evaluation, Dissemination, and Assessment Center.

(1991). Conversational and academic language proficiency in bilingual contexts. *AILA Review, 8*, 75–89.

(2000). *Language, power, and pedagogy: Bilingual children in the crossfire*. Clevedon, England: Multilingual Matters.

(2012). The intersection of cognitive and sociocultural factors in the development of reading comprehension among immigrant students. *Reading and Writing, 25*(8), 1973–1990.

Cunningham A. E., & Stanovich, K. E. (1997). Early reading acquisition and its relation to reading experience and ability 10 years later. *Developmental Psychology, 33*, 934–945.

Curby, T. W., Brock, L. L., & Hamre, B. K. (2013). Teachers' emotional support consistency predicts children's achievement gains and social skills. *Early Education & Development, 24*(3), 292–309.

Curenton, S. M., Craig, M. J., & Flanigan, N. (2008). Use of decontextualized talk across story contexts: How oral storytelling and emergent reading can scaffold children's development. *Early Education and Development, 19*(1), 161–187.

Dale, E. (1965). Vocabulary measurement: Techniques and major findings. *Elementary English, 42*, 82–88.

Davidson, R. G., & Snow, C. E. (1995). The linguistic environment of early readers. *Journal of Research in Childhood Education, 10*, 5–21.

Davison, M. D., Hammer, C., & Lawrence, F. R. (2011). Associations between preschool language and first grade reading outcomes in bilingual children. *Journal of Communication Disorders, 44*(4), 444–458.

de Boysson-Bardies, B., & Vihman, M. M. (1991). Adaptation to language: Evidence from babbling and first words in four languages. *Language, 67,* 297–319.

De Jong, P. F., & Leseman, P. P. M. (2001). Lasting effects of home literacy on reading achievement in school. *Journal of School Psychology, 39*(5), 389–414.

De Temple, J., & Snow, C. E. (2003). Learning words from books. In A. van Kleeck, S. A. Stahl, & E. B. Bauer (Eds.), *On reading books to children: Parents and teachers* (pp. 16–36). Mahwah, NJ: Lawrence Erlbaum Associates.

Deacon, S. H., Commissaire, E., Chen, X., & Pasquarella, A. (2013). Learning about print: The development of orthographic processing and its relationship to word reading in first grade children in French immersion. *Reading and Writing, 26*(7), 1087–1109.

Deacon, S. H., Wade-Woolley, L., & Kirby, J. (2007). Crossover: The role of morphological awareness in French immersion children's reading. *Developmental Psychology, 43*(3), 732.

Demir, O. E., Rowe, M. L., Heller, G., Goldin-Meadow, S., & Levine, S. C. (2015). Vocabulary, syntax, and narrative development in typically developing children and children with early unilateral brain injury: Early parental talk about the "there-and-then" matters. *Developmental Psychology, 51*(2), 161–175.

Denton, C. A., Enos, M., York, M. J., et al. (2015a). Text-processing differences in adolescent adequate and poor comprehenders reading accessible and challenging narrative and informational text. *Reading Research Quarterly, 50*(4), 393–416.

Denton, C. A., Wolters, C. A., York, M. J., et al. (2015b). Adolescents' use of reading comprehension strategies: Differences related to reading proficiency, grade level, and gender. *Learning and Individual Differences, 37,* 81–95.

Dewey, J. (1916). *Democracy and education: An introduction to the philosophy of education.* New York, NY: Macmillan.

Diakidoy, I. A. N., Stylianou, P., Karefillidou, C., & Papageorgiou, P. (2005). The relationship between listening and reading comprehension of different types of text at increasing grade levels. *Reading Psychology, 26*(1), 55–80.

Diamond, A. (2013). Executive functions. *Annual Review Psychology, 64,* 135–168.

Diazgranados, S., Selman, R. L., & Dionne, M. (2016). Acts of social perspective taking: A functional construct and the validation of a performance measure for early adolescents. *Social Development, 25*(3), 572–601.

Dickinson, D. K. (2001). Book reading in preschool classrooms: Is recommended practice common? In D. K. Dickinson & P. O. Tabors (Eds.), *Beginning literacy with language: Young children learning at home and school* (pp. 175–203). Baltimore, MD: Paul H. Brookes.

Dickinson, D. K, Golinkoff, R. M., & Hirsh-Pasek, K. (2010). Speaking out for language: Why language is central to reading development. *Educational Researcher, 39*(4), 305–310.

Dickinson, D. K., McCabe, A., Clark-Chiarelli, N., & Wolf, A. (2004). Cross-language transfer of phonological awareness in low-income Spanish and English bilingual preschool children. *Applied Psycholinguistics, 25*(3), 323–347.

Dickinson, D. K., & Porche, M. V. (2011). Relation between language experiences in preschool classrooms and children's kindergarten and fourth-grade language and reading abilities. *Child Development, 82*(3), 870–886.

Dickinson, D. K., & Tabors, P. (Eds.). (2001). *Beginning literacy with language: Young children learning at home and school.* Baltimore, MD: Paul H. Brookes.

Dickson, W. P. (1982). Two decades of referential communication research: A review and meta-analysis. In C. J. Brainerd & M. Pressley (Eds.), *Verbal processes in children* (pp. 1–33). New York, NY: Springer.

Dittmar, M., Abbot-Smith, K., Lieven, E., & Tomasello, M. (2008). German children's comprehension of word order and case marking in causative sentences. *Child Development, 79*(4), 1152–1167.

Dixon, L. Q., Chuang, H. K., & Quiroz, B. (2012). English phonological awareness in bilinguals: A cross-linguistic study of Tamil, Malay and Chinese English-language learners. *Journal of Research in Reading, 35*(4), 372–392.

Donahue, M. (2014). Perspective-taking and reading comprehension of narratives: Lessons learned from the bean. In C. A. Stone, E. Silliman, B. Ehren, & G. Wallach (Eds.), *Handbook of language and literacy development and disorders* (2nd ed., pp. 323–338). New York, NY: Guilford Press.

Downer, J., Sabol, T. J., & Hamre, B. (2010). Teacher–child interactions in the classroom: Toward a theory of within- and cross-domain links to children's developmental outcomes. *Early Education and Development, 21*(5), 699–723.

Duffy, G. G. (1993). Teachers' progress toward becoming expert strategy teachers. *Elementary School Journal, 94*(2), 109–120.

Duke, N. K., & Carlisle, J. (2011). The development of comprehension. In M. L. Kamil, P. D. Pearson, E. B. Moje, & P. P. Afflerbach (Eds.), *Handbook of reading research* (Vol. 4, pp. 199–228). New York, NY: Routledge.

Duke, N. K., & Pearson, P. (2002). Effective practices for developing reading comprehension. In A. E. Farstrup & S. Samuels (Eds.), *What research has to say about reading instruction* (pp. 205–242). Newark, DE: International Reading Association.

Duncan, G. J., Dowsett, C. J., Claessens, A., Magnuson, K., Huston, A. C., Klebanov, B., . . . Japel, C. (2007). School readiness and later achievement. *Developmental Psychology, 43*, 1428–1446.

Dunn, L. M., Dunn, L. M., Whetton, C., & Burley, J. (1997). *The British Picture Vocabulary Scale* (2nd ed.). London, England: Nelson.

Durand, T. (2011). Latino parental involvement in kindergarten: Findings from the Early Childhood Longitudinal Study. *Hispanic Journal of Behavioral Sciences, 33*, 469–489.

Durgunoğlu, A. Y. (2002). Cross-linguistic transfer in literacy development and implications for language learners. *Annals of Dyslexia, 52*, 189–204.

Durham, R. E., Farkas, G., Hammer, C. S., Tomblin, J. B., & Catts, H. W. (2007). Kindergarten oral language skill: A key variable in the intergenerational transmission of socioeconomic status. *Research in Social Stratification and Mobility, 25*(4), 294–305.

Durkin, D. (1978/1979). What classroom observations reveal about reading comprehension instruction. *Reading Research Quarterly, 14*, 481–533.

Early, D. M., Maxwell, K. L., Ponder, B. D., & Pan, Y. (2017). Improving teacher–child interactions: A randomized controlled trial of Making the Most of Classroom Interactions and My Teaching Partner professional development models. *Early Childhood Research Quarterly, 38,* 57–70.

Edmonds, M. S., Vaughn, S., Wexler, J., et al. (2009). A synthesis of reading interventions and effects on reading comprehension outcomes for older struggling readers. *Review of Educational Research, 79*(1), 262–300.

Eisenberg, A. (2002). Maternal teaching talk within families of Mexican descent: Influences of task and socioeconomic status. *Hispanic Journal of Behavioral Sciences, 24,* 206–224.

Eisenberg, N., Valiente, C., & Eggum, N. D. (2010). Self-regulation and school readiness. *Early Education and Development, 21*(5), 681–698.

Elleman, A. M., Lindo, E. J., Morphy, P., & Compton, D. L. (2009). The impact of vocabulary instruction on passage-level comprehension of school-age children: A meta-analysis. *Journal of Research on Educational Effectiveness, 2*(1), 1–44.

Entwisle, D., Alexander, K., & Olson, L. (2005). First grade and educational attainment by age 22: A new story. *American Journal of Sociology, 110*(5), 1458–1502.

Faggella-Luby, M. N., Graner, P. S., Deshler, D. D., & Drew, S. V. (2012). Building a house on sand: Why disciplinary literacy is not sufficient to replace general strategies for adolescent learners who struggle. *Topics in Language Disorders, 32* (1), 69–84.

Faigenbaum-Golovin, S., Shaus, A., Sober, B., Levin, D., Na'aman, N., Sass, B., . . . Finkelstein, I. (2016). Algorithmic handwriting analysis of Judah's military correspondence sheds light on composition of biblical texts. *Proceedings of the National Academy of Sciences, 113,* 4664–4669.

Fan, S. P., Liberman, Z., Keysar, B., & Kinzler, K. D. (2015). The exposure advantage: Early exposure to a multilingual environment promotes effective communication. *Psychological Science, 26,* 1090–1097.

Fang, Z. (2012). The challenges of reading disciplinary texts. In T. L. Jetton & C. Shanahan (Eds.), *Adolescent literacy in the academic disciplines: General principles and practical strategies* (pp. 34–68). New York, NY: Guilford.

Fang, Z., Schleppegrell, M. J., & Cox, B. M. (2006). Understanding the language demands of schooling: Nouns in academic registers. *Journal of Literacy Research, 38*(3), 247–273.

Farnia, F., & Geva, E. (2013). Growth and predictors of change in English language learners' reading comprehension. *Journal of Research in Reading, 36*(4), 389–421.

Farrar, M. J. (1990). Discourse and the acquisition of grammatical morphemes. *Journal of Child Language, 17*(3), 607–624.

Feinauer, E., Hall-Kenyon, K. M., & Davison, K. C. (2013). Cross-language transfer of early literacy skills: An examination of young learners in a two-way bilingual immersion elementary school. *Reading Psychology, 34* (5), 436–460.

Fernald, A., Perfors, A., & Marchman, V. A. (2006). Picking up speed in understanding: Speech processing efficiency and vocabulary growth across the 2nd year. *Developmental Psychology, 42*(1), 98–116.

Fernald, A., Pinto, J. P., Swingley, D., Weinbergy, A., & McRoberts, G. W. (1998). Rapid gains in speed of verbal processing by infants in the 2nd year. *Psychological Science, 9*(3), 228–231.

Firth, A., & Wagner, J. (1997). On discourse, communication, and (some) fundamental concepts in SLA research. *Modern Language Journal, 8,* 285–300.

Fitzgerald, J., Amendum, S. J., Relyea, J. E., & Garcia, S. G. (2015). Is overall oral English ability related to young Latinos' English reading growth? *Reading & Writing Quarterly, 31*(1), 68–95.

Fivush, R., Haden, C. A., & Reese, E. (2006). Elaborating on elaborations: Role of maternal reminiscing style in cognitive and socioemotional development. *Child Development, 77*(6), 1568–1588.

Florit, E., Roch, M., & Levorato, M. C. (2014). Listening text comprehension in preschoolers: A longitudinal study on the role of semantic components. *Reading and Writing: An Interdisciplinary Journal, 27,* 793–817.

Foorman, B. R., Koon, S., Petscher, Y., Mitchell, A., & Truckenmiller, A. (2015). Examining general and specific factors in the dimensionality of oral language and reading in 4th–10th grades. *Journal of Educational Psychology, 107*(3), 884–899.

Foorman, B. R., Petscher, Y., & Bishop, M. D. (2012). The incremental variance of morphological knowledge to reading comprehension in grades 3–10 beyond prior reading comprehension, spelling, and text reading efficiency. *Learning and Individual Differences, 22*(6), 792–798.

Ford-Connors, E. (2011). Examining middle-school teachers' talk during vocabulary instruction. *Yearbook of the Literacy Research Association, 60,* 229–244.

Ford-Connors, E., & Paratore, J. R. (2015). Vocabulary instruction in fifth-grade and beyond: Sources of word learning and productive contexts for development. *Review of Educational Research, 85*(1), 50–91.

Francis, D. J., Snow, C. E., August, D., Carlson, C. D., Miller, J., & Iglesias, A. (2006). Measures of reading comprehension: A latent variable analysis of the Diagnostic Assessment of Reading Comprehension. *Scientific Studies of Reading, 10*(3), 301–322.

Frazier, B. N., Gelman, S. A., & Wellman, H. M. (2009). Preschoolers' search for explanatory information within adult–child conversation. *Child Development, 80* (6), 1592–1611.

(2016). Young children prefer and remember satisfying explanations. *Journal of Cognition and Development, 17*(5), 718–736.

Frost, R. L. A., Monaghan, P., & Christiansen, M. H. (2016). Using statistics to learn words and grammatical categories: How high frequency words assist language acquisition. In A. Papafragou, D. Grodner, D. Mirman, & J. C. Trueswell (Eds.), *Proceedings of the 38th Annual Conference of the Cognitive Science Society* (pp. 81–86). Austin, TX: Cognitive Science Society.

Fuchs, L. S., Fuchs, D., Hosp, M. K., & Jenkins, J. R. (2001). Oral reading fluency as an indicator of reading competence: A theoretical, empirical, and historical analysis. *Scientific Studies of Reading, 5*(3), 239–256.

García, G. (1991). Factors influencing the English reading test performance of Spanish-speaking Hispanic children. *Reading Research Quarterly, 26,* 371–392.

García, O. (2009). *Bilingual education in the 21st century: A global perspective.* New York, NY: Wiley-Blackwell.

(2014). Countering the dual: Transglossia, dynamic bilingualism and translanguaging in education. In R. S. Rubdy & L. Alsagoff (Eds.), *The global-local interface and hybridity: Exploring language and identity* (pp. 100–118). Bristol, England: Multilingual Matters.

Gee, J. P. (2014). Decontextualized language: A problem, not a solution. *International Multilingual Research Journal, 8*, 9–23.

Genesee, F., Paradis, J., & Crago, M. B. (2004). *Dual language development and disorders: A handbook on bilingualism and second language learning* (Vol. 11). Baltimore, MD: Paul H. Brookes.

Genesee, F., Tucker, G. R., & Lambert, W. E. (1975). Communication skills of bilingual children. *Child Development, 46*, 1010–1014.

Gerde, H. K., & Powell, D. R. (2009). Teacher education, book-reading practices, and children's language growth across one year of Head Start. *Early Education and Development, 20*(2), 211–237.

Gest, S. D., Holland-Coviello, R., Welsh, J. A., Eicher-Catt, D. L., & Gill, S. (2006). Language development subcontexts in Head Start classrooms: Distinctive patterns of teacher talk during free play, mealtime, and book reading. *Early Education and Development, 17*(2), 293–315.

Geva, E. (2006). Second language oral proficiency and second language literacy. In D. August & T. Shanahan (Eds.), *Developing literacy in second-language learners: Report of the national literacy panel on language-minority children and youth* (pp. 123–139). Mahwah, NJ: Lawrence Erlbaum Associates.

Geva, E., & Farnia, F. (2012). Developmental changes in the nature of language proficiency and reading fluency paint a more complex view of reading comprehension in ELL and EL1. *Reading and Writing, 25*, 1819–1845.

Gilbert, J. K., Goodwin, A. P., Compton, D. L., & Kearns, D. M. (2014). Multisyllabic word reading as a moderator of morphological awareness and reading comprehension. *Journal of Learning Disabilities, 47*(1), 34–43.

Girolametto, L., & Weitzman, E. (2002). Responsiveness of child care providers in interactions with toddlers and preschoolers. *Language, Speech, and Hearing Services in Schools, 33*, 268–281.

Girolametto, L., Weitzman, E., & Greenberg, J. (2003). Training day care staff to facilitate children's language. *American Journal of Speech-Language Pathology, 12*(3), 299–311.

(2012). Facilitating emergent literacy: Efficacy of a model that partners speech-language pathologists and educators. *American Journal of Speech-Language Pathology, 21*, 47–63.

Girolametto, L., Weitzman, E., Lefebvre, P., & Greenberg, J. (2007). The effects of in-service education to promote emergent literacy in child care centers: A feasibility study. *Language, Speech, and Hearing Services in Schools, 38*, 72–83.

Goetz, P. J. (2003). The effects of bilingualism on theory of mind. *Bilingualism: Language and Cognition, 6*, 1–15.

Goldberg, H., Paradis, J., & Crago, M. (2008). Lexical acquisition over time in minority first language children learning English as a second language. *Applied Psycholinguistics, 29*(1), 41–65.

Goldin-Meadow, S., Levine, S. C., Hedges, L. V., Huttenlocher, J., Raudenbush, S. W., & Small, S. L. (2014). New evidence about language and cognitive development based on a longitudinal study: Hypotheses for intervention. *American Psychologist, 69*, 588–599.

Goldin-Meadow, S., Mylander, C., de Villiers, J., Bates, E., & Volterra, V. (1984). Gestural communication in deaf children: The effects and noneffects of parental input on early language development. *Monographs of the Society for Research in Child Development, 49*(3), 1–151.

Goldman, S. R., & Snow, C. E. (2015). Adolescent literacy: Development and instruction. In A. Pollatsek & R. Treiman (Eds.), *The Oxford handbook of reading* (pp. 463–478). New York, NY: Oxford University Press.

Goldstein, H. (2003). *Multilevel statistical models*. New York, NY: Arnold.

Goldstein, M. H., King, A. P., & West, M. J. (2003). Social interaction shapes babbling: Testing parallels between birdsong and speech. *Proceedings of the National Academy of Sciences, 100*(13), 8030–8035.

Goodman, K. S. (1965). A linguistic study of cues and miscues in reading. *Elementary English, 42*, 639–643.

Goodman, Y. (1989). Roots of the whole-language movement. *Elementary School Journal, 90*, 113–127.

Goodwin, A. P. (2016). Effectiveness of word solving: Integrating morphological problem-solving within comprehension instruction for middle school students. *Reading & Writing, 29*(1), 91–116.

Goodwin, A. P., Gilbert, J. K., & Cho, S.-J. (2013). Morphological contributions to adolescent word reading: An item response approach. *Reading Research Quarterly, 48*(1), 39–60.

Gort, M. (2006). Strategic codeswitching, interliteracy, and other phenomena of emergent bilingual writing: Lessons from first grade dual language classrooms. *Journal of Early Childhood Literacy, 6*(3), 323–354.

Gort, M., & Sembiante, S. F. (2015). Navigating hybridized language learning spaces through translanguaging pedagogy: Dual language preschool teachers' languaging practices in support of emergent bilingual children's performance of academic discourse. *International Multilingual Research Journal, 9*(1), 7–25.

Gosse, C. S., McGinty, A. S., Mashburn, A. J., Hoffman, L. M., & Pianta, R. C. (2014). The role of relational and instructional classroom supports in the language development of at-risk preschoolers. *Early Education & Development, 25*(1), 110–133.

Gottardo, A., Chiappe, P., Yan, B., Siegel, L., & Gu, Y. (2006). Relationships between first and second language phonological processing skills and reading in Chinese-English speakers living in English-speaking contexts. *Educational Psychology, 26*, 367–393.

Gottardo, A., Javier, C., Farnia, F., Mak, L., & Geva, E. (2014). Bidirectional cross-linguistic relations of first and second language skills in reading comprehension of Spanish- speaking English learners. *Written Language and Literacy, 17*, 62–88.

Gottardo, A., & Mueller, J. (2009). Are first- and second-language factors related in predicting second-language reading comprehension? A study of Spanish-speaking children acquiring English as a second language from first to second grade. *Journal of Educational Psychology, 101*, 330–344.

Gough, P. B., & Hillinger, M. L. (1980). Learning to read: An unnatural act. *Bulletin of the Orton Society, 30*, 179–190.

Graesser, A. C., Singer, M., & Trabasso, T. (1994). Constructing inferences during narrative text comprehension. *Psychological Review, 101*(3), 371–395.

Grant, A., Gottardo, A., & Geva, E. (2011). Reading in English as a first or second language: The case of grade 3 Spanish, Portuguese, and English speakers. *Learning Disabilities Research & Practice, 26*, 67–83.

Graves, M. F. (2016). *The vocabulary book: Learning and instruction* (2nd ed.). New York, NY: Teachers College Press.

Graves, M. F., Baumann, J. F., Blachowicz, C. L. Z., Manyak, P., Bates, A., Cieply, C., Davis, J. R., & Von Gunten, H. (2014). Words, words everywhere, but which ones do we teach? *The Reading Teacher, 67*(5), 333–346.

Gray, S., Carter, A., Briggs-Gowan, M., Jones, S., Wagmiller, R., & Eccles, J. S. (2014). Growth trajectories of early aggression, overactivity, and inattention: Relations to second-grade reading. *Developmental Psychology, 50*(9), 2255–2263.

Greene, R., & Hakuta, K. (2015). Epistemological linguistics: A new, learning-centered branch of linguistics. In R. A. Scott & M. C. Buchmann (Eds.), *Emerging trends in the social and behavioral sciences: An interdisciplinary, searchable, linkable resource.* Retrieved from https://onlinelibrary.wiley.com/doi/book/10.1002/9781118900772

Greenleaf, C., & Valencia, S. (2016). Missing in action: Learning from texts in subject-matter classrooms. In D. A. Appleman & K. A. Hinchman (Eds.), *Adolescent literacies: A handbook of practice-based research* (pp. 235–256). New York, NY: Guilford.

Grimm, K. J., Steele, J. S., Mashburn, A. J., Burchinal, M., & Pianta, R. C. (2010). Early behavioral associations of achievement trajectories. *Developmental Psychology, 46*(5), 976–983.

Grosjean, F. (2010). *Bilingual: Life and reality.* Cambridge, MA: Harvard University Press.

Grøver Aukrust, V., & Snow, C. E. (1998). Narratives and explanations during mealtime conversations in Norway and the U.S. *Language in Society, 27*, 221–246.

Guglielmi, R. S. (2008). Native language proficiency, English literacy, academic achievement, and occupational attainment in limited-English-proficient students: A latent growth modeling perspective. *Journal of Educational Psychology, 100*(2), 322–342.

Guo, Y., Piasta, S. B., Justice, L. M., & Kaderavek, J. N. (2010). Relations among preschool teachers' self-efficacy, classroom quality, and children's language and literacy gains. *Teaching and Teacher Education, 26*(4), 1094–1103.

Hair, E., Halle, T., Terry-Humen, E., Lavelle, B., & Calkins, J. (2006). Children's school readiness in the ECLS-K: Predictions to academic, health, and social outcomes in first grade. *Early Childhood Research Quarterly, 21*, 431–454.

Hakuta, K. (2011). Educating language minority students and affirming their equal rights: Research and practical perspectives. Seventh Annual Brown Lecture in Education Research. *Educational Researcher, 20*, 1–12.

Halliday, M. A. K. (1975). *Learning how to mean: Explorations in the development of language.* London, England: Edward Arnold.

(1993). Towards a language-based theory of learning. *Linguistics and Education, 5* (2), 93–116.

(2004). *The language of science – collected works of M.A.K. Halliday* (Vol. 5). New York, NY: Continuum.

Halliday, M. A. K., & Matthiessen, C. M. I. M. (2004). *An introduction to functional grammar* (3rd ed.). London, England: Arnold.

Hammer, C. S., Hoff, E., Uchikoshi, Y., Gillanders, C., Castro, D. C., & Sandilos, L. E. (2014). The language and literacy development of young dual language learners: A critical review. *Early Childhood Research Quarterly, 29*, 715–733.

Hammer, C. S., Lawrence, F. R., & Miccio, A. W. (2007). Bilingual children's language abilities and early reading outcomes in head start and kindergarten. *Language, Speech, and Hearing Services in Schools, 38*(3), 237–248.

Hammett, L. A., Van Kleeck, A., & Huberty, C. J. (2003). Patterns of parents' extra-textual interactions with preschool children: A cluster analysis study. *Reading Research Quarterly, 38*(4), 442–467.

Hamre, B., Hartfield, B., Pianta, R., & Jamil, F. (2014). Evidence for general and domain- specific elements of teacher-child interactions: Associations with pre-school children's development. *Child Development, 85*(3), 1257–1274.

Hamre, B. K., Justice, L. M., Pianta, R. C., Kilday, C., Sweeney, B., Downer, J. T., & Leach, A. (2010). Implementation fidelity of MyTeachingPartner literacy and language activities: Association with preschoolers' language and literacy growth. *Early Childhood Research Quarterly, 25*(3), 329–347.

Harris, P. L. (2012). *Trusting what you're told: How children learn from others.* Cambridge, MA: Belknap Press/Harvard University Press.

(2017). Tell, ask, repair: Early responding to discordant reality. *Motivation Science, 3,* 275–286.

Harris, P. L., & Corriveau, K. H. (2011). Young children's selective trust in informants. *Proceedings of the Royal Society B, 366,* 1179–1190.

Harris, P. L., & Lane, J. D. (2014). Infants understand how testimony works. *Topoi, 33,* 443–458.

Hart, B., & Risley, T. R. (1995). *Meaningful differences in the everyday experience of young American children.* Baltimore, MD: Paul H. Brookes.

Hayes, D. P., & Ahrens, M. (1988). Vocabulary simplification for children: A special case of "motherese"? *Journal of Child Language, 15,* 395–410.

Heath, S. B. (1983). *Ways with words: Language, life, and work in communities and classrooms.* New York, NY: McGraw-Hill.

(2012). *Words at work and play: Three decades in family and community life.* Cambridge, England: Cambridge University Press.

Hedges, L., & Hedberg, E. (2007). Intraclass correlation values for planning group-randomized trials in education. *Educational Evaluation and Policy Analysis, 29*(1), 60–87.

Hedrick, W. B., Harmon, J. M., & Linerode, P. M. (2004). Teachers' beliefs and practices of vocabulary instruction with social studies textbooks in grades 4–8. *Reading Horizons, 45,* 103–125.

Hemphill, L., & Snow, C. E. (1996). Language and literacy development: Discontinuities and differences. In D. Olson & N. Torrance (Eds.), *The handbook of education and human development: New models of learning, teaching and schooling* (pp. 173–201). Oxford, England: Blackwell.

Henrichs, J., Rescorla, L., Schenk, J. J., Schmidt, H. G., Jadooe, V. W. V., Hofman, A., ... Tiemeier, H. (2011). Examining continuity of early expressive vocabulary development: The Generation R study. *Journal of Speech, Language, and Hearing Research, 54*, 854–869.

Henrichs, L. F. (2010). *Academic language in early childhood interactions: A longitudinal study of 3- to 6-year-old Dutch monolingual children* (Unpublished doctoral dissertation). University of Amsterdam, Netherlands. Retrieved from http://dare.uva.nl/en/record/334829

Hickman, G. P., Bartholomew, M., Mathwig, J., & Heinrich, R. S. (2008). Differential developmental pathways of high school dropouts and graduates. *Journal of Educational Research, 102*(1), 3–14.

Hiebert, E. H., & Kamil, M. L. (2005). *Teaching and learning vocabulary: Bringing research to practice*. New York, NY: Routledge.

Hindman, A. H., Erhart, A. C., & Wasik, B. A. (2012). Reducing the Matthew effect: Lessons from the ExCELL Head Start intervention. *Early Education & Development, 23*(5), 781–806.

Hindman, A. H., Wasik, B. A., & Erhart, A. C. (2012). Shared book reading and Head Start preschoolers' vocabulary learning: The role of book-related discussion and curricular connections. *Early Education & Development, 23*(4), 451–474.

Hipfner-Boucher, K., Lam, K., & Chen, X. (2014). The effects of bilingual education on the English language and literacy outcomes of Chinese-speaking children. *Written Language & Literacy, 17*(1), 116–138.

Hirsh-Pasek, K., Adamson, L. B., Bakeman, R., Owen, M. T., Golinkoff, R. M., Pacee, A., ... Suma, K. (2015). The contribution of early communication quality to low-income children's language success. *Psychological Science, 26*, 1971–1983.

Hoff, E. (2003). The specificity of environmental influence: Socioeconomic status affects early vocabulary development via maternal speech. *Child Development, 71*, 1368–1378.

(2006). How social contexts support and shape language development. *Developmental Review, 26*, 55–88.

(2013). Interpreting the early language trajectories of children from low-SES and language minority homes: Implications for closing achievement gaps. *Developmental Psychology, 49*, 4–6.

Hoff-Ginsberg, E. (1985). Some contributions of mothers' speech to their children's syntactic growth. *Journal of Child Language, 12*(2), 367–385.

Hoover, W. A., & Gough, P. B. (1990). The simple view of reading. *Reading and Writing: An Interdisciplinary Journal, 2*(2), 127–160.

Howard, E. R., Green, J. D., & Arteagoitia, I. (2012). Can yu rid guat ay rot? A developmental investigation of cross-linguistic spelling errors among Spanish–English bilingual students. *Bilingual Research Journal, 35*(2), 164–178.

Howard, E. R., Páez, M. M., August, D. L., Barr, C. D., Kenyon, D., & Malabonga, V. (2014). The importance of SES, home and school language and literacy practices, and oral vocabulary in bilingual children's English reading development. *Bilingual Research Journal, 37*(2), 120–141.

Howes, C. (2008). Measures of classroom quality in prekindergarten and children's development of academic, language, and social skills. *Child Development, 79*(3), 732–749.

Howes, C., Burchinal, M., Pianta, R., Bryant, D., Early, D., Clifford, R., & Barbarin, O. (2015). Ready to learn? Children's pre-academic achievement in pre-kindergarten programs. *Early Childhood Research Quarterly, 23*, 27–50.

Hsin, L., & Snow, C. E. (2017). Social perspective taking: A benefit of bilingualism in academic writing. *Reading and Writing: An Interdisciplinary Journal, 30*, 1193–1214.

Hsu, H. C., & Fogel, A. (2001). Infant vocal development in a dynamic mother–infant communication system. *Infancy, 2*(1), 87–109.

Hu, C. F. (2013). Predictors of reading in children with Chinese as a first language: A developmental and cross-linguistic perspective. *Reading and Writing, 26*(2), 163–187.

Huang, X. Y. (2011). Delayed language development of children in bilingual education. *Journal of Longyan University, 3*, 22.

Hughes, M., & Allen, S. E. M. (2015). The incremental effect of discourse-pragmatic sensitivity on referential choice in the acquisition of a first language. *Lingua, 155*, 43–61.

Hurtado, N., Marchman, V. A., & Fernald, A. (2008). Does input influence uptake? Links between maternal talk, processing speed and vocabulary size in Spanish-learning children. *Developmental Science, 11*(6), 31–39.

Huttenlocher, J., Haight, W., Bryk, A., Seltzer, M., & Lyons, T. (1991). Early vocabulary growth: Relation to language input and gender. *Developmental Psychology, 27*, 236–248.

Huttenlocher, J., Vasilyeva, M., Cymerman, E., & Levine, S. (2002). Language input and child syntax. *Cognitive Psychology, 45*(3), 337–374.

Huttenlocher, J., Waterfall, H., Vasilyeva, M., Vevea, J., & Hedges, L. V. (2010). Sources of variability in children's language growth. *Cognitive Psychology, 61*(4), 343–365.

Hutzler, F., & Wimmer, H. (2004). Eye movements of dyslexic children when reading in a regular orthography. *Brain and Language, 89*, 235–242.

Hwang, J. K., Lawrence, J. F., Mo, E., & Snow, C. E. (2014). Differential effects of a systematic vocabulary intervention on adolescent language minority students with varying levels of English proficiency. *International Journal of Bilingualism, 19*, 314–332.

Hyland, K. (2009). *Academic discourse: English in a global context*. London, England: Continuum.

Ivey, G., & Broaddus, K. (2001). "Just plain reading": A survey of what makes students want to read in middle school classrooms. *Reading Research Quarterly, 36*(4), 350–377.

January, S.-A. A., & Ardoin, S. P. (2012). The impact of context and word type on students' maze task accuracy. *School Psychology Review, 41*, 262–271.

Jared, D., Cormier, P., Levy, B. A., & Wade-Woolley, L. (2011). Early predictors of biliteracy development in children in French immersion: A 4-year longitudinal study. *Journal of Educational Psychology, 103*(1), 119–139.

Jean, M., & Geva, E. (2009). The development of vocabulary in English as a second language children and its role in predicting word recognition ability. *Applied Psycholinguistics, 30*, 153–185.

Jenkins, J. R., Stein, M. L., & Wysocki, K. (1984). Learning vocabulary through reading. *American Educational Research Journal, 21*(4), 767–787.

Jiménez, R., Garcia, G. E., & Pearson, P. D. (1995). Three children, two languages, and strategic reading: Case studies in bilingual/monolingual READING. *American Educational Research Journal, 32*(1), 67–97.

Johnson, I. (2013, April 25). China's Sufis: The shrines behind the dunes. *New York Review of Books*. Retrieved from www.nybooks.com/blogs/nyrblog/2013/apr/25/china-xinjiang-sufi-shrines/

Jones, S. M., Bub, K. L., & Raver, C. C. (2013). Unpacking the black box of the CSRP intervention: The mediating roles of teacher–child relationship quality and self-regulation. *Early Education and Development, 24*(7), 1043–1064.

Jones, S. M., LaRusso, M., Kim, J., Kim, H. Y., Selman, R., Uccelli, P., Barnes, S., ... Snow, C. (in press). Experimental effects of Word Generation on vocabulary, academic language, perspective taking, and reading comprehension in high poverty schools. *Journal for Research on Educational Effectiveness*.

Justice, L. M., & Ezell, H. K. (2004). Print referencing: An emergent literacy enhancement strategy and its clinical applications. *Language, Speech, and Hearing Services in Schools, 35*, 185–193.

Justice, L. M., Mashburn, A., Pence, K. L., & Wiggins, A. (2008). Experimental evaluation of a preschool language curriculum: Influence on children's expressive language skills. *Journal of Speech, Language, and Hearing Research, 51*(4), 983–1001.

Kamil, M. L., Borman, G. D., Dole, J., et al. (2008). *Improving adolescent literacy: Effective classroom and intervention practices: A practice guide* (NCEE No. 2008-4027). Washington, DC: National Center for Education Evaluation and Regional Assistance, Institute of Education Sciences, US Department of Education.

Kan, P. F., & Kohnert, K. J. (2008). Fast mapping by bilingual preschool children. *Journal of Child Language, 35*, 495–514.

Kang, J. Y. (2013). Decontextualized language production in two languages: An investigation of children's word definition skills in Korean and English. *Applied Psycholinguistics, 34*, 211–231.

Karbach, J., Strobach, T., & Schubert, T. (2015). Adaptive working-memory training benefits reading, but not mathematics in middle childhood. *Child Neuropsychology, 21*, 285–301.

Keenan, J. M., & Meenan, C. E. (2014). Test differences in diagnosing reading comprehension deficits. *Journal of Learning Disabilities, 47*(2), 125–135.

Keller, H. (2013). *Cultures of infancy*. Hove, England: Psychology Press.

Kendeou, P., Bohn-Gettler, C. M., White, M. J., & van den Broek, P. (2008). Children's inference generation across different media. *Journal of Research in Reading, 31*, 259–272.

Kermani, H., & Janes, H. A. (1999). Adjustment across task in maternal scaffolding in low-income Latino immigrant families. *Hispanic Journal of Behavioral Sciences, 21*, 134–153.

Kidd, E. (2012). Implicit statistical learning is directly associated with the acquisition of syntax. *Developmental Psychology, 48*(1), 171–184.

Kieffer, M. J. (2008). Catching up or falling behind? Initial English proficiency, concentrated poverty, and the reading growth of language minority learners in the United States. *Journal of Educational Psychology, 100*, 851–868.

(2014). Morphological awareness and reading difficulties in adolescent Spanish-speaking language minority learners and their classmates. *Journal of Learning Disabilities, 47*(1), 44–53.

Kieffer, M. J., & Box, C. D. (2013). Derivational morphological awareness, academic vocabulary, and reading comprehension in linguistically diverse sixth graders. *Learning and Individual Differences, 24*, 168–175.

Kieffer, M. J., & Lesaux, N. K. (2012). Direct and indirect roles of morphological awareness in the English reading comprehension of native English, Spanish, Filipino, and Vietnamese speakers. *Language Learning, 62*(4), 1170–1204.

Kieffer, M. J., Petscher, Y., Proctor, C. P., & Silverman, R. D. (2016). Is the whole greater than the sum of its parts? Modeling the contributions of language comprehension skills to reading comprehension in the upper elementary grades. *Scientific Studies of Reading, 20*(6), 436–454.

Kieffer, M. J., & Vukovic, R. K. (2013). Growth in reading-related skills of language minority learners and their classmates: More evidence for early identification and intervention. *Reading and Writing: An Interdisciplinary Journal, 26*, 1159–1194.

Kilgus, S. P., Methe, S. A., Maggin, D. M., & Tomasula, J. L. (2014). Curriculum-based measurement of oral reading (R-CBM): A diagnostic test accuracy meta-analysis of evidence supporting use in universal screening. *Journal of School Psychology, 52*(4), 377–405.

Kim, Y.-S., Al Otaiba, S., Sidler, J. F., & Greulich, L., & Puranik, C. (2014). Evaluating the dimensionality of first grade written composition. *Journal of Speech, Language, and Hearing Research, 57*, 199–211.

Kim, Y. S. G. (2009). Crosslinguistic influence on phonological awareness for Korean–English bilingual children. *Reading and Writing, 22*(7), 843–861.

(2015). Language and cognitive predictors of text comprehension: Evidence from multivariate analysis. *Child Development, 86*, 128–144.

(2016). Direct and mediated effects of language and cognitive skills on comprehension or oral narrative texts (listening comprehension) for children. *Journal of Experimental Child Psychology, 141*, 101–120.

(2017). Why the simple view of reading is not simplistic: Unpacking the simple view of reading using a direct and indirect effect model of reading (DIER). *Scientific Studies of Reading, 21*, 310–333.

Kim, Y.-S. G., & Phillips, B. (2014). Cognitive correlates of listening comprehension. *Reading Research Quarterly, 49*, 269–281.

(2016). 5 minutes a day: An exploratory study of improving comprehension monitoring for prekindergartners from low income families. *Topics in Language Disorder, 36*, 356–367.

Kim, Y.-S. G., & Pilcher, H. (2016). What is listening comprehension and what does it take to improve listening comprehension? In R. Schiff & M. Joshi

(Eds.), *Handbook of interventions in learning disabilities* (pp. 159–174). New York, NY: Springer.

Kim, Y.-S. G., & Schatschneider, C. (2017). Expanding the developmental models of writing: direct and indirect effects model of developmental writing (DIEW). *Journal of Educational Psychology, 109*, 35–50.

Kintsch, W. (1988). The use of knowledge in discourse processing: A construction-integration model. *Psychological Review, 95*, 163–182.

(1998). *Comprehension: A paradigm for cognition*. Cambridge, MA: Cambridge University Press.

(2004). The construction–integration model of text comprehension and its implications for instruction. In R. B. Ruddell & N. J. Unrau (Eds.), *Theoretical models and processes of reading* (5th ed., pp. 1270–1328). Newark, DE: International Reading Association.

Kirjavainen, M., Theakston, A., & Lieven, E. (2009). Can input explain children's me-for-I errors? *Journal of Child Language, 36*(5), 1091–1114.

Koenig, M., & Harris, P. L. (2005). Preschoolers mistrust ignorant and inaccurate speakers. *Child Development, 76*, 1261–1277.

Kohnert, K., Yim, D., Nett, K., Kan, P. F., & Duran, L. (2005). Intervention with linguistically diverse kindergarten children: A focus on developing home language(s). *Language, Speech, and Hearing Services in Schools, 36*(3), 251–263.

Kong, A., & Pearson, D. P. (2003). The road to participation: The construction of a literacy practice in a learning community of linguistically diverse learners. *Research in the Teaching of English, 38*, 85–124.

Kovács, A., Tauzin, T., Téglás, E., Gergely, G., & Csibra, G. (2014). Pointing as epistemic request: 12-month-olds point to receive new information. *Infancy, 19*, 543–557.

Kovelman, I., Baker, S. A., & Petitto, L. (2008). Age of first bilingual language exposure as a new window into bilingual reading development. *Bilingualism: Language and Cognition, 11*(2), 203–223.

Kroll, J. F., & de Groot, A. (1997). Lexical and conceptual memory in the bilingual: Mapping form to meaning in two languages. In A. M. B. de Groot & J. F. Kroll (Eds.), *Tutorials in bilingualism: Psycholinguistic perspectives* (pp. 169–199). Mahwah, NJ: Lawrence Erlbaum Associates.

Kuhl, P. K. (1991). Human adults and human infants show a "perceptual magnet effect" for the prototypes of speech categories, monkeys do not. *Attention, Perception, & Psychophysics, 50*(2), 93–107.

Kuo, L. J., & Anderson, R. C. (2006). Beyond cross-language transfer: Reconceptualizing the impact of early bilingualism on phonological awareness. *Scientific Studies of Reading, 14*, 365–385.

LaBerge, D., & Samuels, S. J. (1974). Toward a theory of automatic information processing in reading. *Cognitive Psychology, 6*, 293–323.

Lacey, W. K. (1968). *The family in classical Greece*. Ithaca, NY: Cornell University Press.

Laghzaoui, M. (2011). *Emergent academic language at home and at school* (Unpublished doctoral dissertation). Tilburg University, Oisterwijk, Netherlands.

Laing, S. P., & Kamhi, A. G. (2002). The use of think-aloud protocols to compare inferencing abilities in average and below-average readers. *Journal of Learning Disabilities, 35*(5), 436–447.

Lam, K., Chen, X., Geva, E., Luo, Y., & Li, H. (2012). The effects of morphological awareness development on reading achievement in young English Language Learners (ELLs): A longitudinal study. *Reading and Writing, 25*, 1847–1872.

Landry, S. H., Anthony, J. L., Swank, P. R., & Monseque-Bailey, P. (2009). Effectiveness of comprehensive professional development for teachers of at-risk preschoolers. *Journal of Educational Psychology, 101*(2), 448–465.

Landry, S. H., Smith, K. E., Miller-Loncar, C. L., & Swank, P. R. (1997). Predicting cognitive-language and social growth curves from early maternal behaviors in children at varying degrees of biological risk. *Developmental Psychology, 33*, 1040–1053.

Landry, S. H., Swank, P. R., Anthony, J. L., & Assel, M. A. (2011). An experimental study evaluating professional development activities within a state funded pre-kindergarten program. *Reading and Writing: An Interdisciplinary Journal, 24*(8), 971–1010.

Landry, S. H., Swank, P. R., Smith, K. E., Assel, M. A., & Gunnewig, S. B. (2006). Enhancing early literacy skills for preschool children bringing a professional development model to scale. *Journal of Learning Disabilities, 39*(4), 306–324.

LaRusso, M., Kim, H. Y., Selman, R., Uccelli, P., Dawson, T., Jones, S., . . . Snow, C. E. (2016). Contributions of academic language, perspective taking, and complex reasoning to deep reading comprehension. *Journal of Research on Educational Effectiveness, 9*, 201–222.

Ledoux, G., Roeleveld J., Mulder, L., Veen, A., Karssen, M., Van Daalen, M., . . . Fettelaar, D. (2015). *Het onderwijsachterstandenbeleid, werkt het zoals bedoeld?* [Educational disadvantages policy: Does it work as intended?]. Amsterdam, Netherlands: Kohnstamm Instituut.

Leech, K. A., Wei, R., Harring, J., & Rowe, M. L. (2018). A brief parent-focused intervention to improve preschoolers' conversational skills and school readiness. *Developmental Psychology, 54*(1), 15–28.

Leider, C. M., Proctor, P. C., Silverman, R. D., & Harring, J. R. (2013). Examining the role of vocabulary depth, cross-linguistic transfer, and types of reading measures on the reading comprehension of Latino bilinguals in elementary school. *Reading and Writing: An Interdisciplinary Journal, 26*(9), 1459–1485.

Lepola, J., Lynch, J., Laakkonen, E., Silvén, M., & Niemi, P. (2012). The role of inference making and other language skills in the development of narrative listening comprehension in 4- to 6-year old children. *Reading Research Quarterly, 47*, 259–282.

Lervåg, A., & Grøver Aukrust, V. (2010). Vocabulary knowledge is a critical determinant of the difference in reading comprehension growth between first and second language learners. *Journal of Child Psychology and Psychiatry, 51*(5), 612–620.

Lesaux, N. K., Crosson, A. C., Kieffer, M. J., & Pierce, M. (2010). Uneven profiles: Language minority learners' word reading, vocabulary, and reading comprehension skills. *Journal of Applied Developmental Psychology, 31*(6), 475–483.

Lesaux, N. K., & Geva, E. (2006). Synthesis: Development of literacy in language-minority students. In D. L. August & T. Shanahan (Eds.), *Developing literacy in a second language: Report of the national literacy panel* (pp. 53–74). Mahwah, NJ: Lawrence Erlbaum Associates.

Lesaux, N. K., Kieffer, M. J., Faller, S. E., & Kelley, J. G. (2010). The effectiveness and ease of implementation of an academic vocabulary intervention for linguistically diverse students in urban middle schools. *Reading Research Quarterly, 45*, 196–228.

Lesaux, N. K., Lipka, O., & Siegel, L. S. (2006). The development of reading in children who speak English as a second language. *Developmental Psychology, 39*(6), 1005–1019.

Lesaux, N. K., Rupp, A. A., & Siegel, L. S. (2007). Growth in reading skills of children from diverse linguistic backgrounds: Findings from a 5-year longitudinal study. *Journal of Educational Psychology, 99*(4), 821–834.

Lesaux, N. K., & Siegel, L. S. (2003). The development of reading in children who speak English as a second language. *Developmental Psychology, 39*, 1005–1019.

Leseman, P. P. M. (2000). Bilingual vocabulary development of Turkish preschoolers in the Netherlands. *Journal of Multilingual and Multicultural Development, 21*(2), 93–112.

Leseman, P. P. M., Mayo, A. Y., & Scheele, A. F. (2009). Traditional and new media in the lives of young disadvantaged bilingual children. In A. G. Bus & S. B. Neuman (Eds.), *Literacy and media* (pp. 135–150). New York, NY: Falmer Press.

Leseman, P. P. M., Scheele, A. F., Mayo, A. Y., & Messer, M. H. (2007). Home literacy as a special language environment to prepare children for school. *Zeitschrift für Erziehungswissenschaft, 10*(3), 334–355.

Leseman, P. P. M., Scheele, A. F., Messer, M. H., & Mayo, A. Y. (2009). Bilingual development in early childhood and the languages used at home: Competition for scarce resources? In I. Gogolin & U. Neumann (Eds.), *Streitfall Zweisprachigkeit – The bilingualism controversy* (pp. 289–316). Wiesbaden, Germany: VS-Verlag.

Lever, R., & Sénéchal, M. (2011). Discussing stories: On how a dialogic reading intervention improves kindergartners' oral narrative construction. *Journal of Experimental Child Psychology, 108*(1), 1–24.

LeVine, R. A., LeVine, S., Dixon, S., Richman, A., Leiderman, H., Keefer, C. H., & Brazelton, T. B. (1996). *Child care and culture: Lessons from Africa.* Cambridge, England: Cambridge University Press.

LeVine, R. A., LeVine, S., Schnell-Anzola, B., Rowe, M., & Dexter E. (2012). *Literacy and mothering: How women's schooling changes the lives of the world's children.* New York, NY: Oxford University Press.

Lewis, C., Enciso, P. E., & Moje, E. B. (Eds.). (2007). *Reframing sociocultural research on literacy: Identity, agency, and power.* Mahwah, NJ: Lawrence Erlbaum Associates.

Leyva, D., Reese, E., Grolnick, W., & Price, C. (2008). Elaboration and autonomy support in low-income mothers' reminiscing: Links to children's autobiographical narratives. *Journal of Cognition and Development, 9*, 363–389.

Leyva, D., Reese, E., & Wiser, M. (2012). Early understanding of the functions of print: Parent-child interaction and preschoolers' notating skills. *First Language, 32*, 301–323.

Leyva, D., Tamis-LeMonda, C., Yoshikawa, H., Jimenez-Robbins, C., & Malachowski, L. (2017). Grocery games: How ethnically diverse low-income mothers support children's mathematics and literacy. *Early Childhood Research Quarterly, 40*, 63–76.

Leyva, D., Weiland, C., Yoshikawa, H., Snow, C., Barata, C., Rolla, A., & Treviño, E. (2015). Assessing classroom quality in the U.S. and Chile: Factor structure and associations with prekindergarten outcomes. *Child Development, 86*(3), 781–799.

Li, C. J. (2013). *Research on the semantic development of Xinjiang minority young children* (Unpublished master's thesis). East China Normal University, Shanghai, China.

Li, S. G., & Cai, W. L. (2012). Challenges of Xinjiang bilingual education in elementary school. *Journal of Hetian Normal University, 31*(3), 85–87.

Liberman, Z., Woodward, A. L., Keysar, B., & Kinzler, K. D. (2016). Exposure to multiple languages enhances communication skills in infancy. *Developmental Science, 19*, 1–11.

Lieven, E. (2013). Language acquisition as a cultural process. In P. J. Richerson & M. H. Christiansen (Eds.), *Cultural evolution: Society, technology, language, and religion* (pp. 269–283). Cambridge, MA: MIT Press.

(2017). Is language development dependent on early communicative development? In N. J. Enfield (Ed.), *Dependencies in language: On the causal ontology of linguistic systems* (pp. 85–95). Berlin, Germany: Language Science Press.

Lieven, E., & Stoll, S. (2013). Early communicative development in two cultures. *Human Development, 56*, 178–206.

Limbird, C. K., Maluch, J. T., Rjosk, C., Stanat, P., & Merkens, H. (2013). Differential growth patterns in emerging reading skills of Turkish-German bilingual and German monolingual primary school students. *Reading and Writing, 27*, 1–24.

Lin, D., McBride-Chang, C., Aram, D., Levin, I., Cheung, R. Y., Chow, Y. Y., & Tolchinsky, L. (2009). Maternal mediation of writing in Chinese children. *Language and Cognitive Processes, 24*, 1286–1311.

Lindsey, K. A., Manis, F. R., & Bailey, C. E. (2003). Prediction of first-grade reading in Spanish-speaking English-language learners. *Journal of Educational Psychology, 95*(3), 482–494.

Lipka, O., & Siegel, L. S. (2007). The development of reading skills in children with English as a second language. *Scientific Studies of Reading, 11*(2), 105–131.

(2010). The improvement of reading skills of L1 and ESL children using a Response to Intervention (RtI) Model. *Psicothema, 22*, 963–969.

(2012). The development of reading comprehension skills in children learning English as a second language. *Reading and Writing: An Interdisciplinary Journal, 25*, 1873–1898.

Liszkowski, U., Brown, P., Callaghan, T., Takada, A., & de Vos, C. (2012). A prelinguistic gestural universal of human communication. *Cognitive Science, 36*, 698–713.

Lizskowski, U., Carpenter, M., Henning, A., Striano, T., & Tomasello, M. (2004). 12-month-olds point to share attention and interest. *Developmental Science, 7*, 297–307.

LoCasale-Crouch, J., Konold, T., Pianta, R., Howes, C., Burchinal, M., Bryant, . . . Barbarin, O. (2007). Profiles of observed classroom quality in state-funded pre-kindergarten programs and associations with teacher, program, and classroom characteristics. *Early Childhood Research Quarterly, 22*(1), 3–17

Loftus, S. M., Coyne, M. D., McCoach, D. B., Zipoli, R., & Pullen, P. C. (2010). Effects of a supplemental vocabulary intervention on the word knowledge of kindergarten students at risk for language and literacy difficulties. *Learning Disabilities Research & Practice, 25*(3), 124–136.

Logan, G. D. (1992). Shapes of reaction-time distributions and shapes of learning curves: A test of the instance theory of automaticity. *Journal of Experimental Psychology: Learning, Memory, and Cognition, 18*(5), 883–914.

Lohmann, H., & Tomasello, M. (2003). The role of language in the development of false belief understanding: A training study. *Child Development, 74*, 1130–1144.

Lonigan, C., Schatschneider, C., & Westberg, L. (2008). Identification of children's skills and abilities linked to later outcomes in reading, writing, and spelling. In *Developing early literacy: Report of the National Early Literacy Panel* (pp. 55–106). Retrieved from https://lincs.ed.gov/publications/pdf/NELPReport09.pdf

Lonigan, C. J., & Shanahan, T. (2009). *Developing early literacy: Report of the National Early Literacy Panel. Executive summary. A scientific synthesis of early literacy development and implications for intervention.* Washington, DC: National Institute for Literacy.

Lonigan, C. J., & Whitehurst, G. J. (1998). Relative efficacy of parent and teacher involvement in a shared-reading intervention for preschool children from low-income backgrounds. *Early Childhood Research Quarterly, 13*, 263–290.

Loosli, S. V., Buschkuehl, M., Perrig, W. J., & Jaeggi, S. M. (2012). Working memory training improves reading processes in typically developing children. *Child Neuropsychology, 18*, 62–78.

López, L. M. (2012). Assessing the phonological skills of bilingual children from preschool through kindergarten: Developmental progression and cross-language transfer. *Journal of Research in Childhood Education, 26*(4), 371–391.

López, L. M., & Greenfield, D. B. (2004). The cross-language transfer of phonological skills of Hispanic Head Start children. *Bilingual Research Journal, 28* (1), 1–18.

Love, J., Kisker, E. E., Ross, C., Raikes, H., Constantine, J., Boller, K., et al. (2005). The effectiveness of Early Head Start for 3-year-old children and their parents. *Developmental Psychology, 41*(6), 885–901.

Lu, L., & Liu, H. S. (1998). *The Peabody Picture Vocabulary Test–Revised in Chinese.* Taipei, Taiwan: Psychological Publishing.

Lucca, K., & Wilbourn, M. P. (2016). Communicating to learn: Infant's pointing gestures result in optimal learning. *Child Development, 89*, 941–960.

Lüke, C., Grimminger, A., Rohfling, K. J., Liszkowski, U., & Ritterfeld, U. (2017). In infants' hands: Identification of preverbal infants at risk for primary language delay. *Child Development, 88*, 484–492.

Luo, R., Tamis-LeMonda, C., Kuchirko, Y., Ng, F. F., & Liang, E. (2014). Mother–child book-sharing and children's storytelling skills in ethnically diverse, low-income families. *Infant and Child Development, 24*, 402–425.

Luo, Y. C., Chen, X., & Geva, E. (2014). Concurrent and longitudinal cross-linguistic transfer of phonological awareness and morphological awareness in Chinese-English bilingual children. *Written Language & Literacy, 17*(1), 89–115.

Lyon, G. R. (1995). Research initiatives in learning disabilities: Contributions from scientists supported by the National Institute of Child Health and Human Development. *Journal of Child Neurology, 10,* 120–126.

Lyster, S.-A. H., Horn, E., & Rygvold, A.-L. (2010). Ordforråd og ordforrådsutvikling hos norske barn og unge. Resultater fra en utprøving av British Picture Vocabulary Scale II, second edition [Vocabulary and vocabulary development in Norwegian children and youth. Results from testing with British Picture Vocabulary Scale II]. *Spesialpedagogikk, 9,* 35–43.

Ma, R. (2008). Minority education and practice of bilingual teaching in Xinjiang. *Peking University Education Review, 6*(2), 2–41.

MacWhinney, B. (2000). *The CHILDES Project: Tools for analyzing talk* (3rd ed.). Mahwah, NJ: Lawrence Erlbaum Associates.

(2004a). A multiple process solution to the logical problem of language acquisition. *Journal of Child Language, 31*(4), 883–914.

(2004b). A unified model of language acquisition. In J. F. Kroll & A. M. B. de Groot (Eds.), *Handbook of bilingualism: Psycholinguistic approaches* (pp. 49–67). Oxford, England: Oxford University Press.

MacWhinney, B., & Snow, C. (1990). The child language data exchange system: An update. *Journal of Child Language, 17*(2), 457–472.

Maguire, M. J., Hirsh-Pasek, K., & Golinkoff, M. (2006). *A unified theory of word learning: Putting verb acquisition in context.* Oxford, England: Oxford University Press.

Mahon, E. A. (2006). High-stakes testing and English language learners: Questions of validity. *Bilingual Research Journal, 30*(2), 479–497.

Marinova-Todd, S. H., & Hall, E. (2013). Predictors of English spelling in bilingual and monolingual children in Grade 1: The case of Cantonese and Tagalog. *Educational Psychology, 33*(6), 734–754.

Marinova-Todd, S. H., Siegel, L. S., & Mazabel, S. (2013). The association between morphological awareness and literacy in English Language Learners from diverse language backgrounds. *Topics in Language Disorders, 33,* 93–107.

Martin, J., Sokol, B. W., & Elfers, T. (2008). Taking and coordinating perspectives: From prereflective interactivity, through reflective intersubjectivity, to metareflective sociality. *Human Development, 51*(5–6), 294–317.

Martínez-Roldán, C. M. (2015). Translanguaging practices as mobilization of linguistic resources in a Spanish/English bilingual after-school program: An analysis of contradictions. *International Multilingual Research Journal, 9*(1), 43–58.

Martínez, R. A., Hikida, M., & Durán, L. (2015). Unpacking ideologies of linguistic purism: How dual language teachers make sense of everyday translanguaging. *International Multilingual Research Journal, 9*(1), 26–42.

Marulis, L. M., & Neuman, S. B. (2010). The effects of vocabulary intervention on young children's word learning: A meta-analysis. *Review of Educational Research, 80*(3), 300–335.

Mashburn, A. J. (2008). Quality of social and physical environments in preschools and children's development of academic, language, and literacy skills. *Applied Developmental Science, 12*(3), 113–127.

Mashburn, A. J., Pianta, R. C., Hamre, B. K., Downer, J. T., Barbarin, O. A., Bryant, D., ... Vogt, P. (2016). Infant engagement and early vocabulary development: A naturalistic observation study of Mozambican infants from 1; 1 to 2; 1. *Journal of Child Language, 43*(2), 235–264.

Matthews, D., Behne, T., Lieven, E., & Tomasello, M. (2012). Origins of the human pointing gesture? A training study with 9- to 11-month olds. *Developmental Science, 15*(6), 817–829.

Matthews, D., Butcher, J., Lieven, E., & Tomasello, M. (2012). Two-and four-year-olds learn to adapt referring expressions to context: effects of distracters and feedback on referential communication. *Topics in Cognitive Science, 4*(2), 184–210.

Matthews, D., Theakston, A., Lieven, E., & Tomasello, M. (2006). The effect of perceptual availability and prior discourse on young children's use of referring expressions. *Applied Psycholinguistics, 27*, 403–422.

McAdams, D. P. (1988). *Power, intimacy, and the life story: Personological inquiries into identity*. New York, NY: Guilford Press.

McGillion, M., Herbert, J. S., Pine, J., Vihman, M., DePaolis, R., Keren-Portnoy, T., & Matthews, D. (2017). What paves the way to conventional language? The predictive value of babble, pointing, and socioeconomic status. *Child Development, 88*(1), 156–166.

McKeown, M. G., Beck, I. L., Omanson, R. C., & Perfetti, C. A. (1983). The effects of long-term vocabulary instruction on reading comprehension: A replication. *Journal of Literacy Research, 15*, 3–18.

McKeown, M. G., Beck, I., Omanson, R., & Pople, M. (1985). Some effects of the nature and frequency of vocabulary instruction on the knowledge and use of words. *Reading Research Quarterly, 20*, 522–535.

McMaster, K. L., den Broek, P. V. A., Espin, C., White, M. J., Rapp, D. N., Kendeou, P., ... Carlson, S. (2012). Making the right connections: Differential effects of reading intervention for subgroups of comprehenders. *Learning and Individual Differences, 22*, 100–111.

McMurray, B., Horst, J., & Samuelson, L. (2012). Word learning emerges from the interaction of online referent selection and slow associative learning. *Psychological Review, 119*(4), 831–877.

Meins, E., Fernyhough, C., Arnott, B., Leekam, S. R., & Rosnay, M. (2013). Mind-mindedness and theory of mind: Mediating roles of language and perspectival symbolic play. *Child Development, 84*, 1777–1790.

Meneses, A., Uccelli, P., Santelices, M. V., Ruiz, M., Acevedo, D., & Figueroa, J. (2018). Academic language as a predictor of reading comprehension in monolingual Spanish-speaking readers: Evidence from Chilean early adolescents. *Reading Research Quarterly, 31*, 703–723.

Mercer, N., & Howe, C. (2012). Explaining the dialogic processes of teaching and learning: The value and potential of sociocultural theory. *Learning, Culture, and Social Interaction, 1*, 12–21.

Milner, H. R. (2012). Beyond a test score: Explaining opportunity gaps in educational practice. *Journal of Black Studies, 43*(6), 693–718.

Miller, J. F., Heilmann, J., Nockerts, A., Iglesias, A., Fabiano, L., & Francis, D. J. (2006). Oral language and reading in bilingual children. *Learning Disabilities Research & Practice, 21*, 30–43.

Ministry of Education, Chile. (2012/2013). Informe Técnico Simce 2012, 2013. Santiago, Chile: Author.

Mol, S. E., & Bus, A. G. (2011). To read or not to read: A meta-analysis of print exposure from infancy to early adulthood. *Psychological Bulletin, 137*(2), 267–296.

Mol, S. E., Bus, A. G., & de Jong, M. T. (2009). Interactive book reading in early education: A tool to stimulate print knowledge as well as oral language. *Review of Educational Research, 79*(2), 979–1007.

Mol, S. E., Bus, A. G., de Jong, M. T., & Smeets, D. H. (2008). Added value of dialogic parent–child book readings: A meta-analysis. *Early Education and Development, 19*, 7–26.

Moll, H., & Tomasello, M. (2006). Level 1 perspective-taking at 24 months of age. *British Journal of Developmental Psychology, 24*, 603–613.

Murphy, P. K., Wilkinson, I. A. G., Soter, A. O., Hennessey, M. N., & Alexander, J. F. (2009). Examining the effects of classroom discussion on students' comprehension of text: A meta-analysis. *Journal of Educational Psychology, 101*(3), 740–764.

Muter, V., Hulme, C., Snowling, M. J., & Stevenson, J. (2004). Phonemes, rimes, vocabulary, and grammatical skills as foundations of early reading development: Evidence from a longitudinal study. *Developmental Psychology, 40*(5), 665–680.

Nagy, W. E., Berninger, V. W., & Abbott, R. D. (2006). Contributions of morphology beyond phonology to literacy outcomes of upper elementary and middle-school students. *Journal of Educational Psychology, 98*(1), 134–147.

Nagy, W. E., Berninger, V., Abbott, R., Vaughan, K., & Vermeulen, K. (2003). Relationship of morphology and other language skills to literacy skills in at-risk second-grade readers and at-risk fourth-grade writers. *Journal of Educational Psychology, 95*(4), 730–742.

Nagy, W. E., Carlisle, J. F., & Goodwin, A. P. (2014). Morphological knowledge and literacy acquisition. *Journal of Learning Disabilities, 47*(1), 3–12.

Nagy, W. E., & Scott, J. A. (2000). Vocabulary processing. In M. Kamil, P. Mosenthal, P. D. Pearson, & R. Barr (Eds.), *Handbook of reading research* (Vol. 3, pp. 269–284). Mahwah, NJ: Lawrence Erlbaum Associates.

Nagy, W. E., & Townsend, D. (2012). Words as tools: Learning academic vocabulary as language acquisition. *Reading Research Quarterly, 47*, 91–108.

Naigles, L. R., & Hoff-Ginsberg, E. (1998). Why are some verbs learned before other verbs? Effects of input frequency and structure on children's early verb use. *Journal of Child Language, 25*(1), 95–120.

Nakamoto, J., Lindsey, K. A., & Manis, F. R. (2008). A cross-linguistic investigation of English language learners' reading comprehension in English and Spanish. *Scientific Studies of Reading, 12*(4), 351–371.

(2012). Development of reading skills from K–3 in Spanish-speaking English language learners following three programs of instruction. *Reading and Writing, 25*(2), 537–567.

Namy, L. L., Acredolo, L., & Goodwyn, S. (2000). Verbal labels and gestural routines in parental communication with young children. *Journal of Nonverbal Behavior, 24*(2), 63–79.

Nation, I. S. (1990). *Teaching and learning vocabulary.* New York, NY: Newbury House.

National Bureau of Statistics of the People's Republic of China. (2010). *Tabulation on the 2010 Population Census of the People's Republic of China*. Retrieved from www.stats.gov.cn/tjsj/pcsj/rkpc/6rp/indexch.htm

National Center for Education Statistics. (2015a). *The nation's report card: 2015 reading*. Washington, DC: US Department of Education.

(2015b). *The nation's report card: Trends in academic progress 2015*.Washington, DC: National Center for Education Statistics, Institute of Education Sciences, US Department of Education.

(2017). *The nation's report card: Reading 2017*. Washington, DC: Institute of Education Sciences, US Department of Education.

National Governors Association Center for Best Practices & Council of Chief State School Officers. (2010). *Common Core State Standards for English language arts & literacy in history/social studies, science & technical subjects*. Washington, DC: Author.

National Institute of Child Health and Human Development. (2000). Report of the National Reading Panel. Teaching children to read: An evidence-based assessment of the scientific research literature on reading and its implications for reading instruction: Reports of the subgroups (NIH Publication No. 00-4754). Washington, DC: US Government Printing Office.

National Reading Panel. (2000). Report of the National Reading Panel: Teaching children to read: An evidence-based assessment of the scientific research literature on reading and its implications for reading instruction (NIH Publication No. 00-4769). Washington, DC: US Government Printing Office.

Nazzi, T., Bertoncini, J., & Mehler, J. (1998). Language discrimination by newborns: toward an understanding of the role of rhythm. *Journal of Experimental Psychology: Human Perception and Performance, 24*(3), 756–766.

Nelson, K. E. (1977). Facilitating children's syntax acquisition. *Developmental Psychology, 13*(2), 101–107.

(1998). *Language in cognitive development: The emergence of the mediated mind*. Cambridge, England: Cambridge University Press.

Nelson, K., & Fivush, R. (2004). The emergence of autobiographical memory: A social cultural developmental theory. *Psychological Review, 111*(2), 486–511.

Nese, J. F. T., Biancarosa, G., Cummings, C., Kennedy, P., Alonzo, J., & Tindal, G. (2013). In search of average growth: Describing within-year oral reading oral reading fluency growth across Grades 1–8. *Journal of School Psychology, 51*(5), 625–642.

Ness, M. (2011). Explicit reading comprehension instruction in elementary classrooms: Teachers' use of reading comprehension strategies. *Journal of Research in Childhood Education, 25*, 98–117.

Neuendorf, K. A. (2002). *The content analysis guidebook*. Thousand Oaks, CA: Sage.

Newell, G. E., Beach, R., Smith, J., & VanDerHeide, J. (2009). Teaching and learning argumentative reading and writing: A review of the literature. *Reading Research Quarterly, 46*(3), 273–304.

Newport, E., Gleitman, H., & Gleitman, L. (1977). Mother, I'd rather do it myself: Some effects and non-effects of maternal speech style. In C. Snow & C. Ferguson (Eds.), *Talking to children: Language input and acquisition* (pp. 109–150). Cambridge, England: Cambridge University Press.

New York State Education Department. (2014). *Unit III: Researching to deepen understanding unit: Water.* www.engageny.org/resource/grades-7-ela-researching-dee pen-understanding-unit-water

Nicoladis, E., & Genesee, F. (1996). A longitudinal study of pragmatic differentiation in young bilingual children. *Language Learning, 46,* 439–464.

Ninio, A. (1980). Picture-book reading in mother–infant dyads belonging to two subgroups in Israel. *Child Development, 51*(2), 587–590.

Ninio, A., & Snow, C. E. (1996). *Pragmatic development.* Boulder, CO: Westview Press.

Nisbett, R. E., & Wilson, T. D. (1977). Telling more than we can know: Verbal reports on mental processes. *Psychological Review, 84*(3), 231–259.

No Child Left Behind (NCLB) Act of 2001, Pub. L. No. 107-110, § 115, Stat. 1425 (2002).

Nystrand, M. (1997). *Opening dialogue: Understanding dynamics of language and learning in the English classroom.* New York, NY: Teachers College Press.

O'Brien, D., Stewart, R., & Beach, R. (2009). Proficient reading in school: Traditional paradigms and new textual landscapes. In L. Christenbury, R. Bomer, & P. Smagorinsky (Eds.), *Handbook of adolescent literacy research* (pp. 80–97). New York, NY: Guilford.

O'Connor, C., & Michaels, S. (2015). How'd you figure that . . . OUT? What can micro-analysis of discourse tell us about fostering academic language? *Linguistics and Education, 31,* 304–310.

O'Connor, C., & Snow, C. E. (2017). Classroom discourse: What do we need to know for research and for practice? In M. Schober, A. Britt, and D. Rapp (Eds.), *The Routledge handbook of discourse processes* (2nd ed., pp. 315–341). New York, NY: Routledge.

Oakhill, J. V., & Cain, K. (2012). The precursors of reading ability in young readers: Evidence from a four-year longitudinal study. *Scientific Studies of Reading, 16*(2), 91–121.

Ochs, E. (1988). *Culture and Language Development: Language Acquisition and Language Socialization in a Samoan Village.* Cambridge, England: Cambridge University Press.

Ochs, E., & Shohet, M. (2006). The cultural structuring of mealtime socialization. In New directions for child and adolescent development, 2006 (pp. 35–49). Hoboken, NJ: John Wiley.

OECD. (2014). *PISA 2012 results: What students know and can do. Student performance in mathematics, reading, and science* (Vol. 1, rev. ed.). Paris: Author.

O'Reilly, T., Sabatini, J., Bruce, K., Pillarisetti, S., & McCormick, C. (2012). Middle school reading assessment: Measuring what matters under a RTI framework. *Reading Psychology, 33*(1–2), 162–189.

Ouellette, G. P. (2006). What's meaning got to do with it: The role of vocabulary in word reading and reading comprehension. *Journal of Educational Psychology, 98,* 554–566.

Pagani, L. S., Fitzpatrick, C., Archambault, I., & Janosz, M. (2010). School readiness and later achievement: A French Canadian replication and extension. *Developmental Psychology, 46*(5), 984–994.

Pan, B. A., Rowe, M. L., Singer, J. D., & Snow, C. E. (2005). Maternal correlates of growth in toddler vocabulary production in low-income families. *Child Development, 76*(4), 763–782.

Pan, B. A., & Snow, C. E. (1999). The development of conversation and discourse skills. In M. Barrett (Ed.), *The development of language* (pp. 229–250). Hove, England: Psychology Press.

Paradis, J., & Jia, R. (2017). Bilingual children's long-term outcomes in English as a second language: Language environment factors shape individual differences in catching up with monolinguals. *Developmental Science, 20*(1), e12433.

Paribakht, T., & Wesche, M. (1996). Enhancing vocabulary acquisition through reading: A hierarchy of text-related exercise types. *Canadian Modern Language Review, 52*, 155–178.

Park, B. J. (2015). *Investigation of reading skill development of English language learners: A two-year longitudinal study* (Unpublished doctoral dissertation). Retrieved from https://scholarsbank.uoregon.edu/xmlui/handle/1794/19688

Pasquarella, A., Chen, X., Lam, K., Luo, Y. C., & Ramirez, G. (2011). Cross-language transfer of morphological awareness in Chinese-English bilinguals. *Journal of Research in Reading, 34*, 23–42.

Pasquarella, A., Deacon, H., Chen, B. X., Commissaire, E., & Au-Yeung, K. (2014). Acquiring orthographic processing through word reading: Evidence from children learning to read French and English. *International Journal of Disability, Development and Education, 61*(3), 240–257.

Patterson, J. L. (2004). Comparing bilingual and monolingual toddlers' expressive vocabulary size: Revisiting Rescorla and Achenbach (2002). *Journal of Speech, Language, and Hearing Research, 47*(5), 1213–1215.

Paul, R., & Roth, F. P. (2011). Characterizing and predicting outcomes of communication delays in infants and toddlers: Implications for clinical practice. *Language, Speech, and Hearing Services in Schools, 42*(3), 331–340.

Peal, E., & Lambert, W. (1962). The relation of bilingualism to intelligence. *Psychological Monographs, 76*(546), 1–23.

Pearson, B. Z., Fernandez, S. C., Lewedeg, V., & Oller, D. K. (1997). The relation of input factors to lexical learning by bilingual infants. *Applied Psycholinguistics, 18* (1), 41–58.

Pearson, P. D., & Hamm, D. N. (2003). *Reading comprehension assessment: One very resilient phenomenon.* Presentation at the International Reading Association Convention, Orlando, FL. Retrieved from www.ciera.org/library/presos/2003/index .html

Pearson, P. D., Hiebert, E. H., & Kamil, M. L. (2007). Vocabulary assessment: What we know and what we need to learn. *Reading Research Quarterly, 42*(2), 282–296.

Peisner-Feinberg, E., Burchinal, M. R., Clifford, R. M., Culkin, M. L., Howes, C., Kagan, S. L., & Yazejian, N. (2001). The relation of preschool child-care quality to children's cognitive and social developmental trajectories through second grade. *Child Development, 72*(5), 1534–1553.

Pelletier, J. (2006). Relations among theory of mind, metacognitive language, reading skills and story comprehension in L1 and L2 learners. In A. Antonietti, O. L. Sempio, & A. Marcetti (Eds.), *Theory of mind and language in developmental contexts* (pp. 77–92). New York, NY: Springer.

Pelletier, J., & Astington, J. W. (2004). Action, consciousness and theory of mind: Children's ability to coordinate story characters' actions and thoughts. *Early Education and Development, 15,* 5–22.

Pelletier, J., & Beatty, R. (2015). Children's understanding of Aesop's fables: Relations to reading comprehension and theory of mind. *Frontiers in Psychology, 6,* Article 1448.

Perfetti, C., & Stafura, J. (2014). Word knowledge in a theory of reading comprehension. *Scientific Studies of Reading, 18*(1), 22–37.

Peterson, C., Jesso, B., & McCabe, A. (1999). Encouraging narratives in preschoolers: An intervention study. *Journal of Child Language, 26,* 49–67.

Petscher, Y. (2011). The impact of teacher responsivity education on preschoolers' language and literacy skills. *American Journal of Speech-Language Pathology, 20*(4), 315–330.

Pianta, R. C., Belsky, J., Vandergrift, N., Houts, R., & Morrison, F. (2008). Classroom effects on children's achievement trajectories in elementary school. *American Educational Research Journal, 45,* 365–397.

Pianta, R. C., La Paro, K. M., & Hamre, B. K. (2012). *Classroom assessment scoring system (CLASS) manual, Pre-K* (Versión en español). Baltimore, MD: Paul H. Brookes.

Pine, J. M., Freudenthal, D., Krajewski, G., & Gobet, F. (2013). Do young children have adult-like syntactic categories? Zipf's law and the case of the determiner. *Cognition, 127*(3), 345–360.

Place, S., & Hoff, E. (2011). Properties of dual language exposure that influence 2-year-olds' bilingual proficiency. *Child Development, 82*(6), 1834–1849.

Poulsen, M., & Gravgaard, A. K. (2016). Who did what to whom? The relationship between syntactic aspects of sentence comprehension and text comprehension. *Scientific Studies of Reading, 20*(4), 325–338.

Pressley, M., Brown, R., El-Dinary, P. B., & Afflerbach P. (1995). The comprehension instruction students need: Instruction fostering constructively responsive reading. *Learning Disabilities Research and Practice, 10,* 215–224.

Pressley, M., Wharton-McDonald, R., Hampson, J. M., & Echevarria, M. (1998). Literacy instruction in ten grade-4/5 classrooms in upstate New York. *Scientific Studies of Reading, 2,* 159–191.

Prevoo, M., Malda, M., Mesman, J., & van IJzendoorn, M. (2015). Within- and cross-language relations between oral language proficiency and school outcomes in bilingual children with an immigrant background: A meta-analytical study. *Review of Educational Research, 86,* 237–276.

Proctor, C. P., August, D., Carlo, M. S., & Snow, C. (2006). The intriguing role of Spanish language vocabulary knowledge in predicting English reading comprehension. *Journal of Educational Psychology, 98*(1), 159–169.

Proctor, C. P., August, D., Snow, C. E., & Barr, C. D. (2010). The interdependence continuum: A perspective on the nature of Spanish–English bilingual reading comprehension. *Bilingual Research Journal, 33*(1), 5–20.

Proctor, C. P., Carlo, M., August, D., & Snow, C. E. (2005). Native Spanish-speaking children reading in English: Toward a model of comprehension. *Journal of Educational Psychology, 97,* 246–256.

Proctor, C. P., Dalton, D., Uccelli, P., Biancarosa, G., Mo, E., Snow, C. E., & Neugebauer, S. (2011). Improving comprehension online: Effects of deep vocabulary instruction with bilingual and monolingual fifth graders. *Reading and Writing: An Interdisciplinary Journal, 24*, 517–544.

Proctor, C. P., Silverman, R. D., Harring, J. R., Jones, R., & Hartranft, A. M. (2018). *Evaluation of a supplemental, language-based reading program for Spanish- and Portuguese-speaking bilingual learners in fourth and fifth grades.* Unpublished manuscript.

Proctor, C. P., Uccelli, P., Dalton, B., & Snow, C. E. (2009). Understanding depth of vocabulary online with bilingual and monolingual children. *Reading & Writing Quarterly, 25*(4), 311–333.

Purcell-Gates, V., Duke, N. K., & Martineau, J. A. (2007). Learning to read and write genre-specific text: Roles of authentic experience and explicit teaching. *Reading Research Quarterly, 42*, 8–45.

Rabe-Hesketh, S., Skrondal, A., & Pickles, A. (2005). Maximum likelihood estimation of limited and discrete dependent variable models with nested random effects. *Journal of Econometrics, 128*(2), 301–323.

Rall, J., & Harris, P. L. (2000). In Cinderella's slippers? Story comprehension from the protagonist's point of view. *Developmental Psychology, 36*, 202–208.

Ramirez, G., Chen, X., Geva, E., & Kiefer, H. (2010). Morphological awareness in Spanish-English bilingual children: Within and cross-language effects on word reading. *Reading and Writing: An Interdisciplinary Journal, 23*, 337–358.

Ramirez, G., Chen, X., Geva, E., & Luo, Y. (2011). Morphological awareness and word reading in ELLs: Evidence from Spanish- and Chinese-speaking children. *Applied Psycholinguistics, 32*, 601–618.

Ramírez, G., Chen, X., & Pasquarella, A. (2013). Cross-linguistic transfer of morphological awareness in Spanish-speaking English language learners: The facilitating effect of cognate knowledge. *Topics in Language Disorders, 33*(1), 73–92.

Rasinski, T., Homan, S., & Biggs, M. (2009). Teaching reading fluency to struggling readers: Method, materials, and evidence. *Reading & Writing Quarterly, 25*(2–3), 192–204.

Raudenbush, S. W., & Bryk, A. S. (2002). *Hierarchical linear models: Applications and data analysis methods.* London, England: Sage.

Ravid, D., & Tolchinsky, L. (2002). Developing linguistic literacy: A comprehensive model. *Journal of Child Language, 29*, 419–448.

Reese, E. (1995). Predicting children's literacy from mother–child conversations. *Cognitive Development, 10*, 381–405.

Reese, E., & Cleveland, E. (2006). Mother–child reminiscing and children's understanding of mind. *Merrill-Palmer Quarterly, 52*(1), 17–43.

Reese, E., & Cox, A. (1999). Quality of adult book reading affects the children's emergent literacy. *Developmental Psychology, 35*, 20–28.

Reese, E., Leyva, D., Sparks, A., & Grolnick, W. (2010). Maternal elaborative reminiscing increases low-income children's narrative skills relative to dialogic reading. *Early Education and Development, 21*, 318–342.

Reese, E., & Newcombe, R. (2007). Training mothers in elaborative reminiscing enhances children's autobiographical memory and narrative. *Child Development, 78*(4), 1153–1170.

Reese, E., Sparks, A., & Leyva, D. (2010). A review of parent interventions for kindergarten children's language and emergent literacy. *Journal of Early Childhood Literacy, 10*(1), 97–117.

Reschly, A. L., Busch, T. W., Betts, J., Deno, S. L., & Long, J. D. (2009). Curriculum-based measurement oral reading as an indicator of reading achievement: A meta-analysis of the correlational evidence. *Journal of School Psychology, 47*(6), 427–469.

Rescorla, L. (2011). Late talkers: Do good predictors of outcome exist? *Developmental Disabilities Research Reviews, 17*, 141–150.

Resnick, L. B., Levine, J. M., & Teasley, S. D. (Eds.). (1991). *Perspectives on socially shared cognition.* Washington, DC: American Psychological Association.

Reznitskaya, A., & Gregory, M. (2013). Student thought and classroom language: Examining the mechanisms of change in dialogic teaching. *Educational Psychologist, 48*(2), 114–133.

Richman, A. L., Miller, P. M., & LeVine, R. A. (1992). Cultural and educational variations in maternal responsiveness. *Developmental Psychology, 28*(4), 614–621.

Ricketts, J., Nation, K., & Bishop, D. V. (2007). Vocabulary is important for some, but not all reading skills. *Scientific Studies of Reading, 11*(3), 235–257.

Rinaldi, C., & Paez, M. (2008). Preschool matters: Predicting reading difficulties for Spanish-speaking bilingual students in first grade. *Learning Disabilities: A Contemporary Journal, 6*(1), 71–86.

Rogoff, B. (2003). *The cultural nature of human development.* New York, NY: Oxford University Press.

Rollins, P. R. (2003). Caregivers' contingent comments to 9-month-old infants: Relationships with later language. *Applied Psycholinguistics, 24*(2), 221–234.

Romano, E., Babchishin, L., Pagani, L. S., & Kohen, D. (2010). School readiness and later achievement: Replication and extension using a nationwide Canadian survey. *Developmental Psychology, 46*(5), 995–1007.

Roorda, D., Koomen, H., Spilt, J., & Oort, F. (2011). The influence of affective teacher–student relationships on students' school engagement and achievement: A meta-analytic approach. *Review of Educational Research, 81*(4), 493–529.

Rowe, M. L. (2012). A longitudinal investigation of the role of quantity and quality of child-directed speech in vocabulary development. *Child Development, 83*, 1762–1774.

(2013). Decontextualized language input and preschoolers' vocabulary development. *Seminars in Speech and Language, 34*(4), 260–266.

Rowe, M. L., & Goldin-Meadow, S. (2009). Early gesture selectively predicts later language learning. *Developmental Science, 12*(1), 182–187.

Rowe, M. L., Leech, K. A., & Cabrera, N. J. (2017). Going beyond input quantity: Wh-questions matter for toddlers' language and cognitive development. *Cognitive Science, 41*(S1), 162–179.

Rowland, C. F., Pine, J. M., Lieven, E. V., & Theakston, A. L. (2003). Determinants of acquisition order in wh-questions: Re-evaluating the role of caregiver speech. *Journal of Child Language, 30*(3), 609–635.

Rudolph, J. M., & Leonard, L. B. (2016). Early language milestones and specific language impairment. *Journal of Early Intervention, 38*(1), 41–58.

Ruston, H. P., & Schwanenflugel, P. J. (2010). Effects of a conversation intervention on the expressive vocabulary development of prekindergarten children. *Language, Speech, and Hearing Services in Schools, 41*(3), 303–313.

Rydland, V., Grøver, V., & Lawrence, J. (2014). The second-language vocabulary trajectories of Turkish immigrant children in Norway from ages five to ten: The role of preschool talk exposure, maternal education, and co-ethnic concentration in the neighborhood. *Journal of Child Language, 41*, 352–381.

Sabatini, J. P., Bruce, K., Steinberg, J., & Weeks, J. (2015). *SARA reading components tests, RISE forms: Technical adequacy and test design* (Research Report No. RR-15–32). Princeton, NJ: Educational Testing Service.

Sabatini, J. P., O'Reilly, T., Halderman, L. K., & Bruce, K. (2014). Integrating scenario-based and component reading skill measures to understand the reading behavior of struggling readers. *Learning Disabilities Research & Practice, 29* (1), 36–43.

Saffran, J. R. (2001). Words in a sea of sounds: The output of infant statistical learning. *Cognition, 81*(2), 149–169.

Saffran, J. R., Newport, E. L., & Aslin, R. N. (1996). Word segmentation: The role distributional cues. *Journal of Memory and Language, 35*(4), 606–621.

Salomo, D., & Liszkowski, U. (2013). Sociocultural settings influence the emergence of prelinguistic deictic gestures. *Child Development, 84*(4), 1296–1307.

Scammacca, N., Roberts, G., Vaughn, S., & Stuebing, K. K. (2015). A meta-analysis of interventions for struggling readers in grades 4–12:1980–2011. *Journal of Learning Disabilities, 48*(4), 369–390.

Scarborough, H. S. (2009). Connecting early language and literacy to later reading (dis) abilities: Evidence, theory, and practice. In F. Fletcher-Campbell, J. Soler, & G. Reid (Eds.), *Approaching difficulties in literacy development: Assessment, pedagogy and programmes* (pp. 23–38). London, England: Sage.

Scarborough, H. S., & Dobrich, W. (1994). On the efficacy of reading to preschoolers. *Developmental Review, 14*, 245–302.

Schacter, D. L., Addis, D. R., & Buckner, R. L. (2007). Remembering the past to imagine the future: The prospective brain. *Nature Reviews Neuroscience, 8*(9), 657–661.

Scheele, A. F., Leseman, P. P. M., & Mayo, A. Y. (2010). The home language environment of monolingual and bilingual children and their language proficiency. *Applied Psycholinguistics, 31*(1), 117–140.

Scheele, A. F., Leseman, P. P. M., Mayo, A. Y., & Elbers, E. (2012). The relation of home language and literacy to three-year-old children's emergent academic language in narrative and instruction genres. *Elementary School Journal, 112*(3), 419–444.

Schellekens, L., Henrichs, L. F., & Leseman, P. P. M. (2014). *The relation between early first and second language proficiency and academic achievement of Dutch, Moroccan-Dutch and Turkish-Dutch primary school children: A longitudinal study* (Unpublished master's thesis). Utrecht University, Utrecht, Netherlands.

Schleppegrell, M. J. (2001). Linguistic features of the language of schooling. *Linguistics and Education, 12*, 431–459.

    (2004). *The language of schooling: A functional linguistics perspective*. London, England: Lawrence Erlbaum Associates.

Schmerse, D., Lieven, E., & Tomasello, M. (2015). Young children use shared experience to interpret definite reference. *Journal of Child Language*, *42*(5), 1146–1157.

Schmitt, M. B., Pentimonti, J. M., & Justice, L. M. (2012). Teacher–child relationships, behavior regulation, and language gain among at-risk preschoolers. *Journal of School Psychology*, *50*(5), 681–699.

Schmitt, S. A., Pratt, M. E., & McClelland, M. M. (2014). Examining the validity of behavioral self-regulation tools in predicting preschoolers' academic achievement. *Early Education and Development*, *25*(5), 641–660.

Schwanenflugel, P. J., Hamilton, C. E., Neuharth-Pritchett, S., Restrepo, M. A., Bradley, B. A., & Webb, M. Y. (2010). PAVEd for Success: An evaluation of a comprehensive preliteracy program for four-year-old children. *Journal of Literacy Research*, *42*(3), 227–275.

Scott, C. M., & Balthazar, C. H. (2010). The grammar of information: Challenges for older students with language impairments. *Topics in Language Disorders*, *30*(4), 288–307.

Scott, J. A., Jamieson-Noel, D., & Asselin, M. (2003). Vocabulary instruction throughout the day in twenty-three Canadian upper-elementary classrooms. *Elementary School Journal*, *103*, 269–312.

Searle, J. (1969). *Speech acts*. Cambridge, England: Cambridge University Press.

Selman, R. L. (2007). *The promotion of social awareness*. New York, NY: Russell Sage Foundation.

Sénéchal, M., Cornell, E. H., & Broda, L. S. (1995). Age-related changes in the organization of parent-infant interactions during picture-book reading. *Early Childhood Research Quarterly*, *10*, 317–337.

Sénéchal, M., & LeFevre, J. (2003). Parental involvement in the development of children's reading skill: A five-year longitudinal study. *Child Development*, *73*, 445–460.

Sénechal, M., LeFevre, J., Thomas, E. M., & Daley, K. E. (2011). Differential effects of home literacy experiences on the development of oral and written language. *Reading Research Quarterly*, *33*, 96–116.

Sénéchal, M., Ouellette,G., & Rodney, D. (2006). The misunderstood giant: On the predictive role of early vocabulary to future reading. In D. K. Dickinson & S. B. Neuman (Eds.), *Handbook of early literacy research* (Vol. 2, pp. 173–182). New York, NY: Guilford Press.

Shanahan, T., Callison, K., Carriere, C., Duke, N. K., Pearson, P. D., Schatschneider, C., & Torgesen, J. (2010). *Improving reading comprehension in kindergarten through 3rd grade: A practice guide* (Report No. NCEE 2010-4038). Washington, DC: National Center for Education Evaluation and Regional Assistance, Institute of Education Sciences, U.S. Department of Education.

Shavelson, R., & Towne, L. (2002). *Features of education and education research. Scientific research in education*. Washington, DC: National Academy Press.

Shi, R., Werker, J. F., & Cutler, A. (2006). Recognition and representation of function words in English-learning infants. *Infancy*, *10*(2), 187–198.

Shin, J., Deno, S. L., & Espin, C. (2000). Technical adequacy of the maze task for curriculum-based measurement of reading growth. *Journal of Special Education*, *34*, 164–172.

Siegal, M., Iozzi, L., & Surian, L. (2009). Bilingualism and conversational understanding in young children. *Cognition, 110,* 115–122.

Silverman, R. D. (2007). Vocabulary development of English-language and English-only learners in kindergarten. *Elementary School Journal, 107*(4), 365–383.

Silverman, R. D., & Hines, S. (2009). The effects of multimedia enhanced instruction on the vocabulary of English language learners and non-English language learners in pre-kindergarten through second grade. *Journal of Educational Psychology, 101,* 305–314.

Silverman, R. D., Proctor, C. P., Harring, J. R., Doyle, B., Mitchell, M. A., & Meyer, A. G. (2013). Teachers' instruction and students' vocabulary and comprehension: An exploratory study with English monolingual and Spanish-English bilingual students in grades 3–5. *Reading Research Quarterly, 49,* 31–60.

Silverman, R. D., Proctor, C. P., Harring, J. R., Hartranft, A. M., & Guthrie, S. (2014). *Teachers' instruction and students' vocabulary and comprehension in grades 3–5.* Paper presented at the annual meeting of the Society for the Scientific Study of Reading, Santa Fe, NM.

Sim, S., & Berthelsen, D. (2014). Shared book reading by parents with young children: Evidence-based practice. *Australasian Journal of Early Childhood, 39*(1), 50–55.

Singer, J. D., & Willett, J. B. (2003). *Applied longitudinal data analysis: Modeling change and event occurrence.* Oxford, England: Oxford University Press.

Siu, C. T. S., & Ho, C. S. H. (2015). Cross-language transfer of syntactic skills and reading comprehension among young Cantonese–English bilingual students. *Reading Research Quarterly, 50*(3), 313–336.

Skibbe, L., Bindman, S., Hindman, A., Aram, D., & Morrison, F. (2013). Longitudinal relations between parental writing support and preschoolers' language and literacy skills. *Reading Research Quarterly, 48,* 387–401.

Slavin, R. E., & Cheung, A. (2005). A synthesis of research on language of reading instruction for English language learners. *Review of Educational Research, 75*(2), 247–284.

Smith, F. (1971). *Understanding reading: A psycholinguistic analysis of reading and learning to read.* New York, NY: Holt, Rinehart and Winston.

Snow, C. E. (1972). Mothers' speech to children learning language. *Child Development, 43,* 549–565.

(1977a). Mothers' speech research: From input to interaction. In C. E. Snow & C. Ferguson (Eds.), *Talking to children: Language input and acquisition* (pp. 31–50). Cambridge, England: Cambridge University Press.

(1977b). The development of conversation between mothers and babies. *Journal of Child Language, 4*(1), 1–22.

(1983). Literacy and language: Relationships during the preschool years. *Harvard Educational Review, 53*(2), 165–189.

(1990). The development of definitional skill. *Journal of Child Language, 17*(3), 697–710.

(1991a). Language proficiency: Towards a definition. In G. Appel & H. W. Dechert (Eds.), *A case for psycholinguistic cases* (pp. 63–89). Amsterdam, Netherlands: John Benjamins.

(1991b). The theoretical bases for relationships between language and literacy development. *Journal of Research in Childhood Education, 6,* 5–10.

(1993). Families as social contexts for literacy development. *New Directions for Child Development, 61,* 11–24.

(2002). *Reading for understanding: Toward an R&D program in reading comprehension.* Santa Monica, CA: RAND Corporation

(2010). Academic language and the challenge of reading for learning about science. *Science, 328,* 450–452.

(2014). Input to interaction: Three key shifts in the history of child language research. *Journal of Child Language, 41,* 117–123.

Snow, C. E., & Beals, D.E. (2006). Mealtime talk that supports literacy development. *New Directions in Child and Adolescent Development, 111,* 51–66.

Snow, C. E., Burns, M. S., & Griffin, P. (Eds.). (1998). *Preventing reading difficulties in young children.* Washington, DC: National Academies Press.

Snow, C. E., Cancino, H., Gonzalez, P., & Shriberg, E. (1989). Giving formal definitions: An oral language correlate of school literacy. In D. Bloome (Ed.), *Classrooms and literacy* (pp. 233–249). Norwood, NJ: Ablex.

Snow, C. E., & Dickinson, D. K. (1991). Skills that aren't basic in a new conception of literacy. In E. M. Jennings & A. C. Purves (Eds.), *Literate systems and individual lives: Perspectives on literacy and schooling* (pp. 179–191). Albany, NY: State University of New York Press.

Snow, C. E., & Ferguson, C. A. (Eds.). (1977). *Talking to children: Language input and language acquisition.* Cambridge, England: Cambridge University Press.

Snow, C. E., & Lawrence, J. F. (2011). *Word Generation in Boston public schools: Natural history of a literacy intervention.* Washington, DC: Council of the Great City Schools. Retrieved from https://files.eric.ed.gov/fulltext/ED518090.pdf

Snow, C. E., Lawrence, J., & White, C. (2009). Generating knowledge of academic language among urban middle school students. *Journal of Research on Educational Effectiveness, 2*(4), 325–344.

Snow, C. E., Porche, M. V., Tabors, P. O., & Harris, S. R. (2007). *Is literacy enough? Pathways to academic success for adolescents.* Baltimore, MD: Paul H. Brookes.

Snow, C. E., Tabors, P. O., & Dickinson, D. K. (2001). Language development in the preschool years. In D. K. Dickinson & P. O. Tabors (Eds.), *Beginning literacy with language: Young children learning at home and school* (pp. 1–26). Baltimore, MD: Paul H. Brookes.

Snow, C. E., & Uccelli, P. (2009). The challenge of academic language. In D. R. Olson & N. Torrance (Eds.), *The Cambridge handbook of literacy* (pp. 112–133). New York, NY: Cambridge University Press.

Sokolov, J. L., & Snow, C. E. (1994). The changing role of negative evidence in theories of language development. In C. Gallaway & B. J. Richards (Eds.), *Input and interaction in language acquisition* (pp. 38–55). Cambridge, England: Cambridge University Press.

Solis, M., Miciak, J., Vaughn, S., & Fletcher, J. M. (2014). Why intensive interventions matter: Longitudinal studies of adolescents with reading disabilities and poor reading comprehension. *Learning Disability Quarterly, 37*(4), 218–229.

Somers, M.-A., Corrin, W., Sepanik, S., et al. (2010). *The enhanced reading opportunities Study final report: The impact of supplemental literacy courses for struggling ninth-grade readers* (NCEE Report No. 2010-4021). Washington, DC: Institute of Education Sciences, US Department of Education.

Soto Huerta, M. E. (2012). Guiding biliteracy development: Appropriating cross-linguistic and conceptual knowledge to sustain second-language reading comprehension. *Bilingual Research Journal, 35*(2), 179–196.

Southgate, V., Senju, A., & Csibra, G. (2007). Action anticipation through attribution of false belief by 2-year-olds. *Psychological Science, 18*, 587–592.

Sparks, A., & Reese, E. (2013). From reminiscing to reading: Home contributions to children's developing language and literacy in low-income families. *First Language, 33*, 89–109.

Spilt, J. L., Koomen, H. M., & Harrison, L. J. (2015). Language development in the early school years: The importance of close relationships with teachers. *Developmental Psychology, 51*, 185–196.

Stahl, S. A., & Clark, C. H. (1987). The effects of participatory expectations in classroom discussion on the learning of science vocabulary. *American Educational Research Journal, 24*, 541–556.

Stahl, S. A., & Fairbanks, M. M. (1986). The effects of vocabulary instruction: A model based meta-analysis. *Review of Educational Research, 56*, 72–110.

Stahl, S. A., & Nagy, W. E. (2006). *Teaching word meanings*. Mahwah, NJ: Lawrence Erlbaum Associates.

Stahl, S. A., & Vancil, S. (1986). Discussion is what makes semantic maps work in vocabulary instruction. *Reading Teacher, 40*, 62–69.

Stake, R. E. (2006). *Multiple case study analysis*. New York, NY: Guilford Press.

Statistic Bureau of Xinjiang Uyghur Autonomous Region. (2014a). *2014 statistic yearbook of Xinjiang Uyghur Autonomous Region*. Retrieved from www.xjtj.gov.cn/sjcx/zgxj_3740/zgxj2014/201509/t20150902_478515.html

(2014b). *2014 statistic yearbook of Xinjiang Uyghur Autonomous Region*. Retrieved from www.xjtj.gov.cn/sjcx/tjnj_3415/2014xjtjnj/rkjy_2014/201506/t20150630_471951.html

(2016). *2014 child development report of Xinjiang*. Retrieved from www.xjtj.gov.cn/tjfx/201601/t20160125_488524.html

Strasser, K., & del Rio, F. (2014). The role of comprehension monitoring, theory of mind, and vocabulary depth in predicting story comprehension and recall of kindergarten children. *Reading Research Quarterly, 49*, 169–187.

Sun, M. X. (2012). Reflection on the use of bilingual kindergarten textbooks among ethnic minorities in Xinjiang. *Journal of Xinjiang University (Philosophy, Humanities & Social Science), 1*, 94–97.

Sun-Alperin, M. K., & Wang, M. (2011). Cross-language transfer of phonological and orthographic processing skills from Spanish L1 to English L2. *Reading and Writing, 24*(5), 591–614.

Swain, M. (2005). The output hypothesis: Theory and research. In E. Hinkel (Ed.), *Handbook of research in second language teaching and learning* (pp. 471–483). Mahwah, NJ: Lawrence Erlbaum Associates.

Swanson, E., Wanzek, J., McCulley, L., et al. (2016). Literacy and text reading in middle and high school social studies and English language arts classrooms. *Reading & Writing Quarterly, 32*(3), 199–222.

Swanson, H. L., Rosston, K., Gerber, M., & Solari, E. (2008). Influence of oral language and phonological awareness on children's bilingual reading. *Journal of School Psychology, 46,* 413–429.

Swanson, J., Valiente, C., & Lemery-Chalfant, K. (2012). Predicting academic achievement from cumulative home risk: The mediating roles of effortful control, academic relationships, and school avoidance. *Merrill-Palmer Quarterly, 58,* 375–408.

Sweet, A. P. (2005). Assessment of reading comprehension: The RAND reading study group vision. In S. G. Paris & S. A. Stahl (Eds.), *Children's reading comprehension and assessment* (pp. 3–12). London, England: Lawrence Erlbaum Associates.

Tabors, P. O., Roach, K. A., & Snow, C. E. (2001). Home language and literacy environment: Final results. In D. K. Dickinson & P. O. Tabors (Eds.), *Beginning literacy with language* (pp. 111–138). Baltimore, MD: Paul II. Brookes.

Taumoepeau, M., & Reese, E. (2013). Maternal reminiscing, elaborative talk, and children's theory of mind: An intervention study. *First Language, 33*(4), 388–410.

Taumoepeau, M., & Ruffman, T. (2016). Self-awareness moderates the relation between maternal mental state language about desires and children's mental state vocabulary. *Journal of Experimental Child Psychology, 144,* 114–129.

Tenenbaum, H. R., & Leaper, C. (1997). Mothers' and fathers' questions to their child in Mexican-descent families: Moderators of cognitive demand during play. *Hispanic Journal of Behavioral Sciences, 32,* 318–332.

Theakston, A. L., Lieven, E. V., Pine, J. M., & Rowland, C. F. (2004). Semantic generality, input frequency and the acquisition of syntax. *Journal of Child Language, 31*(1), 61–99.

The acquisition of auxiliary syntax: BE and HAVE. *Cognitive Linguistics, 16*(1), 247–277.

Thorndike, E. L. (1917). Reading as reasoning: A study of mistakes in paragraph reading. *Journal of Educational Psychology, 8*(6), 323–332.

Tilstra, J., McMaster, K., van den Broek, P., Kendeou, P., & Rapp, D. (2009). Simple but complex: Components of the simple view of reading across grade levels. *Journal of Research in Reading, 32*(4), 383–401.

Tomasello, M. (1999). *The cultural origins of human cognition.* Cambridge, MA: Harvard University Press.

(2003). *Constructing a language: A usage-based approach to child language acquisition.* Cambridge, MA: Harvard University Press.

(2008). *Origins of human communication.* Cambridge, MA: MIT Press.

Tomasello, M., & Brooks, P. J. B. (1999). Early syntactic development: A construction grammar approach. In M. Barrett (Ed.), *The development of language* (pp. 161–190). Hove, England: Psychology Press.

Tomasello, M., & Farrar, M. J. (1986). Joint attention and early language. *Child Development, 57,* 1454–1463.

Tompkins, V., Guo, Y., & Justice, L. M. (2013). Inference generation, story comprehension, and language in the preschool years. *Reading and Writing: An Interdisciplinary Journal, 26,* 403–429.

Toyama, Y., Hiebert, E., & Pearson, P. D. (2017). An analysis of the text complexity of leveled passages in four popular classroom reading assessments. *Educational Assessment, 22*(3), 139–170.

Trabasso, T., & van den Broek, P. (1985). Causal thinking and the representation of narrative events. *Journal of Memory and Language, 24,* 612–630.

Trapman, M., van Gelderen, A., van Steensel, R., van Schooten, E., & Hulstijn, J. (2014). Linguistic knowledge, fluency and meta-cognitive knowledge as components of reading comprehension in adolescent low achievers: Differences between monolinguals and bilinguals. *Journal of Research in Reading, 37*(S1), S3–S21.

Tsung, L. T., & Cruickshank, K. (2009). Mother tongue and bilingual minority education in China. *International Journal of Bilingual Education and Bilingualism, 12* (5), 549–563.

Tyler, A., & Nagy, W. (1990). Use of derivational morphology during reading. *Cognition, 36*(1), 17–34.

Uccelli, P., & Páez, M. M. (2007). Narrative and vocabulary development of bilingual children from kindergarten to first grade: Developmental changes and associations among English and Spanish skills. *Language, Speech, and Hearing Services in Schools, 38*(3), 225–236.

Uccelli, P., Barr, C. D., Dobbs, C. L., Phillips Galloway, E., Meneses, A., & Sánchez, E. (2015). Core academic language skills (CALS): An expanded operational construct and a novel instrument to chart school-relevant language proficiency in pre-adolescent and adolescent learners. *Applied Psycholinguistics, 36,* 1077–1109.

Uccelli, P., Demir-Lira, Ö. E., Rowe, M., Levine, S., & Goldin-Meadow, S. (2018). Children's early decontextualized talk predicts academic language proficiency in mid-adolescence. Advanced online publication. Child Development. doi:10.1111/cdev.13034

Uccelli, P., & Phillips Galloway, E. (2016). Academic language across content areas: Lessons from an innovative assessment and from students' reflections about language. *Journal of Adolescent & Adult Literacy, 60*(4), 396–404.

Uccelli, P., Phillips Galloway, E., Barr, C. D., Meneses, A., & Dobbs, C. L. (2016). Beyond vocabulary: Exploring cross-disciplinary academic-language proficiency and its association with reading comprehension. *Reading Research Quarterly, 50* (3), 337–356.

Uccelli, P., Phillips Galloway, E., & Qin, W. (in press). The language for school literacy: Widening the lens on language and reading relations during adolescence. In E. B. Moje, P. Afflerbach, P. Enciso, & N. K. Lesaux (Eds.), *Handbook of reading research* (Vol. 5). New York, NY: Routledge.

Uchikoshi, Y. (2005). Narrative development in bilingual kindergarteners: Can Arthur help? *Developmental Psychology, 41,* 464–478.

(2013). Predictors of English reading comprehension: Cantonese-speaking English language learners in the U.S. *Reading and Writing, 26*(6), 913–939.

Uchikoshi, Y., & Marinova-Todd, S. (2012). Vocabulary and early literacy skills of Cantonese-speaking English language learners in the U.S. and Canada. *Reading and Writing: An Interdisciplinary Journal, 25,* 2107–2129.

Uchikoshi, Y., Yang, L., Lohr, B., & Leung, G. (2016) Role of oral proficiency on reading comprehension: Within-language and cross-language relationships. *Literacy Research: Theory, Method, and Practice, 65,* 236–252.

Universidad Diego Portales. (2016). *Un Buen Comienzo: Informe evaluación de impacto* (Unpublished manuscript).

Valdés, G. (2004). Between support and marginalization: The development of academic language in linguistic minority children. *International Journal of Bilingual Education and Bilingualism*, 7, 102–132.

Valdés, G., & Figueroa, R. (1994). *Bilingualism and testing: A special case of bias*. Norwood, NJ: Ablex.

van den Broek, P., & Espin, C. A. (2012). Connecting cognitive theory and assessment: Measuring individual differences in reading comprehension. *School Psychology Review*, *41*, 315–325.

van den Broek, P., Rapp, D. N., & Kendeou, P. (2005). Integrating memory-based and constructionist processes in accounts of reading comprehension. *Discourse Processes*, *39*, 299–316.

van Dijk, M., Blom, E., & Leseman, P. P. M. (2015). The relations between language input and vocabulary development in Dutch, Moroccan-Dutch and Turkish-Dutch preschoolers: A growth modeling approach (Unpublished master's thesis). Utrecht University, Utrecht, Netherlands.

van Dijk, T. A., & Kintsch, W. (1983). *Strategies of discourse comprehension*. New York, NY: Academic Press.

van Lier, L., & Walqui, A. (2012). *Language and the Common Core State Standards*. Stanford, CA: Understanding Language Initiative. Retrieved from http://ell .stanford.edu/sites/default/files/pdf/academic-papers/04-Van%20Lier%20Walqui %20Language%20and%20CCSS%20FINAL.pdf

Vandermaas-Peeler, M., Boomgarden, E., Finn, L., & Pittard, C. (2012). Parental support of numeracy during a cooking activity with four-year-olds. *International Journal of Early Years Education*, *20*, 78–93.

Varghese, N. V. (2014). *From schooling to learning: A Report from the International Working Group on Education (IWGE)*. Paris, France: International Institute for Educational Planning.

Veenendaal, N. J., Groen, M. A., & Verhoeven, L. (2016). Bidirectional relations between text reading prosody and reading comprehension in the upper primary school grades: A longitudinal perspective. *Scientific Studies of Reading*, *20*(3), 189–202.

Venezky, R. L. (1984). The history of reading research. In P. D. Pearson, R. Barr, M. L. Kamil, & P. Mosenthal (Eds.), *Handbook of reading research* (Vol. 1, pp. 3–38). Mahwah, NJ: Lawrence Erlbaum Associates.

Verhoeven, L., & Perfetti, C. (2017). *Learning to read across languages and writing systems*. Cambridge, England: Cambridge University Press.

Verhoeven, L., & van Leeuwe, J. (2008). Prediction of the development of reading comprehension: A longitudinal study. *Applied Cognitive Psychology*, *22*(3), 407–423. (2012). The simple view of second language reading throughout the primary grades. *Reading and Writing*, *8*, 1805–1818.

Vygotsky, L. S. (1978). *Mind in society: The development of higher psychological processes*. Cambridge, MA: Harvard University Press.

Wagner, D. A. (2015). Learning and literacy: A research agenda for post-2015. *International Review of Education*, *61*, 327–341.

Wang, A. S., & Meng, F. L. (2006). The development of Xinjiang bilingual education policy for minority groups. *Journal of Research on Education for Ethnic Minorities*, *17*(2), 22–27.

Wang, M., Anderson, A., Cheng, C., Park, Y., & Thomson, J. (2008). General auditory processing, Chinese tone processing, English phonemic processing and English reading skill: A comparison between Chinese-English and Korean-English bilingual children. *Reading and Writing, 21*(6), 627–644.

Wang, M., Cheng, C., & Chen, S. W. (2006). Contribution of morphological awareness to Chinese-English biliteracy acquisition. *Journal of Educational Psychology, 98*(3), 542–533.

Wang, M., Ko, I. Y., & Choi, J. (2009). The importance of morphological awareness in Korean–English biliteracy acquisition. *Contemporary Educational Psychology, 34*(2), 132–142.

Wang, M., Park, Y., & Lee, K. R. (2006). Korean–English biliteracy acquisition: Cross-language phonological and orthographic transfer. *Journal of Educational Psychology, 98*(1), 148–158.

Wanzek, J., Vaughn, S., Scammacca, N. K., et al. (2013). Extensive reading interventions for students with reading difficulties after grade 3. *Review of Educational Research, 83*(2), 163–195.

Wasik, B. A., & Bond, M. A. (2001). Beyond the pages of a book: Interactive book reading and language development in preschool classrooms. *Journal of Educational Psychology, 93*, 243–250.

Wasik, B. A., Bond, M. A., & Hindman, A. (2006). The effects of a language and literacy intervention on Head Start children and teachers. *Journal of Educational Psychology, 98*, 63–74.

Wasik, B. A., & Hindman, A. H. (2011). Improving vocabulary and pre-literacy skills of at-risk preschoolers through teacher professional development. *Journal of Educational Psychology, 103*(2), 455–469.

Wasik, B. A., Hindman, A. H., & Snell, E. K. (2016). Book reading and vocabulary development: A systematic review. *Early Childhood Research Quarterly, 37*, 39–57.

Watson, A., Painter, K., & Bornstein, M. (2002). Longitudinal relations between 2-year-olds' language and 4-year-olds' theory of mind. *Journal of Cognition and Development, 2*, 449–457.

Watts, S. M. (1995). Vocabulary instruction during reading lessons in six classrooms. *Journal of Reading Behavior, 27*, 399–424.

Weitzman, E., & Greenberg, J. (2002). *Learning language and loving it: A guide to promoting children's social language, and literacy development in early childhood settings* (2nd ed.). Toronto, ON: Hanen Centre.

Weizman, Z. O., & Snow, C. E. (2001). Lexical output as related to children's vocabulary acquisition: Effects of sophisticated exposure and support for meaning. *Developmental Psychology, 37*, 265–279.

Welch-Ross, M. K. (1997). Mother–child participation in conversation about the past: Relationship to preschoolers' theory of mind. *Developmental Psychology, 33*(4), 618–629.

White, C. E. (2004). Closing the gap: Addressing the vocabulary needs of English-language learners in bilingual and mainstream classrooms. *Reading Research Quarterly, 39*, 186–215.

Whitehurst, G. J., Arnold, D. S., Epstein, J. N., Angell, A. L., Smith, M., & Fischel, J. E. (1994). A picture book reading intervention in day care and home for children from low-income families. *Developmental Psychology, 30*, 679–689.

Widdowson, H. (1979). Notional syllabuses. In H. Widdowson (Ed.), *Explorations in applied linguistics* (pp. 247–250). Oxford, England: Oxford University Press.

Williams, K. T. (1997). *Expressive vocabulary test.* Los Angeles, CA: American Guidance Service.

Wilson, P. Y., & Anderson, R. C. (1986). What they don't know will hurt them: The role of prior knowledge in comprehension. In J. Orsanu (Ed.), *Reading comprehension: From research to practice* (pp. 31–48). Hillsdale, NJ: Lawrence Erlbaum Associates.

Wimmer, H., & Perner, W. (1983). Beliefs about beliefs: Representation and constraining function of wrong beliefs in young children's understanding of deception. *Cognition, 13,* 103–128.

Wittrock, M. C. (1990). Generative processes of comprehension. *Educational Psychologist, 14*(4), 345–376.

Wolf, M. K., Crosson, A. C., & Resnick, L. B. (2005). Classroom talk for rigorous reading comprehension instruction. *Reading Psychology, 26,* 27–53.

Wong Fillmore, L., & Snow, C. E. (2000). *What teachers need to know about language* (Contract No. ED-99-CO-0008). Washington, DC: US Department of Education's Office of Educational Research and Improvement, Center for Applied Linguistics.

Wright, T. S. (2012). What classroom observations reveal about oral vocabulary instruction in kindergarten. *Reading Research Quarterly, 47,* 353–355.

Xinjiang Department of Education. (2013). *Xinjiang bilingual education development plan for kindergarten, elementary, middle and high school (2010–2020).* Retrieved from www.xjedu.gov.cn/xjjyt/jyzt/xqjywlxz/xqsyzc/2013/60171.htm

Yeong, S. H., Fletcher, J., & Bayliss, D. M. (2014). Importance of phonological and orthographic skills for English reading and spelling: A comparison of English monolingual and Mandarin-English bilingual children. *Journal of Educational Psychology, 106*(4), 1107–1121.

Yeong, S. H., & Liow, S. J. R. (2012). Development of phonological awareness in English–Mandarin bilinguals: A comparison of English–L1 and Mandarin–L1 kindergarten children. *Journal of Experimental Child Psychology, 112*(2), 111–126.

Yin, R. K. (2009). *Case study research: Design and methods.* Thousand Oaks, CA: Sage.

York, B. N., & Loeb, S. (2014). *One step at a time: The effects of an early literacy text messaging program for parents of preschoolers* (NBER Working Paper No. 20659). Retrieved from www.nber.org/papers/w20659

Yoshikawa, H., Leyva, D., Snow, C. E., Trevino, E., Barata, M. C., Weiland, C., ... Arbour, M. C. (2015). Experimental impacts of a teacher professional development program in Chile on preschool classroom quality and child outcomes. *Developmental Psychology, 51*(3), 309–322.

Yow, W. Q., & Markman, E. M. (2011). Young bilingual children's heightened sensitivity to referential cues. *Journal of Cognition and Development, 12,* 12–31.

Zambrana, I. M., Pons, F., Eadie, P., & Ystrom, E. (2014). Trajectories of language delay from age 3 to 5: Persistence, recovery and late onset. *International Journal of Language and Communication Disorders, 49,* 304–316.

Zhao, J., Dixon, L. Q., Quiroz, B., & Chen, S. (2015). The relationship between vocabulary and word reading among Head Start Spanish–English bilingual children. *Early Childhood Education Journal, 45*(1), 1–8.

Zhou, J., Li, C. J., Du, L. J., Wang, F. X., Chen, S., & Zhang, L. (2014). The development of Mandarin acquisition of Uyghur children in bilingual kindergartens in Xinjiang. *Journal of East China Normal University (Education Science)*, *1*, 65–72.

Ziegler, F., Mitchell, P., & Currie, G. (2005). How does narrative cue children's perspective taking? *Developmental Psychology, 41*, 115–123.

Index

absenteeism, school performance influenced by, 76
abstract systems level, of analysis, 7
academic achievement, bilingualism and, 208–209
academic discourse/language, 46–47
  in adolescence, 47, 123
  bilingual children development of, 205–206
  contextual focus on, 138–139
  cross-disciplinary, 98, 99
  decontextualized language and, 42–43, 98
  defined, 5–6, 98
  discipline-specific, 98
  future research on, 14
  language-mediated learning and, 15
  level of analysis for, 7
  vocabulary knowledge relationship with, 135, 145
  WG Project for, 4
Academic English Language Proficiency instrument, 99–100
academic language exposure, of monolingual and bilingual children, 205–217. See also Development of Academic Language in School and at Home
  academic language development and, 205–206
  bilingualism, academic achievement and, 208–209
  cross-language facilitative effects, 207–208
academic language proficiency
  CALS research program on, 95–96
  Language for School Literacy and, 97
  RC contribution from, 95–96
Academic Language Project, 102
Academic Word List, in WG, 138
achievement, later
  attention skills and, 75–76
  early math skills and, 75
  reading skills and, 75
active role of reader, in RC, 147–148
actual practices level, of analysis, 7

adolescence, 1. *See also* Strategic Adolescent Reading Intervention project
  academic language knowledge in, 47, 123
  CALS and Spanish-speaking in, 107–108
  comprehension in, 171
  language learning, 2
  malleable language proficiency in, 4
  RC struggle of, 95–96
adolescent language and literacy relations, 99–100
  CAL as RC predictor, 96, 100, 102–104
  child decontextualized language and, 96
  language development and social context, 96
advanced decoding skills, 54
affiliation, as social need, 14, 170–171
Africa, multilingualism in, 254
agency, as social need, 14, 170–171
ages
  developmental perspective of, 9–10
  early language skills and literacy proficiencies, 9
  language learning across, 7
  parental input and language development, 9
analysis levels, of discourses, 7
artificial speech stream segmentation, 21
Asia, multilingualism in, 254
assessments
  on language-mediated learning, 15
  need for, 260
attention sharing behaviors, of infants
  cross-cultural studies on, 22
  of first word comprehension, 21–22
  of gaze checking, 21–22
  LuCiD Centre study on, 22–23
  of pointing, 21–22, 26–27
attention skills
  later achievement and, 75–76
  for school readiness, 75–76
audience
  continuum of, 6
  familiar in early childhood, 3
  school indeterminate nature of, 3–4